Succe in Maths

for the Caribbean

Student's Book 4

Althea A Foster
James Rees

PEARSON
Longman

Pearson Education Limited
Edinburgh Gate
Harlow
Essex
CM20 2JE
England
and Associated Companies throughout the World

www.longmancaribbean.com

Carlong Publishers (Caribbean) Limited
33 Second Street
Newport West
Kingston 13
Jamaica

Lexicon Trindad Limited
LP# 48 Boundary Road
San Juan
Trinidad

ISBN-10: 0-582-85327-3   ISBN-13: 978-0-582 85327-0

Prepared for publication by Kamae Design.

Printed in China
GCC/01

CONTENTS

See our companion website at http://www.longmancaribbean.com
for answers to the exercises in this book!

1 Sets

1️⃣ Symbols, Definitions and Operations

Remember?

A set is a collection of objects. A set may be defined by describing or by listing its members. The order in which the members of a set are written does not matter but the set must be described precisely so that it clearly defines a unique set.

A universal set is the set that contains all the members in a problem.

A universal set can have more than one subset, and a subset may itself have subsets.

The complement of a set S is the set of all the members of the universal set that are *not* in the set S.

In the table below are commonly used symbols that represent definitions and operations used in set problems.

Symbol	Meaning
U and ξ	the universal set
{ }	curly brackets (braces) to indicate a set
S'	the complement of set S
Ø and {}	empty or null set
∈	is a member of; belongs to
∉	is *not* a member of; does *not* belong to
⊂	is a subset of
⊄	is *not* a subset of
⊃	contains
⊅	does not contain
n(S)	number of members in set S
{1, 2, 3, ...}	the three dots indicate an infinite set
{a, b, ..., y, z}	the three dots indicate missing members

We can define U = {*fruit*},

where {*fruit*} = {*melon, papaw, mango, plum, banana, orange*}

and F = {*melon, papaw*}, S = {*mango, plum*}.

Since *melon* is a member of the set F, we write *melon* ∈ F; also, *papaw* ∈ F.

F and S are subsets of U, so that we write

  F ⊂ U, S ⊂ U; and, U ⊃ F, U ⊃ S

Example   Given that P = {*a, b, c, d, e, f, g*} is the universal set and
S = {*a, b, c*}, in each of the following use symbols to
(a) list the members of S'
(b) write **(i)** S is a subset of P   **(ii)** P contains S
      (iii) *a* is a member of S **(iv)** *f* does not belong to S.

Answer   **(a)** S' = {d, e, f, g}
      (b) (i) S ⊂ P   **(ii)** P ⊃ S   **(iii)** a ∈ S   **(iv)** f ∉ S

Remember?

A set is represented graphically by enclosing the members in a **Venn Diagram**. The members of the sets are put in a rectangle, a circle, or a loop.

In the sets U = {*fruit*},

where {fruit} = {*melon, papaw, mango, plum, banana, orange*}

and F = {*melon, papaw*} and S = {*mango, plum*},

F and S are subsets of U. These sets
are represented as shown in the Venn diagram
on the right.

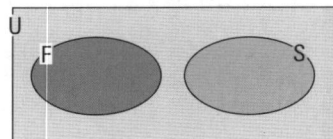

In the Venn diagram **(i)**, the unshaded area
represents F', the complement of the set F,
where F' = {*mango, plum, banana, orange*}.

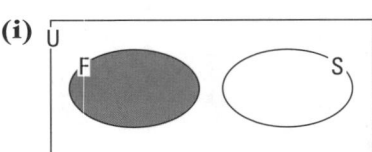

In the Venn diagram **(ii)**, the unshaded
area represents S', the complement of the
set S, where S' = {*melon, papaw, banana, orange*}.

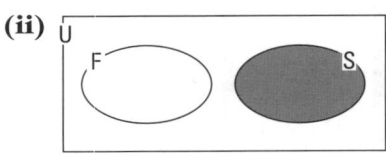

Example The Venn diagram shows a set F and a subset S.

(a) Describe in words
  (i) the set F (ii) the subset S.

(b) List the members of
  (i) the set F (ii) the subset S
  (iii) S', the complement of S.

Answer (a) (i) F = {the first 10 letters of the alphabet}
  (ii) S = {the first 3 letters of the alphabet}

(b) (i) F = {a, b, c, d, e, f, g, h, i, j}
  (ii) S = {a, b, c}
  (iii) S' = {d, e, f, g, h, i, j}

Key Fact

When there is only one loop, the members of the complement of a set are not enclosed in a loop.

Practice

1 Complete the statements below by replacing ☆ with the correct symbol from the following list: ∈ or ∉, ⊂ or ⊄ and ⊃ or ⊅.

(a) boys ☆ {males} (b) {girls} ☆ {females}
(c) keyboard ☆ {computer} (d) 7 ☆ {factors of 35}
(e) {30, 45} ☆ {multiples of 15} (f) metre ☆ {units of weight}
(g) {solids} ☆ {cube, prism, cone} (h) 5 ☆ {factors of 9}
(i) {1.6,$\frac{1}{3}$} ☆ {counting numbers} (j) {animals} ☆ {cat, dog, bird, tree}

2 For each of the following statements, decide whether it is *True* or *False*.

(a) {Friday, Monday} ⊂ {days in a week}
(b) −3 ∈ {negative numbers}
(c) {units of time} ⊃ {hour, second, gram}
(d) {horn, drum, guitar} ∈ {musical instruments}
(e) {fraction, decimal} ⊃ {integers}

1 Name each set described below and list the members.

(a) names of four classmates
(b) six different birds
(c) four integers less than 2
(d) five towns in CARICOM

2 For each set in **B** question 1:
   (i) name and describe the members of a subset
   (ii) list the members of the subset
   (iii) draw a Venn Diagram showing your subset.

C For each Venn diagram given, describe the members of:
(a) the universal set   **(b)** the subset   **(c)** the complement of the subset.

1
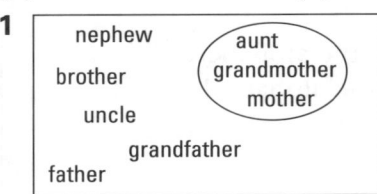

2
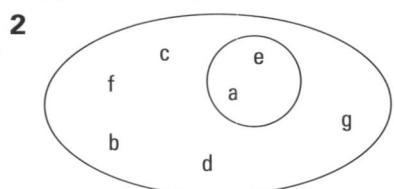

3
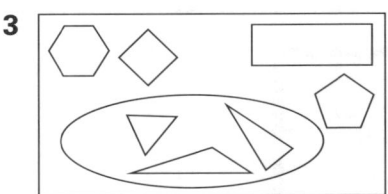

4
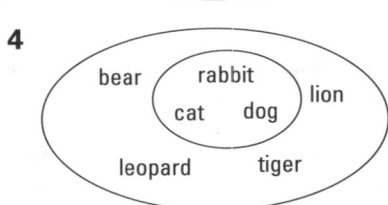

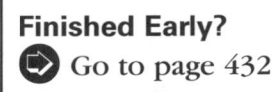

Finished Early?
➡ Go to page 432

Remember?

In an **infinite set**, the list of members is never-ending, so the number of members cannot be counted.

A **finite set** has a definite number of members that can be counted.

There are no members in an **empty set**.

Repeated members in a finite set are counted only *once*.

A **subset** of a finite set is made up of either all of the members, some of the members or none of the members so that the subsets of a finite set include the set itself and the empty set. The subsets that are the set itself or the empty set are called **improper** subsets. For example, the subsets of the set {a, b, c} are { }, {a}, {b}, {c}, {a, b}, {a, c}, {b, c}, {a, b, c}.

When there are n members in a set, the number of subsets is 2^n.

D **1** For each of the following sets, state whether the set is infinite, finite or empty.

(a) {shoes in a shoe factory}

(b) {grains of sand on a beach}

(c) {hours in 1 week}

(d) {letters in the word *Mississippi*}

(e) {teachers in the Caribbean}

(f) {prime numbers between 10 and 20}

(g) {bicycles that move at 30 metres per second}

Key Facts

Ø or {}	represents the empty or null set
{0}	is a set with one member, 0
{Ø}	is a set with one member, Ø

2 For the universal sets given below:

(i) write all the subsets

(ii) state the number of subsets.

(a) U = {x, y}

(b) U = {letters of the word *keen*}

(c) U = {1, 3, 5, 7}

(d) U = {letters of the word *sends*}

Key Facts

Selected members of an infinite set form a finite set. For example, {counting numbers less than 6} = {1, 2, 3, 4, 5}.

Finished Early?

➭ Go to page 432

Further Practice

E In each of the following Venn diagrams:

(i) name and list the members of

(a) the universal set

(b) the subset shown

(c) the complement of the subset

(ii) use symbols to show the relationship between the universal set and the subset.

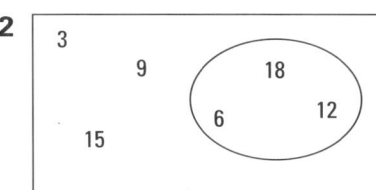

1 | cup, glass, jug, water, coffee, juice, tea

2 | 3, 9, 18, 6, 12, 15

F **1** Name and describe in words the following sets.

(a) {1, 2, 3, 4, ..., 7, 8, 9}

(b) {plumber, teacher, dentist, barber, doctor, beautician, nurse}

(c) {5, 10, 15, 20, 25, 30}

2 Use symbols, in each of the sets named in **F** question 1, to:
   (a) name a subset and list the members
   (b) name the complement of the subset and list the members
   (c) draw a Venn diagram to represent
       the universal set and the subset.

Finished Early?
 Go to page 432

❷ Relations Among Sets

Remember?

Sets that have an equal number of members are called **equivalent** sets.
Repeated members in a set are counted only *once*.

Equivalent sets that have the *same* (or identical) members are **equal** sets.

Equal sets must be equivalent, that is, both sets must have the same
number of members, but *equivalent sets may not be equal sets*.

Example   F = {odd numbers greater than 1 and less than 12}
           and G = {prime numbers greater than 1 and less than 12}.
           (a) List the members of   **(i)** F **(ii)** G.
           (b) State, giving your reason, whether the sets are equal
               or equivalent.
Answer   **(a)** **(i)** F = {3, 5, 7, 9, 11}   **(ii)** G = {2, 3, 5, 7, 11}
           (b) equivalent, since n(F) = n(G) = 5, but the members are
              not the same.

Practice

G For each of the following pairs of sets, state whether the sets are

(i) equivalent   **(ii)** equal   **(iii)** not equivalent.

1 (a) {factors of 10}   **(b)** {1, 2, 5, 10, 5, 2, 1}

2 (a) {three-letter words beginning with *p* and ending with *t*}
   (b) {vowels in the alphabet}

3 (a) {1, 2, 3}   **(b)** {4, 5, 6}

4 (a) {even numbers less than 7}   **(b)** {whole numbers less than 5}

5 (a) {letters of the word *rained*}   **(b)** {letters of the word *drainer*}

6 (a) {all shapes with 4 sides}
   (b) {square, rectangle}

Finished Early?
 Go to page 433

Remember?

The following sets of numbers are infinite sets:

N = {*counting numbers*} = {1, 2, 3, ...}
W = {*whole numbers*} = {0, 1, 2, 3, ...}
Z = {*integers*} = {..., −3, −2, −1, 0, 1, 2, 3, ...}

We see that   N ⊂ W ⊂ Z

Q, {*rational numbers*}, includes fractions and decimals
and R, {*real numbers*}, includes numbers such as $\sqrt{3}$, $\sqrt{17}$ and π.
Q and R are also infinite sets so that   R ⊃ Q ⊃ Z ⊃ W ⊃ N

In solving problems with sets of numbers, we define and use a finite set by *including* **limits**, that is, we state a **range of values**.

For example, we can say '*whole numbers that are less than 30*'
We write L = {whole numbers that are less than 30}
or   L = {0, 1, 2, 3, ..., 28, 29}

The expression '*less than 30*' is a range of values.

The sets M = {*multiples*} and P = {*prime numbers*} are also infinite sets.

   M ⊂ N and P ⊂ N.

If F = {*factors*}, then F ⊂ N.

Key Fact

Since it is impossible to list all the members of an infinite set, a Venn diagram cannot be drawn to represent an infinite set.

Practice

1 List the members of each of the following sets.
   (a) J = {factors of 32}
   (b) K = {multiples of 7}
   (c) X = {odd numbers greater than 10 and less than 20}
   (d) D = {prime numbers between 4 and 20}

2 Describe in words the following sets.
   (a) P = {1, 2, 3, ..., 18, 19, 20}
   (b) S = {2, 4, 6, 8, 10, 12, ...}
   (c) T = {4, 9, 16, 25, 36}
   (d) V = {2, 3, 5}

3 For each of the following sets, state whether the set is infinite, finite or empty.
  (a) {rational numbers}
  (b) {prime numbers between 24 and 29}
  (c) {odd numbers between 10 and 20}
  (d) {factors of 4 greater than 12}
  (e) {fractions that are equal to 0.3}
  (f) {integers less than 0}

4 For each of the sets in question 3 above, when possible:
  (a) state the number of members, using n( )
  (b) list the subsets.

 For each of the following pairs of sets, state whether the sets are:
(i) equivalent   **(ii)** equal   **(iii)** not equivalent.

1 (a) {factors of 21}   **(b)** {1, 3, 7, 21}

2 (a) {fractions less than 1}   **(b)** {fractions between 0 and 1}

3 (a) {odd numbers between 2 and 10} **(b)** {prime numbers less than 10}

4 (a) {multiples of 3 less than 12}   **(b)** {rational numbers less than 9}

> **Finished Early?**
> ➡ Go to page 433

Remember?

In **set-builder notation**, we use the mathematical symbols for *'equal to'*, *'less than'*, *'less than or equal to'*, *'greater than'* and *'greater than or equal to'*, and set symbols to describe a finite set of numbers accurately and briefly. For example, we write

$$L = \{x : x < 30, x \in W\} \text{ or } L = \{x, x \in W : x < 30\}$$

and read this as
'x is such that each member x is less than 30 and x is a member of the set W',
or 'x is a member of the set W such that each member x is less than 30',
    where ':' means 'such that'.
To describe *'the set of multiples of 3 that are less than 30 and greater than 15'*, we write

$$K = \{x : 15 < x < 30, x \in W\} \text{ or } K = \{x, x \in W : 15 < x < 30\}$$

Then, we say that L and K are written in **set-builder notation**. The members of sets L and K must be whole numbers or integers.

Practice

J Write the sets given in **H** questions 1 – 3 using set-builder notation.

Finished Early?

Go to page 433

3 Intersecting Sets

Remember?

If P and Q are two **finite** sets, then the set of members common to both is called the **intersection** and denoted by **P ∩ Q**. Before we can draw the Venn diagram of intersecting sets, as in **(i)**, we have to list the members of the two sets to find the common members.

(i)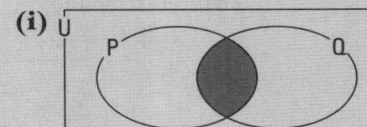

Sets that do not intersect are called **disjoint sets**, as in **(ii)**. The intersection of disjoint sets is the empty set.

(ii)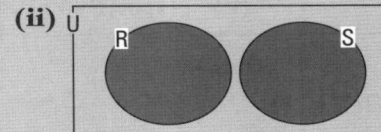

The set formed by combining the members of two sets is the **union** of the sets and is written **P ∪ Q** and shown in **(iii)**. Note that in the union of intersecting sets, we list the common members only once.

(iii)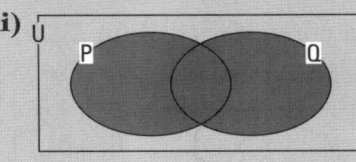

Symbol	Meaning
A ∩ B	A *intersection* B
A ∪ B	A *union* B

Example   U = {whole numbers less than 16}
P = {prime numbers}
Q = {factors of 24}
(a) List the members of   (i) P ∩ Q   (ii) P ∪ Q
(b) Draw the Venn diagram to represent this information.
(c) Hence, write   (i) n(P ∩ Q)   (ii) n(P ∪ Q)

Answer   U = {1, 2, 3, 4, 5, 6, ..., 14, 15}
P = {3, 5, 7, 11, 13}
Q = {1, 2, 3, 4, 6, 8, 12}
(a)   (i) P ∩ Q = {3}
(ii) P ∪ Q = {1, 2, 3, 4, 5, 6, 7, 8, 11, 12, 13}
(b)

U   15   9
P   5   4   12   Q
    11   3   6   2
    7   13   1   8
14   10   5

(c)   (i) n(P ∩ Q) = 1   (ii) n(P ∪ Q) = 11

Practice

K Make six copies of each of the following Venn diagrams.

In a copy of each Venn diagram, shade in each of the following areas:

(a) M'   **(b)** H'   **(c)** M' ∩ H   **(d)** M ∩ H'   **(e)** M' ∪ H   **(f)** M ∪ H'

1
M   H

2
M   H

3
M   H

Finished Early?
➡ Go to page 433

Remember?

The intersection of a set and its subset is the subset as shown by the shaded region in **(i)**.

(i)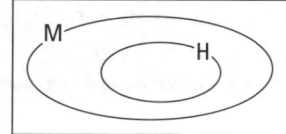

The union of a set and its subset is the set itself as shown by the shaded region in **(ii)**.

(ii)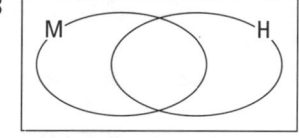

Key Fact

The subsets in a universal set

either intersect and have common members that belong to more than one set

or do not intersect and have no common members in more than one set.

Learn About It

In order to solve problems in which there are more than two subsets, we work through the same steps, that is, we list the members of the universal set and the subsets. Next we check whether there are common members in more than one subset so that we can identify if the subsets intersect in order to list the intersection and union of the sets. Then we can draw the Venn diagram.

Example	U = {letters in the word *athletics*}
	 R = {letters in the word *latest*}
	 S = {letters in the word *health*}
	 T = {letters in the word *hat*}
	 (a) List the members of
	      (i) R ∩ S, R ∩ T, S ∩ T **(ii)** R ∪ S, R ∪ T, S ∪ T
	      (iii) (R ∩ S)' **(iv)** (R ∪ T)'
	 (b) Draw the Venn diagram to represent this information.

Answer	U = {a, t, h, l, e, i, c, s}; R = {l, a, t, e, s};
	 S = {h, e, a, l, t}; T = {h, a, t}
	 (a) **(i)** R ∩ S = {l, a, t, e}, R ∩ T = {a, t}, S ∩ T = {h, a, t}
	      (ii) R ∪ S {l, a, t, e, s, h}, R ∪ T = {l, a, t, e, s, h},
	          S ∪ T = {h, e, a, l, t}
	      (iii) (R ∩ S)' = {i, c, s, h} **(iv)** (R ∪ T)' = {i, c}
	 (b) 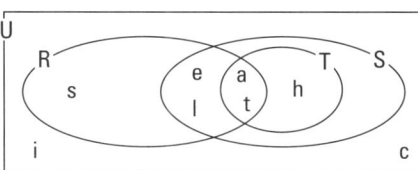

Try It Out

L **(a)** Copy and complete the Venn diagram where X = {p, q, r, s}, Y = {r, s, t, w, a} and Z = {p, s, a, b}.

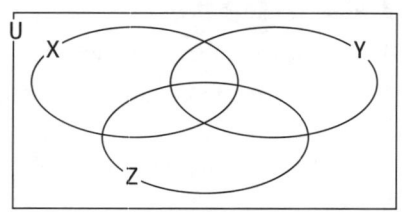

(b) Using your diagram or otherwise, list the members of:

(i) (X ∩ Y) ∪ Z

(ii) (Y ∪ Z) ∩ X

Practice

M Make four copies of each of the following Venn diagrams and for each diagram shade the required sets (a) – (d).

(a) (P ∪ R) ∩ S   **(b)** (P ∩ R) ∪ S

(c) P ∪ (R ∩ S')   **(d)** P ∩ (R ∪ S')

1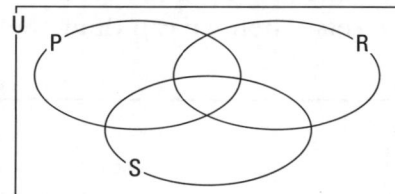

2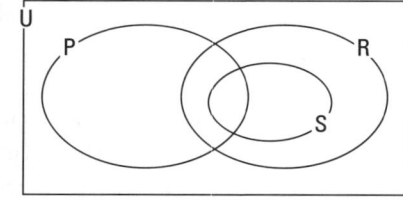

3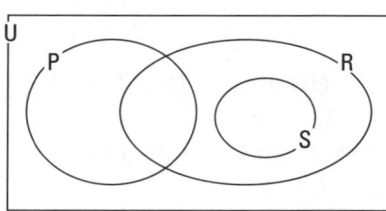

4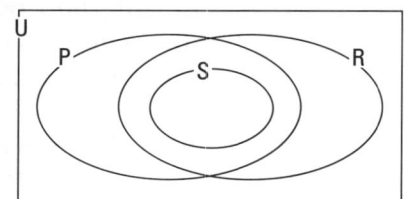

Finished Early?

➡ Go to page 433

N In each of the following Venn diagrams, the number of members in each subset is shown. For each question:

(a) write the equation to show the relation between the numbers of members in each subset and the total number of members in the universal set

(b) find each value of x

(c) calculate   **(i)** $n(A)$ **(ii)** $n(B)$ **(iii)** $n(A \cup B)$ **(iv)** $n(A \cap B)'$.

1

2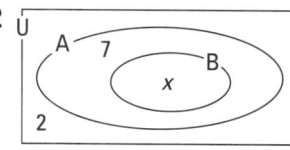

3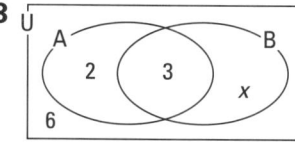

     $n(U) = 11$ $n(U) = 15$ $n(U) = 12$

O The numbers of the members in each of the subsets are shown in the Venn diagram where $U = A \cup B \cup C$ and $n(U) = 37$. Find

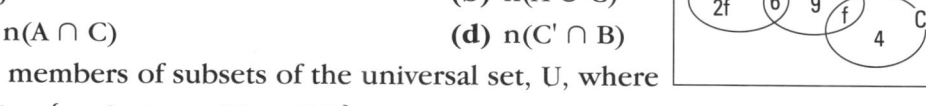

(a) f (b) $n(A \cup C)$

(c) $n(A \cap C)$ (d) $n(C' \cap B)$

P The members of subsets of the universal set, U, where

$$U = \{x : 3 \leqslant x < 30, x \in Z\}$$

are described in each of the following questions. List the members of:

(a) the universal set

(b) each intersection of two subsets

(c) the complement of each intersection

(d) each union of two subsets

(e) the complement of each union.

1 A = {odd numbers greater than 15}
    B = {prime numbers}

2 F = (factors of 120}
    P = {prime factors of 210}
    M = {multiples of 5 less than 20}

Q For each question in **P**, draw the Venn diagram.

> **Finished Early?**
> Go to page 433

Further Practice

R Describe the shaded areas in the following Venn diagrams:

1

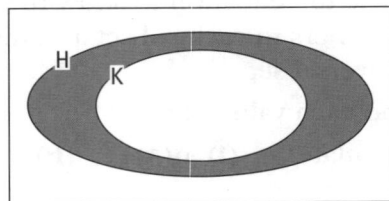

2

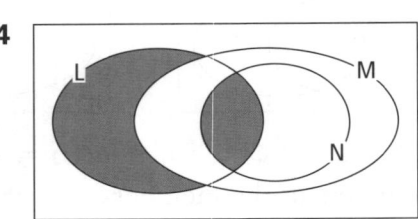

3

4

S For each question:

(a) draw the Venn diagram

(b) list the members of

    (i) each set

    (ii) the intersection of each pair

    (iii) the complement of each intersection

    (iv) the union of each pair

    (v) the complement of each union.

1 K = {letters of the word *arithmetic*}

   M = {letters of the word *rate*}

2 C = {letters of the word *function*}

   D = {letters of the word *count*}

   E = {letters of the word *ion*}

T In each of the following Venn diagrams:

(a) describe the members of each set

(b) for each question, list the members of

    (i) the intersection of each pair

    (ii) the complement of the intersection

    (iii) the union of each pair

    (iv) the complement of the union.

1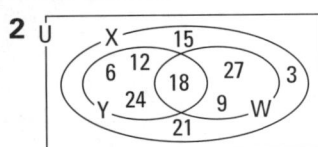

2

Finished Early?
➡ Go to page 433

4 Problem Solving

Remember?

To solve some real-life problems, it is possible to work through the
same steps that we use in set questions, that is,
1 collect the data
2 group the data in sets
3 identify the sets that apply in order to solve the problem
4 list the members of all the sets in the problem
5 check whether there is a universal set and subsets
6 find the intersection or union of the sets involved
7 determine which set is the solution set.

Example	Find the lowest common multiple of 9 and 15.
Thinking	We need to list the set of multiples of 9 and of 15, and identify the common multiples, that is, the intersection of the two sets.
	We can do this by drawing the Venn diagram of the intersection or by looking at the two lists. Then select the smallest member of the intersection.
Working	$S = \{multiples\ of\ 9\}$ $= \{9, 18, 27, 36, 45, 54, 63, 72, 81, 90, 99, ...\}$ $E = \{multiples\ of\ 15\}$ $= \{15, 30, 45, 60, 75, 90, 105, ...\}$ $S \cap E = \{45, 90, ...\}$ The smallest member of $S \cap E$ is 45.
Answer	The lowest common multiple of 9 and 15 is 45.

Practice

Ⓤ In each of the following problems:
(a) use set-builder notation to describe the sets
(b) list the members of the sets   (c) solve the problem.
1 Find the lowest common multiple of 6 and 16.
2 Write the set of prime numbers that are greater than 5 and less than 40.
3 Determine the highest common factor of 52 and 36.
4 Find the smallest perfect square that is greater than 15 and less than 40.

1 In a class of 36, students some students are members of both the Mathematics Club and the Computer Society. 20 students belong to the Mathematics Club and 28 to the Computer Society. There are 6 students who do not belong to either the Mathematics Club or the Computer Society.
  (a) Draw a Venn diagram to represent this information.
  (b) Write an equation and solve it to find the number of students who are members of both the Mathematics Club and the Computer Society.

2 In a group of 11 friends, 6 play tennis, 5 play cricket and 7 play soccer. 3 play tennis and cricket, 2 play cricket and soccer, and 4 play soccer and tennis. Each person plays at least one of these games.

Draw and use a Venn diagram to find how many people play all three games.

3 A company employs 59 people. 52 of the employees are men. 18 people, including all the women, are clerical staff.
  (a) Draw a Venn diagram to show this information.
  (b) Find the number of men who are clerical staff.

4 The subsets of a universal set U are X, Y and Z, where $X \cap Z = \{\}$.

Given that $n(X) = 9$, $n(Y) = 16$, $n(X \cap Y) = 3$, $n(Y \cap Z) = 5$, $n(Y \cup Z) = 16$, $n(X \cup Y \cup Z)' = 2$
  (a) draw and label clearly a Venn diagram to show the above information
  (b) use set notation to write a statement representing the number of members in the universal set
  (c) calculate the value of $n(U)$
  (d) state the relation between Y and Z.

5 Given that U = {all quadrilaterals}, P = {all parallelograms}, R = {rectangles} and S = {squares},
  (a) draw a Venn diagram to show the relationship between P, R and S
  (b) write the following statements in set notation.
    (i) *There are some parallelograms that are not rectangles.*
    (ii) *Quadrilaterals that are not parallelograms or not rectangles are among those which are not squares.*

W Using set notation in each of the following problems,
  (a) (i) describe all the sets
      (ii) rewrite the statements
  (b) draw the Venn diagram
  (c) write the set relation that represents the statement in italics.

1 All the boxes have straight edges.
   Some boxes are made of glass.
   Some boxes are made of wood.
   All gift boxes are made of glass.
      V is a gift box.

2 All the students are fifth-formers.
   Some study Geography and Mathematics.
   Some study Biology and Mathematics.
   No student studies Geography, Biology and Mathematics.
      Danielle studies Geography and Mathematics.
      Tim studies neither Geography nor Biology.

Further Practice

 1 (a) Draw one or more Venn diagrams that illustrate the statements:
   (i) *All bicycles have two wheels.*
   (ii) *All bicycles have handlebars.*

   (b) Can it be deduced that all two-wheeled vehicles have handlebars?

2 (a) If U = {polygons} and T = {triangles}, draw a Venn diagram to
   illustrate the proposition that '*Some isosceles triangles are*
   right-angled'.

   (b) If $s \in$ {scalene triangles}, on the diagram mark s in the set to which
   it belongs.

   (c) What conclusions can be drawn from your diagram?

3 (a) Draw a Venn diagram showing the relationship among the following
   sets:
   U = {people}, W = {women}, M = {mothers}, and
   G = {grandmothers}

   (b) Write the following statements in set notation:
   (i) *There are some people who are mothers but who are **not***
   grandmothers.
   (ii) *People who are not women or who are not mothers are among*
   those who are not grandmothers.

Finished Early?
 Go to page 433

2 Relations and Functions

In this chapter you will learn about …
1 relations
2 functions
3 graphs

1 Relations

Remember?

A **relation** is the rule that describes either a connection between two members of one set, for example, children in a family; or a connection between two members of different sets, for example, students and the games they play.

A relation can be illustrated by drawing an **arrow diagram**. The member of the first set is called the **object** and the member of the second set is called the **image**.

If the members are all in one set, for example, {children in a family} = {Richard, Andrew, Sylvia}, the relation *'is the brother of'* is as shown in the arrow diagram on the right.

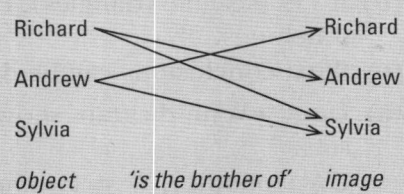

Note that the direction of the arrows indicates the direction of the relation. No arrow goes from Sylvia. Why is this?

When there are two sets, for example,

{students} = {Ann, Damon, John, June, Robert}
and {games} = {tennis, soccer, volleyball, cricket, netball}

and when the relation *'plays'* is between the two sets, so that Ann plays cricket, netball; June plays tennis; Damon plays soccer; John plays soccer, cricket; Robert plays tennis, soccer, volleyball, cricket; the arrow diagram for this relation is as shown below:

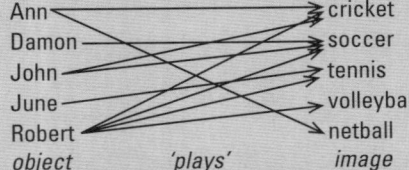

<u>Word Check</u>

an element a member of the sets in a relation

domain the first set of elements in a relation

co-domain the second set of elements in a relation

a mapping diagram an arrow diagram or an arrow graph

Remember?

The corresponding elements in a relation form an **ordered pair**.

The ordered pairs in the relation 'is the brother of' on the set of the children, Richard, Andrew and Sylvia, in the family are (Richard, Andrew), (Richard, Sylvia), (Andrew, Richard), (Andrew, Sylvia); and the pairs in the relation 'plays' on the sets, {students} and {games}, are (Ann, cricket), (Ann, netball), (June, tennis), (Damon, soccer), (John, soccer), (John, cricket), (Robert, tennis), (Robert, soccer), (Robert, cricket) and (Robert, volleyball).

In general, if x represents the object and y the image, we write $x \rightarrow y$, and write the ordered pair as (x, y).

Key Fact

An **object** may have more than one **image**.

Practice

 1 In each of the following examples:

   (a) draw an arrow diagram to show the relation **(b)** list the ordered pairs.

     (i) {3, 4, 5, 6, 8, 10, 12, 20, 21, 24, 25}
       is a multiple of

    (ii) {fly, ant, dove, mosquito, pigeon, crow} and {bird, insect}
       belongs to the species

   (iii) {factors of 12} and {factors of 30}
       is less than or equal to

   (iv) {1, 8, 27, 64} and {1, 2, 3, 4}
       is the cube of

Key Fact

The order of the elements in an ordered pair is significant.

2 For each of the following sets of ordered pairs:
  (a) draw the arrow diagram   **(b)** write the relation.
    (i) (2, 3), (3, 4), (4, 5), (5, 6)
    (ii) (3, 6), (5, 10), (7, 14), (9, 18)
    (iii) (2, 4), (2, 6), (2, 8), (2, 12), (3, 6), (3, 9), (3, 12), (4, 8), (4, 12)

3 Each of the following arrow diagrams shows a relation.
  (a) State the relation.   **(b)** List the ordered pairs.

(i)
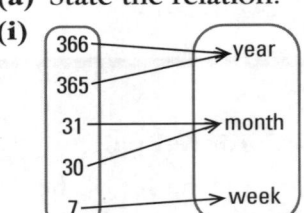

(ii)
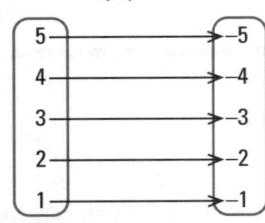

(iii)
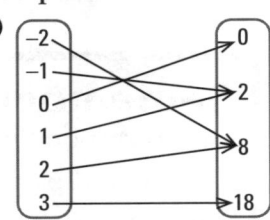

Key Fact

There may be more than one relation
between the members of a set.

B Make up your own relations using:
  (a) members of only one set   **(b)** members of two sets.
  For each example   **(i)** write the relation in words
                      (ii) draw the arrow diagram
                      (iii) list the ordered pairs.

Finished Early?
➡ Go to page 434

Further Practice

C For each of the following examples:
  (a) write the relation in words
  (b) list the ordered pairs.

(i)
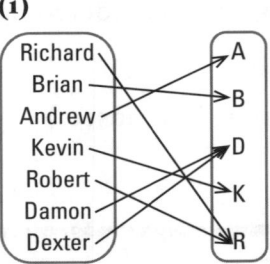

(ii)
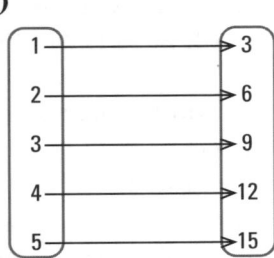

(iii)
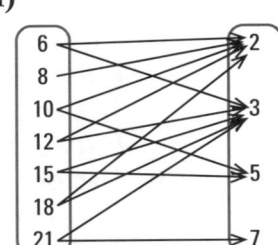

Finished Early?
➡ Go to page 434

Remember?

When the relation is between two sets, a member of the first set can go to one or more members of the second set. The different types of relation can be clearly represented by arrow diagrams:

(i) *many-to-many*

The members of the first set go to more than one member of the second set, more than one image corresponding to more than one object.

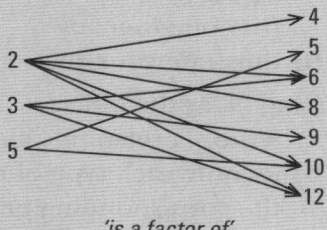

'is a factor of'

(ii) *many-to-one*

Each member of the first set goes to only one member of the second set, at least one image corresponding to more than one object.

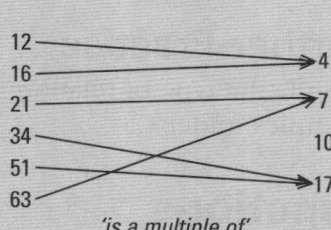

'is a multiple of'

(iii) *one-to-many*

Each member of the first set goes to more than one member of the second set, each image corresponding to only one object.

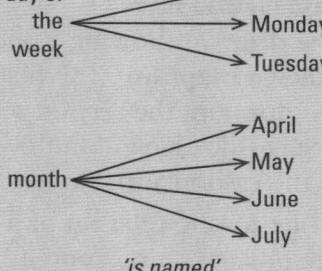

'is named'

(iv) *one-to-one*

Each member of the first set goes to only one member of the second set.

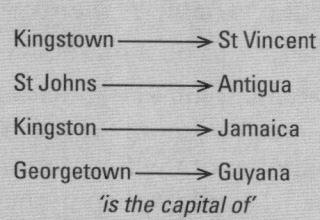

'is the capital of'

Key Fact

The number of members may not be the same in the set of objects and in the set of the images.

Practice

D 1 Identify the type of relation in each of the examples under **A**, questions 1 – 3.

2 **(a)** Give two examples of each of the following types of relations:
      (i) many-to-many   **(ii)** many-to-one
      (iii) one-to-many   **(iv)** one-to-one
  (b) Illustrate your answers on arrow diagrams.

3 Using '9' as the object:
  (a) write six relations, including at least one of each type of relation
  (b) identify each type of relation and list
     the corresponding images.

Further Practice

E Identify the type of relation in each of the examples under **C**.

> **Finished Early?**
> ⮕ Go to page 434

2 Functions

> ### Remember?
>
> The diagram showing a one-to-one relation or a many-to-one relation is called a **mapping**. The first set of elements in the ordered pair is called the **domain**; the second set of elements is called the **range**. We say that an object (the element in the domain) is mapped onto an image (the element in the co-domain). Note that the set of all the **images** is called the range.
>
> A one-to-one relation or a many-to-one relation is called a **function**. If the object is represented by the variable x, and the image is represented by the variable y, then $x \rightarrow y$.
>
> y is said to be a function of x and written as $y = f(x)$ or $f : x \rightarrow y$.
>
> The mapping of a function can be shown in a **mapping table**, usually referred to simply as a **table** or a **table of values**. For example, in the mapping of the function '*is 3 more than*', for whole numbers greater than 1 but less than 6; that is, number $\rightarrow$ number plus 3, that is, $x \rightarrow x + 3$, $\{x : 1 < x < 6, x \in W\}$
>
> This is the equation $y = x + 3$, and for the value $1 < x < 6$ gives us the mapping table on the right.
>
> | x | 2 | 3 | 4 | 5 |
> |---|---|---|---|---|
> | y | 5 | 6 | 7 | 8 |
>
> x is the **independent variable** and y is the **dependent variable**, since the value of y depends on the value of x, when $y = f(x)$.

Key Fact

In the mapping of a function, each object has only one image and all the objects *must* go to at least one image.

Example   **(a)** Illustrate the relation $y = 2x + 1$ for
$x \in \{-2, -1, 0, 1, 2, 3\}$ by means of:
    (i) an arrow diagram   **(ii)** a set of ordered pairs
(iii) a table of values.
(b) Is the relation a function? If yes, say whether it is
one-to-one or many-to-one.
(c) Write down the domain and the range.

Answer   **(a)**   **(i)**

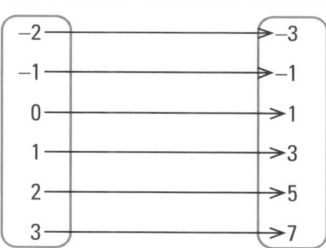

    (ii) $(-2, -3)$, $(-1, -1)$, $(0, 1)$, $(1, 3)$, $(2, 5)$, $(3, 7)$
    (iii)

x	−2	−1	0	1	2	3
y	−3	−1	1	3	5	7

(b) yes; one-to-one
(c) Domain = $\{-2, -1, 0, 1, 2, 3\}$; Range = $\{-3, -1, 1, 3, 5, 7\}$

Key Fact

In a one-to-one mapping, exactly one object is related
to one image, so there is exactly the same number of
elements in the domain and the range.

Practice

F **1** **(a)** State which of the following arrow diagrams illustrate functions, giving reasons for your statement for each relation.
(b) Say which functions are one-to-one and which are many-to-one.

(i)   **(ii)**   **(iii)**

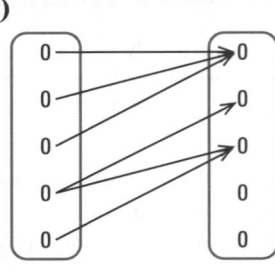
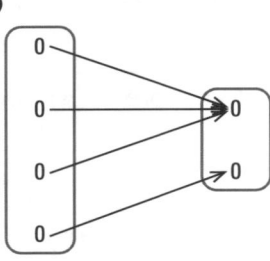

(iv)   **(v)**   **(vi)**

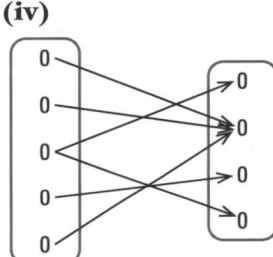
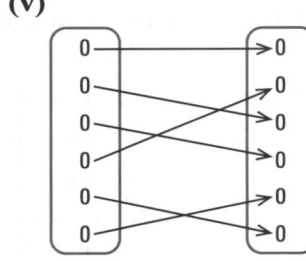
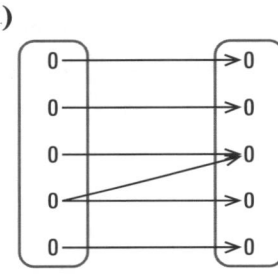

2 Draw an arrow diagram from the domain A = {−1, 0, 2, 5} to the co-domain B = {0, 1, 4, 25} for the relation *'is the square root of'*.

3 **(a)** Draw an arrow diagram for the domain P = {2, 3, 4, 5} and the co-domain R = {4, 6, 8, 10, 12} and the relation *'is a factor of'*.
(b) How many images does '2' have?
(c) How many images does '5' have?
(d) Name this type of relation.

4 A = {b, c, d} and P = {p, s, t, w}.
Relation R_1 is given by {(b, s), (c, w), (d, p), (b, t)} and relation R_2 by {(b, w), (c, p)}.
(a) State whether these relations are functions or not functions. Explain your answer.
(b) For each relation, write down the domain and the range.

5 **(a)** Draw up a table of values for the following functions.
(b) Write the functions as ordered pairs.
    (i) $f : x \rightarrow 2x - 3$, $x \in \{-2, -1, 0, 1, 2, 3\}$
    (ii) $f(x) = x^2 + 1$ where $-3 < x < 4$
    (iii) $y = x^2 - 2x + 4$,
        where $x = -3, -2, -1, 0, 1, 2, 3$

Finished Early?
➡ Go to page 435

> **Word Check**
>
> a **variable** an unknown that can assume a variety of numerical values
>
> a **constant** a fixed numerical value that does not involve any power of a variable

Further Practice

G In the following arrow diagrams:

    (a) identify those which are functions and those which are not functions, giving your reasons

    (b) for each function, write down the domain and the range.

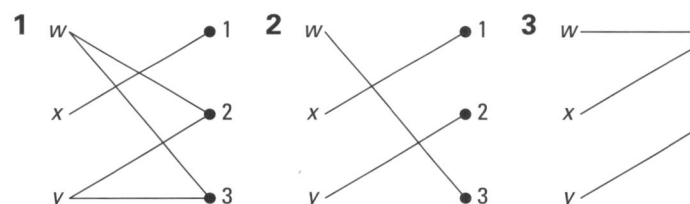 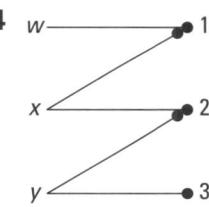

H For each relation shown below:

    (a) list the ordered pairs

    (b) state whether the relation is a function or not, giving your reason

    (c) if the relation is a function, say whether it is one-to-one or many-to-one.

domain	relation	*range*
1 {−3, −1, 0, 1, 2, 3}	$x \rightarrow -x + 1$	{4, 2, −1, −3}
2 {bird, cow, tree, worm}	is	{animal, four-legged}
3 {1, 2, 3, 4, 5}	$x \rightarrow -x$	{−1, −2, −3, −4, −5}
4 {15, 12, 9, 6, 3}	multiple of	{5, 4, 3, 2}
5 {−3, −2, −1, 0, 1, 2}	$x \rightarrow x^2 - 2$	{7, −1, −2, 2}
6 {2, 3, 4, 5, 6, 7}	prime factors of	{10, 12, 14, 16, 18, 20}

> **Finished Early?**
> Go to page 435

> **Key Fact**
> Every function is a relation but relations are **not** always functions.

③ Graphs

Remember?

Two number lines that intersect at right angles at the zero point on each number line are called **Cartesian axes**. The horizontal axis is usually taken as the **x-axis** and the vertical axis as the **y-axis**; the axes divide the grid into four quadrants. The point of intersection of the axes is called the **origin** and is defined by the ordered pair of numbers (0, 0).

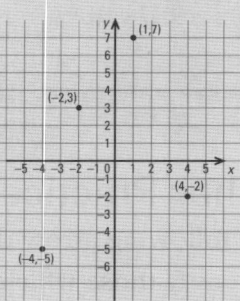

Every point on the grid is defined by (x, y), an ordered pair of numbers called the **coordinates** of the point. Each point uses the scales on the axes (the number lines) to mark its position on the grid; coordinates include fractions and negative numbers.

Therefore, the two corresponding elements in the ordered pairs of a function can be taken as the coordinates of points on a grid; the first element is plotted along the x-axis and the second element along the y-axis. Positive x-values are to the right of the origin and negative x-values are to the left of the origin; positive y-values are upwards from the origin and negative y-values are downwards from the origin. The points are joined to represent a **graph** of the function.

Key Fact

A function can be represented by an arrow diagram, a set of ordered pairs, a table of values or a graph.

Practice

① For each of the following functions:

(a) draw up a table of values

(b) use suitable scales to represent 1 unit on each axis

(c) plot the points on graph paper

(d) draw the graph of the function.

1 $y = 3x - 2$, $-1 < x < 3$

2 $y = x^2 + 3$, $-2 \leqslant x < 4$

3 $y = -x - 2$, $-5 < x \leqslant 4$

4 $y = \frac{1}{2}x^2 - 4$, $-3 \leqslant x < 3$

J For each of the following graphs:

(a) write the coordinates of points on the graph, that is, the ordered pairs of the function [at least 3 in question 1; 5 in question 2]

(b) find the relation between the x-coordinate and the corresponding y-coordinate

(c) write the relation in the form $y = f(x)$.

1

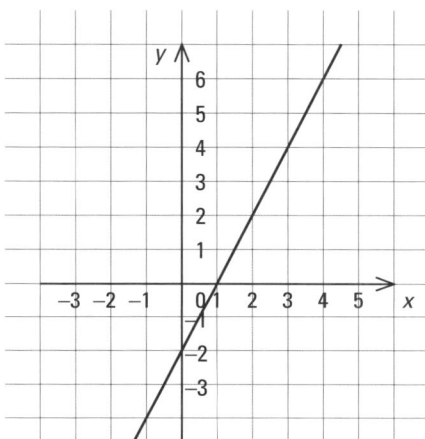

2

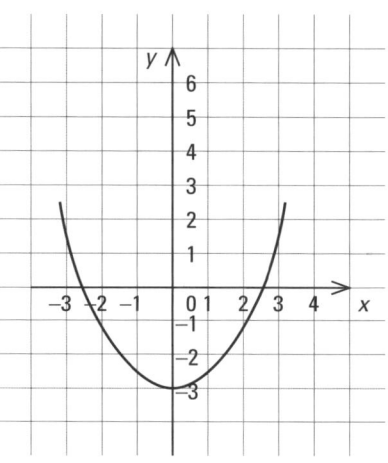

Further Practice

K For each of the following functions:

(a) list the ordered pairs

(b) plot the points and draw the graph.

1 $f : x \rightarrow 2x - 3$, $x \in \{-2, -1, 0, 1, 2, 3\}$

2 $f(x) = x^2 + 1$ where $-3 < x < 4$

3 $y = x^2 - 2x + 4$, where $x = -3, -2, -1, 0, 1, 2, 3$

> **Finished Early?**
> Go to page 435

Remember?

If the graph is a straight line, the function is called a **linear function**. The relation between the elements, x and y, gives the **equation of the line** and is written as $y = f(x)$.

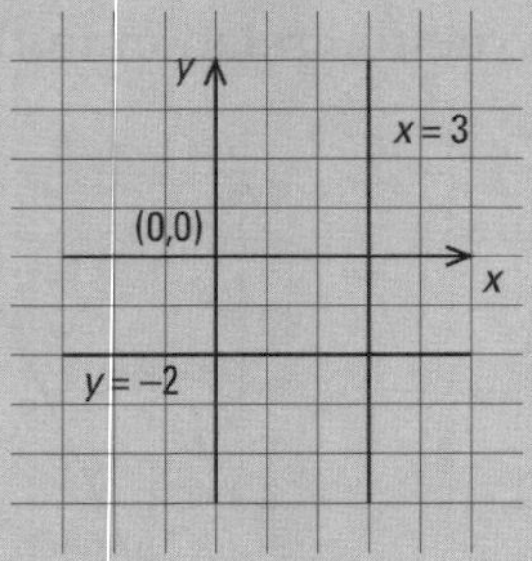

The equation of a line parallel to the y-axis is
$x = a$, where a is a constant.
For example, the x-coordinate of all the points on the line $x = 3$ (as in the diagram) is 3.
The line represents the set of ordered pairs, that is
$\{(3, -2), (3, -1), (3, 0), (3, 2), (3, 5), ...\}$

The equation of a line parallel to the x-axis is
$y = b$, where b is a constant.
For example, the y-coordinate of all the points on the line $y = -2$ (as in the diagram) is –2.
The line represents the set of ordered pairs, that is
$\{(-1, -2), (0, -2), (1, -2), (3, -2), (4, -2), ...\}$

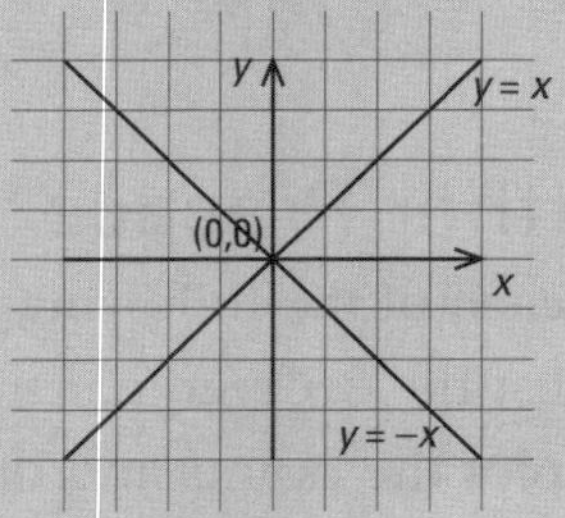

When the y-coordinate = x-coordinate of any point on the line, the equation of the line is $y = x$ (as in the diagram).
The line represents the set of ordered pairs of the function, that is
$\{(-2, -2), (-1, -1), (0, 0), (2, 2), (4, 4), ...\}$

When the y-coordinate = $-(x$-coordinate) of any point on the line, the equation of the line is $y = -x$ (as in the diagram).
The line represents the set of ordered pairs of the function, that is
$\{(-2, 2), (-1, 1), (0, 0), (2, -2), (4, -4), ...\}$

Key Facts

The graph of the function is **a straight line parallel to the y-axis**:
- if all the first members in a set of ordered pairs are the same
- if all the independent variables (x-values) in a table of values are the same.

The graph of the function is **a straight line parallel to the x-axis**:
- if all the second members in a set of ordered pairs are the same
- if all the dependent variables (y-values) in a table of values are the same.

Remember?

In real life, graphs are widely used to show how one quantity varies with another, for example, different kinds of currency, units of measure. We can also use graphs to find out how some quantities, such as temperature, charges, distance and speed, vary with time.
We can also use graphs to **estimate** the value of
either the function y for a given value of the other variable x
or the independent variable x for a known value of the function y.

Practice

1 In exchange for $Y 364.00, a customer received $X 70.00.

   (a) Using a scale of 1 cm to represent $X 10 on the x-axis and 1 cm to represent $Y 50 on the y-axis, draw a graph to show the relation between $X and $Y.

   (b) From your graph, find how many:
      (i) $Y are received for $X 45
      (ii) $X are received for $Y 425.

2 The monthly charges for a utility are a basic rental of $30 plus 20 cents per unit.

The graph shows the charges for 0–400 units. Use the graph to find:

   (a) the charges for 100 units

   (b) the number of units for a charge of $36.50.

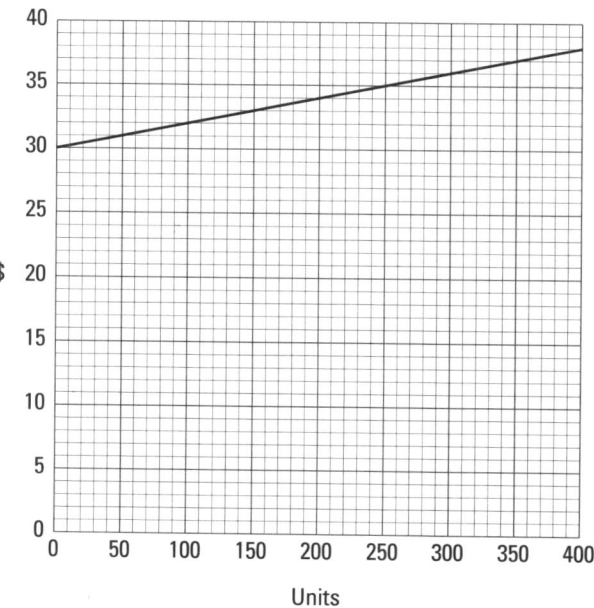

3 The information given in the table below represents a function.

Length of a side of a square (x cm)	1	2	3	4	5	6
Area of square (A cm^2)	1	4	9	16	25	36

(a) Show this on a graph.
(b) Write down the relation between the side, x, and the area, A.
(c) Find: (i) the area of a square of side 2.3 cm
            (ii) the length of a side when the area is 12.96 cm^2.

4 The information given in the table below represents a linear function.

Time (t h)	1	2	3	4	5
Distance from home (d km)	138		214	252	

(a) Show this on a graph.
(b) Complete the table.

> *Hint: use a broken axis on the distance axis.*

(c) Write down the relation between the distance, d, and the time, t.
(d) Find: (i) the distance from home when the time was first noted
            (ii) the time when the distance moved was 153 km.

> **Finished Early?**
> Go to page 435

Further Practice

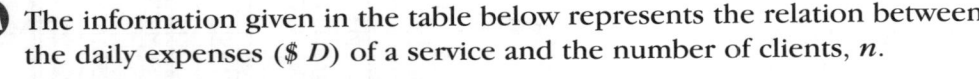 The information given in the table below represents the relation between the daily expenses ($ D) of a service and the number of clients, n.

n	10		50	80	100
D	75	90	135		210

(a) Use a scale of 1 cm to 10 units on each axis to plot these values and draw a suitable graph.
(b) Show that D and n are connected by the linear relation
    $D = a + bn$, where a and b are constants.
(c) Use your graph to find the value of a. Hence, find the value of b.
(d) Complete the table, stating what is represented by the values found.

When the charge ($ C) for the service is $ 5 per client:
(e) Write the relation between the service charge and the number of clients, n.
(f) On the same axes, draw a graph to show this relation.
(g) Estimate the least number of clients before a profit is made.
(h) Use the graph to estimate the profit when there are 40 clients.

> **Finished Early?**
>  Go to page 435

3 Number Theory

1 Number Systems

Remember?

In a number system, there are different symbols called **numerals** for writing numbers. The most common number systems that we use in our day-to-day activities are the **decimal number system**, and the **Roman numeral system** which is an old system that is used mainly for writing dates.

The decimal number system is a **place-value** system based on ten numerals called **digits**, that is, $\{0, 1, 2, 3, ..., 8, 9\}$. The **place** of the digit in a number gives the **value** of that digit in the number.

In the decimal number system, all numbers except **zero** are either **even**, that is, are divisible by 2, $\{2, 4, 6, ...\}$ or **odd**, $\{1, 3, 5, ...\}$.

There are also special names for some numbers, for example, *pair* (2), *dozen* (12), *score* (20) and *gross* (144).

A number that gives the order of something in a list is called an ordinal number, for example, *first*, *tenth*, and so on.

Key Facts

In the decimal place-value system, the value of the digit in each of the different 'places' (or columns) is shown on the right.

The value of the same digit increases by ten times its value as it moves across each of the columns from right to left.

Thus the digit 3 in the tens column has the value 30 and the digit 3 in the millions column has the value 3 000 000.

To indicate the base, we may write 30_{ten}.

| millions | hundred thousands | ten thousands | thousands ($\times 10 \times 10 \times 10$) | hundreds ($\times 10 \times 10$) | tens ($\times 10$) | units (digit) |

Learn About It

The greatest digit in any number in a place-value system is 1 less than the base number, for example, 9 is the largest digit in the decimal system.

We can express any number in an expanded form so that, for example, we write:

$$352_{ten} = 3 \times (10 \times 10) + 5 \times (10) + 2$$
and $\quad 1001_{five} = 1 \times (5 \times 5 \times 5) + 0 \times (5 \times 5) + 0 \times (5) + 1 \; [\, = 126_{ten}]$

Try It Out

1 Complete the table below:

Base number	Greatest digit
10	9
8	
7	
5	
2	

2 Draw up the first four columns for a number in:
(a) base eight   (b) base five.
[*See Key Facts above*]

3 Write the following numbers in expanded form:
(a) 101_{ten} (b) 101_{eight} (c) 101_{two}

4 Find the value of the numbers in 3(b) and 3(c) in base ten.

Practice

B **1** Change the following numbers in base ten to the given bases:
   (a) 23, 234, 2345 to base eight
   (b) 11, 23, 75, 141 to base two.

2 Change the following numbers to base ten:
   (a) 1101_{two} **(b)** 327_{eight}
   (c) 100101_{two}

Further Practice

C **1** Change the following numbers in base ten to the given bases:
   (a) 65, 173, 544 to base eight
   (b) 17, 39, 89, 132 to base two.

2 Change the following numbers to base ten:
   (a) 1111_{two} **(b)** 265_{eight} **(c)** 111101_{two}

> **Finished Early?**
> ➡ Go to page 437

❷ Sets of Numbers

> ## Remember?
>
> In the decimal number system, a **multiple** is defined as the product of a number when multiplied by 1, 2, 3, 4, …, for example, multiples of 3 are 3, 6, 9, 12, 15, … The **common multiples** of two or more numbers are multiples of all the given numbers, for example, common multiples of 3 and 4 are 12, 24, … The **lowest common multiple** (LCM) is the common multiple that has the smallest value, for example, the LCM of 3 and 4 is 12.
>
> A **factor** of any number N is defined as a number that can be divided into N exactly without leaving a remainder, for example, 3 is a factor of 12. The **common factors** of two or more numbers are factors of all the given numbers, for example, common factors of 12 and 30 are 1, 2, 3 and 6. The **highest common factor** (HCF) is the common factor that has the largest value, for example, the HCF of 12 and 30 is 6.
>
> A number that has only two factors, 1 and itself, is called a **prime number**, for example, 5 and 23 are prime numbers. If a number has more than two factors, it is a **composite number**. Factors that are prime numbers are called **prime factors**.
>
> When the prime factors of a number are repeated, we may write them in **index form**, for example, $72 = 1 \times 2 \times 2 \times 2 \times 3 \times 3 = 1 \times 2^3 \times 3^2$. The 3 in 2^3 is called the **index** or **power**. Note that we list only $\{2, 3\}$ as the set of prime factors of 72; we do not repeat the factors 2 and 3.

Key Fact

Factors of a number occur in pairs. One (1) is a factor of every number but one is **not** a prime number.

Remember?

The **square** of a number is the product of a number multiplied by itself, for example, $25 = 5 \times 5$. We can write the square in index form, that is $25 = 5^2$. We also say that squaring a number is **raising a number to the power of 2**.

The **square root** of a number N, written $\sqrt{N}$, is the number that must be squared to get the number N, for example, $\sqrt{25} = 5$. When the square root of a number N is a whole number, we say that the number N is a **perfect square**.

The **cube** of a number is the product given by three of a number multiplied together, for example, $64 = 4 \times 4 \times 4$. We can write the cube in index form, that is $64 = 4^3$. We also say that cubing a number is **raising a number to the power of 3**.

The **cube root** of a number N, written $\sqrt[3]{N}$, is the number that must be cubed to get the number N, for example, $\sqrt[3]{64} = 4$.

Word Check

base the number being multiplied in a power

index/power the number of times a number is multiplied by itself

surd the square root of a number that is not a perfect square

Practice

D 1 (a) For each number in the following sets of numbers list members of the set of multiples.

(i) 3, 4, 9   (ii) 2, 5, 6, 15

(b) For each set of numbers, write the set of common multiples.

(c) For each set of numbers, write the lowest common multiple.

2 (a) List the set of factors of each number in each set of numbers.
  (i) 96, 140, 294   **(ii)** 42, 105, 270, 325
  For each set of numbers, write
  (b) each number as the product of its prime factors using index form
  (c) the set of common factors
  (d) the highest common factor.

3 For each number given, use prime factors to find the square root, writing your answer as a surd if necessary.
  (i) 36   **(ii)** 72   **(iii)** 120   **(iv)** 468   **(v)** 693

4 Tom works an 8-hour shift and then is off-duty for 8 hours. Bob works a 6-hour shift and then is off-duty for 6 hours. They started their shifts together at 7 am on Monday. Find when they next start their shifts at the same time.

5 A small model of a picture is required to make exact copies to be put onto squares of areas of 144, 324 and 900 square units. Calculate the area of the smallest model that can be used.

6 A roll of wall-paper must be cut in equal lengths of 3.5 m, 4.2 m, or 7 m. Find the length of the shortest roll so that it is possible to cut off equal pieces of any of the three lengths.

Finished Early?
 Go to page 438

Further Practice

E 1 Write each number as the product of its prime factors using index form.
  (i) 60   **(ii)** 98   **(iii)** 242   **(iv)** 351   **(v)** 459

2 For each number given, use prime factors to find the square root, writing your answer as a surd if necessary.
  (i) 25   **(ii)** 112   **(iii)** 242   **(iv)** 441   **(v)** 567

3 For each set of numbers below, use prime factors to write the:
  (a) LCM   **(b)**   HCF.
  (i) 36, 54   **(ii)** 110, 231, 363   **(iii)** 28, 63, 98, 147

4 Find the largest number of children who can share 63 plums and 42 mangoes equally.

5 Some screws in a box are counted in heaps of 9 and none are left over. The screws are counted again in heaps of 12 and again none are left over. What is the smallest number of screws in the box?

Key Fact
The square root of a number multiplied by itself equals the number.

Finished Early?
 Go to page 438

Remember?

The sets of multiples and factors, squares and cubes of whole numbers, prime numbers and composite numbers are positive numbers used for counting and so are subsets of the set of natural or counting numbers, N = {1, 2, 3, 4, ...}.

N is a subset of the set of whole numbers, W = {0, 1, 2, 3, 4, ...}, that is N ⊂ W.

Numbers that are used for measuring, for example, quantities such as length, time, temperature, must include both positive and negative whole numbers, and zero. These numbers belong to the **set of integers, Z** where Z = {... –4, –3, –2, –1, 0, +1, +2, +3, +4, ...}.

Positive and negative numbers are together referred to as **directed numbers**. Directed numbers can be shown on a number line:

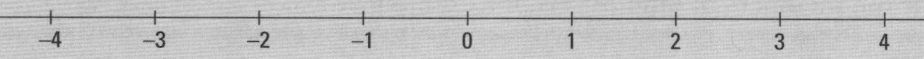

Zero is neither positive nor negative.

Key Facts

To show a directed number we write the symbol, either + or – , with **no space before the number**; for example, –43, –5, +7, +62;

to show the operations of addition or subtraction, we leave a space before and after the symbol, for example, –43 + 4, –5 – 7, 48 + –2.

Remember?

A set of numbers is also required to measure quantities smaller than a unit, that is, numbers that denote parts of a whole or **fractions**. The set of fractions is included in the set called the **set of rational numbers, Q**. Thus the set, Q, includes the integers and fractions, mixed numbers and decimals, that is, numbers that can be written as a ratio, $\frac{n}{d}$, where n and d are integers.

The **set of real numbers, R**, includes the rational numbers as well as numbers that cannot be expressed as a rational number, for example, surds such as $\sqrt{5}$, and π. These numbers are called **irrational numbers**. Approximations are used for their value when working out calculations.

The sets of numbers (except the sets of factors of counting numbers) are infinite sets. Generally, in solving problems it is necessary to define limits for the members of infinite sets, for example, $x : -5 < x < 3, x \in Z$.

Practice

F **1** Arrange the numbers from the smallest to the largest in each of the following groups:

(a) $-5, +3, +1, -1$ (b) $0, -2, +4, +1, -6$ (c) $-3, +3, -4, +4, -5, +5$

2 List any three members of each of the following sets of numbers:

(a) rational numbers   (b) integers
(c) whole numbers   (d) irrational numbers
(e) counting numbers

3 Find the next four terms in each of the following sets of numbers:

(a) $\{1, 2, 4, 8, 16, ...\}$ (b) $\{1, 3, 7, 13, 21, ...\}$
(c) $\{6, 13, 20, 27, 34, ...\}$ (d) $\{1, 1, 2, 3, 5, 8, ...\}$
(e) $\{1, 3, 6, 10, 15, 21, ...\}$
(f) $\{1, 3, 6, 9, ...\}$

Further Practice

G **1** Draw a Venn diagram to show the relation among the sets of rational numbers, natural (counting) numbers, integers and fractions.

2 Find the next four terms in each of the following sets of numbers:

(a) $\{2, 5, 8, 11, 14, ...\}$ (b) $\{0, 1, 3, 6, 10, ...\}$
(c) $\{1, 4, 9, 16, 25, ...\}$ (d) $\{1, 2, 5, 10, 17, ...\}$

Finished Early?
 Go to page 438

3 Fractional Parts

Remember?

We use **fractions** to describe

- **equal parts** of a whole, for example, $\frac{1}{4}$ of the diagram is shaded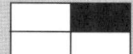
- subsets of a set of **equal elements**, for example, $\frac{2}{3}$ of the circles are black.

In a fraction, the **denominator** is the bottom number and gives the total number of equal parts that the whole or the total is divided into. The **numerator** (the top number) gives the number of parts that you need in the fraction. Generally the numerator is a smaller number than the denominator. If the numerator is a larger number than the denominator, then the fraction is called an **improper fraction**, for example, $\frac{9}{4}$.

Equivalent fractions are fractions that have the same value but which are divided into different numbers of total parts. When the numerator and denominator have no common factors, the fraction is in its **lowest terms**. All the other equivalent fractions have common factors in the numerator and denominator.

A number that is a combination of a whole number and a fraction is called a **mixed number**, for example, $5\frac{3}{4}$.

Percentages are fractions that have a denominator equal to 100 so that a whole or the total is equal to one hundred per cent. The symbol '%' indicates a percentage, that is, $100\% = 1$ and $12\% = \frac{12}{100}$.

Word Check

cancel divide the numerator and the denominator by the same number

express write in symbols or words

represent show or indicate a mathematical concept, generally by using symbols, a table, a diagram, a figure or a graph

Key Fact

A whole number is a fraction with a denominator equal to 1, or when a fraction has a numerator that is a mulutiple of the denominator, for example, $\frac{4}{2}$, $\frac{8}{4}$, $\frac{27}{2}$.

Remember?

The decimal place-value system can be extended to include fractions.

The whole number and the fraction parts are separated by a **decimal point**.

The part of the number to the left of the decimal point is the whole number part; the part to the right of the decimal point is the fraction part.

The decimal part is the numerator of a fraction where the denominator is a power of 10, for example, 0.27 means 27 hundredths, that is $\frac{27}{100}$.

Note that $0.27 = \frac{27}{100} = 27\%$

and that $0.2 = 2 \times 10^{-1}$ and $0.07 = 7 \times 10^{-2}$.

millions	hundred thousands	ten thousands	thousands $(\times 10 \times 10 \times 10) = \times 10^3$	hundreds $(\times 10 \times 10) = \times 10^2$	tens $(\times 10)$	units	tenths $(\div 10) = \times 10^{-1}$	hundredths $(\div 10 \div 10) = \times 10^{-2}$	thousandths $(\div 10 \div 10 \div 10) = \times 10^{-3}$	ten thousands
						0 .	2	7		

Key Facts

Fractions, percentages and decimals are different ways of representing parts of quantities.

A mixed number written as a percentage is greater than 100%.

Practice

 **1** Arrange the following sets of fractions from largest to smallest:

(a) $\{\frac{3}{10}, \frac{4}{5}, \frac{5}{6}, \frac{7}{15}\}$ (b) $\{\frac{5}{6}, \frac{1}{2}, \frac{3}{4}, \frac{2}{3}, \frac{4}{5}\}$

(c) $\{\frac{11}{9}, \frac{7}{5}, \frac{5}{3}, \frac{11}{10}, \frac{7}{6}\}$

2 Arrange the following sets of decimals from smallest to largest:

(a) $\{0.0314, 0.00413, 0.134, 0.00431\}$

(b) $\{5.243, 21.45, 2.435, 4.325, 2.543\}$

Finished Early?

 Go to page 438

Remember?

To write a fraction as a decimal, we can use the numerator of an equivalent fraction with the denominator that is a power of 10 since the decimal number is the numerator with the number of decimal places equal to the number of zeroes in the denominator. Hence
- find the equivalent fraction
- write the numerator with the decimal point in the correct position.

For example, $\frac{3}{5} = \frac{6}{10} = 0.6$; $\frac{7}{20} = \frac{35}{100} = 0.35$

A fraction can also be changed to a decimal fraction by dividing the numerator by the denominator, for example, $\frac{3}{5} = 5\overline{)3.00} = 0.6$.

Fractions that give exact decimal fractions are called **terminating decimals**.

Fractions that cannot be written as equivalent fractions with a denominator that is a power of 10, are never-ending decimal fractions, called **recurring decimals**, for example, $\frac{5}{9} = 0.55555...$ We say that this decimal number is 'zero point 5 recurring' and write it as $0.\dot{5}$.

To write an exact decimal number (terminating decimal) as a fraction, we can write the digits of the decimal part as the numerator. Then the denominator is a power of 10 where the number of zeroes is equal to the number of decimal places. When there are common factors in the numerator and denominator, the fraction can be cancelled to its lowest terms, for example, $0.25 = \frac{25}{100} = \frac{1}{4}$.

To write a recurring decimal as a fraction, write the repeated digit(s) as the numerator and put the same number of 9s as the denominator, for example, $0.142857142857... = \frac{142857}{999999} = \frac{1}{7}$.

To write a decimal number as a percentage, multiply by 100 and include the % symbol, for example, $0.436 = 43.6\%$.

Practice

1 Express each of the following fractions as:

(a) a decimal number   (b) a percentage.

(i) $\frac{1}{4}$ (ii) $\frac{1}{3}$ (iii) $\frac{3}{8}$ (iv) $\frac{2}{9}$ (v) $\frac{2}{5}$ (vi) $\frac{4}{7}$

2 Express each of the following decimals as:

(a) a fraction   (b) a percentage.

(i) 0.5   (ii) 2.6   (iii) 19.6   (iv) 0.045   (v) 15.05

3 Arrange the following numbers from smallest to largest:

$\frac{3}{4}$, 60%, $\frac{5}{8}$, $\frac{13}{10}$, 0.875, $\frac{7}{9}$, $\frac{2}{3}$, 2.5

> **Finished Early?**
> Go to page 438

Further Practice

Given the numbers: 135%, $\frac{5}{8}$, $\frac{3}{4}$, $\frac{49}{10}$, 12%, $\frac{17}{9}$, 342%

(a) write the numbers as decimals

(b) arrange the numbers in order from smallest to largest.

> **Finished Early?**
> Go to page 438

Remember?

Economists and scientists work with very large numbers and very small numbers. To make it easier to read and to write these numbers, we can write

- the digits in the number in groups of three to the left and right of the decimal point; for example, 3 284 129.214 37.
- the numbers in **standard form** (sometimes called **scientific notation**); in standard form we use a decimal number, x, where $1 \leqslant x < 10$, multiplied by a power of 10; usually the number is written correct to 2 or 3 decimal places (d.p.), for example, we will write, correct to 3 d.p.
  the large number   3 284 129.214 37 as 3.284×10^6; and
  the small number   0.000 567 123   as 5.671×10^{-4}

Learn More About It

The **binary system** is a number system based on the two digits 0 and 1. This system is particularly important in today's world since binary numbers are used in computers – when computer switches operate, the digit '1' means *on* and the digit '0' means *off*.

The columns in the binary system have the values shown in the diagram on the right. The value of the digit 1 is multiplied by 2 as it moves across each column from right to left.

sixty-fours	thirty-twos	sixteens $(\times 2 \times 2 \times 2 \times 2)$	eights $(\times 2 \times 2 \times 2)$	fours $(\times 2 \times 2)$	twos $(\times 2)$	units (digit)

Thus, comparing the decimal and the binary systems, we have

Decimal system	Binary system
1	1
2	10
3	11
4	100
5	101
6	110
7	111
8	1000

and so on.

What is 12_{10} in base two?
Since 12 is less than 16, there are no sixteens in 12. To find the number of eights in 12, divide by eight; there is one eight and the remainder is 4; there is one four and the remainder is 0.

Thus, in the decimal and the binary systems
$$12_{10} = (2 \times 2 \times 2) + (2 \times 2) + 0 + 0$$
$$= 1100_2$$

sixty-fours	thirty-twos	sixteens $(\times 2 \times 2 \times 2 \times 2)$	eights $(\times 2 \times 2 \times 2)$	fours $(\times 2 \times 2)$	twos $(\times 2)$	units (digit)
			1	1	0	0

Similarly,
$$151_{10} = (2 \times 2 \times 2 \times 2 \times 2 \times 2 \times 2 \times 2) + 0 + 0$$
$$+ (2 \times 2 \times 2 \times 2) + 0 + (2 \times 2) + (2) + 1$$
$$= 10010111_2$$

one hundred and twenty eights	sixty-fours	thirty-twos	sixteens $(\times 2 \times 2 \times 2 \times 2)$	eights $(\times 2 \times 2 \times 2)$	fours $(\times 2 \times 2)$	twos $(\times 2)$	units (digit)
1	0	0	1	0	1	1	1

Practice

 1 Express each of the following in standard form.
    (a) 52.43, 21.045, 2.435, 432.5, 2 543 271
    (b) 0.0314, 0.004 13, 0.134, 17.504, 0.000 005 043

2 Express each of the following as a decimal number.
    (a) 5.24×10^2, 1.415×10^5, 2.43×10^3, 4.325×10^7
    (b) 3.14×10^{-2}, 4.13×10^{-5}, 3.124×10^{-3}, 1.054×10^{-6}

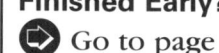

Finished Early?
➡ Go to page 438

Further Practice

 1 Express each of the following in standard form.
    36, 0.3, 0.003, 43 505 643, 0.000 63, 0.000 000 105, 7320

2 Express each of the following as a decimal number.
    4×10^2, 2.6×10^{-7}, 1.07×10^{-3}, 5.55×10^8

Finished Early?
➡ Go to page 438

Unit 1 *Sets, Relations and Number Theory*

Summary of Chapters 1, 2 and 3

Sets

- A set is a collection of objects having a common property and usually named by a capital letter.
- The members of the set are called its **elements**.
- The members may be defined by a description, e.g. {five vowels of the alphabet}, by listing its members, for example, {a, e, i, o, u} or in set-builder notation, for example, {$x : -2 < x < 5$}, $x \in Z$}. Note that the use of set-builder notation shortens the description and provides information about the range of values of the elements. A list of the symbols of set language and their meanings is given in Chapter 1.
- The members of a set can be represented on a **Venn diagram**.
- A set may be an **empty** or **null** set (no elements), a **finite** set (a given number of elements) or an **infinite** set (a never-ending number of elements).
- Sets can be used to illustrate the relationship between all the sets used in the decimal number system. These sets of numbers (except the sets of factors of the counting numbers) are all infinite sets.
- The set that includes all the members of the set in a given problem is termed the **universal set**. Sets that have only some of the members in the problem are called **subsets**. The members of the universal set that do not belong to the subset are called the **complement** of the subset.
- **Equivalent sets** have the same number of elements; **equal sets** have identical elements.
- **Disjoint sets** have no common elements, that is, the sets do not **intersect**. When sets intersect, Venn diagrams can be used to draw conclusions deriving from a number of statements involving terms such as 'all', 'some' and 'none'.

Relations and Functions

- **Relations** and **functions** show a connection between the elements of two sets. The first set is called the **domain** and an element of the domain is called an **object**. The second set is called the **co-domain** and each corresponding element in the co-domain that is connected to an object is called its **image**. A relation may be one-to-one, one-to-many, many-to-one or many-to-many.

- A relation may be described by a **phrase**, an **arrow diagram**, a **table of values**, **ordered pairs**, or a **graph**. A graph can be used to represent a relation by using the ordered pairs as the coordinates of points referred to x- and y-axes in a Cartesian plane. The order of the elements in an ordered pair is important. The points on a graph may be joined by straight lines or a curve.

- A **function** (also referred to as a **mapping**) is a relation in which *every object* in the domain is related to *one and only one image* in the co-domain. Only one object can be mapped onto one image, that is, a **one-to-one** relation, or more than one object may be mapped onto the same image, that is, a **many-to-one** relation. The set of **images** is called the **range**.

- If the ordered pair in a function f is (x, y), then x is the independent variable and y is the dependent variable. The function f may be written as $y = f(x)$, or $f : x \rightarrow y$.

  When the graph is a straight line, the function f is called a linear function, and the relation $y = f(x)$ is called the equation of the line.

Number Theory

- The decimal number system in general use today includes all the sets of numbers required for counting, measuring and working out calculations.

- **N** is the set of **natural (counting) numbers** – these are all **positive** numbers. When the number zero (0) is included, the set becomes **W**, the set of **whole numbers**.

- The set of **positive and negative** whole numbers is called **Z**, the set of **integers**.

- When exact parts of a whole, that is, fractions are included, the set is called **Q**, the set of **rational numbers**.

- When irrational numbers such as π, are included, the set is called **R**, the set of **real numbers**. For these sets therefore, the relation is $N \subset W \subset Z \subset Q \subset R$. Positive and negative numbers are also referred to as **directed numbers**.

- Generally, for everyday purposes, numbers use the base 10 **place-value** system, called the **decimal** or **denary** system. Numbers use symbols called **numerals**. The numerals in the decimal system are 0, 1, 2, 3, 4, 5, 6, 7, 8, 9 and are called **digits**. In a place-value system, the value of a digit depends on its position in the number.

- Numbers written in the base 2 place-value system, called the **binary** system, use only the digits 0 and 1, and are of particular significance for application in the technology related to computers and calculating machines.

- **Odd** numbers and **even** numbers, **prime** numbers and **composite** numbers, **multiples** and **factors,** are subsets of N, while **fractions, mixed numbers, percentages** and **decimals** are subsets of Q.

- **Common factors** and the **highest common factor (HCF), common multiples** and the **lowest common multiple (LCM)** of two or more numbers are useful in simplifying computational exercises and solving real-world problems.

- The **power** of a number is the repeated multiplication, say, n times, of the number. The **root** of a number is the inverse or opposite of the power. The power and root of a number may be an integer, a rational number or a real number.

- The power of a number b, may be given in **index form** by writing b^n, where b is called the **base** and n is called the **index** {plural is indices). Very large numbers and very small numbers may be written using indices in **standard form** or **scientific notation**, that is, $a \times 10^n$, where $1 \le a < 10$ and $n \in Z$.

 # Computation

In this chapter you will learn about ...

① operations and laws
② calculating fractions and decimals
③ using ratios and rates
④ approximation and estimation

① Operations and Laws

Remember?

The four basic arithmetic operations are addition and subtraction, and multiplication and division. These operations are done in a definite order, **BoDMAS**, that is

first: **Brackets**
next: **Powers** [and Roots]
then: **Division and Multiplication** [working from left to right]
last : **Addition and Subtraction**

When there are **nested brackets** (brackets within brackets) always work out the innermost brackets first.

When doing addition, subtraction, multiplication and division, two quantities are combined together to give a result. These are called **binary operations**.

The **electronic calculator** is a tool which can do complicated calculations and when used correctly, can do them faster than most humans. Like all machines, the calculator is most useful when used wisely. It is best to use a calculator only when necessary. Be careful to read the manufacturer's instructions to learn the sequence of entering data and operations for your type of calculator and afterwards check by using small numbers in simple calculations. Many calculator keys perform special functions.

Calculators can store numbers in memory. Check the memory keys on your calculator so you can use them when you do complex calculations. Some special keys are shown in the table on page 48.

Key Fact

An inverse operation reverses the calculation done by another operation. Examples of inverse operations are: addition and subtraction; multiplication and division.

Key	Function	Notes
enter =	Enter data	
CE C DEL AC	Cancel errors, edit commands	These keys allow you to start again if you make a mistake, or to edit your calculation before entering it.
+/− (−)	Change sign, negative numbers	
%	Percentage	Press after a calculation to get answer as a percentage.
x^2	Square	Much quicker than multiplying the number by itself or using the power key.
$\sqrt{}$	Square root	Check for your calculator whether you press it before or after the number.
y^x ^ $y^{1/x}$ $\sqrt[x]{y}$	Powers/roots	Check for your calculator whether you enter the base or the index first.
$^1/_x$	Reciprocal	Works out 1 ÷ the number you enter.
EXP EE	Standard form	To enter 3.4×10^6, key in **3 . 4 EXP 6** NOT **3 . 4 × 1 0 EXP 6**
π	pi	Use in circle calculations.

Memory keys	Function
STO M+ MIN M+	Store
RCL M+ MR	Recall
MCL MC 0 MIN 0 STO M+	Clear
M+	Add to the number in memory
M−	Subtract from the number in memory

Remember?

Operations have particular properties when they obey certain laws. The **commutative law** states that the order of the numbers in the operation does not matter. This is true in addition and in multiplication, for example,

$2 + 5 = 5 + 2$; and $7 \times 3 = 3 \times 7$.

Therefore the basic operations of addition and multiplication are **commutative**; subtraction and division are not since $7 - 2 \neq 2 - 7$; and $12 \div 3 \neq 3 \div 12$.

The **associative law** states that the order in which the numbers in the operation are combined does not matter. This is true in addition and in multiplication, for example, $(2 + 5) + 3 = 2 + (5 + 3)$; and $(7 \times 3) \times 2 = 7 \times (3 \times 2)$.

Therefore the basic operations of addition and multiplication are **associative**; subtraction and division are not since $(7 - 5) - 3 \neq 7 - (5 - 3)$; and $(12 \div 3) \div 2 \neq 12 \div (3 \div 2)$.

Since $3(5 + 2) = 3(5) + 3(2)$ and $3(5 - 2) = 3(5) - 3(2)$, we say that multiplication is **distributive** over addition and subtraction.

Key Facts

Tests of divisibility: any whole number is divisible by

2 if its last digit is even
3 if the sum of its digits is divisible by 3
4 if its last two digits form a number divisible by 4
5 if its last digit is 5 or 0
6 if its last digit is even and the sum of its digits is divisible by 3
8 if its last three digits form a number divisible by 8
9 if the sum of its digits is divisible by 9
10 if its last digit is 0

Learn About It

$5 + 4 = 9$ and $5 \times 4 = 20$

We cannot find any examples in which the sum or the product of two whole numbers is not also a whole number.

Let $a \in W$, and $b \in W$, where $W = \{$whole numbers$\}$.

Then $a + b \in W$ and $a \times b \in W$ for all values of a and b.

We say that *the set of whole numbers is* **closed** *under addition and multiplication*.

This is known as the **law of closure** which states that, if an operation is applied to any two members of a set and the result is also a member of the set, then the set of numbers is closed under that operation.

Try It Out

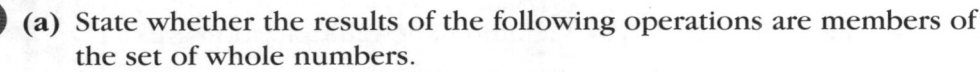

(a) State whether the results of the following operations are members of the set of whole numbers.

    (i) $9 - 4$ **(ii)** $4 - 9$

(b) Is $a - b \in W$ for all values of $a - b$?

(c) What conclusions can you draw about the law of closure applied to the set of whole numbers under subtraction?

Practice

B (a) Work out the results of the division of the following whole numbers:

    (i) $12 \div 4$ **(ii)** $4 \div 12$

(b) Is $a \div b \in W$ for all values of $a \div b$?

(c) What conclusions can you draw about the law of closure applied to the set of whole numbers under division?

> **Word Check**
>
> **binary operation** any operation that combines two quantities to get a result

---

Remember?

The **identity element for addition** is zero (0), that is, when zero is added to any number, the result is the same number so that, for example, $0 + 12 = 12$.

The **identity element for multiplication** is one (1), that is, when any number is multiplied by one, the result is the same number so that, for example, $24 \times 1 = 24$.

Practice

C **1** Find the value of each of the following, using an electronic calculator if necessary:

(a) $29 + 43 \times 7$ (b) $5 \times (71 - 17)$

(c) $(3 + 47) \div 25$ (d) $5 \times 71 - 17$

(e) $3 + 47 \div 25$ (f) $(24 \times 5) \div (18 \div 6)$

2 For each of the calculations in question 1, state the law(s) that the calculation illustrates.

3 For each of the following:

(a) work out the calculation

(b) state the set of numbers, W, Z, Q or R, that the answer belongs to.

(i) $27 \div 7$ (ii) $\sqrt{24 \div 8}$

(iii) $3949 \times 11 \times 0$ (iv) $59 - 25 \times 3$

4 Work out the calculations for the binary operations given below.

(a) $p * q$ means $\frac{2}{3}p \times \frac{1}{4}q$

(i) $18 * 12$ (ii) $24 * (7 * 6)$

(b) $m \# n$ means $m^2 + 3n$

(i) $3 \# 2$ (ii) $(3 \# 2) \# 1$

5 Show whether the binary operations given in question 4 obey:

(a) the commutative law   (b) the associative law.

Key Fact

Generally, if there is *only one example* where a law does not hold for an operation, we say that the operation does not have that property.

Finished Early?

➡ Go to page 438

Further Practice

D For each of the following calculations:

(a) state whether it is *true* or *false*   (b) give a reason for your answer.

1 $42 - 26 = 26 - 42$

2 $35 + (7 \times 4) = 35 + 7 \times 4$

3 $34 + 23 + 0 = 34 + 23$

4 $6 \times (14 + 3) = 6 \times 14 + 6 \times 3$

5 $(20 \div 5) \div 2 = 20 \div (5 \div 2)$

6 $33 \times 1 = 33$

7 $20 \times 5 \times 2 = (20 \times 5) \times 2$

Finished Early?

➡ Go to page 438

Remember?

When working with directed numbers, subtracting a positive number is the same as adding the negative number; subtracting a negative number is the same as adding the positive number.

When two numbers of different signs are multiplied together, the product is negative. When two numbers of the same sign are multiplied together, the product is positive; thus, squaring any number gives a positive answer.

Addition and subtraction are **inverse operations**; so are multiplication and division.

Practice

E Simplify and evaluate the following calculations.

1 $-5 + (-4)$

2 $-7 - (-3)$

3 $9 \times (6 - 13)$

4 $(5 - 9) - 6$

5 $9 - (-6) + (-8)$

6 $-4 + (-3) - 13$

7 $5 \times (-7)$

8 $-13 \times (-6)$

9 $-5 \times (-3) \times (-11)$

10 $15 \div (-3)$

11 $9 \times (-4) \div (-6)$

12 $-12 \div (-4) \div (-3)$

Finished Early?
➡ Go to page 438

Further Practice

F Simplify and evaluate the following calculations.

1 $9 + (-15)$

2 $-16 - (-7)$

3 $19 - (-6) + (-18)$

4 $-7 + (-3) - 1$

5 $-4 \times (-13)$

6 -13×3

7 $4 \times (-4) \div (-8)$

8 $-20 \div (-4) \div (-2)$

Finished Early?
➡ Go to page 438

② Calculating Fractions and Decimals

Remember?

To express one quantity as a fraction of another quantity, the two quantities must be in the same unit, for example, 10 minutes as a fraction of 1 hour must be written as 10 minutes of 60 minutes, and then the fraction becomes $\frac{10}{60} = \frac{1}{6}$, in its lowest terms.

To express one quantity as a percentage of another quantity, work out as a fraction and then multiply the fraction by 100 to write as a percentage.

Word Check

dividend the number that is divided by another number

divisor the number that divides another number

reciprocal the number or expression produced by dividing
1 by a given number or expression

Remember?

To add and to subtract fractions, the fractions must have the same total number of equal parts, that is, the denominators must be the same. For each fraction, find the equivalent fraction with the same denominator, or use a common multiple (usually the LCM) of the denominators. Then, the sum or difference of the fractions is the sum or difference of the numerators.

For example, $\frac{2}{5} + \frac{3}{8}$ must be changed to $\frac{16}{40} + \frac{15}{40} = \frac{31}{40}$;

also, $\frac{2}{5} - \frac{3}{8}$ becomes $\frac{16}{40} - \frac{15}{40} = \frac{1}{40}$.

To multiply a fraction by a whole number:
- multiply the numerator of the fraction by the number, for example, $\frac{2}{5} \times 3 = \frac{6}{5} = 1\frac{1}{5}$, since $\frac{2}{5} \times 3$ means three (two-fifths).

To multiply a fraction by another fraction:
- multiply the numerators together and multiply the denominators together, for example, $\frac{2}{3} \times \frac{4}{5} = \frac{8}{15}$.

Multiplication and division are inverse operations. Dividing a fraction, F, by a whole number or a fraction is the same operation as multiplying F by the reciprocal of the number or the fraction, for example,

(i) $\frac{2}{5} \div 3 = \frac{2}{5} \times \frac{1}{3} = \frac{2}{15}$ (note that $\frac{2}{5} \div 3$ is the same operation
                                          as $\frac{1}{3}$ of $\frac{2}{5}$)

(ii) $\frac{2}{3} \div \frac{4}{5} = \frac{2}{3} \times \frac{5}{4} = \frac{5}{6}$ (cancelling by 2 to write the answer in the
                                          lowest terms)

Practice

G Evaluate the following.

1 $\frac{1}{9} + \frac{2}{3}$ **2** $1\frac{2}{3} - \frac{3}{8}$

3 $9\frac{1}{4} - 6\frac{1}{3} + 1\frac{5}{9}$ **4** $(5\frac{3}{10} - 2\frac{4}{5}) \times 6$

5 $3(3\frac{7}{9} + 2\frac{2}{3})$ **6** $3\frac{1}{7}(6\frac{1}{4} - 5\frac{4}{9})$

7 $3\frac{4}{7} \times \frac{3}{10}$ **8** $6\frac{2}{3} \times 2\frac{5}{8}$

9 $5\frac{1}{2} \div 1\frac{5}{8}$ **10** $11\frac{1}{4} \div 3\frac{1}{3} \times \frac{2}{5}$

11 $\dfrac{3\frac{4}{7} \times \frac{3}{10}}{2\frac{2}{3} \times \frac{3}{8}}$ **12** $\dfrac{4\frac{2}{5} \div 3\frac{2}{3}}{1\frac{5}{6} \div 2\frac{3}{4}}$

> **Finished Early?**
> 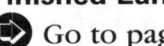 Go to page 439

H **1** In a box there are footballs, tennis balls and basketballs; $\frac{1}{4}$ of the balls are footballs and $\frac{1}{3}$ are basketballs. There are 30 tennis balls. Find the total number of balls in the box.

2 In each of the following, express the first quantity as a fraction of the second quantity.

     (a) $ 200, $ 240   **(b)** 110 m, 3 km   **(c)** 350 g, 8 kg

> **Finished Early?**
> 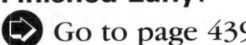 Go to page 439

Further Practice

I Evaluate the following.

1 $3\frac{1}{2} + 2\frac{5}{8} - 3\frac{1}{4}$ **2** $1\frac{1}{2} + 2\frac{3}{4} \times 1\frac{2}{3}$

3 $\dfrac{1\frac{4}{9} + \frac{3}{9}}{3\frac{1}{5}}$ **4** $\dfrac{4\frac{1}{3} - 3\frac{5}{6}}{1\frac{5}{6} + 2\frac{3}{4}}$

5 $5\frac{1}{2} \times \frac{3}{11}$ **6** $5\frac{3}{10}(2\frac{4}{5} - 2\frac{5}{8})$

7 $3\frac{4}{7} \div 1\frac{5}{8}$ **8** $1\frac{1}{4} \div \frac{1}{3} \div 1\frac{2}{5}$

9 $\dfrac{7 \times \frac{3}{10}}{1\frac{2}{3} \times \frac{3}{8}}$ **10** $\dfrac{2\frac{2}{5} \div 1\frac{2}{3}}{2\frac{2}{5} \times 1\frac{2}{3}}$

> **Finished Early?**
> Go to page 439

Remember?

To add and subtract decimals, group digits of the same place value together. It is useful to write the numbers in a column with the decimal points under one another.

To multiply a decimal number by powers of 10, keep the decimal point fixed. Then, as the power of 10 increases by 1, the digits in the number (including zero) move one place to the *left*. When the place to the right in the whole number part becomes empty, we write a zero in order to keep the value of the number correct. Note that if the place is after the decimal point, there is no need to have a place holder, for example, $25.46 \times 10 = 254.6$ but $3.57 \times 10\,000 = 35\,700$.

When decimal numbers are multiplied, the number of decimal places in the product is equal to the sum of the decimal places in the numbers, for example, $0.26 \times 0.35 = 0.0910$, written as 0.091.

Practice

J Calculate 257×33, and use the result to find the value of:

1 2.57×3.3 **2** 25.7×3.3

3 25.7×0.33 **4** 0.257×33

5 0.257×3.3 **6** 0.257×0.33

Finished Early?
Go to page 439

Remember?

To divide a decimal number by powers of 10, keep the decimal point fixed and as the power of 10 increases by 1 in the divisor, the digits in the number (including zero) move one place to the *right*. When the place to the right of the decimal point becomes empty, we write a zero in order to keep the value of the number correct, for example, $3.07 \div 1000 = 0.003\,07$

When a number is divided by a decimal number, make the divisor a whole number and move the decimal point the same number of places in the dividend to have an equivalent division, that is, to keep the value of the division the same, for example, $0.245 \div 0.35 = 24.5 \div 35 = 0.7;\ 10.8 \div 0.24 = 1080 \div 24 = 45$

Practice

K Calculate the following without using a calculator.
- **(a)** 43.028 + 2.3007
- **(b)** 34.503 – 3.4503
- **(c)** 3.012 × 0.007
- **(d)** 7.5012 ÷ 0.012
- **(e)** (0.23 + 0.17) × 0.6
- **(f)** (8.3 – 7.94) ÷ 0.3
- **(g)** $\dfrac{6.44 + 2.07}{15.2 - 12.9}$
- **(h)** $\dfrac{1.8 \times 0.5}{0.45 \times 8}$

2 Write the elements of each of the following sets in order from the smallest to the largest, indicating clearly the method used.
- **(a)** $\{38\%, \frac{3}{4}, 0.66, \frac{3}{8}, 0.77, 70\%\}$
- **(b)** $\{5.24 \times 10^2, -1.415 \times 10^5, 2.43 \times 10^3, 4.325 \times 10^2\}$
- **(c)** $\{2.66, \frac{8}{3}, 300\%, 3.25, \frac{13}{5}, 275\%\}$
- **(d)** $\{3.14 \times 10^{-2}, 4.13 \times 10^{-5}, 3.124 \times 10^{-3}, 1.054 \times 10^{-6}\}$

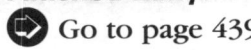

Finished Early?
⇨ Go to page 439

Further Practice

L **1** Calculate the following without using a calculator.
- **(a)** 70.032 + 8.2319
- **(b)** 76.428 – 46.72
- **(c)** 5.213 × 2.01
- **(d)** 2.4375 ÷ 0.0013
- **(e)** 0.05(3 – 0.8)
- **(f)** (1.62 – 0.77) ÷ 0.34
- **(g)** $\dfrac{2.03 + 1.09}{0.08}$
- **(h)** $\dfrac{1.14 \times 0.7}{11.5 - 9.4}$

2 Work out each of the following, writing your answer in the simplest form.
- **(a)** $\frac{7}{40}$ as **(i)** a decimal **(ii)** a percentage
- **(b)** 4.28 as **(i)** a percentage **(ii)** a mixed number

Finished Early?
⇨ Go to page 439

3 Using Ratios and Rates

Remember?

A **ratio** is a comparison between two or more quantities of the same kind; we may compare different lengths, various prices, distances, and so on.

In order to express the comparison as a ratio, the quantities must be measured in the **same units**, for example, the different lengths must all be measured in centimetres, or all in metres; prices must all be in dollars, or all in cents, and so on.

When quantities of different kinds are compared, the comparison is called a **rate**, for example, when distance moved is compared with time, the rate is **speed**, measured, for example, *in kilometres per hour*; when the wages received is compared with the number of hours worked, the **rate of pay** is *dollars per hour*.

A ratio can be written, for example, as *Length A : Length B =* $20 \, cm : 30 \, cm$, and read as 'the ratio of Length A compared to Length B is 20 cm compared to 30 cm', where ':' stands for 'compared to'.

If you multiply or divide all the numbers in a ratio by the same number, then the ratio is the same, and you get an **equivalent ratio**.

Since the units of the quantities in a ratio are the same, there are no units in a ratio. Hence, the ratio can be expressed as a fraction, for example, if Length A : Length B = $20 \, cm : 30 \, cm$, then we can write the ratio as

$\dfrac{\text{Length A}}{\text{Length B}} = \dfrac{20 \, cm}{30 \, cm} = \dfrac{20}{30} = \dfrac{2}{3}$, in its lowest terms.

Note that $20 : 30$ and $2 : 3$ are equivalent ratios.

Hence, to compare ratios, first write as fractions and then apply the same rules as for fractions.

If the order of the quantities being compared is changed, then the order of the numerical terms in the ratio is also changed, for example, if $A : B = 2 : 3$, then $B : A = 3 : 2$.

Key Fact

The ratio $n : 1$ means the first quantity is n times the second.

Practice

M Simplify the following ratios.

1 350 : 210

2 17 : 85

3 5 cm to 1 km

4 0.5 litres to 200 ml

5 3 km to 15 m

6 \$ 12 to 40 cents

7 $2\frac{3}{4} : 1\frac{5}{6}$

8 1.5 kg to 600 g

> **Finished Early?**
> Go to page 439

N Write the above ratios under **M** in the form $n : 1$ or $1 : n$.

> **Finished Early?**
> Go to page 439

Further Practice

⊙ Simplify the following ratios and then write the ratios in the form $n : 1$ or $1 : n$.

1 56 : 72

2 91 : 18.2

3 30 cm to 1 m 10 cm

4 40 cents to \$ 4

5 500 cc to 3 litres

6 $2\frac{1}{10} : \frac{3}{4}$

> **Finished Early?**
> Go to page 439

Remember?

Quantities may be 'shared' or divided in a given ratio. Then, the total number of 'shares' or parts in the ratio is taken as the whole or total; and each 'share' or part of the ratio is a fraction of the whole, for example, to divide \$ 20 in the ratio 2 : 3:

Total number of parts = 2 + 3 = 5

The shares/parts are $\frac{2}{5}$ of \$ 20 and $\frac{3}{5}$ of \$ 20.

Key Fact

Ratios can be among more than two terms, for example, X : Y : Z = 3 : 5 : 2.

Remember?

A quantity may also be increased or decreased in a given ratio, for example, if the time to complete a task is 6 hours, and if the time is increased in the ratio 4 : 3, that is, $(\frac{4}{3} \times 6)$ hours, then the new time is 8 hours, or if the time is decreased in the ratio 2 : 3, that is, $(\frac{2}{3} \times 6)$ hours, then the new time is 4 hours.

Practice

P Divide each of the following in the given ratio.

1 $ 250, 2 : 3

2 15 m, 7 : 3

3 5 litres, 2 : 2 : 1

4 30 kg, 1 : 1.5 : 2.5

> **Finished Early?**
> ➡ Go to page 439

Q In each of the following, change the amount in the given ratio.

1 $ 3224, 5 : 8

2 12 h, 4 : 3

3 4 litres, 3 : 2

4 900 cm, 2 : 5

> **Finished Early?**
> ➡ Go to page 439

R **1** Cement, sand and gravel are mixed to make concrete. The ratio used is cement : sand : gravel = 2 : 3 : 1.
(a) Find the mass of each material in 33 kg of cement.
The ratio of the mixture is changed. The sand is decreased in the ratio 2 : 3, and the gravel is increased in the ratio 3 : 2.
(b) Find the ratio of the materials in the new mixture.

2 The profits of a business are divided so that J's share : K's share = 5 : 3.
(a) J received $ 2000, find K's share.
(b) Find the total amount of the profits.
K's share was changed in the ratio 10 : 9. Calculate
(c) the new ratio of J's share : K's share
(d) the amount each receives if the profits do not change.

> **Finished Early?**
> Go to page 439

Further Practice

S For each of the following, complete the ratio.

1 $300\,\text{m}$ to $?\,\text{km} = 4 : 5$ **2** $3 : 4 : 2 = ? : 12 : ?$

3 $3 : ? : 2 = \$6 : \$22 : ?$ **4** $15 : 6 = ? : 1$

T For each of the following, find the new value after changing the amount in the given ratio.

1 $24\,\text{cm}^2$, $4 : 3$ **2** $\$210$, $5 : 12$

U **1 (a)** $\$3960$ is shared among Alan, Bill and Carl in the ratio $3 : 2 : 4$. Calculate the amount that each person receives.

    (b) Increase Alan's share in the ratio $5 : 3$, and decrease Carl's share in the ratio $3 : 4$. Write the new ratio of the shares for Alan, Bill and Carl.

    (c) Calculate the new amount that each person receives.

2 Tim studied Mathematics, English and Science for 50 minutes, 30 minutes and 45 minutes respectively.

Ann studied Mathematics, English and Science for 40 minutes, 40 minutes and 45 minutes respectively. For each student:

    (a) find the ratio of the times spent on the three subjects

    (b) work out the fraction of the total time spent on each subject

    (c) compare the proportion of time spent on each subject by each student.

Finished Early?
Go to page 439

Remember?

Two quantities may be compared in two ways

- Both quantities increase or decrease in a constant ratio. This is called **direct proportion**.

  The two quantities are **directly proportional**, and one quantity is a multiple of the other; for example, if there are 12 pens in a box, and C, the number of boxes, increases in a given ratio, then p, the number of pens, increases in the same ratio, and C is directly proportional to p so that $C = 12p$.

  The graph relating directly proportional quantities (C and p) is a straight line that passes through the origin.

- As one quantity increases in a given ratio, the other quantity decreases in the same ratio. This is called **inverse proportion** for example, given a lighted candle, as the number of minutes increases in a given ratio, the length of the candle decreases in the same ratio.

The **unitary method** can be used in solving problems of direct or inverse proportion as follows:

- write statements with the quantity to be found at the end
- decide whether the problem is direct or inverse proportion
- state the given facts in the first line
- find the rate for 1 unit
- work out the required calculations.

Practice

 1 12 pens cost $ 75, how many pens can be bought for $ 100?

2 30 cows eat the grass in a field in 5 days. Find the number of days that the grass in a field of equal size would last 3 cows eating at the same rate.

3 A computer uses 3 ink cartridges to make 80 copies of a document. Work out **(a)** the number of copies that 10 cartridges will make

(b) the number of cartridges required to make 500 copies.

Finished Early?

➡ Go to page 439

Further Practice

 1 A bus is moving at a constant speed. The bus goes 72 km in 1 hour 30 minutes.
Calculate **(a)** the distance covered in 40 minutes
(b) the time taken to move 300 km.

2 The distance d between the legs of a ladder and the height h of the ladder are in a constant ratio. $h = 0.64$ m when $d = 0.4$ m, calculate:
(a) d when $h = 2$ m **(b)** h when $d = 0.6$ m.

> **Finished Early?**
> ⇨ Go to page 439

④ Approximation and Estimation

Remember?

To round a number is to give an approximate value of the number.
In the **decimal place-value system**, look at the digit in the column to the right of the digit to be rounded,
round up, if that digit is greater than or equal to 5;
round down, if that digit is less than 5;
for example, 437 to the nearest ten is 440, and to the nearest hundred is 400.

We can also round any number N to a given number of **significant figures** (s.f.); start to count from the non-zero digit having the highest value on the left of the number. Then, the same rules as before apply, for example, 2175 correct to 1 s.f. is 2000; correct to 2 s.f. is 2200; and correct to 3 s.f. is 2180. Note that the accuracy of the approximation increases as the number of significant figures increases.

Remember that a zero in the 'middle' of a number must be counted since it is a place-holder and not including it as a significant number will change the value of the non-zero digits, and hence the value of the number N.

We can give **approximate** values of decimal numbers by rounding to a given number of **decimal places** (d.p.) using the same rules as for whole numbers, for example, correct to 2 d.p., 3.274 is 3.27 and 24.508 is 24.51.

Key Fact

A number rounded
to the nearest ten is less accurate than the number itself;
to the nearest hundred is less accurate than one rounded
to the nearest ten;
to the nearest thousand is less accurate than one
rounded to the nearest hundred; and so on.

Remember?

When working out calculations, it is useful to first make an **estimate** of the accurate answer by rounding off the numbers to the nearest whole number or to one significant figure.

An estimate helps to prevent some errors and also provides a check whether the answer is sensible or not – this is especially important when using calculators.

In working out the cost of items in real-life situations, an estimate assists in checking for numerical errors in calculations and in making decisions for purchase or not. Use familiar known measures to assist in estimating unknown values, for example, your hand-span (20 cm approximately), lengths of 1 cm, a 1 metre ruler, a 1 kg pack of sugar/flour, a 1 litre carton of juice/milk.

Practice

 Work out the following calculations to the given degree of accuracy.

1 43.0357   **(a)** nearest ten   **(b)** to 2 d.p.   **(c)** to 3 s.f.

2 3.142 × 6.75   **(a)** exactly   **(b)** to 2 d.p.   **(c)** to 3 s.f.

3 $\sqrt{3.142 \times 4.1^3}$ **(a)** nearest whole number   **(b)** to 2 d.p.   **(c)** to 3 s.f.

4 52.88 ÷ 1.26   **(a)** nearest whole number   **(b)** to 2 d.p.   **(c)** to 3 s.f.

Ⓨ State the range of values, by giving the largest possible value and the smallest possible value, of the following.

1 10.4 sec, correct to the nearest 0.1 sec

2 23.72 kg, correct to the nearest 0.01 kg

Key Fact

A measurement that is given to a higher degree of accuracy than the measuring instrument is an example of **false accuracy**.

Choose and use approximate values to estimate whether the given answers are correct. Write C if correct; I if incorrect.

(a) 39.028 + 2.0307 = 59.34 (2 d.p)   (b) 76.831 – 3.4503 = 42.3 (3 s.f.)
(c) 3.012 × 0.007 = 21.08 (3 s.f.)   (d) 3.012 ÷ 0.101 = 3.3 (1 d.p.)

AA

1 For the answers in **Z** that are incorrect, work out the calculation to the given degree of accuracy.

2 Write the following numerical values with the most appropriate degree of accuracy.

(a) a national budget of $ 10 342 421 592.31
(b) the length of a page measured with a 20 cm ruler is 11.456 cm
(c) the weight of a child on a bathroom scale is 6.325 kg

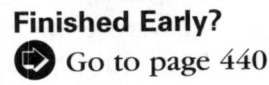

Finished Early?
➡ Go to page 440

Further Practice

AB Choose and use approximate values to estimate whether the given answers are correct. If correct, write C. If incorrect, work out the calculation to the given degree of accuracy.

1 0.06505 + 19.034 = 25.54 (2 d.p.)

2 852.07 – 76.431 = 8.36 (3 s.f.)

3 0. 012 × 5. 01 = 60.1 (3 s.f.)

4 23.65 ÷ 0.11 = 2.2 (1 d.p.)

5 $\sqrt{324.689}$ = 18.1 (1 d.p.)

6 12.47 + 5 × 2.4 = 42 (2 s.f.)

Finished Early?
➡ Go to page 440

5 Consumer Arithmetic

In this chapter you will learn about ...
1. profit and loss
2. mortgages and hire purchase
3. bills and invoices
4. interest
5. wages, salary and income tax
6. exchange rates

1 Profit and Loss

Remember?

The **cost price** of an item is the total amount of money paid to obtain the item.

The **selling price** is the amount it is sold for. If the selling price is higher than the cost price, then the seller makes a **profit**. If the selling price is less than the cost price, then the seller makes a **loss**.

Example   Ravi bought a car for $10 000. He tries to sell it for a 35% profit.
(a) How much is his selling price?
He finally agrees to sell the car for $12 300.
(b) What percentage profit does he make?

Working   (a) 35% profit means 135% of the cost price.

$$\text{Selling price} = \frac{135}{100} \times \$10\,000$$

$$= 1.35 \times \$10\,000$$

$$= \$13\,500$$

(b) Profit = $12 300 – $10 000 = $2300

$$\% \text{ profit} = \frac{\$2300}{\$10\,000} \times 100\%$$

$$= 23\%$$

Answer   (a) $13 500   (b) 23%

Example   A trader sells a toaster for a 30% profit. His selling price is $19.50. How much did he buy the toaster for?

Working   30% profit is 130% of the original price.

So   130% = $19.50

$$1\% = \frac{\$19.50}{130} = \$0.15$$

$$100\% = \$0.15 \times 100 = \$15.00$$

Answer $15.00

Practice

A **1** A trader buys a washing machine for $450. She sells it for a 25% profit.
(a) How much profit does she make?
(b) How much does she sell the washing machine for?

2 *Home Store* buys 100 tables for $50 each. It costs them $3000 to store all the tables.
(a) What is the cost price of each table?
They sell the tables for $100 each.
(b) What percentage profit do they make on each table?

3 A grocer buys apples at 85 ¢ per kilogram. Unfortunately, he realises that he has too many so he sells them for 68 ¢ per kilogram.
(a) What percentage loss does he make?
His total loss was $4.25.
(b) How many kilograms of apples did he buy?

4 *Drinkies* coffee shop just sells cups of coffee. The coffee beans cost $780 per day, the milk $420 per day, water $270 per day and labour costs $500 per day. The shop is rented for $1200 per week.

 (a) How much does it cost to run *Drinkies* for a week?

A cup of coffee costs $2.50.

 (b) How many cups must they sell to cover the costs of running *Drinkies* for a week?

 (c) Last week they sold 7125 cups of coffee. How much profit did they make?

B 1 Hyacinth wants to sell a CD for $10.80. This would give her a 20% profit. She actually only sells it for $10.35. What percentage profit does she makes?

2 Jon sold his car for $10 370, getting a 22% profit. Lucinda sold her car for $10 560 for a 20% profit. Whose car cost the most originally?

3 Carl bought a bike for $120. He sold it to Karim for a 15% profit. Karim then sells the bike to Lyra for a 5% profit. How much more did Lyra pay for the bike than Carl (in percent)?

Remember?

The **marked price** is the selling price on the tag/label.

A **discount** is a reduction to the marked price.

When an item is sold, **sales tax** usually has to be paid. This is sometimes called **Value Added Tax (VAT)**. Sales tax is paid on the marked price of an item.

Practice

C 1 A clothes shop is having a '75% off' sale. How much does Brian pay for the following items?

 (a) Trousers: marked price $152

 (b) A tie: marked price $95.

2 *Sam's Spades* is giving a 40% discount on all spades. The marked price is $18.

 (a) How much does a spade cost?

The VAT on each spade is 17.5%.

 (b) How much is the VAT?

3 Kirsten pays $5.85 for a book that normally costs $7.50.

   (a) What discount did she get on the book?

The sales tax on the book is 8%.

   (b) The shop bought the book for $4.20, what
      percentage profit did they make on the sale?

> **Finished Early?**
> ➡ Go to page 441

❷ Mortgages and Hire Purchase

Remember?

Some items such as houses and cars are too expensive to pay the **cash price** in one go. Instead the item could be paid for by **hire purchase**. Usually the buyer makes a one-off payment called a **deposit** or a **down-payment**. The remainder is called the outstanding balance. This is paid in **installments**.

Usually **interest** is paid on the outstanding balance.

When buying a house we often get a loan to help pay for it. This loan is usually called a **mortgage**.

Example   Mr and Mrs Edmunds want to buy a house for $75 000. To pay for it they take out a mortgage from their bank. To repay the mortgage they must pay the bank a deposit of 5%, and then pay installments of 0.6% per month for 20 years.
How much do they repay for the mortgage?

Working   The deposit is 5% of $75 000

$$= \frac{5}{100} \times \$75\,000 = 5 \times \$750 = \$3750$$

So the deposit is $3750.

The installments are 0.6% of $75 000 per month.

One installment $= \frac{0.6}{100} \times \$75\,000$

$$= 0.6 \times \$750 = 6 \times \$75 = \$450$$

The installments are paid for 20 years which is

$20 \times 12 = 240$ months.

So total repaid by installments

$$= 240 \times \$450 = \$108\,000$$

Total repaid = deposit + installments

$$= \$3750 + \$108\,000$$

$$= \$111\,750$$

Answer   They repay $111 750.

Example   Michelle wants to buy a new vacuum cleaner. The cash price
is $650. She pays a 15% deposit and 18 monthly installments
of $38.
(a) How much does she pay for the vacuum cleaner?
(b) What percentage interest does she pay on the
outstanding balance?

Working   (a) The total paid for the vacuum cleaner is the 15% deposit
plus 18 installments of $38.

$$\text{Deposit} = 15\% \text{ of } \$650$$
$$= \frac{15}{100} \times \$650$$
$$= 15 \times \$6.50$$
$$= \$97.50$$

The installments come to 18 × $38 = $684.
So the total cost of the vacuum cleaner is:

$$\text{cost} = \$97.50 + \$684$$
$$= \$781.50$$

(b) The outstanding balance is the difference between the
cost price of the vacuum cleaner and the deposit.

$$\text{Outstanding balance} = \$650 - \$97.50 = \$552.50$$

The interest paid on the outstanding balance

$$= \$684 - \$552.50$$
$$= \$131.50$$

$$\text{Percentage interest} = \frac{\$131.50}{\$552.50} \times 100\%$$
$$= 23.800...\%$$
$$= 23.8\% \text{ to 1 decimal place}$$

Answer   (a) $781.50   (b) 23.8% (to 1 decimal place)

Practice

D **1** Linda is buying a car on hire purchase. She pays a ten per cent deposit,
then $270 a month for 60 months.
(a) How much does she pay for the car?
(b) How much interest does she pay on the outstanding balance?

$15 950

2 Freddy needs a new oven. He chooses one that needs a $50 down-payment and $50 per month for 1 year. Alternatively, he can pay cash and get a 15% discount. What is the cash price of the oven?

3 *Homely Houses* has two mortgage options.

	Deposit	Installments
Mortgage A	7%	300 monthly installments of 0.5%
Mortgage B	3%	250 monthly installments of 0.7%

Terence and Jamelia want to buy a $150 000 house.
(a) Which mortgage should they take?
(b) What percentage profit do *Homely Homes* make on each mortgage?

③ Bills and Invoices

Remember?

A **bill/invoice** is a list showing how much has to be paid for services carried out or goods bought.

Utility bills and invoices are sent out by commercial businesses to indicate the payment that must be made for services (such as telephone, water, electricity, gas) and goods bought.

Energy consumption is often measured in **kilowatt-hours (kWh)**. 1 kilowatt-hour is the equivalent of 1 kilowatt of energy being used for 1 hour.

Practice

E **1** Calculate the amount owed to the electricity board in each of these cases.

	Previous	Present	kWh used	Rate ($per kWh)	Amount
	05934	06161	6161 − 5934 = 227	0.89	227 × 0.89 = $202.03
a	00356	00478		0.73	
b	01295	01566		0.55	
c	532981	535187		0.435	
d	000177	000208		0.66	

2 The table shows how *Sparky Electricity* calculate their bills. Calculate the amount owed in the following readings.

Fixed rate	$11.75
First 100 kWh	$0.44 per kWh
Next 250 kWh	$0.39 per kWh
Over 350 kWh	$0.30 per kWh
VAT	17.5%

  (a) Previous: 248135
   Present: 248201
  (b) Previous: 004195
   Present: 004473
  (c) Previous: 017862
   Present: 018281
  (d) Previous: 984560
   Present: 986355

3 Petula is changing her telephone supplier. Her new supplier has three tariffs.

	Fixed charge	Daytime rate	Evening rate
Tariff A	$10 per month	7 ¢ per minute	10 ¢ per minute
Tariff B	$5 per month	9 ¢ per minute	11 ¢ per minute
Tariff C	$15 per month	Free	12 ¢ per minute

Petula expects to spend an average of 10 minutes per day on the phone during the daytime, and about 25 minutes in the evening. Which tariff should she use? (Assume a 30-day month).

4 Mr Weekes receives his monthly phone bill. Local calls cost 22 ¢ per minute, international calls $2.50 per minute. He pays a tariff charge of $40 per month. This gives him the first hour of local calls and the first 15 minutes of international calls free. He also owes money from his previous bill. How much is his bill?

Line rental	$15.50
Tariff charge	$40.00
Local calls	513 min
International calls	36 min
Money owed	$7.43
VAT	17.5%

4 Interest

Remember?

When money is borrowed it is usually repaid with interest. The amount borrowed is called the **principal**. The **rate of interest** is the extra amount you have to pay **per annum (p.a.)**.

Similarly, we can **invest** principal into a bank and receive interest on the principal.

The **simple interest** on the principal is given by:

$$I = \frac{PRT}{100}$$

where I is the interest
P is the principal
R is the rate of interest (a percentage)
T is the time for which the loan is agreed (in years)

The **amount** is the principal plus the interest.

Learn About It

Example Theodore borrows $2000 from the bank. The bank charges simple interest at 4.5% per annum, and Theodore pays back $2585.
How long does it take him to pay back the loan?

Working The interest paid, I, is $2585 − $2000 = $585
R = 4.5%, P = $2000
We need to find T, the time in years taken to pay back the loan.

Rearrange $I = \frac{PRT}{100}$ to give:

$$T = \frac{100}{PR} I = \frac{100 \times 585}{2000 \times 4.5}$$

$$= \frac{585}{90}$$

$$= 6.5$$

Answer 6.5 years

Practice

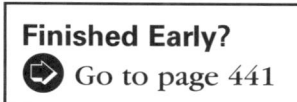

1 Kenny borrows $550 from *Easy Money* bank. They charge 6.8% simple interest, and Kenny pays it back over 3 years.
(a) How much does Kenny repay?
Sunita also takes a loan from *Easy Money* at the same rate of interest. She pays $275.40 interest and pays the loan back over $4\frac{1}{2}$ years.
(b) How much was the principal?

2 Four friends take loans from different banks. Copy and complete the table.

	Principal	Rate of interest	Repayment period	Interest	Amount
Clive	$400	7.2%	2 yrs		
Rosemary	$2250		8.5 yrs		$3053.25
Everton		5.8%		$504.60	$1954.60
Reese			3.5 yrs	$157.50	$907.50

3 Vivian invests $1200 in a savings account. The rate of interest is 4.5%.
(a) How much is in the account after three years?
After 3 years he adds another $900.
(b) How much is in the account after a further 2 years?

Finished Early?
➡ Go to page 441

Learn More About It

When we calculate simple interest, the interest paid at the end of each year is calculated as a percentage of the principal. The interest doesn't change from year to year.

Usually we calculate interest with a slightly different method, called **compound interest**. The principal is borrowed (or invested) and the interest paid at the end of the first year is calculated as a percentage of the principal, just as it is for simple interest. But now the interest is added to the principal. The interest at the end of the second year is calculated as a percentage of the principal + the first year's interest. The second year's interest is then added to the principal + the first year's interest ... and so on.

For example, the principal is $100 and the rate of interest is 10%.

Principal: $\Rightarrow$ Interest at end of 1st year: $\Rightarrow$ Amount at end of 1st year:
$100   10% of $100 = $10 $100 + $10 = $110

Amount at end of 2nd year: Interest at end of 2nd year: $\Leftarrow$
$110 + $11 = $121 $\Leftarrow$ 10% of $110 = $11

$\Rightarrow$ Interest at end of 3rd year: $\Rightarrow$ and so on.
      10% of $121 = $12.10

The total interest paid = amount – principal.

Try It Out

G Copy and complete the table.

Compound interest	At the end of the 1st year Interest	2nd year Amount	At the end of the 3rd year Interest	Amount	At the end of the Interest	Amount
$700 at 5% $450 at 12%						

Practice

H **1** Find the final amount and total compound interest paid on:
     (a) $340 at 7% p.a. for 2 years
     (b) $190 at 9% p.a. for 2 years
     (c) $1200 at 15% p.a. for 3 years.

2 Vincent borrowed $9000 from his bank at a rate of 12% p.a. compound interest. If he doesn't make any repayments, then how much will he owe after 3 years?

3 How long does it take for the money owed on a loan of $2400, borrowed at 8% compound interest, to reach $2799.36?

4 Honour has $500 that she wants to invest in a savings account for 3 years. She has to choose an account:
A1 savings pays 8% compound interest per annum
Easycash pays 8.5% simple interest per annum.
Which account should she use?

Remember?

Many products, such as cars and computers, lose value as they get older. This is called **depreciation**. Some products may actually increase in value as they get older. This is called **appreciation**.

Example	David owns a stove, worth $325. He expects 20% depreciation every year. How much is the stove worth in 2 years?
Working	If the table depreciates 20% every year, then its value at the end of the year is 100% − 20% = 80% of its value at the beginning of the year.
	So after 1 year the stove is worth

$$80\% \text{ of } \$325 = \frac{80}{100} \times \$325$$
$$= 0.8 \times \$325$$
$$= \$260$$

At the end of the second year the stove is worth
$$80\% \text{ of } \$260 = \$208$$

Answer	$208

Practice

1 A car is worth $25 456. It depreciates in value by 15% every year. How much is it worth after 3 years (to the nearest cent)?

2 Carl bought a television for $850. It lost 10% of its value in the first year.
(a) How much is it worth after 1 year?
The television depreciates 12% every year after the first.
(b) How much is the television worth 3 years after buying it?
(c) What percentage of its original value has been lost?

3 Chandice owns a vintage table that her gran gave her. She takes it to an antiques shop to evaluate it. The expert says it is worth $325, and will appreciate at 35% per annum.
(a) How much will it be worth in 3 years?
She accidentally chips the surface on the way out of the antiques shop. The expert says it is now worth only $190 and will appreciate at 20% per annum.
(b) How much has the chipped surface cost her after 3 years?

Further Practice

J 1 Calculate how much each of these items is worth after 3 years.

    (a) A car worth $24 000 that appreciates at 15% per annum.

    (b) A computer worth $700 that depreciates at 30% per annum.

2 Theresa has taken a loan of $2000 from her bank. The bank charges 25% interest at the end of each year. She repays $100 per month.

    (a) How much has she repaid by the end of the first year?

    (b) How much interest does the bank charge at the end of the year?

    (c) How many months into the second year does she pay off the loan?

3 Chantal borrows $2400 from the bank. The bank charges 12% interest per annum. He makes monthly repayments to the bank. At the end of the first year the bank charges him $72 interest.

Calculate:

    (a) how much he owed at the end of the first year

    (b) how much his monthly payments are

    (c) after how many months of the second year he pays off the loan.

Finished Early?
➡ Go to page 441

⑤ Wages, Salary and Income Tax

Remember?

When you do paid work you will be paid either a wage or a salary. **Wages** are usually paid by the hour, day or week. Sometimes someone earning wages can work outside their normal hours, called **overtime**. The employee is usually paid at a higher rate such as at time-and-a-half or double time.

A **salary** is earnings paid over a longer period than a wage, usually monthly. Someone earning a salary is not usually allowed to do overtime.

Practice

K **1** Mrs Ali charges by the hour. Her normal hours are 9 am to 5 pm Monday to Friday. She gets $35 per hour when she does normal hours.
If she works at any other time on a weekday, then she gets time-and-a-half.
If she works at the weekend, then she gets double time.
Calculate how much Mrs Ali earns during these weeks when:
  (a) She does a normal week.
  (b) She works until 8 pm on Thursday and does 4 hours on Sunday.
  (c) She leaves work 2 hours early on Wednesday, but has to work
    2 hours late on Thursday.
  (d) She gets Monday off, but starts at 7:30 am on Tuesday and does
    $6\frac{1}{2}$ hours on Saturday.

2 Mr Boon works $7\frac{1}{2}$ hours a day for 22 days a month. He has a 6-month contract and gets paid $1221 every month. He occasionally has to work overtime for which he gets paid triple his usual rate.
How much does he get paid during his contract when:
  (a) He just does his normal hours.
  (b) He does a total of 59 hours overtime.
  (c) He takes 4 days unpaid holiday, but works 102 hours overtime.

Remember?

Income is money earned through work or investments.

Income tax is deducted from a person's income and goes to the government. Some of a person's income is non-taxable, called **allowances**. Income tax is usually paid on a sliding scale. The first part of the taxable income is paid at a certain rate, the next part at a higher rate, and so on.

Practice

L

Tax-free allowances (per year)		Tax rates (per year)
Personal allowance	= $8000	10% on first $3000
Spousal allowance	= $5000	25% on next $8000
(if not working)		40% on next $24 000
Per child (at school)	= $900	50% on the remaining
Per child (at university)	= $1300	
Mortgage interest	= all	
National insurance	= first $1500	
contributions		

Use the table to calculate the income tax to be paid in the following cases.

(a) Brian Young earns $27 379 every year. He is unmarried with no children. He pays mortgage interest of $1700 a year, and pays national insurance of $90 a month.

(b) Marsha earns $63 419 per year. She is single and has two children at school. Her mortgage interest repayments are $8250 per year and national insurance contributions are $4700 per year.

(c) Alvin and Lacena Best are married. They have one child at university. Alvin is currently out of work; Lacena earns $23 000 every year. They have mortgage interest payments of $1350 per year and pay national insurance of $660 per year.

6 Exchange Rates

Remember?

Most countries have their own currency. When trade is done between countries, or people move from country-to-country, the money needs to be changed from one currency to another. This is done using **exchange rates**.

Exchange rates vary from day to day and they can be different for buying and selling currencies.

Learn About It

The exchange rates between some currencies at the time of writing are given in the table.

	Bds$	EC$	Ja$	TT$	Pesos	US$	UK£
Bds$1.00	1	1.35	30.87	3.10	5.72	0.50	0.28
EC$1.00	0.74	1	22.85	2.30	4.23	0.37	0.20
Ja$1.00	0.03	0.04	1	0.10	0.19	0.02	0.01
TT$1.00	0.32	0.44	9.96	1	1.85	0.16	0.09
Pesos 1.00	5.72	0.24	5.40	0.54	1	0.09	0.05
US$1.00	2.00	2.70	61.59	6.19	11.41	1	0.55
UK£ 1.00	3.63	4.91	112.20	11.27	20.79	1.82	1

Sometimes the organisation exchanging the money will charge you a percentage of the currency called **commission**.

Practice

1 Use the exchange rate table to convert 150 United States dollars (US$150) into the following currencies.
(a) Barbados dollars (Bds$)   (b) Jamaican dollars (Ja$)
(c) Mexican Pesos   (d) United Kingdom pounds (UK£)

2 Devon wants to convert 1350 Trinidad and Tobago dollars (TT$1350). He has to pay 10% commission. Use the exchange rate table to calculate how much of the following currencies he would get.
(a) US dollars   (b) East Caribbean dollars (EC$)
(c) Jamaican dollars   (d) Barbados dollars

1 Clova works in Trinidad. She needs to go to the United States on business, so she exchanges TT$800 into US currency. The bank buys her dollars at a rate of US$0.15 for each TT$.
(a) How many US dollars does she get?
Clova has to cancel her trip. The bank buys the US$ back from her at a rate of TT$6.17 for each US$.
(b) How much money has she lost in the two transactions?

2 Roger is traveling from Miami to St Kitts. He exchanges US$1750 into East Caribbean dollars, and pays 7% commission.
(a) How many EC$ does he receive?
He doesn't spend any money in St Kitts before traveling to Barbados. He gets Barbados dollars, and pays 8% commission.
(b) How many Bds$ does he get?

3 Ato leaves Trinidad with TT$5600. He travels to Jamaica where he spends Ja$15 000. He then converts the remainder into Mexican Pesos. How many Pesos does he get?

Unit 2 *Arithmetic*
Summary of Chapters 4 and 5

Computation
- The order in which the basic arithmetic operations are done is given by BODMAS:
  first: *Brackets*
  next: *pOwers and roots*
  then: *Division and Multiplication*
  last: *Addition and Subtraction.*
- Addition and multiplication obey the **associative** and **commutative** laws. Multiplication is **distributive over addition and subtraction**.
- The **law of closure** states that if an operation is applied to two members of a set and the result of the operation is also a member of the set, then the set is **closed** under the operation.
- To change a number in other bases to a base 10 number, expand the number using the powers of the base for each digit and add these values. To change a base 10 number to a base n number, divide repeatedly by n until the quotient is zero and further division is impossible. The remainders in each line of working, reading upwards, give the required number in base n.
- To add fractions, use **equivalent fractions** having a common denominator, add the numerators and then write the result in its simplest form by reducing the fraction to its lowest terms.
- To multiply fractions, multiply numerator by numerator, and denominator by denominator; write the product in the lowest terms.
- To divide by a fraction, multiply by the reciprocal of the fraction.
- To change a fraction to an equivalent percentage, multiply the fraction by 100 and write the % symbol.
- To change a fraction to a decimal, divide the numerator by the denominator.
- When adding or subtracting decimals, add or subtract digits of the same value.
- When multiplying decimals, make sure that the number of decimal places in the product of the given numbers is the sum of the decimal places in the given numbers.

- In order to compare quantities of the same kind, **ratios** are used. When the quantities are in the same units, the ratio can be expressed as a fraction. Quantities may also be shared or divided in a given ratio.

- Two quantities are **directly proportional** if both quantities increase or decrease in a constant ratio; or **inversely proportional** if, when one quantity increases, the other quantity decreases in the same ratio, or vice versa.

- If quantities are of different kinds, the quantities are compared in the form of a **rate**.

- To give approximate answers for the results of calculations, round each number to a given degree of accuracy, for example, to the nearest digit, ten, hundred, …, to a number of significant figures, or to a number of decimal places.

- Using approximate values, generally one significant figure, the **estimation** of the result of a calculation is useful to prevent errors and to provide a check of the correctness and accuracy of the answer.

Consumer Arithmetic

- The **cost price** of an item is the total amount of money paid to obtain an item.

- The **selling price** is the amount an item is sold for. If the selling price is higher than the cost price, then the seller makes a **profit**. If the selling price is less than the cost price, then the seller makes a **loss**.

- The **marked price** is the selling price on the tag/label of an item.

- A **discount** is a reduction to the marked price.

- When an item is sold, **sales tax** usually has to be paid. This is sometimes called **Value Added Tax (VAT)**. Sales tax is paid on the marked price of an item.

- **Hire purchase** is the process by which you can pay a deposit on an item, and then pay the **outstanding balance** in installments. **Interest** is usually paid on the outstanding balance.

- A **mortgage** is a hire purchase for buying a house.

- A **bill/invoice** is a list showing how much has to be paid for services carried out or goods bought.

- Utility bills and invoices are sent out by commercial businesses to indicate the payment that must be made for services and goods bought.

- When money is borrowed it is usually repaid with interest. The amount borrowed is called the **principal**. The **rate of interest** is the extra amount you have to pay **per annum (p.a.)**.
- The **simple interest** on the principal is given by:
$$I = \frac{PRT}{100}$$
- If **compound interest** is being paid, then the interest to be paid at the end of each year is added to the outstanding balance.
- Some items will lose value over a period of time. This is called **depreciation**. If an item increases in value over time, then it **appreciates**.
- **Wages** are usually paid by the hour, day or week. A **salary** is usually paid monthly.
- **Income** is money gained through work and investments.
- **Income tax** is paid on any income. **Allowances** are tax-free.
- **Exchange rates** are used to change money from one currency into another.

6 Angles, Shapes and Solids

In this chapter you will learn about ...
1. angles and lines
2. angles in triangles and quadrilaterals
3. properties of polygons
4. properties of solids

1 Angles and Lines

Remember?

Angles are formed when two lines meet or intersect at a point, P. The lines are called the *arms* of the angle and P is the vertex.

Angle is a measure of 'turning' or rotation between the two arms.

By definition, *the sum of the angles round a point is 360°.*

Angles are classified according to their measure as follows:

acute angle, between 0° and 90°

right angle, quarter of a complete turn, 90°

obtuse angle, between 90° and 180°

straight angle, half of a complete turn, 180°

reflex angle, between 180° and 360°

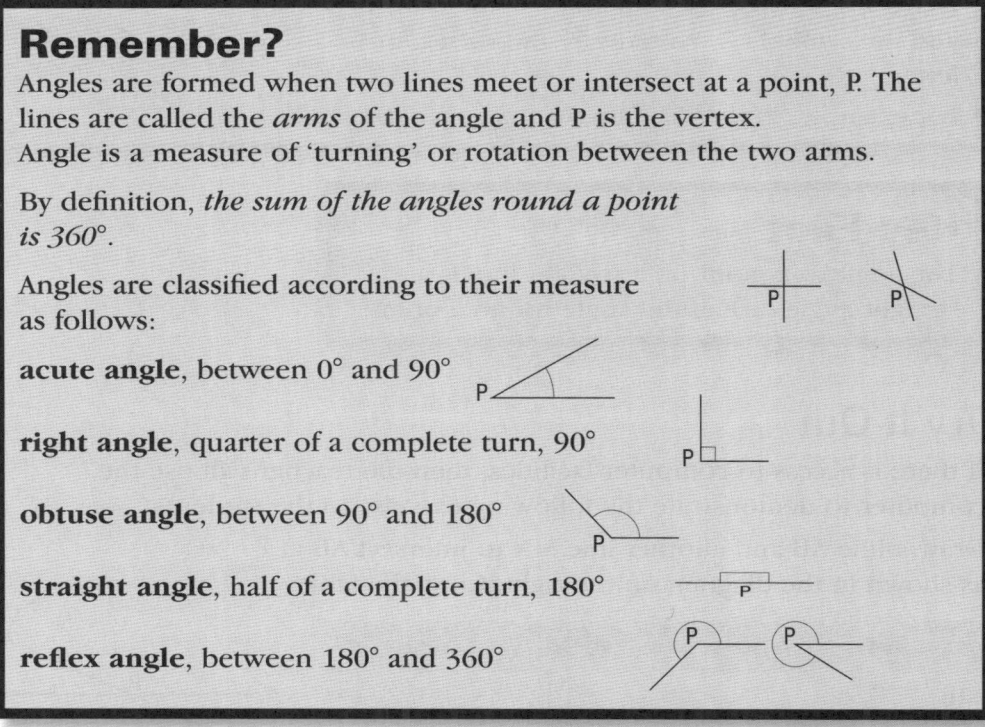

Word Check

classify separate into different groups

measure size in given units

degree unit for measuring angles

° symbol for angle measure

protractor instrument for measuring and drawing angles

adjacent next to one another and touching

revolution 'turning' through 360°

Key Fact

Generally, an angle is named using the arms of the angle and the symbol, $\wedge$, to indicate the vertex, or by a single letter.

For example, in the diagram, we may say $M\hat{H}N$ or x.

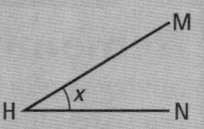

Key Fact

The angle at a point on a straight line is a straight angle or half the angle round a point.

Ⓐ Try It Out

If there is access to computer facilities, then the teacher will use the computer to demonstrate the following exercise to the students.

Draw a line AB and another line MN to intersect AB at P, as shown in the diagram on the right. Copy the table.

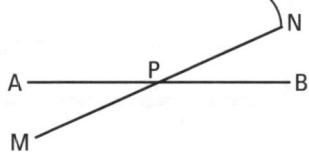

	$B\hat{P}N$	$N\hat{P}A$	$A\hat{P}M$	$M\hat{P}B$
(i)				
(ii)				

With a protractor, measure the angles between the two lines and record the values in row **(i)** of the table. Increase the angle BPN and record the new values of the angles in row **(ii)** of the table. Repeat for a total of six sets of values. Discuss the results.

Remember?

As the angle between two lines is changed, the measure of the angle b changes from $0°$ to $180°$, and of d changes from $180°$ to $0°$, that is, the adjacent angles on a straight line add up to $180°$. When the lines intersect, the vertically opposite angles are equal, that is, $f_1 = f_2$ and $h_1 = h_2$

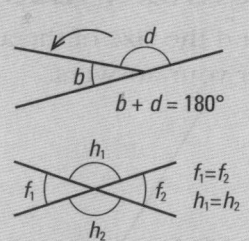

$b + d = 180°$

$f_1 = f_2$
$h_1 = h_2$

Ⓑ Practice

Find the size of the angle marked x in each of these diagrams. Give reasons for your answers.

1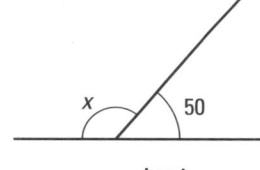

2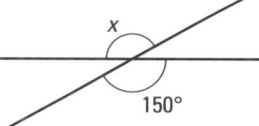

3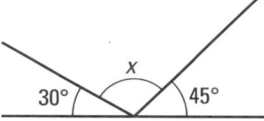

4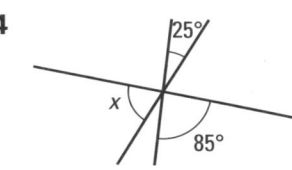

5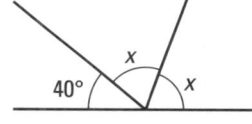

6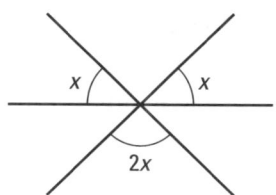

Ⓒ **1** Calculate the angle between the position of the hour hand of a 12-hour clock at 1:00 and the position of the hour hand at 5:00.

2 The minute hand of a 24-hour clock is pointing to 24 and the angle between the hands is $150°$. Calculate the time.

Further Practice

D Find the size of the angle marked x in each of these diagrams. Give reasons for your answers.

1
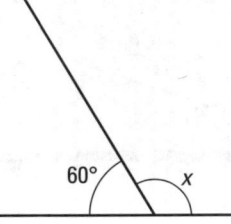

2
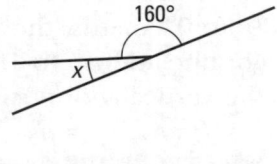

3
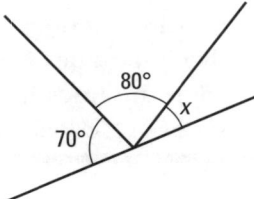

4
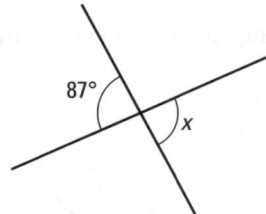

5
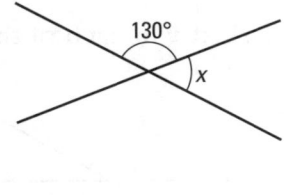

6
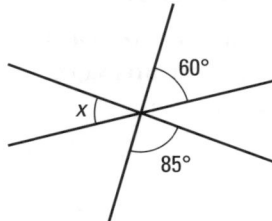

Key Fact

Parallel lines are shown in a diagram by arrowheads pointing in the same direction.

Finished Early?

➡ Go to page 442

Try It Out

E If there is access to computer facilities, then the teacher will use the computer to demonstrate the following exercise to the students.

Draw two parallel lines AB and MN.
Draw a transversal, XY, to intersect AB and MN, as shown in the diagram on the right.
Mark and measure the angles, c_1 and c_2.
Draw other diagrams, each time changing the position of XY and measuring the new values of c_1 and c_2.

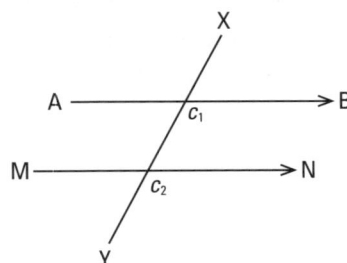

Did you find that the angles, c_1 and c_2, are equal for all positions of XY?
These angles are called **corresponding angles** because they are in similar positions.
Discuss whether there are other corresponding angles.
Describe their positions by referring to the parallel lines, AB and MN, and to the transversal XY.

Draw a new diagram and consider the angle v_1
shown in the diagram.

Then $c_2 = v_1$ (vertically opposite angles)

Therefore, since $c_1 = c_2 = v_1$

Then $c_1 = v_1$

These are called **alternate angles**.

Discuss whether there are other
alternate angles.

Describe their positions by referring to the parallel lines,
AB and MN, and to the transversal XY.

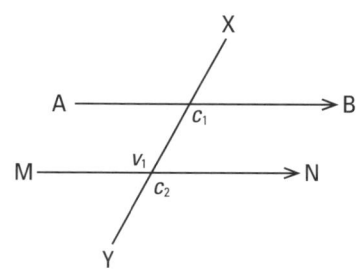

Draw a new diagram and consider another angle i_1
as shown in the diagram.

Then $i_1 + v_1 = 180°$ (adjacent angles on a
straight line)

And since $c_1 = v_1$

Then $i_1 + c_1 = 180°$

The angles i_1 and c_1 are called **allied**
or **co-interior angles**.

Discuss whether there are other allied angles.

Describe their positions referred to the parallel lines, AB and MN, and to
the transversal XY.

Word Check

parallel straight lines that are always the same
distance apart

intersecting cutting one another

transversal line that cuts two or more lines

interior angles angles between the two lines that are
cut by a transversal

exterior angles angles outside the two lines that are
cut by a transversal

adjacent next to, touching

Remember?

When *parallel lines* are crossed by a transversal, ST, there are interior angles *i*, as shown in the diagram and exterior angles, *e*.

Interior angles add up to 180°, that is,
$$i_1 + i_2 = 180°$$
and $i_3 + i_4 = 180°$.

The alternate angles *a* are equal.

The corresponding angles *c* are equal.

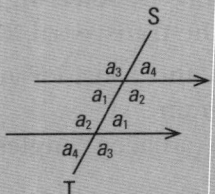
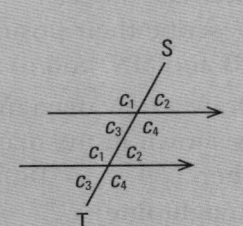

Practice

F In each of the following diagrams, the lines marked with arrows are parallel. Find the size of the angle marked *x* in each of the diagrams.

Give reasons for your answers.

1

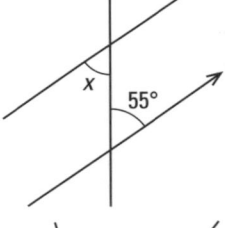

55°

2

125°

x

3

75°

x

60°

4

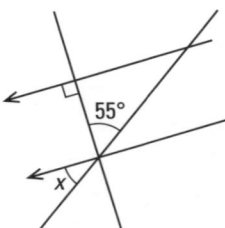

55°

x

5

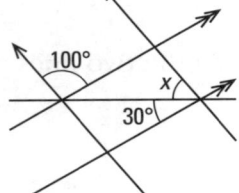

100°

x

30°

6

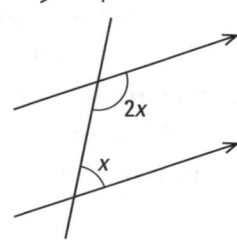

2*x*

x

7

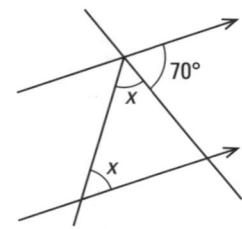

70°

x

x

8

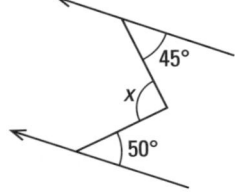

45°

x

50°

Practice

G Calculate the unknown angles in each of the following:

1

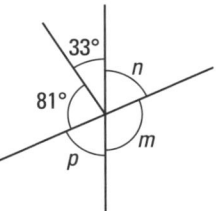

33°
n
81°
m
p

2

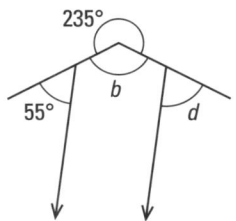

235°
b
55°
d

3

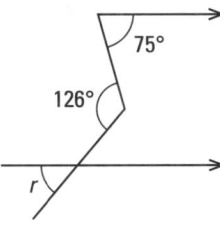

75°
126°
r

4

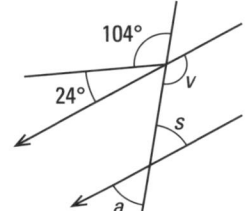

104°
v
24°
s
a

5

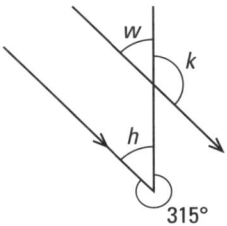

w
k
h
315°

6

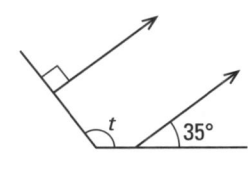

t
35°

Further Practice

H In each of the following diagrams, the lines marked with arrows are parallel. Find the size of the angle marked *x* in each of the diagrams. Give reasons for your answers.

1

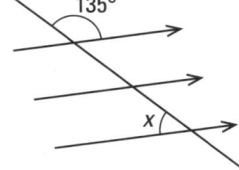

135°
x

2

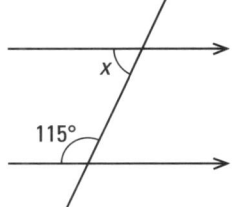

x
115°

3

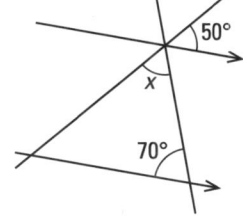

50°
x
70°

4

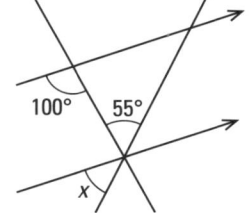

100° 55°
x

5

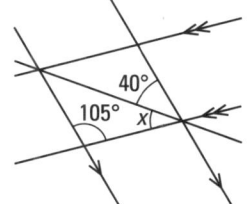

40°
105° x

6

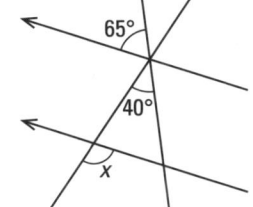

65°
40°
x

Finished Early?
 Go to page 442

❷ Angles in Triangles and Quadrilaterals

Remember?

Triangles are two-dimensional plane shapes with three straight sides and three angles.

Triangles are classified according to their angles:
acute-angled (all angles less than 90°), **right-angled** (one angle is 90°) and **obtuse-angled** (one angle is greater than 90°);
and according to their sides:
scalene (all three sides unequal), **isosceles** (only two sides equal) and **equilateral** (three sides equal).

Congruent triangles have exactly the same shape and size so that all the sides and angles of one triangle are equal to all the sides and angles of the other.

Two triangles are congruent if: three sides of each are equal (*SSS*);
or two sides and the angle included between these sides of each are equal (*SAS*);
or two angles and a corresponding side of each are equal (*AAS*);
or in two right-angled triangles, the right angle, hypotenuse and a corresponding side of each are equal (*RHS*).

Try It Out

❶ If there is access to computer facilities, then the teacher will use the computer to demonstrate the following exercise to the students.

Draw two parallel lines BA and YX.
Draw the transversal, MN,
to intersect BA and YX,
as shown in diagram **(i)** on the right.
The corresponding angles c_1 and c_2 are equal.

(i)

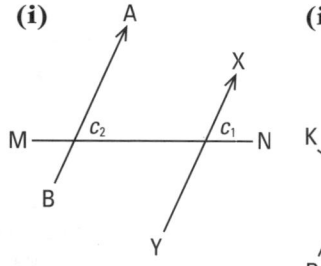

Draw the transversal, KL,
to intersect BA and YX,
as shown in diagram **(ii)** on the right.
The alternate angles a_1 and a_2 are equal.

(ii)

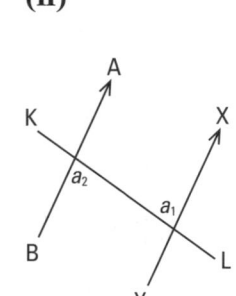

Draw, on one diagram, both transversals, KL and MN, and the corresponding and alternate angles as shown in diagram **(iii)**.

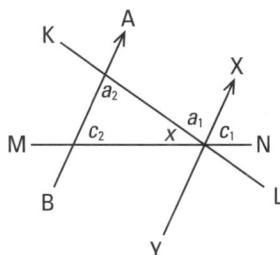

Since x, a_1 and c_1 are adjacent angles on a straight line,

$$x + a_1 + c_1 = 180°.$$

Also, since $c_1 = c_2$ and $a_1 = a_2$

Then $x + a_2 + c_2 = 180°$, that is, *the sum of the angles of a triangle is 180°*.

Practice

J Let students do the following exercise working in pairs. If there is access to computer facilities, students use the Classwork sheet in the computer program *Triangles* on the CD. Otherwise they use centimetre-squared paper of side 12 cm and their exercise books.

1 Given the triangle on the right, change the position of the vertex B along the horizontal line so that the triangle is:
   (a) right-angled   **(b)** isosceles
   (c) acute-angled and scalene
   (d) obtuse-angled and scalene.

2 Draw triangles that are congruent to the given triangle and to each of your own triangles.

3 Given the triangle on the right, change the position of the vertex C along the vertical line so that the triangle is:
   (a) right-angled and scalene
   (b) right-angled and isosceles.

4 Given the triangle on the right, move the vertex A to obtain the following:
   (a) an obtuse-angled isosceles triangle
   (b) a right-angled isosceles triangle
   (c) a right-angled scalene triangle
   (d) an acute-angled scalene triangle.

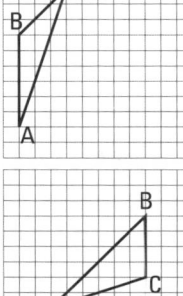

5 Using each of the triangles from questions 3 and 4, draw congruent triangles.

Key Fact

In an isosceles triangle, the angles opposite the equal sides are equal; in an equilateral triangle, all the angles are equal to 60°; in a scalene triangle, the largest angle is opposite the longest side.

Word Check

grid point point where the horizontal and vertical lines on squared paper (grid) intersect

two-dimensional two values are needed to give the position of a point on a plane surface

Further Practice

1 Change the position of the vertex A along the vertical line so that the triangle is:
   (a) right-angled and isosceles
   (b) obtuse-angled and isosceles.

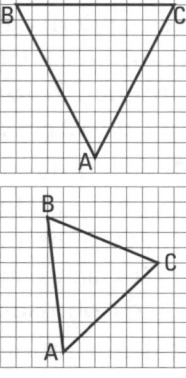

2 Move the vertex B to obtain the following:
   (a) an acute-angled isosceles triangle
   (b) a right-angled isosceles triangle
   (c) a right-angled scalene triangle
   (d) an obtuse-angled isosceles triangle.

3 Using each of the triangles from questions 1 and 2, draw congruent triangles.

Finished Early?
➡ Go to page 443

Remember?

Quadrilaterals are plane shapes with four straight sides and four angles. The opposite vertices are joined by a straight line called a **diagonal**. A diagonal cuts the quadrilateral into two triangles. Since the sum of the angles of a triangle is 180°, then the sum of the angles of a quadrilateral is 360°.

There are different kinds of special quadrilaterals: rectangle, square, parallelogram, rhombus, kite, trapezium and isosceles trapezium.

Key Fact

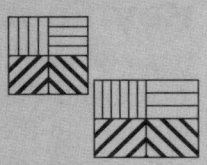

Since the angles at the vertices of four squares meet at a point (360°), the angle at each vertex is 90°.

Similarly, the angle at each vertex of a rectangle is 90°.

Example Using centimetre-squared paper,

(a) draw a kite

(b) draw the diagonals

(c) write down the lengths of the diagonals

(d) write down the position of the mid-points of the diagonals

(e) if the diagonals meet at 90°, show this on the diagram.

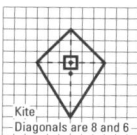

Answer

Kite
Diagonals are 8 and 6

Practice

L **1** Draw (a) a parallelogram with two angles of 45°

(b) a trapezium with an angle of 45°

(c) a kite with one angle of 90°.

2 For each of the following, draw the shapes and then answer the questions (b) – (e) as in the above *Example*:

(i) two different rhombuses (ii) two different trapeziums

(iii) two different isosceles trapeziums (iv) two different parallelograms

(v) two different kites

Word Check

bisect cut into two equal parts

angle bisector line that bisects an angle

M Work in pairs to review the angle, side, diagonal and angle bisector properties of special quadrilaterals.

Use *either* centimetre-squared paper of side 12 cm and your exercise book *or* the *Introduction Screen*, the *Diagonals Screen* and the *Angle Bisectors Screen* of the computer program *Properties of quadrilaterals*.

For each special quadrilateral:

(a) draw a copy of the shape, and ask questions such as: are there equal sides? parallel sides? equal angles? right angles? is a square a rectangle?

(b) mark on your copy: the equal sides, the parallel sides, equal angles, angles that are equal to 90°

(c) copy the following table (on page 95) and complete the first three columns (one row has been done as an example)

(d) draw another copy of the shape, and draw the diagonals

(e) ask questions such as: are the diagonals equal in length? do they cross at right angles? at the mid-points?

(f) draw the angle bisectors

(g) ask questions such as: are both diagonals angle bisectors? does one diagonal bisect the angle of the quadrilateral?

(h) complete the last four columns of the table (one row has been done as an example).

Shape	All names	Sides	Angles	Diagonals			
				same length	intersect at right angles	intersect at mid-points	bisect angle of quadrilateral
Rectangle	rectangle parallelogram	opposite sides parallel and equal	all angles equal to 90°				
Square							
Parallelogram							
Rhombus				no	yes	yes	yes
Kite							
Trapezium							
Isosceles trapezium							

3 Properties of Polygons

Remember?

A plane surface with straight edges or sides is called a **polygon**.
Polygons with all the sides of equal length and all the angles of equal
size are called **regular**.
If all the vertices point outwards, the polygon is a **convex polygon**; if
one or more point inwards, the polygon is a **concave polygon**. Polygons
may also be grouped according to the number of sides as follows:

No. of Sides	3	4	5	6	7	8
Name	Triangle	Quadrilateral	Pentagon	Hexagon	Heptagon	Octagon
Regular	△	▢	⬠	⬡	⬡	⯃
Convex (irregular)	△	▽	⬠	⬡	⬡	▢
Concave (irregular)		◁	⊿	⌂	⬡	⊏

Some other special names are: **nonagon** (9 sides), **decagon** (10 sides),
undecagon (11 sides), **dodecagon** (12 sides).
Plane surfaces (flat shapes) also include the **circle** ◯

and parts of a circle such as the **semi-circle** ◠,

the **quadrant** ◲ , the **sector** ◁ and the **segment** ◠.

Key Facts

A circle is the plane surface traced out when a point moves so that it is
at a fixed distance called the radius, r, from a fixed point, the centre.
The curved line traced out is called the circumference, C where
$C = 2\pi r$. Any part of the circumference is called an arc. A straight line
joining any two points on the circumference is called a chord; a chord
passing through the centre is a diameter, d so that $d = 2r$.

Remember?

The **interior angles** of a polygon are as shown in **(i)**.
The sum of the interior angles varies as the number of sides changes.

The **exterior angles** of a polygon are the angles formed when one side is produced or extended as in **(ii)**. Hence, the sum of the exterior angle and the interior angle next to it is 180°.

The sum of all the exterior angles is 360°.
In a regular polygon with n sides, all the interior angles are equal so that each interior angle is equal to the sum of the interior angles divided by n; all the exterior angles are equal so that each exterior angle is equal to $360° \div n$; and each interior angle is equal to $180° - (360° \div n)$.

Key Fact

The diagonals from any vertex of an n-sided polygon cut the polygon into $(n - 2)$ triangles.

Practice

N Complete the following table.

Polygons	No. of sides	No. of triangles	Sum of the interior angles	Regular Polygons	
				Interior angle	Exterior angle
Triangle	3	1	180°		
Quadrilateral	4	2			
Pentagon	5				
Hexagon					
Heptagon					
Octagon					
Nonagon					
Decagon					
Polygon	n				

Remember?

A **line of symmetry** (or **axis of symmetry**) divides a plane shape so that both parts are exactly the same. A plane shape can have one or more lines of symmetry.

When a plane shape is rotated about a point and fits upon itself in more than one position, the shape has **rotational symmetry** (or **point symmetry**).

The **order** of symmetry is the number of times the shape fits upon itself. Since any shape fits upon itself after one complete revolution, rotational symmetry is always of order greater than one.

Key Fact

All regular polygons have lines of symmetry. For example, an equilateral triangle has three lines of symmetry; that is, line symmetry of order 3. Each line divides the triangle into two congruent right-angled triangles.

Word Check

symmetrical two or more parts exactly similar in size, shape and position about a line or point

congruent equal or the same in all respects

centre of rotation point about which a shape is rotated

Practice

⊙ **1** Calculate the size of each interior angle of a regular dodecagon, that is, a 12-sided polygon.

2 Find the value of the unknown angles in each of the following shapes:

(a)

130° 85°
110°
x
75°

(b)

135° 135°
120°
y
170°
y
130°
110°

(c)

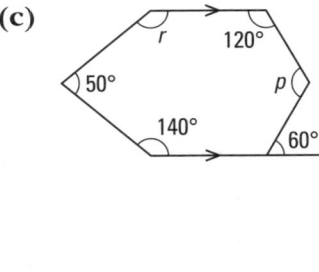

r 120°
50°
p
140°
60°

3 Calculate the number of sides in each of the regular polygons in which:
   (a) exterior angle = 18°   **(b)** interior angle = 156°

4 For each of the following:

  (a) copy the shape and draw in all the lines of symmetry

  (b) state the order of rotational symmetry.

    (i)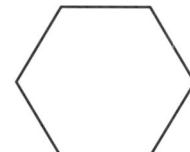
    (ii)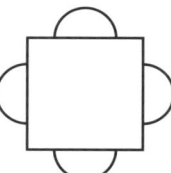

Further Practice

P **1** Find the value of the unknown angles in each of the following shapes:

  (a)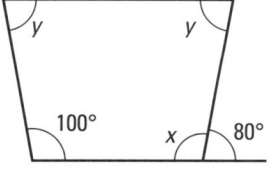
  (b)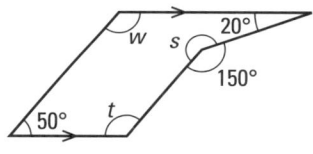

2 For each of the following:

  (a) state the order of rotational symmetry

  (b) copy the shape and draw in all the lines of symmetry.

    (i)
    (ii)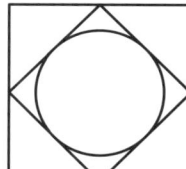

Finished Early?

 Go to page 443

4 Properties of Solids

Remember?

Solids take up space and are enclosed by **faces** (or surfaces). The face of a geometrical solid may be **plane** (flat) or **curved**. The line where two faces meet is called an **edge**. Most solids have edges – flat faces meet along straight edges and curved faces meet along curved edges. Three or more edges meet at a corner or point called a **vertex**.

A **prism** is a solid with a uniform cross-section. Cuboids, cubes and cylinders are prisms. The cross-sections of a cuboid are rectangles or squares, the cross-section of a cube is a square, and of a cylinder is a circle.

Other prisms are named from their cross-sections, for example, a hexagonal prism.

A **pyramid** is a solid which has a plane shape as the base and triangular faces meeting at a point called the **apex** (that is, a vertex). Pyramids are named from their bases, for example, square-based pyramids, hexagonal-based pyramids.

A **right pyramid** is one with the vertex above the centre of the base.

A **cone** is a solid similar to a pyramid but with a plane circular base.

Key Facts

A composite solid may be made by joining different basic solids, or by removing a basic solid from another solid.

In **(i)**, a cuboid and a pyramid are joined – the common face is shaded.

In **(ii)**, a cylinder is removed from a cuboid.

(ii)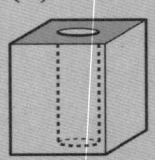

(i)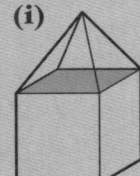

Word Check

base the side of a shape or face of a solid from which the height is measured

cross-section the plane face that is perpendicular to the axis of the figure

uniform the same, or constant

polyhedron a solid with straight edges and plane faces

tetrahedron a polyhedron with four faces, usually a triangular-based pyramid

Key Fact

A solid has mirror symmetry when there is a plane that divides the solid into two exactly equal parts.

Practice

Q In each of the following:
- **(a)** draw the composite solid formed
- **(b)** write down the number of planes of symmetry
- **(c)** if there are planes of symmetry, mark in one plane of symmetry.

1 Two cuboids, which have the same dimensions: x, w and h, joined so that the cross-section is in the shape of **(i)** an 'L' **(ii)** a 'T'.

2 A cube of side $2x$ units from which a cube of side x units is removed from one corner.

3 A cone joined to a hemi-sphere where the radii of the hemi-sphere and the base of the cone are equal and the plane faces form the common face.

4 Three cuboids which have dimensions: x, w and h; x, w and $2h$; and x, w and $3h$ stacked one on top of another, tallest to shortest.

Further Practice

R Draw the following composite solids and mark one plane of symmetry:

1 A pyramid with a square base joined to a cuboid with a square cross-section of equal area.

2 Three cuboids which have the same dimensions and the composite solid forms a 'U'.

3 A cylinder of height r with a cross-section of radius r joined to a cone with a base of radius r and height r and the common face is the circular cross-section.

4 A pyramid of height $2h$ from which a pyramid of height h is removed.

Remember?

A **net** of a solid is the plane shape obtained when the solid is cut along its edges and the faces are flattened out, and therefore is equal to the total surface area of the solid. The following are examples of some common solids and their nets:

Solids		Faces	Edges	Vertices	Net
Cuboid		6	12	8	
Cylinder		3	2	–	
Prism (triangular)		5	9	6	
Pyramid (square-based)		5	8	5	
Cone		2	1	1	

Practice

S (a) Sketch the following solids.

(b) Draw the nets.

(c) Write the length of each edge in your drawings.

1 A cylinder of height p and base radius r that is open at one end.

2 A closed box with the base having dimensions x and w, and height h.

3 A container made from a cone of height $4h$ and base radius $4r$, from which a cone of height h and base radius r is removed, which is open at both ends.

Key Fact

Any plane through the centre of a sphere gives two hemi-spheres that are identical to each other.

Remember?

The plan and the elevations are two-dimensional drawings of a solid.

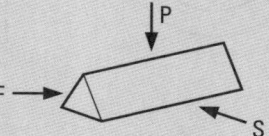

A **plan** is the view when looking down on a solid [P].

Plan

The **front elevation** and the **side elevation** are the views when looking at the solid at the front [F] or at the side [S].

FE   SE

Key Fact

When drawing the plan and elevations of an object, hidden edges are shown as broken lines and vertices as dots.

Practice

T Draw the plan, the front elevation and the side elevation of each of the following solids.

1

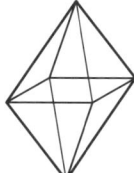

2

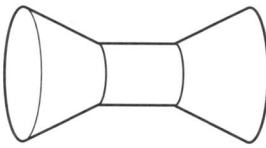

3

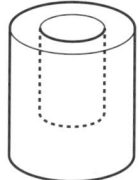

U Sketch and describe the solid for each of the following:

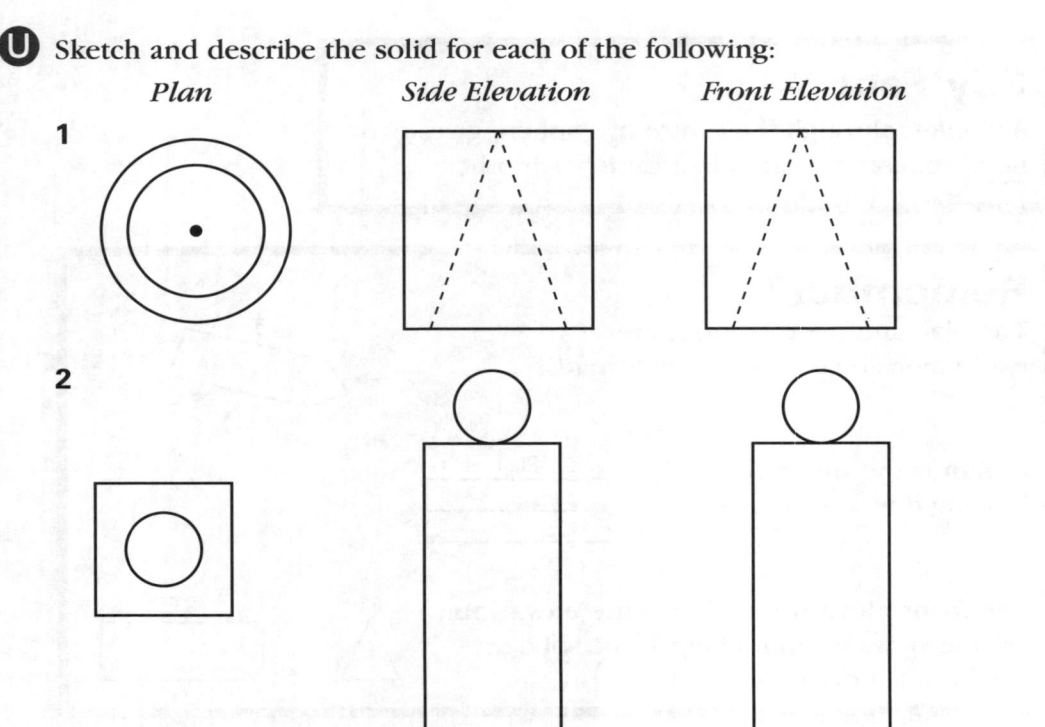

	Plan	*Side Elevation*	*Front Elevation*
1			
2			

Finished Early?
➡ Go to page 444

7 Units of Measurement

In this chapter you will learn about ...
1. basic units of measurement
2. perimeter and area
3. volume and capacity
4. accuracy in measurement

1 Basic Units of Measurement

Remember?

The basic units of measurement refer to the measurement of length, mass and time. In the metric system of units, the basic unit of length is the **metre**, the basic unit of mass is the **gram** and the basic unit of time is the **second**.

In the measurement of length and of mass, prefixes are used to name decimal multiples of the basic units in order to define units for larger and smaller quantities, as shown in the table.

| Prefix | Abbreviations | | Relationship to basic unit | |
	length	mass	length	mass
kilo	km	kg	1000 m	1000 g
hecto	hm	hg	100 m	100 g
deca	dam	dag	10 m	10g
metre / gram	m	g	1 m	1 g
deci	dm	dg	0.1 m	0.1 g
centi	cm	cg	0.01 m	0.01 g
milli	mm	mg	0.001 m	0.001g

The kilometre [1000 m], the metre [1000 mm] and the millimetre are the most commonly used units of length. Similarly, the kilogram, the gram and the milligram are the units of mass in wide use for practical purposes; a unit for larger masses is the **tonne** where 1 tonne = 1000 kg.

Key Facts

1 metre was taken as 1 ten-millionth part of the distance between the North Pole and the Equator.

1 gram is the mass of 1 cubic centimetre of water at a temperature of 4°C.

Practice

A Change each of the following measurements to the unit given.

1 57 m   to   **(i)** cm   **(ii)** mm   **(iii)** km

2 3 kg 28 g   to   **(i)** g   **(ii)** kg   **(iii)** tonne

3 458 mm   to   **(i)** cm   **(ii)** m   **(iii)** km

4 524 kg   to   **(i)** tonne   **(ii)** g   **(iii)** mg

B Work out the following calculations.

1 27 m + 3 m 52 cm + 441 cm

2 44 kg 265 g − 29 kg 550 g

3 625 kg 42 g × 9   (give answer in tonne kg g)

4 474 km 82 m ÷ 7

> **Finished Early?**
> 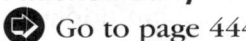 Go to page 444

Key Fact

Since 1 gram is a very small unit, 1 kilogram has become the standard unit of mass.

SI units (Système International d'Unités) is a system of units derived from *m.k.s.* units, that is, metre/kilogram/second units, and is the system internationally used for scientific purposes.

Remember?

Units of time	Abbreviations	Relationship to basic unit
1 second	1 s	1 s
1 minute	1 min	60 s
1 hour	1 h	3600 s [= 60 min]

Time is written in different ways:
- the **12-hour clock** which uses the abbreviations *am* to indicate time after 12 midnight and before 12 midday [noon] and *pm* to indicate time after 12 midday and before 12 midnight.
- the **24-hour clock** which registers time starting at 00:00 hrs at midnight through 12:00 hrs at midday, and 23:59 hrs at 1 minute before midnight. These times may also be written without including 'hrs', that is, as 00:00, 12:00 and 23:59; or 00.00, 12.00, 23.59; or 0000, 1200 and 2359.

Key Fact

The units of time use multiples of 60 and not the decimal system.

Remember?

Speed is the rate at which distance changes with time. In practice, the speed of a moving object is an average value over a period of time. Generally, high speeds over long distances are measured in *km per hour*; smaller units are used for low speeds over short distances or for short periods, for example, *m per min, m per sec, cm per sec, mm per sec*.

Key Fact

By drawing a graph of distance as a function of time or a graph of speed as a function of time, the speed or acceleration at a specific instant of time can be found.

Remember?

The unit for measuring temperature is the **degree**. Two scales in wide use are the Celsius scale and the Fahrenheit scale (mainly in the United States of America). In the SI system of units of measurement, the scale used is the Kelvin scale. Two points on the three scales are used to compare and convert temperatures on the different scales.

	°C	°F	K
Freezing point of water	0	32	273
Boiling point of water	100	212	373

Since 100 Celsius degrees = 180 Fahrenheit degrees = 100 Kelvin,

Then, $1\ C° = \dfrac{9}{5}\ F° = 1\ K.$

Practice

C **1** A bus leaves Grantsville at 23:15 and does not stop until it arrives at Huntsbay at 01:35. The distance between the towns is 104 km. Calculate:

(a) the time of the journey

(b) the average speed of the bus.

2 (a) Draw a graph to show the relation between temperatures on the Celsius and Fahrenheit scales between −10 °C and 100 °C.

(b) Use the graph to find the equivalent temperature in each of the following:

(i) 140 °F in °C   **(ii)** −5 °C in °F

3 The table gives corresponding values of time and the speed of an object moving uniformly from rest.

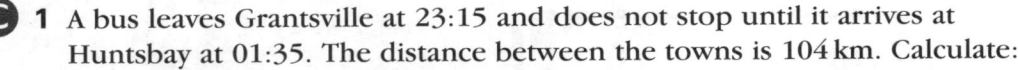

Time	08:00	08:02	08:04	08:06	08:08
Speed km/h	0	3	6	9	12

(a) Draw a graph to represent the given values.

(b) Use the graph to find:

(i) the time when the speed is 10 km/h

(ii) the speed at 08:05.

Finished Early?

 Go to page 444

2 Perimeter and Area

Remember?

The **perimeter** is the total length of the outside boundary of any flat two-dimensional surface, that is, the sum of the lengths of all the sides. The perimeter of a circle is called the **circumference**.

The **area** of a shape is the measure of the surface enclosed within the sides of the shape. The formulae for some basic shapes are:

	Sides	Perimeter	Area
Rectangle	l and w	$2(l + w)$	$l \times w$
Square	l	$4l$	l^2
Parallelogram	l and h	$2(l + h)$	$l \times h$
Triangle	x, y and b	$x + y + b$	$\frac{1}{2}(b \times h)$
Circle	r [radius]	$2\pi r$ [circumference]	πr^2

Key Fact

The metric units of perimeter are the units of length, that is, metre (m), centimetre (cm), kilometre (km), etc; the units of area are based on a square of side of unit length and are given by m², cm², km², etc.

Word Check

hectare an SI unit of area, equal to 10 000 m²

congruent equal in all respects; exactly the same

Key Fact

The distances we measure of a point from a line and the distance between parallel lines is always the perpendicular distance.

Remember?

To find the perimeter or area of compound shapes:
- split the compound shape into basic shapes, usually rectangles, squares, triangles or parallelograms
- calculate the values for the basic shapes
- find the sum or difference of these values.

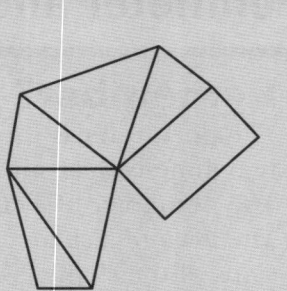

Practice

 If there is access to computer facilities, then the teacher will use the computer program to review areas of plane shapes. Students work through the following exercise.

1 Find the area of each of the following parallelograms:

(i)

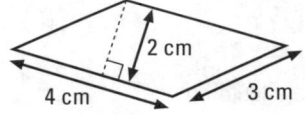

2 cm
4 cm
3 cm

(ii)

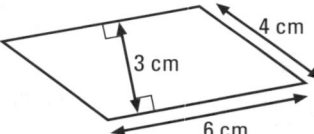

4 cm
3 cm
6 cm

(iii)

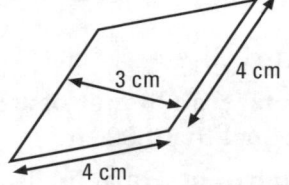

3 cm
4 cm
4 cm

(iv)

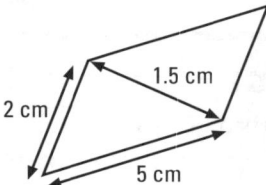

1.5 cm
2 cm
5 cm

2 For each of these parallelograms, draw on squared paper a rectangle which has the same area.

(i)

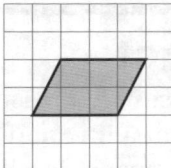

(ii)

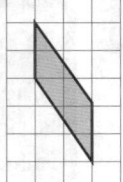

(iii)

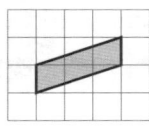

(iv)

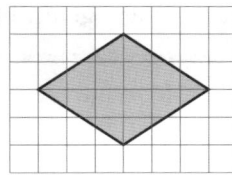

3 Find the area of each of the following triangles:

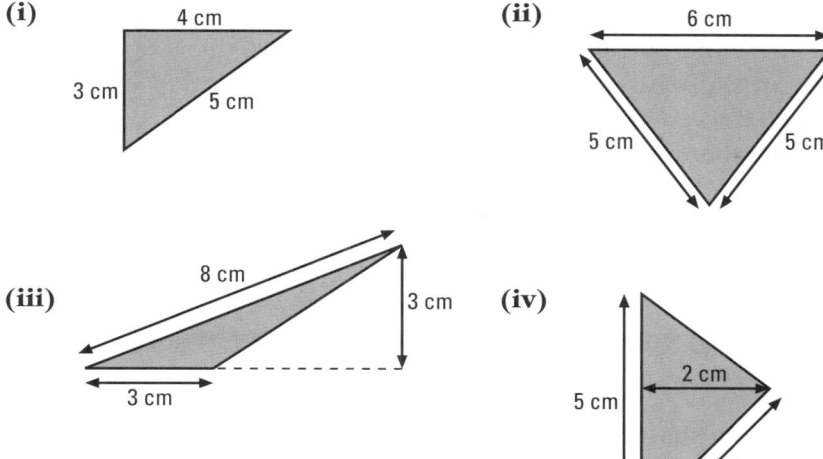

4 Find the area of each of the following shapes:

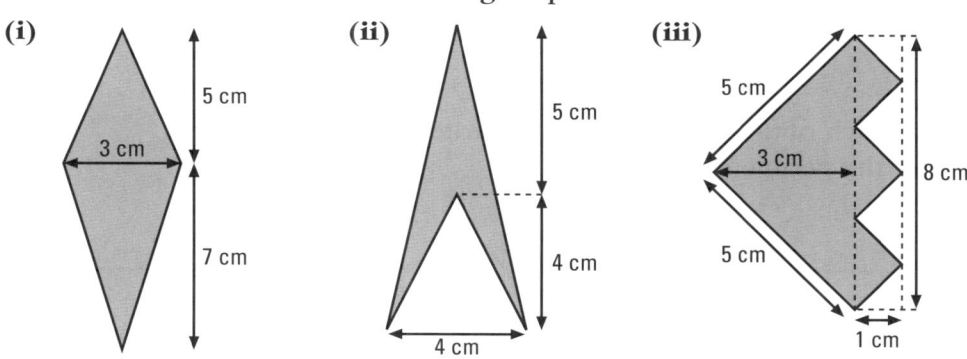

5 Find the area of each of these shapes. Each is made from congruent parallelograms.

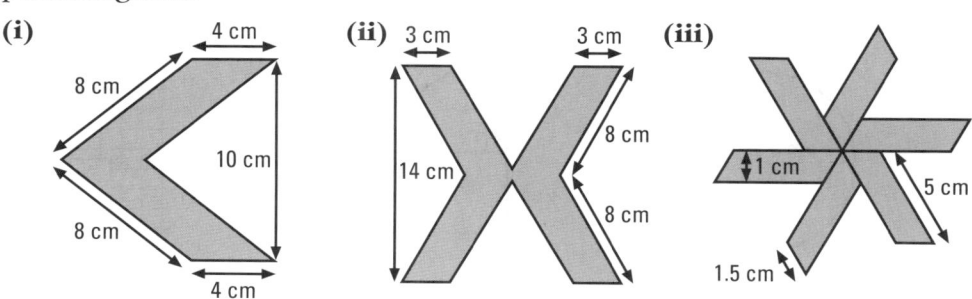

Key Fact

When you know the perimeter or area of a shape and the formula (or an expression) to calculate this value, you can use algebra to find an unknown length in the shape by
- representing the unknown length by a letter
- substituting the letter in the formula or expression
- forming an equation using the known value of the perimeter or area
- solving the equation.

Practice

E 1 For the following shapes, calculate:
(a) the area **(b)** the perimeter. When necessary, take $\pi = \frac{22}{7}$.

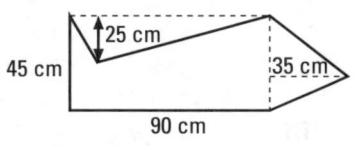

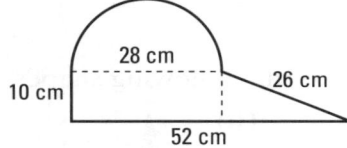

2 For each of the following shapes, write an expression for:
(a) the perimeter, *P*

    (i)   **(ii)**   **(iii)**

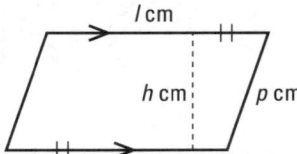

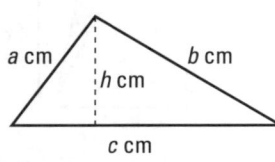

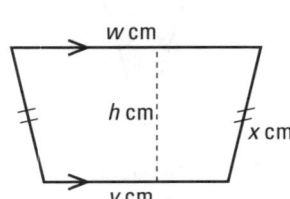

(b) the area, *A*.

    (i)   **(ii)**   **(iii)**

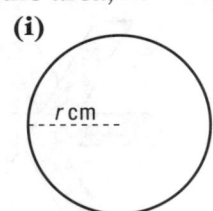

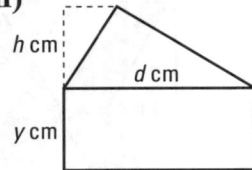

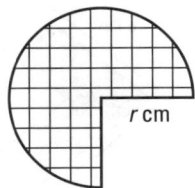

3 Using the values below for the shapes given in question 2, work out each of the unknown lengths:

  (a) **(i)** $l = 16$, $h = 8$, $P = 52$, $p = ?$
    (ii) $a = 10$, $b = 18$, $P = 54$, $c = ?$
    (iii) $w = 32$, $y = 20$, $h = 16$, $P = 92$, $x = ?$
  (b) **(i)** $A = 6.16$, $r = ?$
    (ii) $h = 10$, $d = 23$, $A = 345$, $v = ?$
    (iii) $A = 105$, $r = ?$

Remember?

The **surface area** of a solid is the sum of the areas of all the faces of the solid. The formulae for some common solids are given below:

	Solid	Net	Surface area
Cuboid		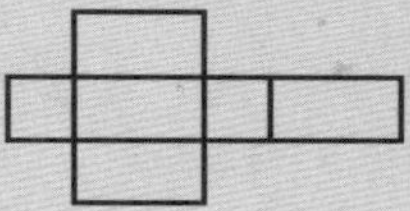	six rectangular faces $2wh + 2lh + 2wl$
Cylinder			one rectangular face and two circular end faces $2\pi rh + 2\pi r^2$
Prism (triangular)			two triangular end faces and three rectangular faces
Pyramid (square-based)			square base and four triangular faces
Cone			circular base of radius r and sector of a circle of radius l
Sphere			$4\pi r^2$

Practice

F Calculate the surface area of the following solids.

1

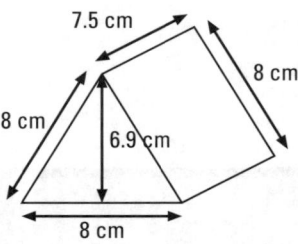

7.5 cm
8 cm
8 cm
6.9 cm
8 cm

2

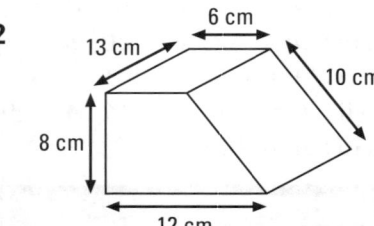

6 cm
13 cm
10 cm
8 cm
12 cm

3

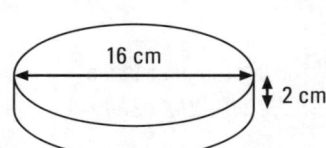

16 cm
2 cm

4

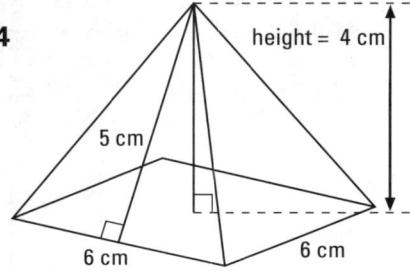

height = 4 cm
5 cm
6 cm
6 cm

5

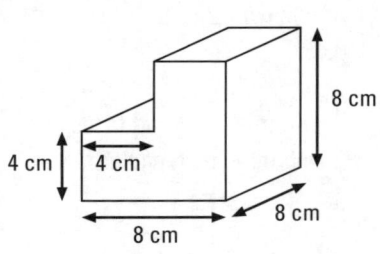

8 cm
4 cm
4 cm
8 cm
8 cm

6

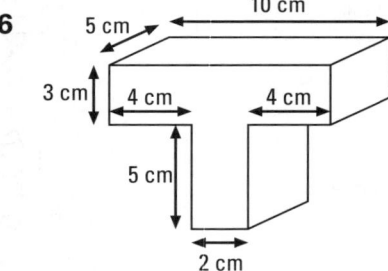

10 cm
5 cm
3 cm
4 cm
4 cm
5 cm
2 cm

7

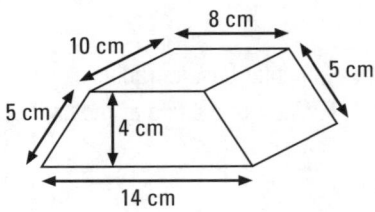

8 cm
10 cm
5 cm
5 cm
4 cm
14 cm

8

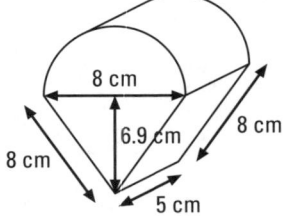

8 cm
8 cm
6.9 cm
8 cm
5 cm

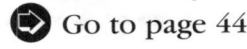

Finished Early?
Go to page 445

③ Volume and Capacity

Remember?

The **volume** of a solid gives a measure of the amount of matter in the solid and thus a measure of the space that the solid occupies.

The **capacity** gives a measure of the amount of space within a cavity and thus is a measure of the fluid that can occupy the space.

The formulae for some common solids are given below:

Solids		Volume
Cuboid		length × width × height $l \times w \times h$
Cylinder		area of cross-section × height $\pi r^2 \times h$
Prism (triangular)		area of cross-section × length $\frac{1}{2} bh \times l$
Pyramid		$\frac{1}{3}$ × area of base × height $\frac{1}{3} \times A \times h$
Cone		$\frac{1}{3} \times \pi r^2 \times h$
Sphere		$\frac{4}{3} \pi r^3$

Word Check

fluids liquids and gases

Key Fact

The metric units of volume are based on a cube of edge of unit length and are given by m³, cm³ [or cc], km³, etc.

The metric units of capacity are based on the litre [l].

(1 litre = 1 dm³ = 1000 cc and 1 millilitre [ml] = 1 cc)

Practice

G Calculate the volume of the solids given under **Practice F**.

Practice

H Two containers with lids are shown in the following diagrams. For each container, calculate:

(a) the surface area   **(b)** the capacity.

1   **2**

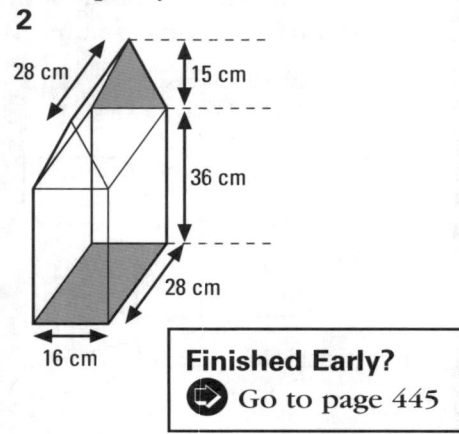

Finished Early?
➡ Go to page 445

4 Accuracy in Measurement

Learn About It

When you use a measuring instrument such as a ruler, a protractor, or a balance, there is always the chance that the measurement may not be accurate. Error may occur because the markings on the instrument itself are not exact and correctly placed, as in the diagram on the right.

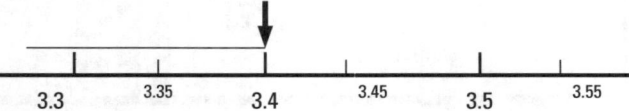

However, the error may be due to *human error*, that is, the person reading the measurement may have been slightly incorrect as shown in the diagram below.

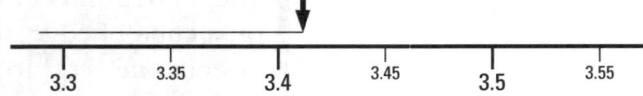

Measurements therefore should be stated approximately. For example, when the length, l cm, of the line shown above is stated correct to 1 d.p., or to 2 s.f., or to the nearest mm, the measurement given must be between 3.35 cm and 3.45 cm. Then the length is stated as 3.4 cm.

If the measurement was less than 3.35 cm, then it would be stated as 3.3 cm and if the measurement was greater than 3.45 cm, it would be stated as 3.5 cm.

Therefore, we write $3.35 \leqslant l < 3.45$. Since $3.35 - 3.4 = -0.05$ and $3.45 - 3.4 = +0.05$, we say that *the greatest possible error* is -0.05 cm, that is ± 0.05 cm.

Note that this does not mean that the error must be 0.05 cm. The error may be less than 0.05 cm but it **cannot be more** than 0.05 cm. The measurement may be written as: length of line, l cm $= 3.4 \pm 0.05$ cm or $3.35 \leqslant l < 3.45$.

> ### Word Check
> **error** difference between the stated measurement and the correct one
>
> **approximate** not exact but close enough to be of practical use

Try It Out

I Write the greatest and smallest possible values of the following measurements.

1 52 g correct to 2 s.f.　　　　**2** 85.8 km correct to 1 d.p.

3 2.54 litres correct to 2 d.p.　　**4** 45° correct to the nearest degree

5 7.2 cm correct to the nearest mm

J State the greatest possible error for each measurement given in **I**.

Learn More About It

The accuracy of calculations that use measurements depends on the accuracy of the measurements. The results of these calculations should be given to the same degree of accuracy as the measurements.

For example, the sides of a rectangle are measured as $l = 4.6$ and $w = 2.1$ correct to 1 d.p. Then the greatest and smallest possible values of l are 4.65 and 4.55, and of w are 2.15 and 2.05.

The perimeter using only the measured values will be 13.4; the greatest possible value of the perimeter is $2(4.65 + 2.15) = 13.6$ and the smallest possible value is $2(4.55 + 2.05) = 13.2$.

The perimeter can then be written as $P = 13.4 \pm 0.2$ or $13.4 \leqslant P < 13.6$.

The area using only the measured values will be 9.7 correct to 1 d.p; the greatest possible value of the area is $4.65 \times 2.15 = 10.0$ correct to 1 d.p. and the smallest possible value is $4.55 \times 2.05 = 9.3$ correct to 1 d.p. The area can then be written as $A = 9.7 \pm 0.3$ or $9.3 \leqslant A < 10.0$.

Key Fact

In order to find the greatest value of the difference of two measurements, say, $a - b$, use the greatest value of a and the smallest value of b.

When the calculation of measurements is the division of two values, say, $y \div x$, in order to find the greatest value of the calculation, use the greatest value of y and the smallest value of x.

Word Check

maximum largest or greatest possible value

minimum smallest or least possible value

Try It Out

K Work out the greatest and smallest possible values of the following calculations.

1 Sum of two masses of 52 g and 35 g correct to 2 s.f.

2 Area of a rectangle with sides of length 5.8 cm and 2.7 cm correct to 1 d.p.

L Find the greatest possible error for each calculation given above in **K**.

Key Fact

A scale drawing is a copy of an actual object in which the scale of the drawing is the ratio of corresponding lengths, for example, if the scale of a map is 1 : 100 000, then a length of 2.6 cm on the map represents (2.6 × 100 000) cm or 2.6 km on the ground.

Practice

M 1 The sides of a tile measure 30 cm and 25 cm correct to the nearest whole number. Find the largest and smallest possible values of the surface area that one tile covers.

2 A shopkeeper states that the weights of three melons are 2.1 kg, 5.3 kg, and 3.2 kg.

(a) Calculate:

(i) the maximum and the minimum weight of each melon

(ii) the greatest possible total weight of the three melons

(iii) the least possible total weight of the three melons.

(b) The shopkeeper charges \$4.00 per kg for the melons. Calculate the difference between the money he receives for his stated weights and the greatest and least amounts he may get.

3 An athlete runs a distance of 800 m, to the nearest metre, in 3 minutes, measured to the nearest minute.

(a) Write the greatest and least possible values of the distance and the time.

(b) Work out the greatest and least possible values of the speed in ms^{-1}.

4 The distance between two towns on a map is measured as 12 cm correct to the nearest centimetre. The scale of the map is 1 : 25 000. Calculate the greatest and least possible values of:

(a) the map distance   **(b)** the actual distance in km.

> **Finished Early?**
>  Go to page 446

Further Practice

 **1** Two of the angles of a triangle are measured as 55° and 80°, correct to the nearest degree. Find the greatest and least values of the third angle of the triangle.

2 The radius of a circular disk is measured as 8.6 cm correct to 1 d.p. Calculate the greatest and smallest values for:

(a) the length of tape that will fit around its circumference

(b) the area of paper to cover both top and bottom circular surfaces.

> **Finished Early?**
> Go to page 446

Unit 3 *Measurement*

Summary of Chapters 6 and 7

Angles, Solids and Shapes

- When lines meet or intersect at a point, **angles** are formed; the lines forming the angle are called the **arms** and the point is called the **vertex** (plural – vertices). An angle is a measure of rotation and is measured using a **protractor**.

- In one complete **revolution** there are 360 **degrees**, written 360°. Angles may be **acute** (>0° and <90°), **right-angled** (90°), **obtuse** (>90° and <180°), **straight** (180°) or **reflex** (>180°).

- When a straight line 'stands' on another straight line, the **adjacent angles on the straight line** add up to 180°.

- When a number of straight lines meet at a point (or vertex), the sum of **the angles at the point** is 360°, and the **vertically opposite angles** are equal.

- When parallel lines (lines that never meet no matter how much they are lengthened) are 'cut' by another line, the **alternate angles** and **corresponding angles** formed are equal.

- Most geometrical solids have **faces**, **edges** and **vertices**. Flat faces meet along straight edges and curved faces meet along curved edges. Edges meet at a point called a **vertex**.

- A **net** of a solid is the plane shape obtained when a solid is cut along the edges and then flattened out.

- The common solids include **prisms** (**cubes**, **cuboids** and **cylinders**), **pyramids**, **cones** and **spheres**.

- A **polygon** is any closed shape that has three or more straight sides. Polygons may be divided into groups according to the number of their sides – **triangles** (3 sides), **quadrilaterals** (4 sides), **pentagons** (5 sides), **hexagons** (6 sides) and so on. These groups are further classified according to the relationship of their sides and angles, for example. **Scalene triangles, acute-angled, right-angled** and **obtuse-angled triangles, isosceles triangles; rectangles, kites, trapeziums, parallelograms** and **rhombuses**.

- A **regular polygon** has equal sides and angles, for example, **equilateral triangles** and **squares**. As the number of sides of a regular polygon increases, the shape approaches the shape of a **circle**.

- The sum of the **angles of a triangle** is 180°, and **of a quadrilateral** is 360°. The sum of the **interior angles** of an n-sided polygon may be written either as

    $(n - 2) \times 180°$ or $(2n - 4) \times 90°$.

- The sum of the **exterior angles** of any polygon is 360°.

- The **plan**, **front elevation** and **side elevation** are two-dimensional drawings of a solid – the plan being viewed from vertically above, and the elevations directly from the front and from the side respectively.

- A **line of symmetry** divides a plane shape into two parts which are identically equal. A solid has **mirror symmetry** when the reflection of one part in the line of symmetry looks like the other part.

- If a plane shape fits upon itself in more than one position when it is rotated about a point, then the shape has **point** (or **rotational**) **symmetry**. The **order** of point symmetry is the number of times the shape fits upon itself when rotated about the point.

Units of Measurement

- The basic quantities – **length**, **mass** and **time** – are now more often measured using the **SI system of units** in which the respective basic units of measurement are **metre**, **kilogram** and **second**. The units of length and mass are decimal systems and their subdivisions are identified by prefixes, for example, *milli*, *centi*, and *kilo*; the units of time do not follow the decimal system. Time is written in different ways including the **24-hour clock**.

- In the SI system of units the unit used to measure **temperature** is the **Celsius degree** – other systems use the Kelvin and the Fahrenheit scales.

- The **perimeter** of a shape is the outline or the measure of the outline of a shape and therefore has units of length. The **area** of a shape is a measure of the surface; the units of area are (units of length)^2.

- The **volume** of a solid is a measure of the space the solid occupies; the units of volume are (units of length)^3.

- The **capacity** of a container is a measure of the space inside the container. The basic unit of capacity is the **litre** which is a fluid measure and is a measure of the space inside a container of internal volume 1000 cubic centimetres.

    Formulae for standard plane shapes and solids are listed in tables in Chapter 7.

- A **scale drawing** of a plane figure is such that while the shape remains the same, the size is different. The **scale** gives the ratio (when both sets of measurement are in the same units) or rate (the two sets of measurements are different) by which the dimensions of the original figure is reduced. The scale used must always be given on a scale drawing.

- Most measuring instruments give measurements which are correct to only 2 or 3 significant figures (s.f.). The difference between the stated reading and the correct reading is called the **error** in the measurement. In addition there is human error. Hence, the answer to a calculation based on numbers obtained from measurements should not contain more significant figures than the measurements. Generally, the answer should have one less significant figure, for example, measurements to 2 s.f. should give an answer to 1 s.f.

8 Algebraic Processes

1 Algebraic Expressions

Remember?

In algebra we use letters to represent different numerical values. An **algebraic expression** therefore generally includes **terms** that are variable and are represented by letters, and a constant term that is a number. Variable terms may also contain numbers and letters that are multiplied together or divided. The $\times$ sign is usually omitted so that

$4xy$ means $4 \times x \times y$.

The number in a variable term is called the numerical **coefficient**.

The terms in an expression are either added together or subtracted and so are connected by a + or a − sign; for example, there are three terms in the expression: $x + 4xy - 2y^3$.

Like terms are terms that have the same variable or set of variables, for example, $3x$, $5x$ and $-2x$ are called terms in x; xy and $-3xy$ are terms in xy. Like terms can be added and subtracted, that is, can be **grouped**.

Grouping terms is one method for **simplifying** algebraic expressions.

Terms that are not like terms are **unlike terms**. For example, x, $\frac{x}{y}$, y^3, $3a$ and $-5b$ are unlike terms and cannot be grouped, so the

expression $x + \frac{x}{y} - y^3 + 3a - 5b$ cannot be simplified further.

When the powers of all the variables in the expression are equal to 1, the expression is called a **linear expression**, for example, $2x + 5y$.

When the highest power of the variables of any term in the expression is equal to 2, the expression is called a **quadratic expression**, for example, $y^2 - 4x + xy - y + 3$.

Key Facts

A letter replaces *only* a numerical value and does not include a unit of measurement. The numerical value may be whole or fractional, positive or negative.

Remember?

When grouping the like terms in an algebraic expression, the terms can be treated as directed numbers and added together using the commutative property and the associative property (see Chapter 4). The order of operations used when simplifying expressions is BoDMAS, that is the same as for arithmetic.

Word Check

variable letter that stands for different values

unknown variable whose value is not known

constant same for all values as the variable changes

Remember?

When removing a bracket, each term in the bracket is multiplied by the term outside the bracket, for example,

$3(x - 2y) = 3x - 6y$.

If the multiplier is negative, then the sign of each term inside the bracket is changed after multiplication, for example,

$-2ab(3x - 2y) = -6abx + 4aby$.

Key Fact

The order of the same variables in a term does not matter so that xy and yx are like terms, but note that xy and Xy are unlike terms.

Practice

A Simplify the following expressions.

1 $6a + 3 - 2a$

2 $\frac{1}{2}f - \frac{2}{3}g + \frac{1}{4}f + \frac{1}{3}g + 2$

3 $4uv - vu + 2uw - 3v^2 + 2u^2$

4 $6y^3 - 3xy - x^2 + 2xy$

5 $4u^2v - v^2u + 2uw^2 - 3vu^2 + 2w^2u$

6 $y^3 - 5x^2y - 4y^2 + 3xy^2 - yx^2$

B Remove the brackets and simplify the following.

1 $-\frac{1}{3}(3jk + 6k - j)$

2 $(m^2 + 2mn - n^2)mn$

3 $(x + 3y)x - (2x - 3y)y$

4 $d(d^2 - 2d + 1) - d(d^2 - 2)$

5 $(t^2 - 3)t^2 + (2t^3 + 2t^2 - 3)2t$

Further Practice

C Simplify each of the following expressions.

1 $c + 7 - 2c - 4b - 3c$

2 $3k + 3m - 2 - 6k - 3m - 2n$

3 $\frac{2}{3}ab - 2bc - 4bc + \frac{1}{3}ab$

4 $a^2 + 4ac + 2a^2 - 8ac$

D Remove the brackets and simplify the following.

1 $3a(a - b)$

2 $-\frac{1}{2}c(2c - 1)$

3 $(fg^2 - f^2g)f$

4 $(3v - w)v + (2w + v)w$

5 $(h - 2k + 3)k - (k + 2h - 1)h$

2 Laws of Indices

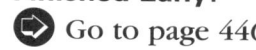

> **Finished Early?**
> ⇨ Go to page 446

Learn About It

We know that 4^2 is the index form for 4×4.

Similarly, x^2 is the index form for $x \times x$.

$$16 = (4 \times 4) \text{ and } 64 = (4 \times 4 \times 4)$$

Expanding the product 16×64 in terms of the factors, we get

$$16 \times 64 = (4 \times 4) \times (4 \times 4 \times 4) = (4 \times 4 \times 4 \times 4 \times 4)$$

We can write the above product using indices:

$$4^2 \times 4^3 = 4^5$$

Similarly, we can write the product $x^2 \times x^3$ in expanded form:

$$x^2 \times x^3 = (x \times x) \times (x \times x \times x) = (x \times x \times x \times x \times x)$$

and then using indices, we see that

$$x^2 \times x^3 = x^5$$

Try It Out

 **(a)** Write each of the following products in expanded form.

(b) State the result in index form.

1 $a^2 \times a^5$ **2** $b^3 \times b^4$ **3** $c \times c^4$

The results show that

$$a^2 \times a^5 = a^7 = a^{2+5}$$
$$b^3 \times b^4 = b^7 = b^{3+4}$$
$$c^1 \times c^4 = c^5 = c^{1+4}$$

In general, $x^m \times x^n = x^{m+n}$.

Similarly, for the inverse process of division
expanding $1024 \div 64$ in terms of the factors, we get

$$1024 \div 64 = (4 \times 4 \times 4 \times 4 \times 4) \div (4 \times 4 \times 4) = (4 \times 4)$$

We can write the above using indices:

$$4^5 \div 4^3 = 4^2$$

Similarly, we can write $x^5 \div x^3$ in expanded form:

$$x^5 \div x^3 = (x \times x \times x \times x \times x) \div (x \times x \times x) = (x \times x)$$

and then using indices, we see that

$$x^5 \div x^3 = x^2$$

Try It Out

 (a) Write each of the following in expanded form.

(b) State the results in index form.

1 $a^6 \div a^2$ **2** $b^5 \div b^4$ **3** $c^3 \div c^7$

These results show that using indices:

$$a^6 \div a^2 = a^4 = a^{6-2}$$
$$b^5 \div b^4 = b^1 = b^{5-4}$$
$$c^3 \div c^7 = \frac{1}{c^4} = c^{3-7} = c^{-4}$$

Therefore, in general,
$x^m \div x^n = x^{m-n}$.

> ### Key Fact
> As shown in question 3, $c^{-4} = \frac{1}{c^4}$.
> In general, $x^{-m} = \frac{1}{x^m}$.

We can write $(16)^3 = 16 \times 16 \times 16$ in terms of factors as

$$(4 \times 4)^3 = (4 \times 4) \times (4 \times 4) \times (4 \times 4)$$

and using indices as $(4^2)^3 = 4^6$.

Similarly, we can write $(x \times x)^3$ in expanded form as

$$(x \times x)^3 = (x \times x) \times (x \times x) \times (x \times x) = (x \times x \times x \times x \times x \times x)$$

and then using indices as $(x^2)^3 = x^6$.

Try It Out

G (a) Write the following in expanded form.

(b) State the result in index form.

1 $(a^2)^4$ **2** $(b^3)^2$ **3** $(c^2)^3$

The results show that

$(a^2)^4 = a^8 = a^{2\times4}$

$(b^3)^2 = b^6 = b^{3\times2}$

$(c^2)^3 = c^6 = (c)^{2\times3}$

In general, $(x^m)^n = x^{mn}$.

Example Simplify the following. (a) $2d^4 \times 4d^3$ (b) $12ab^3c^5 \div 3bc^6$

Working (a) $2 \times 4 \times d^{4+3}$

(b) $12 \div 3 \times a \times b^{3-1} \times c^{5-6}$

Answer (a) $8d^7$

(b) $\dfrac{4ab^2}{c}$

Practice

H Simplify the following.

1 $a^4 \times 4a^3$ **2** $p^6r^5q^5 \div pq^2$ **3** $3d^2 \times 5bd^3$

4 $3xy^4 \times 2yz^3$ **5** $9h^2k^5 \div 3h^3jk^3$ **6** $12ab^5c^5 \div 3b^5c^3$

7 $(2a^3f)^3$ **8** $3(hkn^2)^3 \times (3hk)^2$ **9** $(a^3x^2y)^3 \div 2xy^2$

Key Fact

From the results of question 6, $b^0 = 1$

In general, $x^0 = 1$

Learn More About It

We know that $\sqrt{5} \times \sqrt{5} = 5^1$.

Writing $\sqrt{5} = 5^s$, then $5^s \times 5^s = 5^1$.

Since $x^m \times x^n = x^{m+n}$, $5^{2s} = 5^1 \rightarrow 2s = 1$.

Therefore, $s = \frac{1}{2}$

and $5^{\frac{1}{2}} \times 5^{\frac{1}{2}} = 5^{\frac{1}{2}+\frac{1}{2}} = 5^1 = 5$.

Also, since $5^{\frac{1}{3}} \times 5^{\frac{1}{3}} \times 5^{\frac{1}{3}} = 5^{\frac{1}{3}+\frac{1}{3}+\frac{1}{3}} = 5^1 = 5$,

$\sqrt[3]{5} = 5^{\frac{1}{3}}$

Key Facts

The laws of indices can be stated as

$$x^m \times x^n = x^{m+n}$$
$$x^m \div x^n = x^{m-n}$$
$$(x^m)^n = x^{mn}$$
$$x^{-m} = \frac{1}{x^m}$$

Key Facts

In the **laws of indices**, x stands for a number (or for a letter replacing a number); and x, m, and n may be whole numbers, fractions or decimals, positive or negative.

When x, m and n are mixed numbers, these numbers must be changed to improper fractions before applying the laws of indices.

Example Simplify the following: **(a)** $(2\frac{1}{4})^{-\frac{3}{2}}$ **(b)** $\sqrt{7\frac{1}{5}c^2} \div 1\frac{4}{5}$

Working   **(a)** $[(9 \div 4)^{\frac{1}{2}}]^{-3}$

$= [(3^2)^{\frac{1}{2}} \div (2^2)^{\frac{1}{2}}]^{-3}$

$= 3^{-3} \div 2^{-3}$

$= (\frac{1}{3})^3 \div (\frac{1}{2})^3$

$= (\frac{1}{3})^3 \times (\frac{2}{1})^3$

$= (\frac{2}{3})^3 = \frac{8}{27}$

(b) $\sqrt{7\frac{1}{5}c^2} \div 1\frac{4}{5}$

$= (\frac{36}{5}c^2 \div \frac{9}{5})^{\frac{1}{2}}$

$= [(\frac{36}{5} \times \frac{5}{9})c^2]^{\frac{1}{2}}$

$= [4c^2]^{\frac{1}{2}}$

$= [2 \times 2 \times c \times c]^{\frac{1}{2}}$

$= 2c$

Answer   **(a)** $\frac{8}{27}$ **(b)** $2c$

Key Fact

In $2a^{\frac{3}{2}}$ only a is raised to the power $\frac{3}{2}$;

but in $(2a)^{\frac{3}{2}}$ both 2 and a are raised to the power $\frac{3}{2}$.

Practice

1 Simplify the following.

1 $9^{-\frac{1}{2}}$

2 $\frac{1}{8}^{\frac{1}{3}}$

3 $(16b^6)^{\frac{1}{2}}$

4 $\sqrt{1\frac{7}{9}}$

5 $2x^{-1} \times 3x^3$

6 $2x^{-1} \times (3x)^3$

Further Practice

J Simplify the following.

1 $(36)^{-\frac{3}{2}}$

2 $27^{\frac{1}{3}\frac{1}{3}}$

3 $(16k^4)^{\frac{3}{4}}$

4 $2h^{-3} \times 3h^{-2}$

5 $(2y)^{-1} \times (2y)^3$

6 $(4v)^{-2} \times (2v)^4$

Finished Early?

 Go to page 447

❸ Substitution and Formulae

Remember?

Substitution is the process in which letters are replaced by numbers in order to work out the numerical value of an algebraic term or expression.

A **formula** is a general rule for a relation among different variables. If the value of one of the variables is not known, substitution of a numerical value for each of the other variables in the formula leads to the calculation of the value of the unknown. The unknown is called the **subject of the formula**. For example, if the amount received is the unknown in the formula *Amount = Principal + Interest*, then substituting numbers for *P* and *I* gives the value of *A*.

If another variable, say *I*, becomes the unknown, then the variables in the formula are rearranged so that *I = A − P*. This process is called **changing the subject of the formula**.

Key Fact

Units are not stated in a formula, but the quantities that the variables represent must be given in appropriate units.

Practice

K **1** If $v = -1$, $x = -2$, $y = 3$, find the value of:

   (a) vx (b) vy (c) $3x^2$ (d) $(3x)^2$

   (e) $3v + 2x$ (f) $2y + 4v - x$ (g) $vx^2 + y^2$ (h) $(vx - y)^2$

   (i) $\dfrac{x + y}{2}$ (j) $\dfrac{2v - y}{5}$ (k) $\dfrac{xy(v - 3)}{4vy}$ (l) $\dfrac{(vx - y)^2}{v - xy}$

2 $P = 2h + 2w$:

   Evaluate: **(a)** P when $h = 12$ and $w = 9$

                   (b) h when $P = 34$ and $w = 7$.

3 Evaluate $4y^2 + 3y - 2$ when $y =$

   (a) 2   **(b)** –2   **(c)** 0   **(d)** –3   **(e)** –1

4 Find the value of $x^2y - 4y^2 + 3xy^2 - x^2$ when $x = 3$, and $y = -2$.

5 Evaluate the following given that $r = -3$, $s = 2$ and $t = -1$.

   (a) $r^2 - 5tr - 4t^2$ **(b)** $3srt - rs^2$ **(c)** $\dfrac{tsr}{5tr - 3sr}$

6 The formula for the circumference of a circle is $C = 2\pi r$. Find the circumference of the base of a cylindrical tank if its radius is 0.7 metres.

7 $2700 is the interest I paid on a principal P of $20\,000 after 3 years. Calculate R, the rate paid, using the formula, $I = \dfrac{PTR}{100}$, where T is time.

L In each of the following, make the given letter the subject of the formula:

   1 $K = C + 273$ C **2** $P = 2l + 2b$ b

   3 $t = s + \frac{1}{2}r$ s **4** $t = s + \frac{1}{2}r$ r

   5 $I = \dfrac{PTR}{100}$ T **6** $v = u + at$ t

Finished Early?
➡ Go to page 447

Remember?

In a **binary operation**, two quantities are combined to give a result. All or some of the four basic arithmetic operators – addition, subtraction, multiplication and division – may be used to define other binary operators, for example, finding the average of two numbers uses addition and division.

We can use the symbol ⬭ to represent finding the average of a and b, so we can write $a \circ b$ to represent $(a + b) \div 2$.

Then $14 \circ 8 = (14 + 8) \div 2 = 11$.

And $23 \circ (14 \circ 8) = 23 \circ 11 = (23 + 11) \div 2 = 17$.

Practice

 1 Given that $j \, \Phi \, k = 3j + k$, find the value of:

    (a) $2 \, \Phi \, 3$ **(b)** $2 \, \Phi \, (2 \, \Phi \, 3)$

2 Given that $x \, ☼ \, y = x^2 + y^3$:

    (a) find the value of **(i)** $-2 \, ☼ \, -3$ **(ii)** $(-2 \, ☼ \, -3) \, ☼ \, 1$

    (b) find the value of **(i)** y, if $4 \, ☼ \, y = 24$ **(ii)** x, if $x \, ☼ \, -3 = -2$.

3 *A binary operation is defined as twice the first number divided by the square of one third the second number.*

    (a) Write the above statement using the symbol $\varnothing$ to identify the operation.

    (b) Hence, calculate **(i)** $2 \, \varnothing \, 3$ **(ii)** $(2 \, \varnothing \, 3) \, \varnothing \, 6$.

Finished Early?

➡ Go to page 447

---

❹ Expansion and Factorisation

Remember?

Expansion refers to the multiplication of algebraic expressions within brackets; then each term inside each bracket must be multiplied by each term inside the other bracket. For example, $(a + b)(x + y)$ may be written as $a(x + y) + b(x + y)$ *or* $(a + b)x + (a + b)y$. Both methods result in the same final terms, that is, $ax + ay + bx + by$.

Expansions to be noted in particular are:

$(a + b)(a + b) = (a + b)^2 = a^2 + 2ab + b^2$

$(a - b)(a - b) = (a - b)^2 = a^2 - 2ab + b^2$

$(a + b)(a - b) = a^2 - b^2$

Key Fact

When there are two terms in an expression, it is called a **binomial expression**.

Practice

 Expand each of the following.

1 $(a + 3)(b + 1)$ **2** $(c - 2)(d + 1)$ **3** $(2f - 3)(g - 1)$

4 $(2k + 3)(2k - 1)$ **5** $(3m + 2)^2$ **6** $(x + 3y)(2x + y)$

7 $(d - 2r)(d + r)$ **8** $(d + 2)(d + 2)$ **9** $(t - 3)(t - 3)$

10 $(2d + 1)^2$ **11** $(2x - 3y)^2$ **12** $(3 - 2y)^2$

13 $(n + 1)(n - 1)$ **14** $(3v - 1)(3v + 1)$ **15** $(x - 2y)(x + 2y)$

Further Practice

Expand each of the following.

1 $(d + 2)(d + 5)$ **2** $(2 - t)(3 - t)$

3 $(3n + 1)(n - 1)$ **4** $(a + 2b)(3a + b)$

5 $(3 + g)(3 + g)$ **6** $(m - 2n)^2$

> **Finished Early?**
> 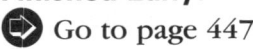 Go to page 447

> **Finished Early?**
> Go to page 447

Learn About It

Factorisation is the reverse process of expansion. To factorise an expression completely, we must find the common factors and, in particular, the highest common factor of all the terms in the expression.

In factorisation, an algebraic expression is written as the product of two or more simpler expressions, for example, $2x + 4y = 2(x + 2y)$; $2ab + bc - bd = b(2a + c - d)$; $3mn + 6m^2 = 3m(n + 2m)$.

Try It Out

Factorise each of the following expressions.

1 $14b - 7de$ **2** $5xy - 7xz$ **3** $16vw + 6uv$

4 $3apr - art$ **5** $2r^4h + 3r^2h^3$ **6** $4(l - b)h - 8(l - b)k$

> ## Key Fact
> The common factor can be a constant, a variable term or a binomial expression, or any combination of these factors.

Practice

 Factorise each of the following expressions.

1 $6d + 3cd$ **2** $hk - 2k^2$ **3** $-3g - 12rg$

4 $2k + 2k^3 + 2$ **5** $3(c + 2) + 2(c + 2)^2$ **6** $6x + 3yx - x^2$

7 $rd^2 - 2rd + 4dr^2$ **8** $4bc + 6bcd + 2b$ **9** $3t^3 - 3t^2 - 3st$

Further Practice

Finished Early?
➡ Go to page 447

R Factorise each of the following expressions.

1 $10m + 5n$ **2** $3vw - uv$ **3** $x(y + 1)^2 + 2b(y + 1)$

4 $2d^2 + d$ **5** $-5x^2 - 10x + 10$ **6** $8(3 - f)g - 2(3 - f)^2$

Finished Early?
➡ Go to page 448

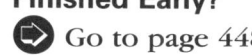 **5** Algebraic Fractions

> ## Remember?
> The same rules and operations that apply to numerical fractions apply to algebraic fractions, for example,
> - equivalent fractions can be made by multiplying or dividing the numerator and denominator by the same quantity
> - fractions can only be added and subtracted if they have common denominators.

Example   Simplify each of the following:

1 $\dfrac{x + 1}{3} - \dfrac{2x}{5}$ **2** $\dfrac{2x - 1}{5x} - \dfrac{4x - 3}{10x}$ **3** $\dfrac{3w}{w - 1} - \dfrac{w}{w + 2}$

Answer

1 $\dfrac{x + 1}{3} - \dfrac{2x}{5}$

$= \dfrac{5(x + 1) - 3(2x)}{15}$

$= \dfrac{5x + 5 - 6x}{15}$

$= \dfrac{5 - x}{15}$

2 $\dfrac{2x - 1}{5x} - \dfrac{4x - 3}{10x}$

$= \dfrac{2(2x - 1) - (4x - 3)}{10x}$

$= \dfrac{4x - 2 - 4x + 3}{10x}$

$= \dfrac{1}{10x}$

3 $\dfrac{3w}{w - 1} - \dfrac{w}{w + 2}$

$= \dfrac{3w(w + 2) - w(w - 1)}{(w - 1)(w + 2)}$

$= \dfrac{3w^2 + 6w - w^2 + w}{(w - 1)(w + 2)}$

$= \dfrac{2w^2 + 7w}{(w - 1)(w + 2)}$

$= \dfrac{w(2w + 7)}{(w - 1)(w + 2)}$

Practice

S Simplify each of the following.

1 $\dfrac{2x}{3} + \dfrac{x-1}{2}$

2 $\dfrac{y-4}{2} - \dfrac{y}{6} + \dfrac{1-y}{3}$

3 $\dfrac{a+3}{3} + \dfrac{2a-1}{2}$

4 $\dfrac{c-2}{2} - \dfrac{2-c}{6}$

5 $\dfrac{f+3}{3} + 4f$

6 $3k - \dfrac{2k-5}{3}$

7 $\dfrac{w+4}{w+1} + \dfrac{2w-1}{w+2}$

8 $\dfrac{1}{2} - \dfrac{3-m}{m+6}$

9 $\dfrac{2d-3}{d+3} - \dfrac{4-d}{d-2}$

10 $\dfrac{3v+5}{3} + 2v$

Finished Early?
 Go to page 448

Further Practice

T Simplify each of the following.

1 $\dfrac{u+2}{2} + \dfrac{2u-1}{4}$

2 $\dfrac{w-1}{3} - \dfrac{1-w}{4}$

3 $\dfrac{h}{h+3} + 4h$

4 $y - \dfrac{2y-3}{3}$

5 $\dfrac{p-3}{2p+1} - \dfrac{1-p}{p-2}$

6 $\dfrac{3v+5}{v+3} + 2$

Finished Early?
 Go to page 448

9 Linear Equations and Inequalities

In this chapter you will learn about ...
1. linear equations
2. identities
3. linear inequalities
4. simultaneous linear equations

1 Linear Equations

Remember?

When an algebraic expression is put equal to another algebraic expression or equal to a numeric value, the statement is called an **equation**.

In a linear equation the highest power of every variable is equal to 1. There may be more than one variable in a linear equation, for example, $3x + 2y = 5x$ is a linear equation in two variables, x and y; and $3x + 2 - 4x = 1$ is an example of a linear equation in one variable, x.

To **solve** an equation is to find the value of the unknown that makes the equation true, that is, the value of the unknown that makes the left-hand side (LHS) of the equation equal to the right-hand side (RHS).

In the **balance method** of solving an equation, the same term is added to or subtracted from both sides of the equation, or both sides are multiplied or divided by the same constant in order to make the expressions on both sides continue to 'balance'.

Key Facts

If there are brackets on either side of the equation, then multiply out the brackets before collecting like terms.

If there are fractions, then multiply *each* term in the equation (including terms that are not fractions) by the LCM of the denominators of the fractions.

Example Solve the following equation. $5x + 3 = x - 5$

Working (*Collect like terms – the terms with the unknown on one side of the equation and constants on the other side; divide by the coefficient of the unknown.*)

$5x - x = -5 - 3$ (*subtract x from both sides; subtract 3 from both sides*)

$4x = -8 \rightarrow x = -2$ (*dividing both sides by 4*)

Answer $x = -2$

Key Fact

It is a good practice to check that your solution is correct by substituting your answer in each side of the original equation to confirm that the two sides of the equation are equal. In the Example above,

$\text{LHS} = 5(-2) + 3 = -7; \text{RHS} = -2 - 5 = -7 = \text{LHS}$

Example Solve the following equation.

$$\frac{x}{2} + \frac{3x + 1}{4} = 4 - \frac{5x}{2}$$

Working $\dfrac{x}{2} + \dfrac{3x + 1}{4} = 4 - \dfrac{5x}{2}$

$$\frac{2(x) + (3x + 1)}{4} = 4(4) - 2(5x)$$

$\therefore 2x + 3x + 1 = 16 - 10x$

$2x + 3x + 10x = 16 - 1$

$15x = 15$

Answer $x = 1$

Check Substitute $x = 1$ in LHS and in RHS.

$\text{LHS} = \dfrac{1}{2} + \dfrac{3 + 1}{4} = \dfrac{3}{2}; \text{RHS} = 4 - \dfrac{5}{2} = \dfrac{3}{2} = \text{LHS}$

Practice

A Solve the following equations.

1 $2a + 3 = 5a$

2 $\frac{1}{2}f - \frac{1}{4}f = 2$

3 $\frac{y}{2} - \frac{y}{3} = \frac{2}{3}$

4 $\frac{3d}{2} - \frac{1}{2} = 3 - \frac{d}{4}$

5 $\frac{2b}{3} = \frac{b - 1}{2}$

6 $\frac{x + 1}{4} = \frac{2x - 3}{3}$

7 $\frac{h + 1}{h} = \frac{h - 1}{2h}$

8 $\frac{2 + n}{4 + n} = \frac{3n - 2}{3n}$

B Remove the brackets and solve the following equations.

1 $-\frac{1}{3}(3k) = 5k - 9$

2 $4(m - 2) - 2(2m - 3) = m$

3 $4(u - 2) = 3(2u - 3)$

4 $6y - 3(y - 2) = 0$

5 $4 - (1 + 2y)2 - (2 - 3y)3 = 11$

6 $4(-2d + 1) + 3(d - 2) = -7$

Key Facts

Solving an equation is the inverse of forming an equation.
Remember when forming an equation we can use a **flow chart**
to assist in identifying the order of the arithmetic operations.
Using a flow chart to do the inverse operations in the reverse
order gives the solution of the equation.

Further Practice

C Solve each of the following equations.

1 $c + 7 = 2c - 3$

2 $-3k + 5 = 2(2k - 1)$

3 $\frac{2}{3}b = 1 + \frac{1}{2}(b - 1)$

4 $(a + 4) - (2 - a) - 3 = 0$

5 $3 - \frac{k}{3} = 2k - \frac{5}{3}$

6 $\frac{x + 1}{4} = \frac{2x - 3}{3}$

7 $\frac{2t - 1}{2t} = \frac{t - 3}{1 + t}$

8 $\frac{4 + d}{d + 2} = \frac{3d - 2}{1 - 3d} + 2$

> **Finished Early?**
> Go to page 448

Remember?

Algebraic equations can be used to solve many word problems. The steps in working out the solution of the problem are

1 identify the unknown and the units to measure its value
2 define the unknown by a letter
3 write the data in terms of the unknown as an algebraic equation
4 solve the equation applying the rules for removing brackets, clearing fractions, expanding expressions, BoDMAS, etc.
5 give the solution of the word problem
6 check the answer by substituting the solution in the word problem.

Example	Andy has \$50 and Rob has \$30. If each week Andy saves \$3 and Rob saves \$5, calculate
	(a) the number of weeks they must save before they both have the same amount of money
	(b) the total amount that each boy has at that time.
Working	(*The unknown variable is the number of weeks so that we need to define the number of weeks.*)
	Let the number of weeks be n.
	After n weeks, Andy has saved $\$(50 + 3n)$
	and Rob has saved $\$(30 + 5n)$.
	Since the amounts are equal, $30 + 5n = 50 + 3n$
	$5n - 3n = 50 - 30$
	$2n = 20$
	$n = 10$
Check	Andy saved $= \$(50 + 3 \times 10) = \$80$
	Rob saved $= \$(30 + 5 \times 10) = \$80$
Answer	**(a)** 10 weeks **(b)** \$80

Practice

D In each of the following:

(a) write an equation to represent the data

(b) solve the equation to find the value of the unknown

(c) check your solution.

1 A rectangle is w cm wide. Its length is 3 cm more than its width. Its perimeter is 70 cm.

2 $500 was shared among three students. George received $$x$. Ann received twice as much as George and Ben got $40 less than George.

3 A fruit vendor bought m oranges at 75 ¢ each. There were 12 bad oranges. He sold the remainder at $1.10 each and made a profit of $28.80.

4 A man worked t hours overtime. He gets $30 an hour for ordinary time and $45 an hour for overtime. His wages for a total of 48 hours were $1485.

E In each of the following questions:

(a) identify the unknown and define it with a letter

(b) write an equation to represent the data

(c) solve the equation

(d) check your solution.

1 Notebooks with ruled pages cost $3.60 each. A notebook with plain pages costs 80 ¢ less. Brenda spent $32.80 and bought a total of 10 notebooks. How many of each kind did she buy?

2 The price of a pack of nuts increases by 15 ¢. The old price was 90% of the new price. Calculate the old and the new prices.

3 In the isosceles triangle shown, the third side is half the length of each equal side. The perimeter of the triangle is 15 cm. Calculate the length of the sides.

4 Find two consecutive odd numbers such that seven times the smaller number is 17 more than six times the larger number.

5 Two cars, A and B, moved towards each other from two stations 240 km apart. The average speed of car A was twice the average speed of car B. The cars met after $2\frac{1}{2}$ hrs. Calculate the speeds of the cars.

Further Practice

Finished Early?
➡ Go to page 448

F In each of the following questions:

(a) write an equation to represent the data

(b) solve the equation

(c) answer the question

(d) check your solution.

1 In a basket, there is a total of 41 citrus fruits. There are n grapefruits, $3n$ oranges, $2n$ tangerines, $(n + 2)$ mandarins and 4 portugals. Find the number of each kind of fruit.

2 A woman spent $\frac{1}{5}$ of her salary on food and gave $\frac{1}{10}$ to charity. She had $4060 remaining. Calculate her salary.

3 A boy 'jogs' for $\frac{1}{2}$ hour at 8 km/h and then walks for t hours at 6 km/h. He travels a total distance of 13 km. Calculate the value of t.

4 A column is 30 cm taller than another column. The taller column is one and a quarter times as tall as the shorter column. Find the heights of the two columns.

5 A rectangular room is 1.5 m longer than it is wide. There are two doorways, each 1.3 m wide. The length of skirting board required for the base of the walls is 27.2 m. Find the length of each wall.

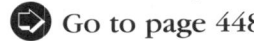

Finished Early?
➡ Go to page 448

2 Identities

Learn About It

The statement $3x + 4 = 1$ .... (1)

is true *only* when $x = -1$.

We can show that the statement

$3x + 4 \equiv 3(x + 1) + 1$ .... (2)

is true for all values of x.

Similarly, $(d + 1)(d + 3) = 0$ .... (3)

is true *only* when $d = -1$ or when $d = -3$

and $(d + 1)(d + 3) \equiv d^2 + 4d + 3$ .... (4)

is true for all values of d.

(1) and (3) are examples of an **equation**.

(2) and (4) are examples of an **identity**.

> **Key Fact**
>
> $\equiv$ is the symbol used to indicate an identity.

Try It Out

G **(a)** State whether each of the following is an equation or an identity.

(b) Give a reason for your answer.

1 $3x + 4 = 5 - 2x$

2 $(3y + 1) - z = 3 + 3(z + y) - 2(1 + 2z)$

3 $(d + 2)2d = d^2 + d(d + 1)$

4 $(c + 2)(c - 3) = c^2 - c - 6$

Learn More About It

In a linear equation, there is *only* one specific value that satisfies the equation, that is, only one solution of the equation. In an equation where the power of the variable is greater than one, there may be more than one solution.

Since there are no specific values that satisfy an identity, we cannot solve an identity. However, in an identity, we can show that:

(i) the terms on one side of the identity can be rearranged and written in the same format as the other side of the identity

(ii) the terms on both sides of the identity can be rearranged and written in a common format.

Example	Show that the following statement is an identity: $2(a + bc^2) + 3 \equiv 3(bc^2 + 1) - (bc^2 - 2a)$
Working	LHS $= 2a + 2bc^2 + 3$ RHS $= 3bc^2 + 3 - bc^2 + 2a = 2bc^2 + 3 + 2a$ LHS $=$ RHS
Answer	Since both sides of the statement can be written in the same format, the statement is an identity.

Try It Out

H Show that each of the following statements is an identity.

1 $3x + 4 \equiv \frac{1}{2}(8 + 6x)$

2 $(3a - b) + 1 - b \equiv b + 5 + 3(a - b) - 4$

3 $(2d + 1)d \equiv d^2 + d(d + 1)$

4 $(x + y)(2y + 1) \equiv 3y^2 + x + y(2x - y + 1)$

Practice

I For each of the following either:

(a) solve the statement if it is an equation *or*

(b) show that the statement is an identity.

1 $2(x + 3y) + x = 3x + 2y$

2 $2 + \frac{m}{3} = 2m - \frac{4}{3}$

3 $2(f + 4)(2 - f) - 3f + 2 = (2 - 3f)(1 - 2f) - 8(f^2 - 2)$

4 $a^2 + 5a + 1 = (a + 2)^2 + 2a$

5 $12b^4c^3 \div 3bc^3 = 32$

J Show that each of the following statements is an identity.

1 $3(x + 1) - 2(x - 1) \equiv 5 + x$

2 $2(a - 2b) + b \equiv 3(a - b) - a$

3 $m^2 + (m + 2)n \equiv m(m + n) + 2n$

4 $(j + k)(k + j) \equiv 2(k^2 + j^2 + kj) - (j^2 + k^2)$

> **Finished Early?**
> ➡ Go to page 448

Further Practice

K For each of the following either:

(a) solve the statement if it is an equation *or*

(b) show that the statement is an identity.

1 $5h - 2 = 3h + 4$

2 $\dfrac{2t - 1}{2t} - \dfrac{t + \frac{1}{2}}{1 + t} = \dfrac{-1}{2t(1 + t)}$

3 $8(y^4)^{\frac{3}{4}} + 1 = 8y^3 - \frac{1}{4}y$

> **Finished Early?**
> ➡ Go to page 448

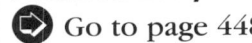

③ Linear Inequalities

> ## Remember?
> A statement that shows that one number is bigger or smaller than another includes one of the two inequality symbols, namely:
> $<$ (less than) or $>$ (greater than)
> and is called an **inequality**, for example, $7 > 3$ and $5 < 9$.
> **Linear inequalities** are algebraic statements that link algebraic expressions that are not equal. These statements use the inequality symbols above as well as the following two symbols:
> $\leqslant$ (less than or equal to) and $\geqslant$ (greater than or equal to).
> Examples of linear inequalities are $x < 8$ and $3y \geqslant 1$.
> The numerical values that satisfy a linear inequality are called a **solution set**. There is no limit to the values that satisfy inequalities defined by the symbols $<$ or $>$. Such a solution set is called a **range** of values.
> A solution set may be between two numerical values, for example, $-2 \leqslant x < 8$, that is, the numbers that are -2 or more but less than 8. Such a set of numbers with a maximum and a minimum is called a **limited range**.
> The method of solving a linear inequality is similar to that used for an equation, for example, to solve $x + 3 > 5$, we write:
> $x + 3 - 3 > 5 - 3 \rightarrow x > 2$

> ### Key Fact
> When solving a linear inequality for a limited range, it is necessary to carry out any operation in all three parts; for example, to solve for x in $-4 < 2x < 6$, we have to divide all three parts by 2 so that we get $-2 < x < 3$.

Practice

L Solve the following linear inequalities.

1 $x + 3 > 1$ **2** $2y < 6$ **3** $3d - 1 \leqslant 5$

4 $\frac{h}{3} > 2$ **5** $-2 \leqslant j + 3 < 2$ **6** $2(m + 4) \geqslant 12$

7 $4(x - 2) < 3x - 5$ **8** $\frac{x + 7}{2} > 5$ **9** $\frac{3x + 1}{2} > \frac{2x - 1}{3}$

M For each of the following, write an inequality for the unknown values.

1 A boy is now n years old. In 5 years, he will be over 21 years of age.

2 The pass mark in an examination was 45 out of a total of 100. Andy earned p marks and passed. June got f marks and failed.

3 The passing grade on a test was m%. Ann earned 75% and passed. Ken earned 65% and did not pass.

4 A team had to spend $700 or less to buy 12 medals; n medals cost $70 each and the remainder cost $50 each.

5 The side of a square is s cm and its perimeter is P cm. The square has an area of less than $100\,\text{cm}^2$.

Further Practice

N Solve the following linear inequalities.

1 $2y > 6 - y$ **2** $x - 3 < 1$ **3** $3p \leqslant 15$

4 $2(n + 2) \geqslant 10$ **5** $\frac{a}{2} > 1$ **6** $-1 \leqslant h - 2 < 3$

7 $4(x - 2) < 3x - 5$ **8** $\frac{2x + 3}{3} \leqslant \frac{5}{6}$ **9** $\frac{x + 3}{2} > \frac{x - 1}{5}$

O For each of the following, write the linear inequality to give the solution set.

1 An obtuse angle is $x°$.

2 One truck carries a load of more than 3 tonnes but less than 4 tonnes. The total mass carried by six trucks is t tonnes.

3 A bus must travel a distance of 120 km in not less than $1\frac{1}{2}$ hours and not more than 3 hours. The average speed is v km/h.

> **Finished Early?**
>  Go to page 449

Key Fact

Note that $\ngtr$, *not greater than*, is the same as $\leqslant$, *less than or equal to*, and $\nless$, *not less than*, is the same as $\geqslant$, *greater than or equal to*.

Remember?

A number line may be used to illustrate the range when solving an inequality. If the end values of the range are not included, then this is illustrated by an empty circle; for example:

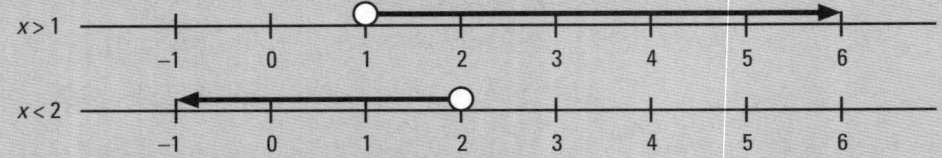

If the end values are included, then this is shown by a shaded circle:

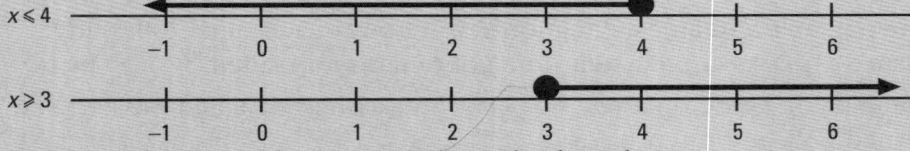

For a limited range, there are circles at both ends:

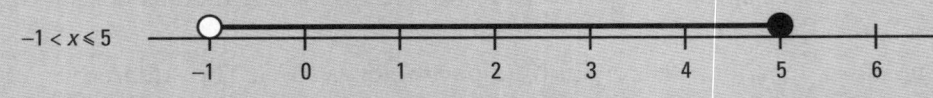

Example	(a) Solve the linear inequality: $x - 2 \leqslant 3$
	(b) Show the range on a number line.
Working	$x - 2 + 2 \leqslant 3 + 2$
Answer	$x \leqslant 5$

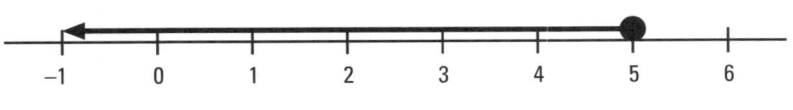

Practice

P The diagrams below are the graphs of linear inequalities.

Express each inequality in the form $a * x * b$, where a and b are numbers, and $*$ may be $<$ or $\leqslant$.

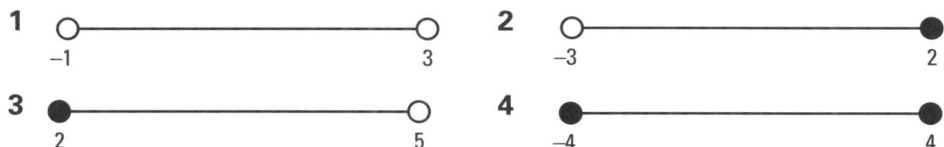

Practice

Q For each of the linear inequalities defined in M on page 143:

(a) find the solution set **(b)** write the solution using set notation

(c) illustrate the range on a number line.

Further Practice

R The diagrams below are the graphs of linear inequalities. Express each inequality in the form a * x * b, where a and b are numbers, and * may be < or ≤.

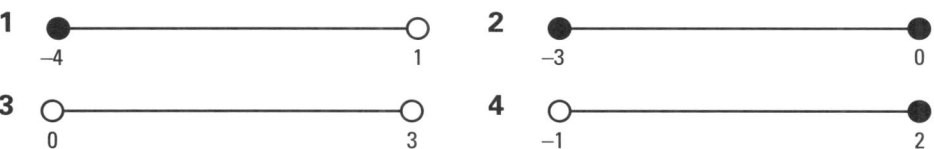

Further Practice

S For each of the linear inequalities defined in O on page 143:

(a) find the solution set **(b)** write the solution using set notation

(c) illustrate the range on a number line.

Remember?

A number line may be used to illustrate the range when solving simultaneous inequalities. Each of the inequalities $x > -1$ and $x \leqslant 5$ is shown on the separate number lines below.

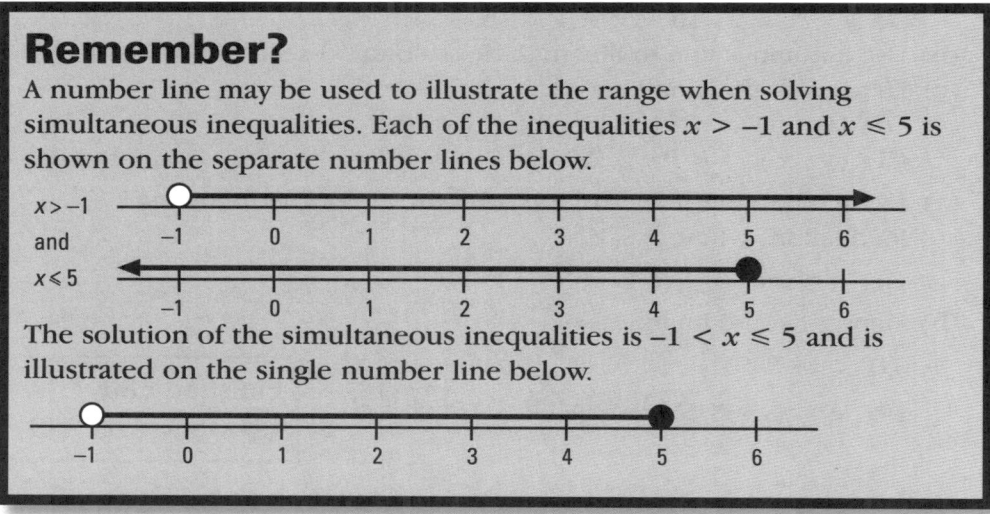

The solution of the simultaneous inequalities is $-1 < x \leqslant 5$ and is illustrated on the single number line below.

Example **(a)** Solve each of the following linear inequalities:
    (i) $3x + 4 < 7$ **(ii)** $5x \geqslant 2x - 9$
(b) What range satisfies both inequalities?
(c) Draw a graph to represent this range.

Working & Answer
(a) **(i)**
$$3x + 4 \quad < 7$$
$$3x + 4 - 4 < 7 - 4$$
$$3x < 3$$
$$x < 1$$

(ii)
$$5x \qquad \geqslant 2x - 9$$
$$5x - 2x \geqslant 2x - 2x - 9$$
$$3x \geqslant -9$$
$$x \geqslant -3$$

(b) $-3 \leqslant x < 1$
(c) The graph is the number line shown below.

Key Fact

The solutions of an inequality may be written using set notation, for example, $\{x : x > 3, x \in W\}$ or $\{x : -1 < x \leqslant 3, x \in W\}$

Practice

1 (a) Find the solution set for each of the following inequalities.
    (i) $x + 5 < 9$ **(ii)** $2x + 1 \geqslant -5$
(b) Use a number line to illustrate these solution sets.
(c) Hence, list the members of
    (i) $\{x : x + 5 < 9\} \cap \{x : 2x + 1 \geqslant -5\}$
    (ii) $\{x : x + 5 < 9\} \cup \{x : 2x + 1 \geqslant -5\}$

2 (a) Using a number line, find the solution set for the following inequalities where $x \in Z$.

(i) $-3 \leqslant x < 6$ **(ii)** $0 < x + 4 \leqslant 9$

(b) Hence, list the members of:

(i) $\{x : -3 \leqslant x < 6\} \cap \{x : 0 < x + 4 \leqslant 9\}$
(ii) $\{x : -3 \leqslant x < 6\} \cup \{x : 0 < x + 4 \leqslant 9\}$

Finished Early?
 Go to page 449

Further Practice

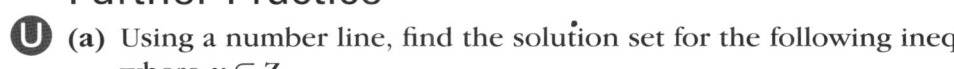 **(a)** Using a number line, find the solution set for the following inequalities where $x \in Z$.

    (i) $3x + 7 < 34$ **(ii)** $-7 < 2x - 3 \leqslant 9$

(b) Hence, list the members of

    (i) $\{x : 3x + 7 < 34\} \cap \{x : -7 < 2x - 3 \leqslant 9\}$

    (ii) $\{x : 3x + 7 < 34\} \cup \{x : -7 < 2x - 3 \leqslant 9\}$

> **Finished Early?**
> ➡ Go to page 449

Learn About It

We know that $5 > 3$ (1)

   and $-5 < -3$.

Note that, multiplying both sides of (1) by -2,

we get $-10 < -6$, that is, the inequality sign in (1) is reversed.

Again, we know that $2 < 7$ (2)

   and $-2 > -7$.

Multiplying both sides of (2) by -2,

we get $-4 > -14$, that is, the inequality sign in (2) is reversed.

We know that $15 > 12$ (3)

   and $-15 < -12$.

Note also that, dividing both sides of (3) by -3,

   we get $-5 < -4$, that is, the inequality sign in (3) is reversed.

Again, we know that $24 < 36$ (4)

   and $-24 > -36$.

Dividing both sides of (4) by -12,

   we get $-2 > -3$, that is, the inequality sign in (4) is reversed.

Also, if we start with the inequality $-3 > -7$, we see that $3 < 7$.

Therefore, we can state a general conclusion that:

when the $+$ or $-$ sign on both sides of an inequality are changed, the inequality sign must be reversed.

The same rule holds true for a linear inequality so that, for example,

if $x > 5$, then $-x < -5$; and if $-3x < -6 \rightarrow x > 2$.

Try It Out

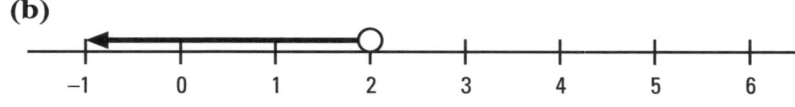

Solve the following inequalities.

1 $1 - x < -2$ **2** $-2x \geqslant 3$ **3** $3(2 - x) > 2$ **4** $2(x + 3) \leqslant 3(2 + 3x)$

Example	**(a)** Solve the linear inequality: $2x - 1 > 4x - 5$

(b) Show the range on a number line.

Working   **(a)** $2x - 1 + 1 > 4x - 5 + 1$
& Answer $2x - 4x > 4x - 4x - 4$
                    $-2x > -4$
                    $x < 2$

(b)

```
◄─────────────────────○──┼────┼────┼────┼────┼
   ┼     ┼    ┼    ┼    ┼    ┼    ┼    ┼    ┼
  -1     0    1    2    3    4    5    6
```

Check   Let $x = 1$; LHS: $2(1) - 1 = 1$; RHS: $4(1) - 5 = -1$
           Let $x = -2$; LHS: $2(-2) - 1 = -5$; RHS: $4(-2) - 5 = -13$
           Since $1 < 2$ and $-2 < 2$, and the inequality is true, the
           solution set is correct.

Practice

(a) Solve the following linear inequalities for the set of rational numbers.

(b) Write the solution using set notation.

(c) Illustrate the range on a number line.

1 $2 - 3x > 1$ **2** $7 \leqslant 15 + 2y$

3 $4(1 - 2f) < 6$ **4** $5t \geqslant 2t + 6$

5 $-1 < 1 - n < 2$ **6** $3 < 4 - 2h < 7$

 1 Twice a number subtracted from 3 is less than 15.

(a) Write the linear inequality to represent this information.

(b) Find the solution set that satisfies this condition.

2 Janet has $210. She buys three shirts, all at the same price, and gets more than $27 change.

(a) Write a linear inequality to represent this information.

(b) Find the maximum cost of one shirt.

3 The longest side of a triangle must be 5 cm more than the shortest side and 2 cm more than the third side. The perimeter of the triangle is greater than 21 cm but not greater than 28 cm.

(a) Write algebraic expressions for the sides of the triangle.

(b) Write a linear inequality for the perimeter.

(c) Given that the lengths of the sides are whole numbers, find the corresponding values for the sides of the triangles that satisfy these conditions.

Further Practice

 (a) Solve the following linear inequalities, where $x \in Q$.

(b) Write the solution set using set notation, that is $\{x : x \quad \}$.

(c) Illustrate the range on a number line.

1 $5 - 2x \leqslant 3$ **2** $-7 \leqslant 3x + 5 < 8$

3 $2(3 - 4x) > x - 3$ **4** $3x \geqslant 7x + 8$

 1 A woman's weekly salary is $1500. After paying rent and buying food, she must not have less than $600. Her food bill is half the amount that she pays for rent. Find the maximum amount that she can pay for rent.

2 Three times a whole number is subtracted from 46. The result is less than 20. Work out the four smallest values of the original number.

Finished Early?

 Go to page 449

④ Simultaneous Linear Equations

Remember?

There is an infinite set of pairs of values that satisfy the variables in a linear equation with two unknowns, for example, in $2x + 3y = 1$, the pairs of values include $(5, -3)$, $(2, -1)$, $(0, \frac{1}{3})$, $(\frac{1}{2}, 0)$, ...

In order to find only one pair of values that satisfy the variables in such an equation, we must have another equation that is true at the same time. These two equations are called **simultaneous linear equations**. Generally, there are two non-graphical methods of solving simultaneous linear equations.

Method 1, by **substitution**: use one equation to obtain an expression for one of the variables, say x, in terms of the other variable, y; substitute this expression in the other equation and solve the linear equation in y; substitute for y in either of the given equations to find the value of x.

Method 2, by **elimination**: make the coefficients of the same variable, say x, in the two equations numerically equal by multiplying all the terms in one (or both) of the equations by a constant; then eliminate that variable (x) by adding or subtracting corresponding terms of the equations; and solve the linear equation in one variable, y; then substitute as in Method 1 to find x.

It is wise to check the solutions found by substituting the two values in the other given equation – not the one used to find the value of the second unknown.

Example	Solve the following pair of simultaneous equations.
	$3x + 2y = 2$ (1)
	$2x - y = 6$ (2)
Working	**Method 1**:
	(Write y in terms of x; substitute for y, solve for x, then y)
	From (2): $-y = -2x + 6 \rightarrow y = 2x - 6$
	Substituting for y in (1): $3x + 2(2x - 6) = 2$
	$3x + 4x - 12 = 2$
	Collecting terms and simplifying: $7x = 2 + 12$
	Then, dividing both sides by 7: $x = 2$
	Then, substituting for x in (1): $3(2) + 2y = 2$
	Solving for y: $2y = 2 - 6$
	$y = -2$
Check	Substitute values in (2): LHS $= 2(2) - (-2) = 6 =$ RHS
Answer	$x = 2, y = -2$

Key Fact

When the coefficient of one of the variables is 1, it is usually easier to use the substitution method. Note that in the example above, we may use the other equation to express y in terms of x, but this involves fractions since using (1) gives $y = \frac{1}{2}(2 - 3x)$.

Example	Solve the following pair of simultaneous equations. $3x + 2y = 2$ (1) $2x - y = 6$ (2)
Working	**Method 2**: *(Multiply (2) by 2, add (1) and (3), solve for x, then y)* (2) × 2: $\qquad 4x - 2y = 12 \qquad$ (3) $\qquad\qquad\quad 3x + 2y = 2 \qquad$ (1) (1) + (3): $\qquad 7x = 14$ Dividing both sides by 7: $x = 2$ Substituting for x in (1): $3(2) + 2y = 2$ Solving for y: $\qquad\qquad 2y = 2 - 6$ $\qquad\qquad\qquad\quad y = -2$
Check	Substitute values in (2): LHS = $2(2) - (-2) = 6$ = RHS
Answer	$x = 2, y = -2$

Key Fact

When the coefficients of the same variable in the two equations are numerically equal, it is generally easier to use the elimination method – subtracting when the signs are both positive or both negative, and adding when the signs are different.

Example Solve the following pair of simultaneous equations.

$$5m + 3n - 2 = 0$$
$$3m - 32 = 7n$$

Working $5m + 3n = 2$ (1)

$3m - 7n = 32$ (2)

(1) × 3: $15m + 9n = 6$ (3)

(2) × 5: $15m - 35n = 160$ (4)

(3) − (4): $44n = -154$

$$n = -\frac{154}{44} = -\frac{7}{2}$$

Substituting for n in (2)

$$3m - 7(-\tfrac{7}{2}) = 32$$

$$3m + \frac{49}{2} = 32$$

$$3m = 32 - \frac{49}{2}$$

$$3m = \frac{15}{2}$$

$$m = \frac{5}{2}$$

Answer $m = \frac{5}{2}, n = -\frac{7}{2}$

Check Substituting for m and n in (1)

LHS $= 5(\tfrac{5}{2}) + 3(-\tfrac{7}{2}) = \frac{25}{2} - \frac{21}{2} = 2 =$ RHS

Practice

 For each of the following pairs of simultaneous equations:

(a) select the method of solving the equations

(b) state the reason for your choice

(c) solve the equation.

1 $x + y = 6$
$2x - 3y = 2$

2 $3x - y = 4$
$x - y = 2$

3 $3x + 2y = 1$
$2x + 3y = -1$

4 $x + 2y = -4$
$3x - 2y = 12$

5 $\frac{1}{2}x + y = 2$
$x - \frac{1}{4}y = -5$

6 $3x - y + 5 = 0$
$x - 2y = 0$

7 $\frac{2x}{3} + y - 1 = x + \frac{y}{3} = 4$

8 $3x - y = x + y = 3$

9 $\dfrac{x + y}{3} = \dfrac{2y - 1}{2} = 2x - y$

10 $3(x - 2y) = 2(x + 1)$
$2x - y = 2(2 + y) + 3$

Key Fact

Numbering the given equations and each step of working assists in making the method of solution clearer as well as in making it easier to check the working.

Further Practice

 Solve the simultaneous equations.

1 $x + 3y = -4$
$x - y = 4$

2 $2x - y = 4$
$3x + y = 11$

3 $4x + 3y - 2 = 0$
$x - 2y - 5 = 1$

4 $5x = y + 3$
$3x - 2 = y$

5 $\frac{1}{2}x - \frac{1}{3}y = \frac{2}{3}$
$\frac{3}{2}x + \frac{5}{3}y = \frac{2}{3}$

6 $5(x + y) = 2(x + 3y) + 1$
$3(x + 2y) - 7 = x + 3y + 1$

7 $\frac{3}{4}(4x + y) = 4$
$2x = \frac{3}{5}(2x - 3y)$

8 $3x - y + 12 = 5x + 2y + 4 = x + y$

Finished Early?

 Go to page 449

Remember?

Sometimes a graphical method can be used to solve simultaneous equations by drawing the graphs of both linear equations on the same axes. The coordinates of the point of intersection of the two lines are the values of the variables that satisfy both equations.

Practice

 (a) On a single set of axes use a suitable scale to draw the graphs of the straight lines given in **AA**.

(b) Hence, find the solution of each pair of simultaneous equations.

> ### Key Fact
>
> It is often necessary to rearrange the terms in the equation with y on the LHS in order to draw up the table of values.

Further Practice

 Solve each pair of simultaneous equations in **AB** questions 1–6 by drawing on the same axes the graphs of the given linear functions.

> ### Remember?
>
> Sometimes we can identify the variables in a real-life problem, write the data as algebraic expressions, and form simultaneous linear equations. By solving the equations, we get the solution of the problem.

Practice

 1 If 2 is added to the numerator and to the denominator of a fraction, then the new fraction becomes $\frac{5}{9}$. If 3 is subtracted from the numerator and from the denominator of the fraction, then the new fraction becomes $\frac{1}{2}$. Find the fraction.

2 In a test Dani scored 17 more marks than Fred. If Dani had scored twice as many marks she would have scored 7 more marks than three times Fred's score. Find the marks each student scored.

3 The figure on the right shows the dimensions of a rectangle in centimetres.

    (a) Write two equations in x and y.

    (b) Solve the equations for x and y.

    (c) Find the dimensions of the rectangle.

$(3x + y - 3)$ cm

$(2y - 1)$ cm $(x + 2)$ cm

$(5y - 4)$ cm

4 The sum of the digits of a two-digit number is 12. When the digits are interchanged, the number increases by 18. Find the original number.

5 The volume of water held in 3 barrels and 5 tanks is 43.6 k*l* and the volume held in 2 barrels and 3 tanks is 26.4 k*l*. Find the volume held in one barrel and in one tank.

6 The weight of 6 televisions and 2 radios is 53 kg; the weight of 3 televisions and 4 radios is 34 kg. Find the average weight of one television and one radio.

7 The total daily wages bill for 3 unskilled and 5 skilled workmen was $780 and for 5 unskilled and 3 skilled workmen it was $660. Assuming a 6-hour day, find the hourly rate paid to an unskilled and to a skilled workman.

8 The maximum number of cars that can be parked at a terminus is 60. When a bus parks at the terminus, it uses the same area as 3 cars. The daily rate for parking 1 bus is $100 and for parking 1 car is $50. Find the number of buses and of cars parked on a day when the terminus was full and the amount of money received was $2600.

Further Practice

AF **1** Find two numbers that have a sum of 98 and a difference of 16.

2 Andy travels a total distance of 56 km in 5 hours, moving at 10 km/h for s hours and at 12 km/h for t hours. Find the value of s and of t.

3 Half of Rob's money plus one-third of Dan's is $32.50. Two-fifths of Dan's money plus one-quarter of Rob's money is $21.50. Calculate the amount of money that Rob and Dan each has.

4 The figure on the right is an equilateral triangle.
  (a) Write two equations in x and y.
  (b) Solve the equations for x and y.
  (c) Find the perimeter of the triangle.

$(2y-1)$ cm $\qquad$ $(x+2)$ cm

$(2x+y-1)$ cm

5 Ann has $3.20 in 10 ¢ coins and 25 ¢ coins. She has twenty coins altogether, find how many of each type of coin she has.

John also has twenty coins but has 45 ¢ more than Ann, find how many of each type of coin he has.

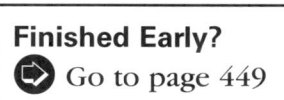

Finished Early?
➡ Go to page 449

Unit 4 *Algebra 1*

Summary of Chapters 8 and 9

Algebraic Expressions

- An **algebraic expression** generally includes both **letters** or **variables** that stand for unknown values, and numbers that are called **constants**. The letter replaces only the numerical value and not the unit of measurement of the quantity. The number multiplying the letter in a variable term is called the **coefficient** and may be an integer, a rational number or a real number.

- In a simple algebraic expression, the coefficient and/or a letter or a constant constitute a **term**. Terms are connected by plus or minus signs. To simplify algebraic expressions, terms may be grouped, for example, **like terms** may be combined; also all the positive terms may be collected and then all the negative terms and the resulting positive and negative terms combined using the same order of operations (BoMDAS) as for arithmetic.

- If there are algebraic fractions in the expression, then apply the same rules as for numerical fractions and find the simplest common denominator. To simplify expressions with terms raised to different powers, the **laws of indices** are used.

- When the powers of all the variables in an expression are equal to 1, the expression is called a **linear expression**. When the highest power of at least one of the variable terms in an expression is equal to 2, the expression is called a **quadratic expression**.

- Simplifying expressions may involve removing brackets or finding common factors. The form of the expression changes but its value does *not* change. To remove brackets, multiply *each* term inside the bracket by the multiplier; to multiply the terms within brackets, *each* term inside each bracket is multiplied by *each* term inside the other bracket; this process is called **expansion**.

- To write an expression as a product of two or more simpler expressions (or **factors**), find the HCF of the terms in the expression. This process is called **factorisation** and may be used to simplify calculations. Factorisation is the inverse operation of expansion.

- A **formula** is an algebraic statement of a relation between quantities denoted by variables (letters). The statement is true for all *corresponding values* of the quantities in the *correct ratio*. The value of one of the variables called the *subject of the formula* is found by substituting the known values of the other variables in the formula. When another variable becomes the unknown and the variables are rearranged, it is called *changing the subject of the formula*.

- In a **binary operation** two elements are combined to produce a 'result' according to given combinations of the basic arithmetic operations of addition, subtraction, multiplication and division. The associative, commutative, distributive and closure properties may also apply to these binary operations.

Linear Equations and Inequalities

- When an algebraic expression is put equal to another algebraic expression or equal to a numeric value, the statement is called an **equation**.

- The process of finding the value of the letter (representing the unknown value) that makes the statement true or that *satisfies the equation* is called *solving the equation*. Note that in solving an equation it is often necessary to first simplify algebraic expressions.

- In the **balance method** of solving an equation, the same mathematical operation – addition or subtraction of the same constant or variable, multiplication or division by the same number or variable – is applied to both the left-hand side (LHS) and the right-hand side (RHS) of the equation until only the letter is on one side of the equation. All the rules for mathematical operations when removing brackets, clearing fractions and expanding expressions apply in finding the **solution**.

- In solving a *word problem*, the first step is to identify the unknown variable and define it by a letter. Next, use the given data to identify the order of mathematical operations that lead to the equation, paying particular attention to any relevant units. The value(s) of the solution must always be checked against the data given in the problem.

- A **flow chart** may be used to illustrate the order of operations in forming the equation. By using another flow chart in which the inverse operations are done in the reverse order, the solution of the equation may be found.

- An algebraic statement in which the LHS is equal to the RHS for *all values* of the unknown is called an **identity**. *An identity can only be shown to be true but cannot be solved*. This is done by rearranging the terms on one side or on both sides of the statement. The symbol ($\equiv$) is used to identify an identity.

- An algebraic statement in which the expressions or quantities on the two sides of the statement are not equal is an **inequality**. The symbols used to connect the LHS and the RHS of the inequality are $<$, $>$, $\leq$, $\geq$, $\neq$.

- The solution set for a **linear inequality** is a **range** or a **limited range** of values. In solving an inequality algebraically, the inequality is reversed when the inequality is multiplied (or divided) by a *negative number*.

- A **linear inequality** or **simultaneous linear inequalities in one variable** may be represented graphically on a *number line*. When the end values of the range are included in the solution set, this is indicated by a shaded circle at the end of the number line. When the end values are not included, the circle is an open circle. The **solution set** of simultaneous linear inequalities in one variable is the intersection of the solution sets of each inequality, that is, of the number lines.

- The graph of a linear function is called a *linear equation in two variables*. Generally, there are two non-graphical algebraic methods for solving simultaneous linear equations in two variables. By **substitution** of one variable in terms of the other variable or by **elimination** of one of the variables, the value of the other variable is found. Using that value in one of the given equations, the value of the second variable is found. The solutions should always be checked in the other given equation.

10 Statistics

In this chapter you will learn about ...
1. types of data
2. collecting data
3. presenting data
4. averages and spread
5. cumulative frequency and percentiles

1 Types of Data

Learn About It

Henry measures the height of the pupils in his class. These are his results (in centimetres):

176	163	165	160	169
172	169	170	159	167
167	165	161	164	170
166	163	172	162	168

This list of numbers is called the **raw data**. It is just the original data, before it is organised.

Henry's data is **continuous**. He has obtained the data by **measuring**. Notice the heights are all round numbers. A pupil could be 172.31423705... cm tall, but Henry can't measure this accurately with his tape measure, so he measures the height to the nearest centimetre.

Rose sits at the side of the road and notes the colour of the cars that pass by during the morning. She puts her data in a table:

Colour	Tally	Frequency
Red	٧Ѝ ٧Ѝ ٧Ѝ ٧Ѝ ‖	22
Blue	٧Ѝ ٧Ѝ ٧Ѝ ‖‖	19
Green	٧Ѝ	5
Other	٧Ѝ ٧Ѝ ١	11

This data is obtained by counting so it is called **discrete data**. Notice that the frequencies are all integers. Clearly it isn't very likely that half a car is going to drive past.

There are two other ways of describing data. **Qualitative data** describes something about the object, for example the colour of a car. **Quantitative data** is numerical, and it can be discrete or continuous.

> ## Word Check
>
> **discrete data** data that is obtained by counting
>
> **continuous data** data that is obtained by measurement
>
> **qualitative data** data that describes a characteristic
>
> **quantitative data** data that is numerical

Try It Out

A Which of the following variables are qualitative and which are quantitative? If the variable is quantitative, then is it discrete or continuous?

1 The age of the cars in the school car park.

2 The make of the cars in the school car park.

3 The number of words on a page of this book.

4 The volume of water in a cup.

5 The size of a box of popcorn (small, medium or large).

6 The amount of air you breathe in an hour.

> **Finished Early?**
> Go to page 450

❷ Collecting Data

> ## Remember?
> When data is collected it can be put into a tally chart.
> If there is a small amount of data, then it can be put into an **ungrouped frequency table**, like the one Rose used earlier.
> If there is a large amount of data, then it can be put into a **grouped frequency table**.
> The groups of data are called **classes**.
> The **modal class** is the class with the highest frequency.

Learn About It

This grouped frequency table shows the heights of some trees, measured to the nearest metre. You can see that 9 trees are between 0 and 5 metres tall, 13 trees are between 6 and 10 metres tall, and so on. By adding the frequencies of all the classes we know that there are 50 trees in total.

Height, H (in m)	Frequency
$0 \leqslant H < 5$	9
$5 \leqslant H < 10$	13
$10 \leqslant H < 15$	17
$15 \leqslant H < 20$	7
$20 \leqslant H < 25$	4
	50

Lower class limit　　Upper class limit

The advantage of using a grouped frequency table, instead of the raw data, is that it is easier to see the distribution of the heights of the trees, that is, how the heights vary. However, you don't have any information about each individual tree. For example, a tree in the last class is bigger than or equal to 20 m and less than 25 m tall, but we don't know exactly how tall.

Usually, we assume all the trees in a class have a height equal to the **mid-point** of the class. For example, we say that all the trees in the class $10 \leqslant H < 15$ are

$$\frac{10 + 15}{2} = 12.5 \text{ m tall.}$$

The **lower class limit** is the smallest height in the class. The **upper class limit** is the largest height in the class. So for the class $0 \leqslant H < 5$ the lower class limit is 0 and the upper class limit is 5.

Look at the second class in the table, for trees between 5 and 10 metres high. Remember that the heights have been measured to the nearest metre. So a tree that was measured to be 5 metres high could actually be only 4.5 m tall (or as much as 5.499... m). Similarly a tree that measured 10 m could actually be as much as 10.499... m tall. So the trees in the class $5 \leqslant H < 10$ might actually be between 4.5 m and 10.5 m tall. We call 4.5 the **lower class boundary** and 10.5 the **upper class boundary**.

In general:

the lower boundary $= \dfrac{\text{lower limit of this class} + \text{upper limit of the class below}}{2}$

the upper boundary $= \dfrac{\text{upper limit of this class} + \text{lower limit of the class above}}{2}$

The size of the class, or **class interval** = upper boundary – lower boundary. So the width of the class $5 \leqslant H < 10$ is $10.5 - 4.5 = 6$m.

Height, H (in m)	Lower boundary	Upper boundary	Class interval
$0 \leqslant H < 5$	0.0	5.5	5.5
$5 \leqslant H < 10$	4.5	10.5	6
$10 \leqslant H < 15$	9.5	15.5	6
$15 \leqslant H < 20$	14.5	20.5	6
$20 \leqslant H < 25$	19.5	25.5	6

Key Fact

For grouped data the classes must **not** overlap.

Word Check

lower limit the smallest value in a class

upper limit the largest value in a class

lower boundary halfway between the lower limit of one class and the upper limit of the previous class

upper boundary halfway between the upper limit of one class and the lower limit of the next class

mid-point the average of the upper and lower class limits

class interval the difference between the upper and lower boundaries

class width the same as the class interval

The same data could be divided into different classes, with different intervals. However, if you use too many classes, then you lose the advantage of putting data into groups. If you don't use enough classes, then you lose information. For example, you could use a different grouped frequency table:

Height, H (in m)	Frequency
$0 \leqslant H < 25$	50

This table doesn't tell you very much about the trees. All 50 trees could be 1 m tall, or they could all be 25 m tall.

Try It Out

B Below are the heights of 20 rose bushes, measured to the nearest centimetre:

67	53	72	84	45
70	64	79	55	67
59	71	87	48	69
50	74	63	66	80

(a) Copy and complete the table:

Height, h, cm	Tally	Frequency
$40 \leqslant h < 50$		
$50 \leqslant h < 60$		
$60 \leqslant h < 70$		
$70 \leqslant h < 80$		
$80 \leqslant h < 90$		

(b) What are the lower and upper limits of each class?

(c) Which is the modal class?

(d) **(i)** Any rose bush with height at least 50 cm but less that 70 cm is a C bush. How many rose bushes are a C?

  (ii) Any rose bush more than 90 cm high gets an A. How many rose bushes got an A?

(e) **(i)** Work out the mid-point of each class.

  (ii) Assume that each rose bush is the height in the middle of their class. Use this to estimate the total height of the rose bushes.

(f) Copy this table and fill in the class boundaries and the width of each class.

Mark	Lower class boundary	Upper class boundary	Class interval
40–49	39.5		
50–59			10
60–69			
70–79			
80–89		89.5	

Practice

 1 The table shows the ages of shoppers
going into the shop *Comfy Clothes*
on a Tuesday.

Age of shopper, age (yr)	Frequency
15 < age ≤ 25	15
25 < age ≤ 35	10
35 < age ≤ 40	9
40 < age ≤ 45	14
45 < age ≤ 50	25
50 < age ≤ 55	17
55 < age ≤ 65	6
65 < age ≤ 75	3

    (a) What are the lower and upper
boundaries of the second class?

    (b) What is the class interval of the
fifth class?

    (c)   **(i)** How many people 45 years old
or under entered the shop?

      (ii) How many people over the
age of 50 entered the shop?

      (iii) How many people between the ages of 36 and 50 went into
Comfy Clothes?

    (d) Give an estimate of the total age of all the people going into the
shop.

2 The data below shows the number of words on thirty pages of a book.

251	281	263	305	298	266
290	281	268	306	282	269
255	309	285	264	284	290
261	288	289	257	294	301
267	258	285	297	307	260

    (a) Organise this data into a grouped frequency table, using appropriate
classes.

    (b) What are the lower and upper boundaries of your second class? What
is its interval?

    (c) Do you notice anything unusual about the data? If so, what?

> **Finished Early?**
> ⇨ Go to page 450

🔟3 Presenting Data

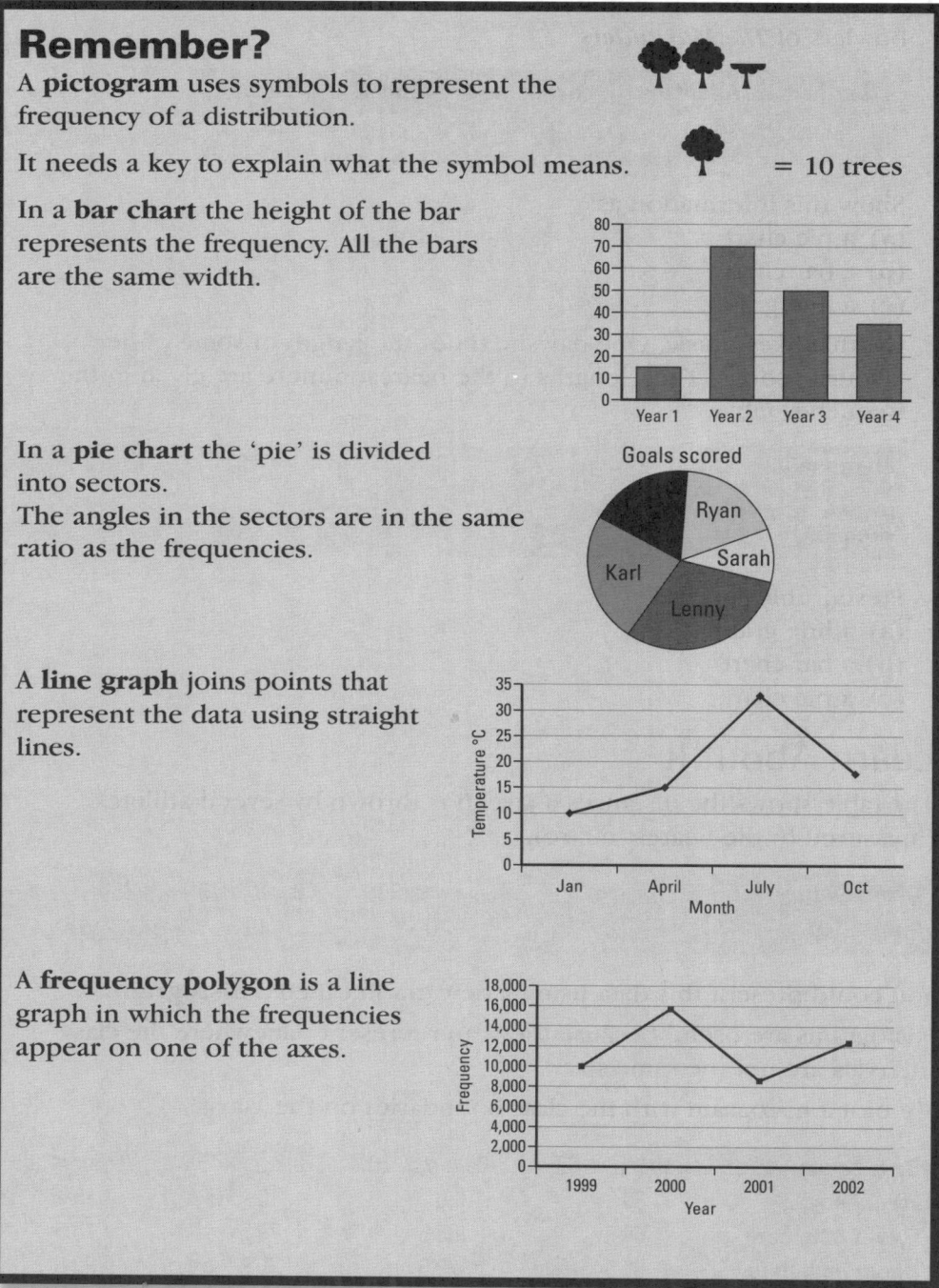

Remember?

A **pictogram** uses symbols to represent the frequency of a distribution.

It needs a key to explain what the symbol means.   = 10 trees

In a **bar chart** the height of the bar represents the frequency. All the bars are the same width.

Goals scored

In a **pie chart** the 'pie' is divided into sectors.
The angles in the sectors are in the same ratio as the frequencies.

A **line graph** joins points that represent the data using straight lines.

A **frequency polygon** is a line graph in which the frequencies appear on one of the axes.

Practice

D **1** The table shows the number of wickets taken in a cricket match by the bowlers of *The Marauders*.

Curtis	Alfonse	Ryan	Matt	Lucas
3	8	4	1	2

Show this information as:
(a) a pie chart
(b) a bar chart
(c) a line graph.

2 Cynthia likes music. One day she times the length of some of her favourite songs. Their lengths to the nearest minute are given in the frequency table.

Duration (min)	1	2	3	4	5	6	7
Frequency	4	8	17	11	3	0	1

Present this data as:
(a) a line graph
(b) a bar chart
(c) a pie chart.

Learn About It

The table shows the distances a javelin is thrown by several athletes (measured to the nearest metre).

Distance (m)	$60 < d \leqslant 65$	$65 < d \leqslant 70$	$70 < d \leqslant 75$	$75 < d \leqslant 80$
Frequency	30	20	10	15

You could present this data using a new graph called a **histogram**.

Histograms are useful because they can represent data where the class intervals are not the same size.

We plot a histogram with the class boundaries on the *x*-axis:

Distance (m)	$60 < d \leqslant 65$	$65 < d \leqslant 70$	$70 < d \leqslant 75$	$75 < d \leqslant 80$
Frequency	30	20	10	15
Lower boundary	60.5	65.5	70.5	75.5
Upper boundary	65.5	70.5	75.5	80.5

The histogram for the javelin throwers' data is shown below.

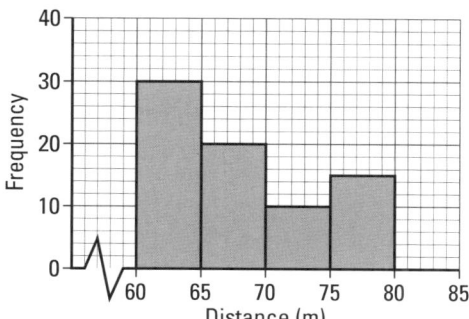

Another way we can present the data is using a frequency polygon. This is like a line graph, in which the frequency is plotted against the mid-point of the class. The points are then joined by straight lines to make a polygon

This is the frequency polygon for the javelin throwers' data shown in the histogram.

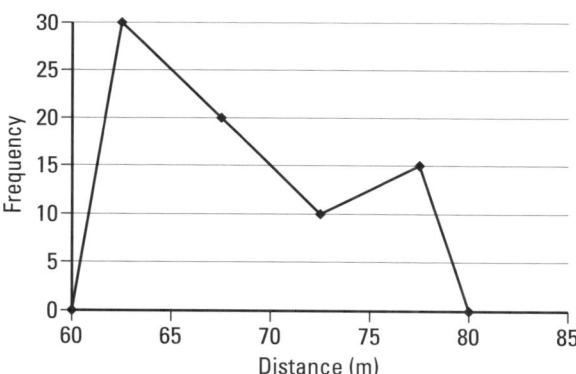

Try It Out

E The table below shows the chest sizes of some men who bought clothes at *Comfy Clothes*.

Chest size (cm)	$65 < s \leqslant 75$	$75 < s \leqslant 85$	$85 < s \leqslant 95$	$95 < s \leqslant 105$	$105 < s \leqslant 115$
Frequency	14	24	26	15	8
Lower limit					
Upper limit					
Mid-point					

(a) Copy and complete the table, filling in the upper and lower boundaries and mid-points.
(b) Display the data in a histogram.
(c) Draw the frequency polygon.

Practice

F *Easy Vid* make video cassettes. The table shows the length of some of their "3 hour" videos.

Length (min)	$165 < l \leqslant 170$	$170 < l \leqslant 175$	$175 < l \leqslant 180$	$180 < l \leqslant 185$
Frequency	24	17	29	36

(a) Draw a histogram to represent the data.
(b) What percentage of the videos lasted longer than 3 hours?

G The histogram shows the lengths of a number of steel tubes.

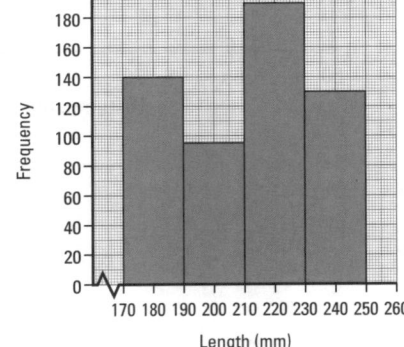

(a) Using the histogram, copy and complete this grouped frequency table.

Length (mm)	$170 < l \leqslant 190$	$190 < l \leqslant 210$	$210 < l \leqslant 230$	$230 < l \leqslant 250$
Frequency				

(b) Use the table to draw a frequency polygon.

Finished Early?
➡ Go to page 450

4 Averages and Spread

Remember?

An average of a set of data values is a value that approximately represents all the data items. For a given set of data values, there are three different types of average:

- The **mean** is the sum of all the data values divided by the total number of data items.
- The **median** is the value of the middle data item when the values are written in numerical order.

  If there are an even number of data items, then the median value is the mean of the two middle data values.

- The **mode** is the data value that occurs most often. A set of data values can have more than one mode.

In grouped data the mean is estimated by using the mid-points of the classes. The range is estimated by using the mid-points of the first and last classes.

A **comparison** table compares facts like the mean, median and range. It can be used to compare different sets of data.

Learn About It

Example   Stan and Kyle both run the 400 m. The table shows the times they ran 400 m in during a year.

Time (t seconds)	$50 < t \leqslant 55$	$55 < t \leqslant 60$	$60 < t \leqslant 65$	$65 < t \leqslant 70$
Stan	2	5	7	3
Kyle	0	5	9	4

    (a) For Stan and Kyle, work out the
       (i) mean speed
      (ii) median speed
      (iii) range of speeds.
    (b) Make a comparison table and compare the results for Stan and Kyle.

Working & Answer   First find the mid-points of the classes.

Time	$50 < t \leqslant 55$	$55 < t \leqslant 60$	$60 < t \leqslant 65$	$65 < t \leqslant 70$
Mid-point	52.5	57.5	62.5	67.5

(a) (i) Stan's mean

$$= \frac{(52.5 \times 2) + (57.5 \times 5) + (62.5 \times 7) + (67.5 \times 3)}{2 + 5 + 7 + 3}$$

$$= \frac{1032.5}{17}$$

$= 60.74\ldots$ seconds

$= 60.7$ seconds (to the nearest 0.1 of a second)

Kyle's mean

$$= \frac{(52.5 \times 0) + (57.5 \times 5) + (62.5 \times 9) + (67.5 \times 4)}{0 + 5 + 9 + 4}$$

$$= \frac{1120}{18}$$

$= 62.22\ldots$ seconds

$= 62.2$ seconds (to the nearest 0.1 of a second)

(ii) The times are already in numerical order.
Stan ran in 17 races so his median time is the 9th value in the table. This is in the class $61 < t \leqslant 65$. So we assume the median is the mid-point.
Stan's median time $= 62.5\,$s

Kyle ran in 18 races, so his median time is the average of the 9th and 10th values. Both the 9th and 10th values are in the class $61 < t \leqslant 65$.
So Kyle's median time $= 62.5\,$s

(iii) The range uses the mid-points of the first and last classes.
So Stan's range is given by:
range $= 67.5 - 52.5 = 15\,$s
Kyle didn't run a time less than 55 seconds, so the first class for Kyle is $55 < t \leqslant 60$.
Kyle's range $= 67.5 - 57.5 = 10\,$s

(b)

	Mean	Median	Range
Stan	60.7	62.5	15
Kyle	62.2	62.5	10

Stan's mean time is slightly lower than Kyle's, but the medians are the same. So Stan appears to run slightly faster than Kyle.
Kyle's range is smaller than Stan's, so Kyle is more consistent.

Try It Out

H Work out the mean, median, mode and range for these sets of data.

1 10, 14, 19, 12, 18

2 0.5, –0.3, –0.2, 0.1, –0.3, 0.2, –0.6, –0.4

3 125, 119, 120, 117, 125, 132, 123, 117, 115, 130

1 Find the mean, median, mode and range of this data.

I **2** The table shows the ages of shoppers going into *Comfy Clothes*. Estimate

No. of pets	0	1	2	3	4
Frequency	9	6	6	6	3

the
(a) mean
(b) median
(c) range.

Age of shopper, age (yr)	Frequency
15 < age ≤ 25	15
25 < age ≤ 35	10
35 < age ≤ 40	9
40 < age ≤ 45	14
45 < age ≤ 50	25
50 < age ≤ 55	17
55 < age ≤ 65	6
65 < age ≤ 75	3

Learn More About It

The three different types of average all have their advantages and disadvantages:

Average	Advantages	Disadvantages
Mean	• Uses all the data • The best 'mathematically'	• Affected by extreme values
Median	• Easy to calculate • Not affected by extreme values	• Does not use all the data
Mode	• Easy to calculate • Not affected by extreme values • Can be used for qualitative data	• Does not use all the data

Try It Out

J Work out the mean, median and mode for these sets of data. Which do you think best represents the data?

1 2, 3, 18, 4, 3   **2** 1, 1, 3, 4, 7, 8   **3** 1, 1, 1, 10, 10, 10

Practice

K

1 Ajay's mean result after four exams was 75%. After his English exam the mean dropped to 70%. What was his result in English?

2 Susie counted the number of words per line on a page of her book. She recorded the results in a table.

Words per line	$0 < w \leqslant 10$	$10 < w \leqslant 20$	$20 < w \leqslant 30$
Page 25	[redacted]	18	14

She worked out that the mean number of words per line on page 25 is 15. Unfortunately she has smudged one of the entries. What was it?

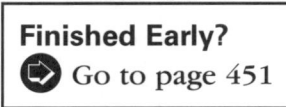

Finished Early?
Go to page 451

5 Cumulative Frequency and Percentiles

Learn About It

The table shows the weights of 200 pupils in a school.

Weight (kg)	$45 \leqslant w < 50$	$50 \leqslant w < 55$	$55 \leqslant w < 60$	$60 \leqslant w < 65$	$65 \leqslant w < 70$
Frequency	26	56	68	36	14

So we know that there are 26 pupils weighing less than 50 kg, 56 pupils weighing between 50 and 55 kg, and so on.

How many pupils are there weighing less than 55 kg? According to the table there are $26 + 56 = 82$ pupils who weigh less than 55 kg. This is called the **cumulative frequency**.

To find the number weighing less than 60 kg we add the 68 pupils weighing between 55 and 60 kg, to give a cumulative frequency of 150 pupils. This is continued until all the pupils are included in the cumulative frequency.

These results can be summarised in a cumulative frequency table.

Weight (kg)	**Upper limit**	**Frequency**	**Cumulative frequency**
$45 \leqslant w < 50$	50	26	$(0 + 26 =)$ 26
$50 \leqslant w < 55$	55	56	$(26 + 56 =)$ 82
$55 \leqslant w < 60$	60	68	$(82 + 68 =)$ 150
$60 \leqslant w < 65$	65	36	$(150 + 36 =)$ 186
$65 \leqslant w < 70$	70	14	$(186 + 14 =)$ 200

We can plot the cumulative frequency against the upper boundary on a graph, and join the points with a smooth curve.

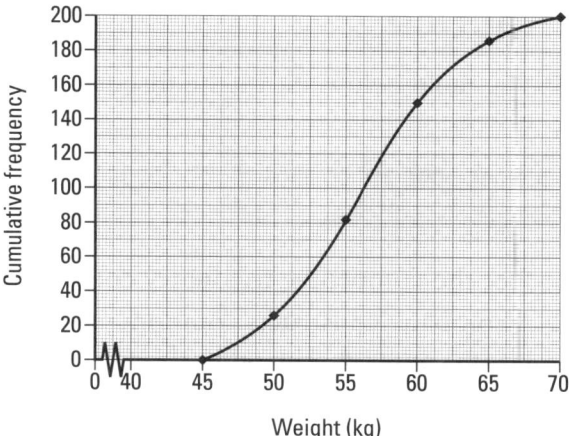

Weight (kg)

This S-shape curve is known as an **ogive**, and appears regularly when plotting cumulative frequencies.

Try It Out

L A company makes shelves of various lengths. The frequencies are given in the table below.

Length (cm)	Frequency	Upper limit	Cumulative frequency
$0 < l \leqslant 25$	18		
$25 < l \leqslant 50$	23		
$50 < l \leqslant 75$	39		
$75 < l \leqslant 100$	41		
$100 < l \leqslant 125$	19		
$125 < l \leqslant 150$	10		

Copy and complete the table.

Practice

 1 The table below shows the distances Kenny threw the javelin in a season.

Distance (m)	$45 \leqslant d < 50$	$50 \leqslant d < 55$	$55 \leqslant d < 60$	$60 \leqslant d < 65$	$65 \leqslant d < 70$
Frequency	11	22	47	43	22

Plot the cumulative frequency curve for the data.

2 A company constructs components for machinery; their lengths need to be very precise. The table shows the numbers of the various sizes the company makes.

Size (cm)	$1.0 \leqslant s < 1.2$	$1.2 \leqslant s < 1.4$	$1.4 \leqslant s < 1.6$	$1.6 \leqslant s < 1.8$	$1.8 \leqslant s < 2.0$	$2.0 \leqslant s < 2.2$
Frequency	89	134	254	298	287	230

Plot the cumulative frequency curve for the data.

Learn More About It

We have already seen one measure of the spread of data: the range. But in the same way that there are several 'averages' of a set of data, there are also other ways of measuring the spread. One of these uses **quartiles**.

25% of the data values are less than or equal to the **lower quartile**, Q_1.
50% of the data values are less than or equal to the second quartile, Q_2.
75% of the data values are less than or equal to the **upper quartile**, Q_3.

The **interquartile range** is given by
interquartile range = upper quartile – lower quartile.

It measures the spread of the middle half of the data.

The **semi-interquartile range** is half the interquartile range.

So how do we find the quartiles using a cumulative frequency curve?
To find the lower quartile:

- Calculate 25% of the total frequency.
- Find this point on the vertical axis.
- Draw a horizontal line across to the curve.
- Draw a vertical line from there down to the horizontal axis.
- Read off the value on the horizontal axis.

We do a similar thing for the median (start with 50%) and the upper quartile (start with 75%).

Look back at the pupils' weights example at the beginning of this section. 25% of the total frequency is 50 pupils. So find 50 on the vertical axis. Draw a line across to the curve, and then down to the horizontal axis, as shown on the diagram.

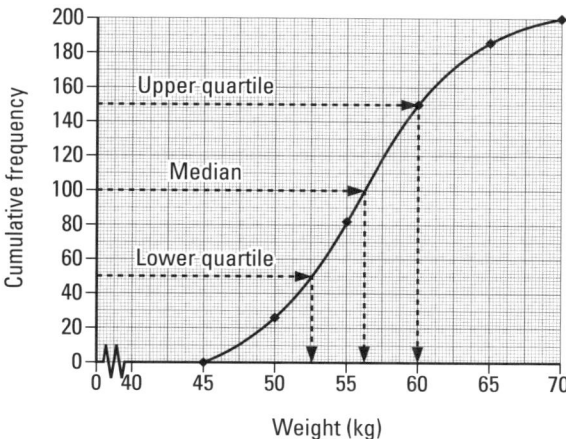

We can see that the line meets the horizontal axis at about 52. So the lower quartile is 52 kg, that is 25% of the pupils weigh less than 52 kg.

Similarly we can see that the median is about 56 kg and the upper quartile is about 59.5 kg.

So the interquartile range is 59.5 – 52 = 7.5 kg and the semi-interquartile range is 7.5 ÷ 2 = 3.75 kg.

If we want to know what percentage of pupils weigh less than, say, 65 kg, we can reverse the process. Find 65 on the horizontal axis, draw a line up to the curve, then across to the vertical axis. The value is about 190. So 190 out of the 200 pupils weigh less than 65 kg. 190 out of 200 is 95%. So 95% of pupils weigh less than 65 kg.

Try It Out

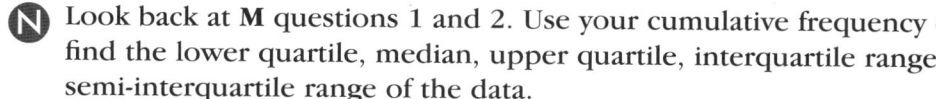

Look back at **M** questions 1 and 2. Use your cumulative frequency curves to find the lower quartile, median, upper quartile, interquartile range and semi-interquartile range of the data.

The lower quartile is sometimes known as the 25th **percentile** because 25% of the observations in the data are less than the lower quartile. Similarly the upper quartile is also called the 75th percentile.

Sometimes we may want to consider different percentages. 10% of the observations are smaller than the 10th percentile; 68% of observations are smaller than the 68th percentile.

Practice

Energon say their batteries last for 25 hours. The table shows the life of some *Energon* batteries.

Life (hr)	$20 < t \leqslant 22$	$22 < t \leqslant 24$	$24 < t \leqslant 26$	$26 < t \leqslant 28$	$28 < t \leqslant 30$
Frequency	15	25	43	28	9
Cumulative frequency					

(a) Copy the table and complete the cumulative frequency row.
(b) Plot the cumulative frequency curve.
(c) Use the curve to calculate the lower quartile, median and upper quartile.
(d) Work out the semi-interquartile range.
(e) What percentage of batteries last less than 23 hours?

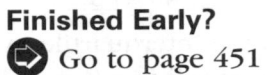

Finished Early?
Go to page 451

11 Probability

In this chapter you will learn about …

1 theoretical and experimental probability
2 related and unrelated events
3 expected outcomes
4 possibility spaces

1 Theoretical and Experimental Probability

Remember?

The **probability** of an event is a numerical measure of the likelihood of the event occurring. P(X) is the probability of X happening.

If P(X) = 0, then X definitely cannot happen. X is an **impossible event**.
If P(X) = 1, then X definitely will happen. X is a **sure event**.
If P(X) = 0.5 = $\frac{1}{2}$, then it is equally likely that X will and X won't happen.

The probability of an event occurring must be between 0 and 1.

The probability that X doesn't happen = 1 – probability X does happen.

Theoretical probability uses mathematical rules to work out probabilities.

Experimental probability uses experiments to work out probabilities.

A **trial** is an action that can be repeated, for example, one flip of a coin.

Learn About It

Example	Emmanuel rolls a fair 6-sided die. He rolls the die once.
	(a) What is the probability that he rolls a 4?
	(b) What is the probability that he doesn't roll a 4?
	(c) What is the probability that he rolls a 9?
	(d) Is it more likely that he rolls a 1 or that he rolls a 6?
Thinking	'Fair' means that that each outcome is equally likely.
Answer	**(a)** There are 6 sides on the die, so there are 6 possible outcomes and each is equally likely.

So the chance of rolling a 4 is 1-in-6.

So $P(4) = \frac{1}{6}$

(b) The probability that he doesn't roll a 4 is $1 - P(4)$.

So $P(\text{not } 4) = 1 - P(4) = 1 - \frac{1}{6} = \frac{5}{6}$

(c) The die doesn't have a 9 on it. So Emmanuel cannot possibly roll a 9.

Therefore $P(9) = 0$

(d) Each number on the die is equally likely to appear so he is just as likely to roll a 1 as a 6.

The example of Emmanuel throwing his die is an example of theoretical probability. We used maths to work out the probabilities.

But what do we do if we want to know the likelihood that someone in your class is over 180 cm tall, or the probability that Honour will score a goal in her next soccer match?

We deal with this sort of problem by using experimental probability. Experimental probability can be used when the theoretical probability cannot be calculated. We estimate the experimental probability by carrying out trials.

To estimate the probability of Honour scoring a goal in a match we could work out how many goals she has scored in her matches so far. If she has scored 12 goals in 20 matches, then we can reasonably assume that her chances of scoring in her next match are 12-in-20.

So $P(\text{Honour scores}) = \frac{12}{20} = \frac{3}{5} = 0.6$

So it is more likely that she will score in the next match than not score. In this example the trials are the matches that Honour plays in, and for each trial (match) we count the number of goals she scores.

Example   The table shows the heights of all the pupils in a maths class.

Height (cm)	$150 < h \leqslant 160$	$160 < h \leqslant 170$	$170 < h \leqslant 180$	$180 < h \leqslant 190$
Frequency	4	7	9	5

   (a) What is the probability that a pupil in the class is over 180 cm tall?
   (b) What is the probability that a pupil is between 161 and 180 cm tall?
   (c) What is the probability that a pupil is between 151 and 190 cm tall?

Answer   **(a)** There are $4 + 7 + 9 + 5 = 25$ pupils in the class.
   5 of them are over 180 cm tall. So:
   $P(\text{height} > 180\,\text{cm}) = \frac{5}{25} = \frac{1}{5}$

   (b) There are 7 pupils between 161 and 170 cm tall and 9 between 171 and 180 cm tall.
   So there are 16 pupils who are between 161 and 180 cm tall.
   $P(\text{height between 161 and 180 cm}) = \frac{16}{25}$

   (c) All the pupils in the class are between 151 and 190 cm tall, so any pupil must be between 151 and 190 cm tall.
   $P(\text{height between 151 and 190 cm}) = 1$

Key Fact

In both the above examples we can see that:

$$\text{probability} = \frac{\text{number of desired outcomes}}{\text{number of possible outcomes}}$$

Try It Out

A 1 The pointer is spun. What is P(white)?

2   A fruit is chosen at random.
   What is P(banana)? What is P(apple)?

Learn More About It

We can use the set notation we learnt about in Chapter 1 to help with probabilities. We know that the probability of a particular outcome is given by:

$$\text{probability} = \frac{\text{number of desired outcomes}}{\text{number of possible outcomes}}$$

In set notation this can be written as:

$$P(X) = \frac{n(X)}{n(U)}$$

where X = the set of desired events

and   U = the set of all possible events.

n(X) means the number of elements in the set X.

Example	Ann chooses a capital letter at random from the alphabet. What is the probability that it is a vowel?
Working	The set of all possible events is the whole of the alphabet, that is U = {A, B, C, ..., Y, Z}
	So n(U) = 26.
	The desired events are the vowels.
	So X = {A, E, I, O, U}
	and n(X) = 5.
	So the probability that Ann chooses a vowel is:
	$P(X) = \dfrac{n(X)}{n(U)} = \dfrac{5}{26}$
Answer	$\dfrac{5}{26}$

Practice

B **1** *Electrize* make batteries. Three in every 50 batteries don't work. What is the probability of buying a battery that works?

2 A grocer has 100 oranges and 50 apples. Three of the oranges have gone bad and two apples have gone bad.
  (a) What is the probability of buying a bad orange?
  (b) What is the probability of buying a bad apple?
  (c) Are you more likely to buy a bad orange or a bad apple?

3 180 *Bright light* light-bulbs are tested to see how long they last. The results are in the table.

Time (hr)	1–100	101–150	151–200	201–300
Frequency	12	84	45	39

(a) What is the probability that a light-bulb lasts more than 100 hours?

(b) What is the probability that a light-bulb will last between 101 and 200 hours?

(c) *Long Lite* make light-bulbs that last for exactly 200 hours. Are you better off buying your light-bulbs from *Long Lite* or *Bright Lite*? Why?

4 The table shows the scores of 100 students in a Maths exam.

Mark	0–10	11–20	21–30	31–40	41–50	51–60	61–70	71–80	81–90	91–100
Frequency	3	7	6	9	13	20	16	12	9	5
Cumulative frequency										

(a) Copy and complete the table.

What is the probability that a student chosen at random gets:

(b) at least 31 marks and no more than 40 marks

(c) less than 61 marks

(d) more than 80 marks

(e) between 20.5 marks and 50.5 marks?

C **1** One letter is chosen at random from the word PROBABILITY.

(a) What is the probability that the letter is B?

(b) What is the probability that the letter chosen is a B or an I or a T?

(c) What is the probability that a P and then a B are chosen?

2 What is the probability that a letter chosen at random from the alphabet is not in the word PROBABILITY?

D **1** Jimmy has 2 green socks, 2 red socks and 4 black socks in his drawer. He decides he wants to wear his green socks, and picks out a sock at random.

(a) What is the probability that it is green?

(b) He is lucky and picks out a green sock. Having put on that sock he pulls another sock out at random.

What is the probability he gets the other green sock?

[*Hint: How many socks are left in the drawer?*]

2 Letitia has a pack of playing cards. She picks out a card at random.

(a) What is the probability that she picks out a Heart?

(b) What is the probability that she picks out a Queen?

(c) What is the probability that she picks out the Queen of Hearts?

Letitia takes the Queen of Hearts out of the pack and throws it away. She then chooses a card at random.

(d) What is the probability that she picks out a Heart?

(e) What is the probability that she picks out a Queen?

(f) What is the probability that she picks out the Queen of Hearts?

Finished Early?

➡ Go to page 452

2 Related and Unrelated Events

Learn About It

Suppose we toss a coin once. What is the probability that we get both a head *and* a tail? It is impossible. We can only get a head *or* a tail, we can't get both. So P(head and tail) = 0. We say that 'getting a head' and 'getting a tail' are **mutually exclusive** events.

> ### Word Check
>
> **mutually exclusive** events that cannot happen together

If we toss a coin once, then what is the probability of getting a head **or** a tail? When we toss a coin the only possible results are 'getting a head' **or** 'getting a tail', so getting a head or a tail is a sure event, that is, P(head **or** tail) = 1. We can look at this in another way. Remember that P(head) = P(tail) = $\frac{1}{2}$.

So:

$$P(\text{head } \mathbf{or} \text{ tail}) = P(\text{head}) + P(\text{tail}) = \frac{1}{2} + \frac{1}{2} = 1$$

Key Fact

If two events X and Y are mutually exclusive then:

P(X **and** Y) = 0

P(X **or** Y) = P(X) + P(Y)

Now suppose that we draw a card at random from a pack. Are the events 'the card is a Jack' and 'the card is a Club' mutually exclusive? No, it is possible to get a card that is both a Jack and a Club – the Jack of Clubs. So the events are not mutually exclusive.

So what is the probability that we draw a Jack **or** a Club? There are 52 cards in the pack, how many of these are Jacks or Clubs? There are 4 Jacks and 13 Clubs in the pack. But we have counted the Jack of Clubs twice, once in the Jacks and once in the Clubs. We can only count each card once, so we must take one away from the total. So there are $4 + 13 - 1 = 16$ cards in the pack which will give us a Jack or a Club. So P(Jack **or** Club) $= \frac{16}{52} = \frac{4}{13}$.

Writing this in symbols gives:

$$P(Jack \text{ or } Club) = P(Jack) + P(Club) - P(both \text{ Jack and Club})$$
$$= \frac{4}{52} + \frac{13}{52} - \frac{1}{52}$$
$$= \frac{16}{52}$$
$$= \frac{4}{13}$$

In general, if A and B are not mutually exclusive then:

$$P(A \text{ or } B) = P(A) + P(B) - P(both \text{ A and B})$$

Try It Out

E **1** Which of the following combinations of events are mutually exclusive and which are not?

(a) Roll one die: get a 1, get a 6.

(b) Roll two dice: get a 1, get a 6.

(c) Take a card from a pack: get a Queen, get a red card.

(d) A random letter of the alphabet: it is in the word APPLE, it is in the word COCONUT.

(e) A random letter of the alphabet: it is in the set {b, f, o, r, w}, it is a vowel.

(f) Two dice are rolled: the sum is 12, the product is 30.

Practice

F **1** Eldece has 4 red socks, 2 blue socks and a green sock in her drawer. If she draws a sock at random from the drawer, what is the probability that the sock is:

(a) blue

(b) red or green

(c) red, green or blue?

2 On a road the probability that a motor vehicle is a car is $\frac{4}{5}$ and the probability it is a motorbike is $\frac{1}{10}$.

Find:

(a) P(car or motorbike)

(b) P(neither car nor motorbike).

3 A card is drawn at random from a pack. Find the probability that it is:

(a) an Ace or a Heart

(b) a King or a black card.

Learn More About It

Suppose we have a bag with four marbles in it: two red and two blue. If a marble is chosen at random from the bag, what is the probability that it is red? There are two red marbles in a bag with four marbles in it so P(red) = $\frac{1}{2}$. If the marble is returned to the bag and another is taken from the bag, what is the probability that it is red? Again there are two red marbles in a bag with four marbles in it, so P(red) = $\frac{1}{2}$. In this case, the result of taking the second marble from the bag is not affected by the result of taking the first marble from the bag. We say that the two events are **independent**.

Word Check

independent events events in which the
    result of one has no effect on the other

What is the probability that we draw a red marble and then a blue marble from the bag? Suppose that we labelled the marbles R_1, R_2, B_1 and B_2. We can list all the possible ways of taking two marbles from the bag:

2nd marble 1st marble	R1	R2	B1	B2
R_1	R_1R_1	R_1R_2	R_1B_1	R_1B_2
R_2	R_2R_1	R_2R_2	R_2B_1	R_2B_2
B_1	B_1R_1	B_1R_2	B_1B_1	B_1B_2
B_2	B_2R_1	B_2R_2	B_2B_1	B_2B_2

Looking at the table we can see that there are 16 possible ways of taking two marbles from the bag, four of these ways give a red then a blue marble so P(1st marble red **and** 2nd marble blue) = $\frac{4}{16}$ = $\frac{1}{4}$.

Notice also that P(1st marble red) $= \frac{1}{2}$ and P(2nd marble blue) $= \frac{1}{2}$.

So:

P(1st marble red) × P(2nd marble blue)

$= \frac{1}{2} \times \frac{1}{2}$

$= \frac{1}{4}$

$=$ P(1st marble red **and** 2nd marble blue)

So P(1st marble red **and** 2nd marble blue)

$=$ P(1st marble red) × P(2nd marble blue).

This is actually true in general for independent events.

Now suppose that we have the same bag of marbles and that we take a marble at random from the bag. The probability that this is a red marble is $\frac{1}{2}$. This time we do

> ## Key Fact
>
> If A and B are two independent events then:
>
> P(A and B) = P(A) × P(B)

not put the marble back in the bag, so there are only three marbles left in the bag. What is the probability that the second marble is blue? It depends on what the first marble was. If the first marble was red, then two of the three remaining marbles are blue so P(2nd marble blue) $= \frac{2}{3}$. However, if the first marble was blue then only one of the three remaining marbles is blue, so P(2nd marble blue) $= \frac{1}{3}$. The probability of the second event is **dependent** on the result of the first event.

This time the probability of taking a red marble and then a blue marble is:

P(1st marble red **and** 2nd marble blue)

$=$ P(1st marble red) × P(2nd marble blue given that the first marble is red)

$= \frac{1}{2} \times \frac{2}{3}$

$= \frac{1 \times 2}{2 \times 3}$

$= \frac{2}{6}$

$= \frac{1}{3}$

> ## Word Check
>
> **dependent events**
> events in which the result of one event affects the result of the other

This rule works for all dependent events.

Key Fact

If the result of B depends on the result of A then:

P(A and B) = P(A) × P(B given that A happened)

Try It Out

G Which of the following events are independent and which are not?

1 Rolling a die and tossing a coin.

2 Taking a card out of a pack, replacing it, and then taking another card.

3 Taking a sock at random from a drawer, putting it on, then taking another sock.

4 Leaving the house late for work, arriving late for work.

Practice

H 1 Eldece rolls a die and tosses a coin. What is the probability that she gets:
   (a) a 2 and a head
   (b) an even number and a tail
   (c) a head and a 7.

2 A bag contains four red marbles, three blue marbles and two green marbles. Marbles are taken at random from the bag. Find the probabilities of these events.
   (a) A red marble is taken, replaced, then a blue marble is taken.
   (b) A green marble is taken, replaced, then a marble that isn't red is taken.
   (c) A blue marble is taken, left out of the bag, then a red marble is taken.
   (d) Three red marbles are taken out one after the other, without replacing any of them.

3 Everton is taking cards at random from a pack.

   Find the following probabilities if **(i)** he replaces each card after taking it out and **(ii)** he doesn't replace the cards.
   (a) The Ace of Spades then the Ace of Clubs
   (b) A Heart then a Diamond
   (c) Three Kings in a row

3 Expected Outcomes

Learn About It

If we tossed a coin 10 times how many times should we expect it to land heads and how many times tails?

When a coin is tossed the probability that it lands heads is $\frac{1}{2}$. So we can reasonably expect a coin to land heads up about $\frac{1}{2}$ the time. So when we toss the coin 10 times we expect it to be heads 5 times. If we expect it to be heads 5 times, then we must expect it to be tails the other 5 times. This is called the **expected frequency**.

Of course when we toss a coin 10 times it usually won't be heads exactly 5 times, but it is the most likely ('expected') outcome.

In general the expected frequency, E(X), of an outcome, X, is given by:

$$E(X) = P(X) \times n$$

where P(X) is the probability of X occurring

and n is the number of trials.

Example	Michael takes 15 shots at a basketball net.
	He scores 11 but misses 4.
	If he took 200 shots, how many could he expect to score?
Working	Michael scored 11 out of 15 shots, so the probability of scoring is $\frac{11}{15}$.
	If he took 200 shots, then he could be expected to score $\frac{11}{15} \times 200 = 146.7$
Answer	146.7

As we have seen the expected frequency isn't necessarily an integer. It is a mathematical way of working out what might happen.

Try It Out

1 The spinner is spun 700 times.

How many times should we expect the spinner to point to grey?

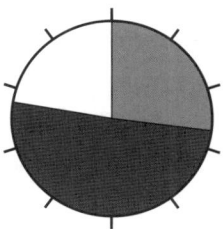

2 The probability that *Slow Coach* will win a horse race is 0.08. If he runs in 55 races during his career, how many races can he be expected to win?

3 The chance of winning a lottery game is 1-in-1000.
  (a) If 273 500 people play the game, how many winners should
    we expect?
  (b) The prize is $2000 dollars for each person who wins. How much
    prize money should we expect to be paid out?

Practice

1 At *Borewood School* 80% of students pass maths and 75% pass physics.
  (a) 195 pupils take the maths exam. How many can be expected to fail?
  (b) 164 pupils take the physics exam. How many more fail physics than
    maths?

2 A fast food restaurant sells burgers, fries and milkshakes.
  Last week it had 5000 customers. 3500 customers bought a burger, 2750
  bought fries and 2100 bought a milkshake.
  (a) What is the probability that a customer will want
      (i) a burger? **(ii)** fries? **(iii)** a milkshake?
  This week the restaurant expects 7500 customers.
  (b) How many burgers, fries and milkshakes should the restaurant stock?

3 Dan wants to know how many people in his town are more than 190 cm
  tall. There are 5742 people in his town. He measures the height of 150
  of them.

Height (cm)	Frequency
< 190	133
≥ 190	17

  What is the expected number of people in his town who are more than
  190 cm tall?

Finished Early?
 Go to page 452

4 Possibility spaces

Remember?
Some situations depend on two events, not just one.
A **possibility space diagram** is a two-way table showing all the possible
outcomes of the two events.

Example   A pair of dice are rolled and the numbers added.
This is repeated 90 times.
How many times should we expect the sum to be
(a) 11?   **(b)** 5?   **(c)** neither 11 nor 5?

Working   Make a possibility
space diagram.
There are 36 possible
values for the sum
of the numbers on
two dice.

+	1	2	3	4	5	6
1	2	3	4	5	6	7
2	3	4	5	6	7	8
3	4	5	6	7	8	9
4	5	6	7	8	9	10
5	6	7	8	9	10	11
6	7	8	9	10	11	12

(a) There are 2 ways of adding the numbers to make 11.
So $P(\text{sum 11}) = \frac{2}{36} = \frac{1}{18}$

The expected number of trials in which the sum comes
to 11 is
$E(\text{sum 11}) = \frac{1}{18} \times 90$

$= \frac{90}{18}$

Answer $= 5$

Working   **(b)** There are 4 ways of adding the numbers to make 5.
So $P(\text{sum 5}) = \frac{4}{36}$

The expected number of trials in which the sum comes
to 5 is
$E(\text{sum 5}) = \frac{4}{36} \times 90$

$= \frac{1}{9} \times 90$

Answer $= 10$

Working   **(c)** In the 90 trials the sum is expected to be 11 in 5 trials
and expected to be 5 in 10 trials. So the sum isn't
expected to be either 11 or 5 in any of the other trials.
So we expect the sum to be neither 11 nor 5 in
$90 - 5 - 10 = 75$ trials.

Answer   75 trials

Try It Out

K Create the possibility space diagram for these experiments.

1 Tossing a coin twice.

2 Rolling two dice and multiplying the numbers that land face up.

3 Tossing a coin and rolling a dice.

Practice

L **1** A coin is tossed twice. What is the probability of getting:
  (a) two tails?   **(b)** a head and a tail in any order?
  (c) a head then a tail?

2 Two dice are thrown and the numbers are multiplied together.
  What is the probability of getting:
  (a) 30?   **(b)** an odd number?   **(c)** a result less than 11?

3 Sarah and Donnie play a game. Sarah tosses a coin and Donnie rolls
  a die. If the coin is a head or the die is a 6 (or both) Sarah wins,
  otherwise Donnie wins.
  (a) What is the probability that **(i)** Sarah wins?   **(ii)** Donnie wins?
  (b) They play the game 30 times. How many times should we expect:
    (i) Sarah to win?
    (ii) Donnie to win?

M **1** An 8-sided die is rolled and a 5-sided spinner
  is spun and the highest number, H, is taken.
  (a) Copy and complete the possibility space
    diagram.

	1	2	3	4	5	6	7	8
1								
2								
3								
4								
5								

  (b) Find:
    (i) P($H = 5$)
    (ii) P($H \geq 3$)
  (c) What is the probability that the number on the spinner is higher than
    the number on the die? [*Hint: You may need to make a new
    possibility space diagram.*]

Finished Early?
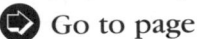 Go to page 190

Unit 5 *Statistics and Probability*

Summary of Chapters 10 and 11

Statistics

- Data can be **discrete** or **continuous**. It can also be **qualitative** or **quantitative**.
- Discrete data is obtained by counting.
- Continuous data is obtained by measuring.
- Qualitative data describes a characteristic.
- Quantitative data is numerical.
- Small amounts of data can be put in an ungrouped frequency table. Larger amounts need to go in a **grouped frequency table**.
- A group of data is called a **class**. The class with the largest frequency is called the **modal class**.

Height, H (cm)	Frequency
$0 < H \leqslant 5$	6
$6 < H \leqslant 10$	9
$10 < H \leqslant 15$	15 ← Modal class

Lower class limit | Upper class limit

- The mean, median and range of data in a grouped frequency table are found using the mid-points of the classes.
- The **lower class boundary** is the smallest possible value that goes in that class. The **upper class boundary** is the largest possible value that goes in that class.
- A **histogram** is used to present data from a grouped frequency diagram.
- The **cumulative frequency** is the sum of all the frequencies up to and including the present class.
- The **ogive** is the S-shaped curve that often occurs when plotting cumulative frequencies.
- 25 per cent of data values are less than or equal to the **lower quartile**. 75 per cent of data values are less than or equal to the **upper quartile**.
- The **interquartile range** is the difference between the upper quartile and the lower quartile.

Probability

- The probability of an event occurring is:

  $$\text{probability} = \frac{\text{number of desired outcomes}}{\text{number of possible outcomes}}$$

- For any event X:

  $P(X) = 0$ X cannot happen

  $P(X) = 1$ X will happen

  $P(X) = \frac{1}{2}$ equal chance that X will or won't happen

- In set notation this can be written as:

  $$P(X) = \frac{n(X)}{n(U)}$$

  where   X = the set of desired events

  and   U = the set of all possible events.

- **Mutually exclusive** events are events that cannot happen at the same time.

- If two events, X and Y, are mutually exclusive then:

  $P(X \textbf{ and } Y) = 0$

  $P(X \textbf{ or } Y) = P(X) + P(Y)$

- **Independent events** are events in which the result of one has no effect on the other.

- If A and B are two independent events then:

  $P(A \text{ and } B) = P(A) \times P(B)$

- **Dependent events** are events in which the result of one event affects the result of the other.

- If the result of B depends on the result of A then:

  $P(A \text{ and } B) = P(A) \times P(B \text{ given that A happened})$

- The **expected frequency**, E(X), of an outcome, X, is given by:

  $E(X) = P(X) \times n$

  where   P(X) is the probability of X occurring

  and n is the number of trials.

- A **possibility space diagram** is a two-way table showing all the possible outcomes of the two events.

12 Geometry and Trigonometry 1

In this chapter you will learn about ...
1. constructions
2. Pythagoras' theorem
3. trigonometric ratios
4. angles of elevation and depression
5. bearings
6. trigonometric ratios of special angles
7. trigonometric identities

1 Constructions

Remember?

- You can construct angles of 60° and 90° using a ruler and compasses.

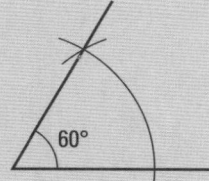

- You can bisect an angle using a ruler and compasses.

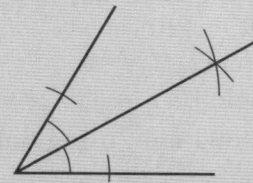

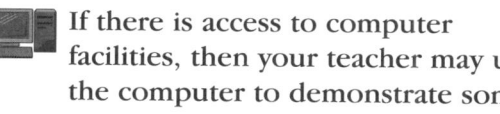 If there is access to computer facilities, then your teacher may use the computer to demonstrate some constructions.

 Ruler, compasses, protractor

Word Check

construct draw accurately

construction lines light lines to help you construct a diagram

Try It Out

(A) Construct these angles, using only a ruler and compasses.

Note: Always leave your construction lines on your answer.

1 60°   **2** 30°   **3** 45°   **4** 22.5°

5 120°   **6** 165°   **7** 225°   **8** 300°

Practice

(B) Construct these triangles, using only a ruler and compasses.

1

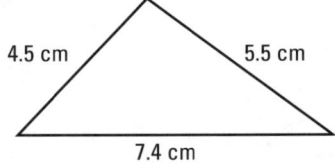

4.5 cm   5.5 cm

7.4 cm

2

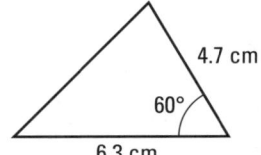

4.7 cm

60°

6.3 cm

2

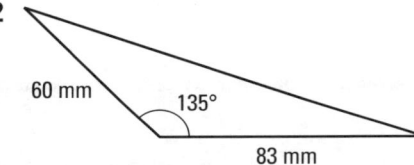

60 mm   135°

83 mm

4

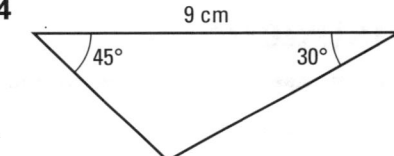

9 cm

45°   30°

5

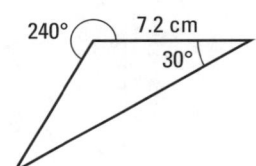

240°   7.2 cm

30°

(C) **1** Construct these triangles, using only a ruler and compasses. Measure and state the lengths of any other sides, and the sizes of the other angles.

(a) Triangle ABC: AB = 9 cm, AC = 7 cm, angle CAB = 120°.

(b) Triangle XYZ: XY = 5 cm, XZ = 12 cm, YZ = 13 cm.

(c) Triangle TUV: angle UTV = 60°, TV = 11 cm, angle UVT = 15°.

2 Construct an equilateral triangle with sides of length 84 mm, using only a ruler and compasses.

3 Triangle RST is isosceles. RS is 6 cm, ST is 11 cm and angle SRT is obtuse.

(a) State the length of RT. [*Hint: Sketch the triangle.*]

(b) Construct triangle RST.

(c) Measure and state the size of angle SRT.

D 1 Construct these shapes using only a ruler and compasses.

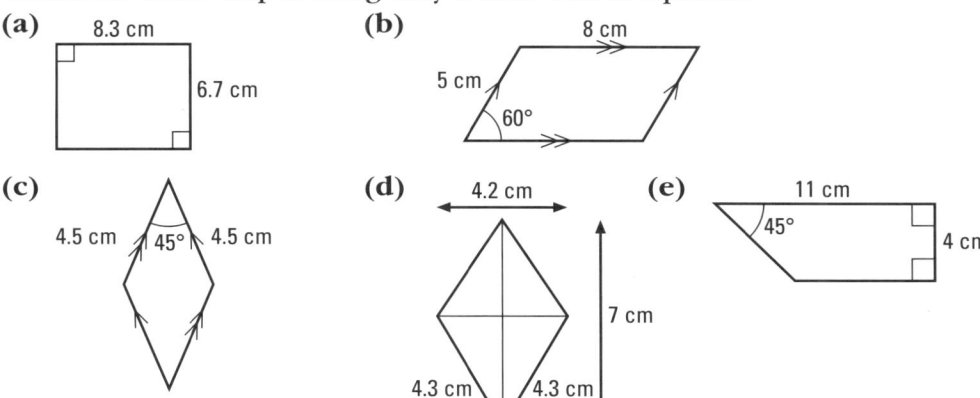

(a) 8.3 cm   6.7 cm

(b) 8 cm   5 cm   60°

(c) 4.5 cm   45°   4.5 cm

(d) 4.2 cm   7 cm   4.3 cm   4.3 cm

(e) 11 cm   45°   4 cm

2 (a) Using ruler and compasses only, construct a quadrilateral ABCD, with AB = CD = 6 cm, AD = 9 cm, angle BAD = 60° and angle ADC = 120°.

(b) Measure and state the length of BC, to the nearest mm, and the size of angle BCD to the nearest degree.

(c) What shape have you drawn?

3 (a) Using ruler and compasses only, construct a quadrilateral RSTU with RS = 35 mm, RU = 83 mm, angle SRU = 45°, angle RST = 120° and angle RUT = 30°.

(b) Measure and state the lengths of ST and TU.

> **Finished Early?**
> ⇨ Go to page 453

② Pythagoras' Theorem

Remember?

The **hypotenuse** is the longest side in a right-angled triangle; the side opposite the right-angle.

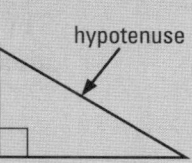

hypotenuse

Pythagoras' theorem

In a right-angled triangle, the square of the hypotenuse is equal to the sum of the squares of the other two sides.

In other words: If c is the length of the longest side and a and b the lengths of the other sides, $c^2 = a^2 + b^2$.

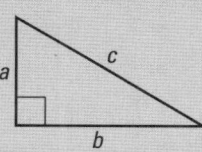

Learn About It

We can use Pythagoras' theorem to work out the length of the hypotenuse of a right-angled triangle when we know the length of the two shorter sides. However, what if we know the hypotenuse and want to find one of the shorter sides?

Well, we can rearrange Pythagoras' theorem:

$$c^2 = a^2 + b^2$$
$$c^2 - b^2 = a^2 \qquad \textit{(Subtract } b^2 \textit{ from both sides.)}$$
$$a^2 = c^2 - b^2 \qquad \textit{(Turn the formula around.)}$$

So we can find the length of one of the shorter sides using the hypotenuse and the other side.

Example	Find the length of the side a, and the area of the triangle.
Working	The length of the hypotenuse is $10\,$cm, and the length of one of the shorter sides is $8\,$cm.

So by using Pythagoras' theorem:
$$c^2 = a^2 + b^2$$
$$10^2 = a^2 + 8^2$$
$$a^2 = 10^2 - 8^2$$
$$= 100 - 64$$
$$= 36$$
$$a^2 = 36, \text{ so}$$
$$a = \sqrt{36} = 6\,\text{cm}.$$

The area of a triangle is $\frac{1}{2} \times$ base $\times$ height.
The base of the triangle is $8\,$cm.
The height of the triangle is $6\,$cm.
$$\text{area} = \frac{1}{2} \times 8 \times 6$$
$$= 4 \times 6$$
$$= 24\,\text{cm}^2$$
So the area is $24\,\text{cm}^2$.

Answer $a = 6\,$cm, area $= 24\,\text{cm}^2$

Try it out

E **1** Find the length of the unknown side and the area of the triangle.

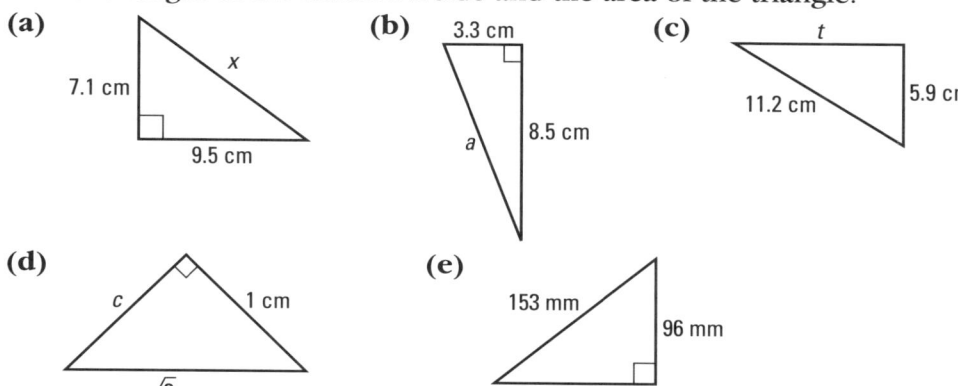

(a)

7.1 cm x 9.5 cm

(b) 3.3 cm a 8.5 cm

(c) t 11.2 cm 5.9 cm

(d) c 1 cm √2 cm

(e) 153 mm 96 mm a

Practice

F Work out the sizes of the unknown lengths.

1

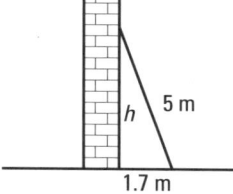

h 5 m 1.7 m

2

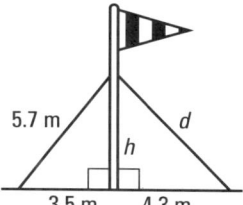

5.7 m h d 3.5 m 4.3 m

3

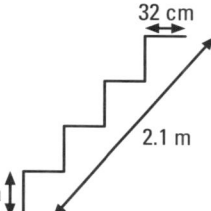

32 cm 2.1 m a

G **1** The rules of soccer say that a soccer pitch must
be between 90 m and 120 m in length and between
45 m and 90 m in width.
What are the smallest and largest possible distances
between opposite corner flags?

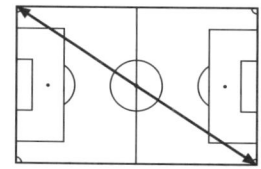

2 Everton wants to fly from Trinidad
to the Caicos islands. If he flies with
Shortflight, then he can go direct. If
he decides to use *Longway Airlines*,
then he has to change in Jamaica.
   (i) If he uses *Shortflight*, then how
      far is the flight?
   (ii) How much further is the journey
      if he flies by *Longway Airlines*?

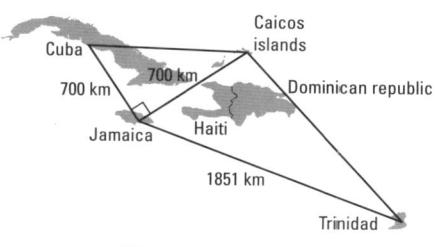

Cuba Caicos islands 700 km 700 km Dominican republic Jamaica Haiti 1851 km Trinidad

Finished Early?
➡ Go to page 453

Learn More About It

We can also use Pythagoras' theorem to find the lengths of sides in more complicated shapes.

Example   Find c.

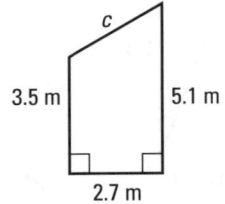

Working   Divide the trapezium into a rectangle and a right-angled triangle.

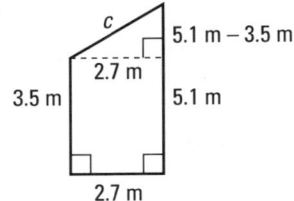

The triangle has short sides of length 2.7 m and 5.1 m − 3.5 m = 1.6 m

So using Pythagoras' theorem:
$$c^2 = 2.7^2 + 1.6^2$$
$$= 9.85$$
So $c = \sqrt{9.85} = 3.1384.... = 3.14$ m (to the nearest cm).

Answer $c = 3.14$ m

Try It Out

H Find the unknown sides.

1
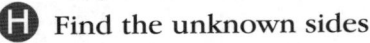
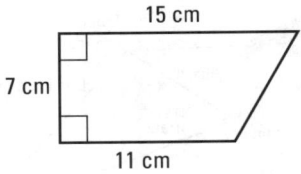

2
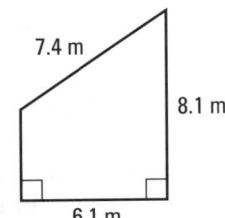

I **1** Find the length BE.

2 Hence find BC.

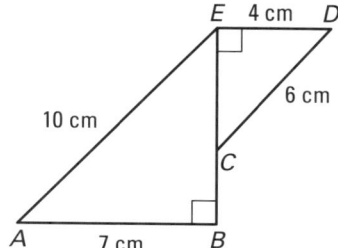

Practice

J **1** The diagram shows a shovel of a digger. How long is the sloping side?

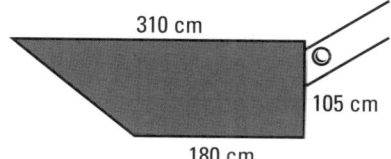

2 An equilateral triangle has sides 17 cm in length. Calculate its height.

3 The 'infield' of a baseball pitch is a square with sides of length 90 feet. The 'bases' are on the corners of the infield.

What is the distance (in a straight line) between first and third bases?

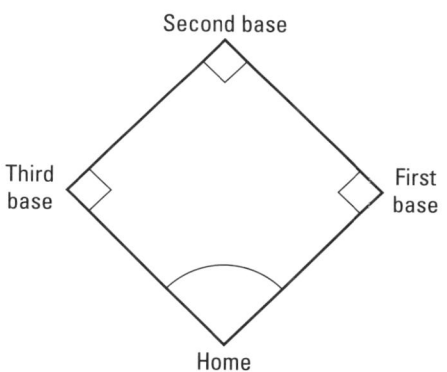

4 A $6\frac{1}{2}$ m tall flag pole holds a triangular flag. The pole is supported by a cable. How long is the cable?

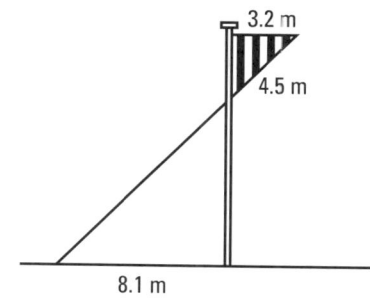

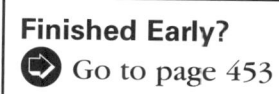

> **Finished Early?**
> ➡ Go to page 453

③ Trigonometric Ratios

Learn About It

Imagine you are flying a kite on a long piece of string.

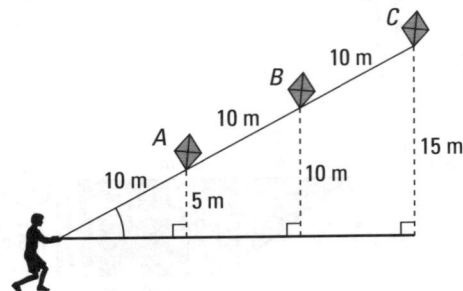

Suppose you let out 10 m of string and the kite reaches a height of 5 m above the ground. If you let out another 10 m of string, then the kite increases its height by another 5 m. Let out another 10 m of string and the height increases by 5 m, and so on.

Let's look at the ratio of the height of the kite to the length of string at A, B and C.

At A: $\dfrac{\text{height of kite}}{\text{length of string}} = \dfrac{5\,\text{m}}{10\,\text{m}} = \dfrac{1}{2} = 0.5$

At B: $\dfrac{\text{height of kite}}{\text{length of string}} = \dfrac{10\,\text{m}}{20\,\text{m}} = \dfrac{1}{2} = 0.5$

At C: $\dfrac{\text{height of kite}}{\text{length of string}} = \dfrac{15\,\text{m}}{30\,\text{m}} = \dfrac{1}{2} = 0.5$

So, as long as the angle between the string and the ground stays the same, the ratio $\dfrac{\text{height of kite}}{\text{length of string}}$ stays the same, no matter how much string is let out. This ratio is known as the **sine** of the angle.

For a general right-angled triangle the sine (usually written **sin**) of an angle A is given as:

$$\sin A = \frac{\text{length of the side opposite the angle}}{\text{length of the hypotenuse}}$$

Usually we are not particularly interested in the sine of an angle. If you want to know the size of the angle itself. You can find this by using the $\sin^{-1}$ function on your calculator. How you get it depends on your type of calculator, but usually you should press:

| 2nd F | then | sin |

or | Inv | then | sin |

Example   For triangle ABC find the sine of the angle at B and the size of the angle at B.

Working   The side opposite B is 9.2 cm long.
The hypotenuse is 14.7 cm long.
So

$$\sin B = \frac{9.2}{14.7} = 0.6258... = 0.63 \text{ to 2 decimal places.}$$

To work out the size of the angle you must take the **inverse sine** of $\frac{9.2}{14.7}$.

Press 2nd F or Inv then sin then (9.2 ÷ 14.7) to get 38.7446... .
So B = 38.7446...° = 38.7° to 1 decimal place.

Answer   sin B = 0.63 to 2 decimal places and B = 38.7° to 1 decimal place.

Try it out

K **1** Find the sizes of the marked angles.

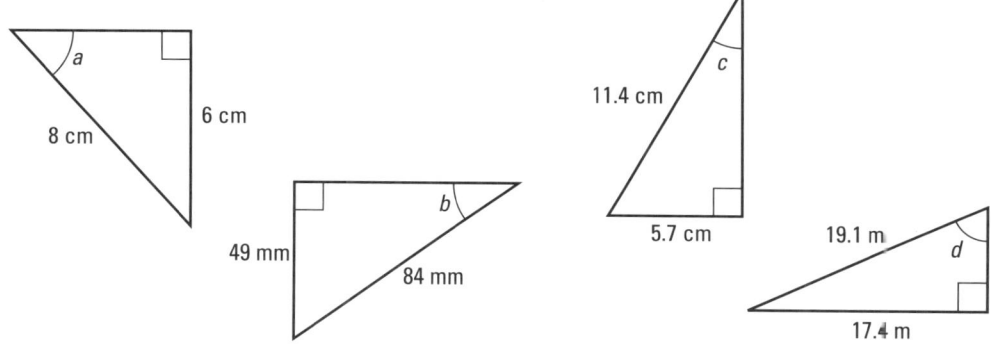

2 Find the lengths of the unknown sides.

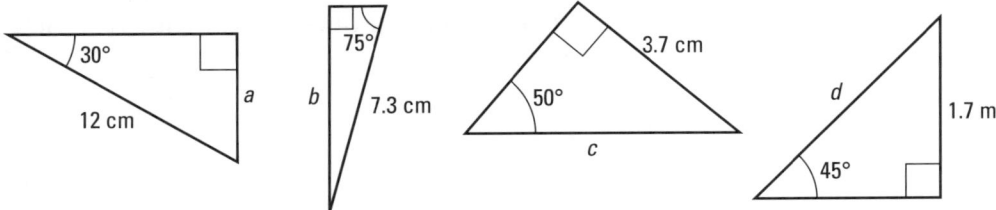

Learn More About It

We have seen how to find the size of an angle if we know the length of the side opposite the angle and the length of the hypotenuse. What if we only know the lengths of the shorter sides, or if we know the length of the hypotenuse and the side next to the angle?

The shorter side next to the angle given is called the **adjacent** side.

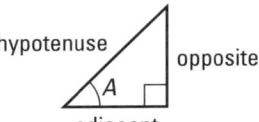

There are two new trigonometric ratios that use the length of the adjacent side: the **cosine** and the **tangent** (usually shortened to **cos** and **tan**).

We already know that:

$$\sin A = \frac{\text{length of the side opposite the angle}}{\text{length of the hypotenuse}}$$

You can get the cosine of an angle using:

$$\cos A = \frac{\text{length of the side adjacent to the angle}}{\text{length of the hypotenuse}}$$

You can get the tangent of an angle using:

$$\tan A = \frac{\text{length of the side opposite the angle}}{\text{length of the side adjacent to the angle}}$$

Key Fact

You can shorten the names of the sides of the triangles to get:

$$\sin A = \frac{\text{opp}}{\text{hyp}} \qquad \cos A = \frac{\text{adj}}{\text{hyp}} \qquad \tan A = \frac{\text{opp}}{\text{adj}}$$

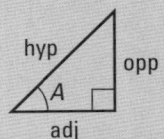

Notice that the length of the hypotenuse is always larger than the other two sides so sin A ⩽ 1 and cos A ⩽ 1.

Example Use the tangent ratio to find the length of AB.

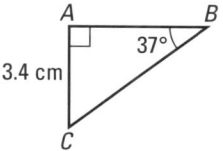

Working We know the angle at B is 37°, and we know the length of AC, which is opposite the angle.

We want to find the length of AB, the side adjacent to the angle.

We can use the tangent ratio:

$$\tan A = \frac{\text{opp}}{\text{adj}}$$

So $\tan 37° = \dfrac{13.4}{AB}$

Rearrange this to get:

$$AB = \frac{13.4}{\tan 37°}$$

$$= 13.4 \div \tan 37°$$

Press tan then 3 then 7 on your calculator to get:
$\tan 37° = 0.7535...$

So

$$AB = 13.4 \div 0.7535...$$
$$= 17.7824...$$
$$= 17.8 \text{ cm to 1 decimal place.}$$

Answer AB = 17.8 cm to 1 decimal place.

It can be difficult to remember which sides to use with which ratio. Does sine use the opposite and the hypotenuse? Or was it the adjacent?

To help you remember you can use SOHCAHTOA:

S i n e
O p p o s i t e
H y p o t e n u s e
C o s i n e
A d j a c e n t
H y p o t e n u s e
T a n g e n t
O p p o s i t e
A d j a c e n t

Example   Find the size of the angle A.

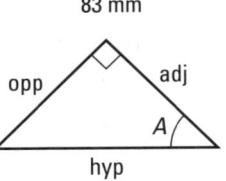

Working   Work out which side is the hypotenuse
and which sides are adjacent and opposite
You know the length of the side adjacent
to the angle and the length of the
hypotenuse. Using SOHCAHTOA you
can see that:

$$\cos A = \frac{adj}{hyp}$$

So:

$$\cos A = \frac{57}{83}$$

Hence A = $\cos^{-1}$ (57 ÷ 83)

$\qquad$ = 46.6268...°

$\qquad$ = 46.6° to 1 decimal 1 place.

Answer   A = 46.6° to 1 decimal place.

Try It Out

L **1** Identify the hypotenuse and the sides adjacent to and opposite the
marked angles.

(a) 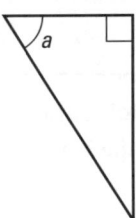 (b) 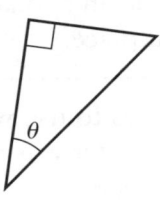 (c)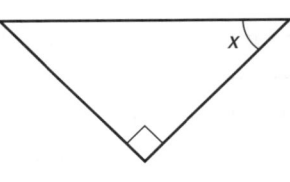

2 Calculate the sizes of the marked angles.

(a) 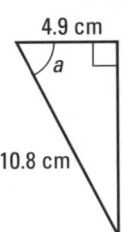 (b) 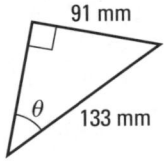 (c)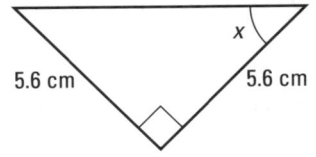

Practice

 Find the sizes of the marked angles and sides.

1

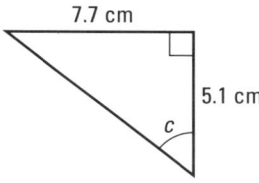

7.7 cm

5.1 cm

c

2

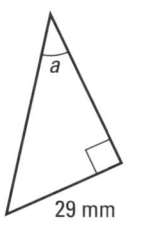

a

29 mm

3

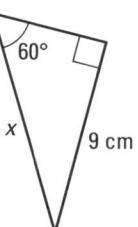

60°

x

9 cm

4

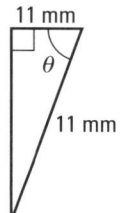

11 mm

θ

11 mm

5

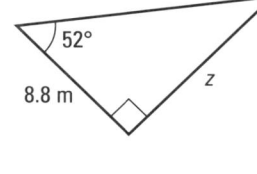

52°

8.8 m

z

6

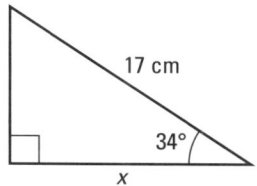

17 cm

34°

x

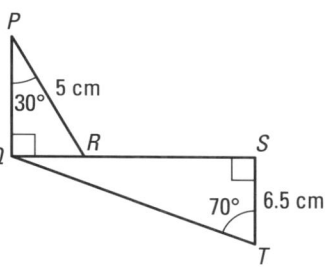

1 Calculate:
   (a) QR
   (b) QS
   (c) RS.

P

5 cm

30°

Q   R   S

70°   6.5 cm

T

2 Calculate:
   (a) AB
   (b) BC.

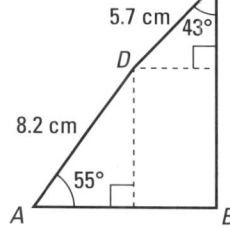

C

5.7 cm   43°

D

8.2 cm

55°

A   B

3 Calculate:
   (a) the length a
   (b) the angle θ.

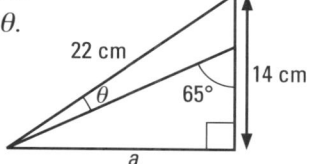

22 cm

θ   65°   14 cm

a

4 Calculate WX.

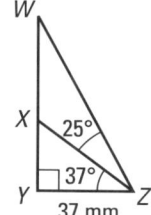

W

X   25°

37°

Y   37 mm   Z

Further Practice

For each of these triangles, calculate the sizes of all angles and the lengths of all the sides.

1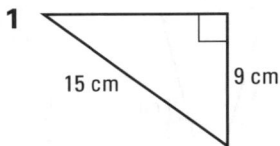

2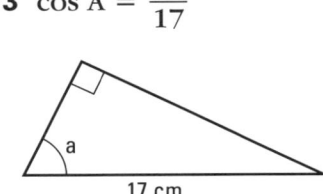

3 $\cos A = \dfrac{8}{17}$

Finished Early?

Go to page 454

4 Angles of Elevation and Depression

Learn About It

We have already met some practical uses of trigonometry. In the following sections we meet some more.

Imagine that you are looking up at a friend standing on a wall. The angle between a horizontal line extending from your eyes and your line of sight is called the **angle of elevation**.

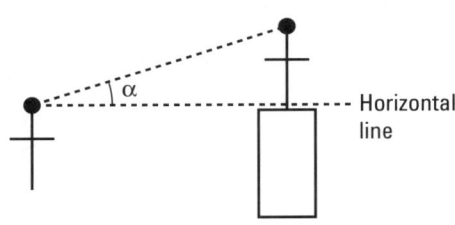

α is the angle of elevation

If your friend is looking down at you, then the angle between a horizontal line extending from their eyes and their line of sight is called the **angle of depression**.

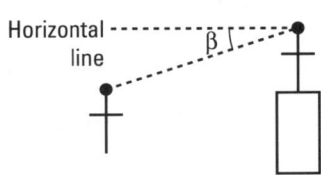

β is the angle of depression

Notice that the angle of elevation and the angle of depression are alternate angles and so are equal.

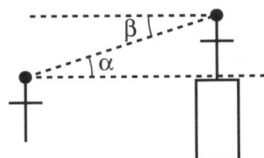

Word Check

angle of elevation the angle between the horizontal and a 'line of sight' above the horizontal

angle of depression the angle between the horizontal and a 'line of sight' below the horizontal

---

Example   Kenmore is standing 2 m away from a wall. Rhema is standing on the wall. Kenmore is 1.8 m tall, Rhema is 1.5 m tall and the wall is 2 m tall.
(a) What is the angle of elevation of Rhema from Kenmore?
(b) What is the angle of depression of Kenmore from Rhema?

Thinking   Begin by drawing a simple diagram.

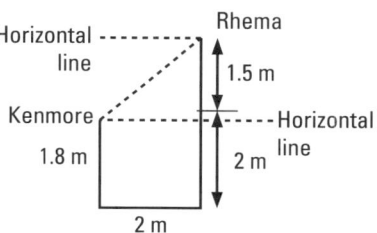

Working   (a) α is the angle of elevation.

$$\alpha = \tan^{-1} \frac{(3.5 - 1.8)}{2}$$

$$= \tan^{-1} \frac{1.7}{2}$$

$$= 40.4° \text{ (to 1 d.p.)}$$

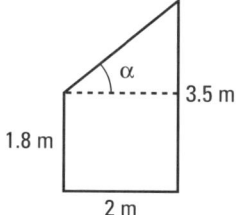

(b) The angle of depression, β, is the same as the angle of elevation.

Answer   (a) 40.4°   (b) 40.4°

Practice

 **1** Curtley is standing at the top of a 15 m tall building. He is looking at a passer-by standing 55 m from the bottom of the building.

What is the angle of depression of the passer-by from Curtley?

2 A monkey is looking at a bunch of bananas in a tree. The monkey is 3.2 m from the tree and the bananas are 4.3 m above the monkey. What is the angle of elevation of the bananas from the monkey?

3 An aircraft is 1250 m from the start of a runway and 375 m above the runway. What is the angle of depression of the start of the runway from the aircraft?

Ⓠ **1** A boat is 250 m from the bottom of a cliff. The angle of depression of the boat from the top of the cliff is 32°.
  (a) What is the angle of elevation of the top of the cliff from the boat?
  (b) Calculate the height of the cliff to the nearest metre.
  (c) A surfer is 30 m from the bottom of the cliff. Calculate the angle of depression of the surfer from the top of the cliff.

2 Clyde and Deon are walking towards a block of flats 43 m high. The angle of elevation of the top of the building from Clyde is 32° and from Deon it is 24°. How far apart are Clyde and Deon? (Assume that they form a straight line from the building.)

⑤ Bearings

Learn About It

When a ship is travelling from one place to another the captain always needs to know exactly where the ship is. To do this he needs to know the distance the ship is from a particular place and in which direction. The direction is given as an angle called a **bearing**.

Bearings are based on the points on the compass. North is at a bearing of 000°, north-east is at 045° and so on.

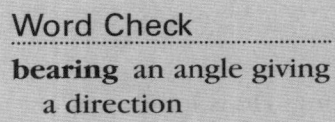

Word Check

bearing an angle giving a direction

Key Fact

The bearing from a particular point is the angle measured *clockwise* from *north*. It is always written as a *three-digit number*.

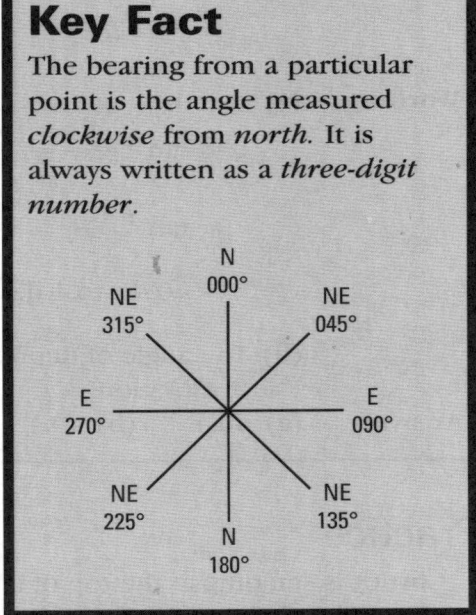

Example   A ship leaves harbour and travels 60 km south-east to reach a lighthouse.
(a) What is the bearing of the lighthouse from the harbour?
(b) Calculate how far south and how far east the ship has travelled, to the nearest kilometre.
(c) What is the bearing of the harbour from the lighthouse?

Working   (a) The ship is travelling SE. Measuring clockwise from north the angle is 135°.
This is already a three-digit number, so it is the bearing of the ship from the harbour.

(b) The ship has travelled 60 km at a bearing of 135°.

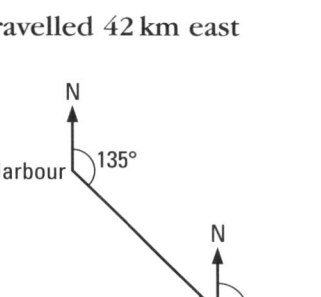

The distances south and east are the lengths of two sides of a right-angled triangle.
Distance east $= 60 \times \sin 45°$
$\qquad\qquad = 42.42\ldots$ km
Distance south $= 60 \times \cos 45°$
$\qquad\qquad\quad = 42.42\ldots$km
To the nearest km the ship has travelled 42 km east and 42 km south.

(c) The bearing of the lighthouse from the harbour is 135°.

From the diagram the bearing of the harbour from the lighthouse is
$180° + 135° = 315°$.

Answer   (a) 135°   (b) 42 km south, 42 km east   (c) 315°

Try It Out

Ruler and protractor

R **1** For each case write down the bearing of B from A.

(a) 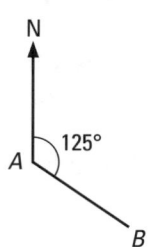 **(b)** 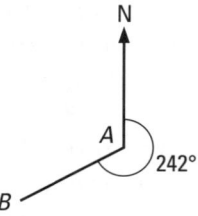 **(c)**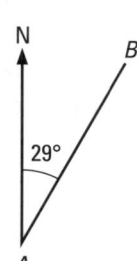

2 Use a ruler and a protractor to draw the following bearings. Remember to mark north on your diagram.

(a) 090° (b) 225° (c) 133° (d) 015°
(e) 180° (f) 300°

S **1** Calculate the bearing of:

(a) B from A
(b) C from A
(c) A from B
(d) A from C.

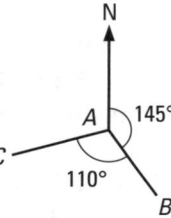

2 Calculate the bearing of:

(a) Q from P
(b) R from P
(c) P from Q
(d) P from R.

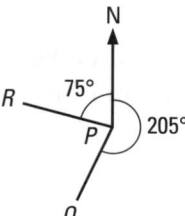

Practice

T **1** Three aeroplanes take off from Piarco International airport. Using a scale of 1 cm to 10 km make a scale drawing of their journeys.

(a) One plane travels 50 km at a bearing of 330°.
(b) The second plane travels at a bearing of 045° for 75 km and then turns and flies due south for 100 km.
(c) The final plane flies due west for 38 km. It then turns through an angle of 50° clockwise and flies for 52 km. Finally, it flies due north for 30 km.

2 At the end of their journeys each plane in question 1 returns directly to the airport. Measure how far the plane has to fly and at what bearing. Give your answers to the nearest km and degree.

U Use trigonometry to answer the following questions.

1 A plane flies 180 km at a bearing of 016.3°. To four significant figures, how far north of its original position is it?

2 A yacht sails 37 km at a bearing of 111°. Calculate how far east of its original position it is, to the nearest one hundred metres.

3 Joel cycles 13 km due west and then cycles 170 km due north. What is the bearing of his final position from his original position to one decimal place?

4 Sandie walks 857 m at a bearing of 330°. Then she walks 242 m at a bearing of 062°. To the nearest metre, how far north of her original position is she?

V Use trigonometry to answer the following questions.

1 A boat takes passengers on a tour of some islands. The boat begins at island A and goes 33 km on a bearing of 073° to reach island B. The boat then moves on to island C which is 44 km away on a bearing of 163° from island B.
   (a) To one decimal place, how far north of island A is island B?
   (b) To one decimal place, how far east of island A is island B?
   (c) Calculate the angle ABC.
   (d) Calculate the distance between A and C.

2 An aircraft takes off from point A and flies 140 km due east. It then turns due south and flies for another 80 km to reach point B.
   (a) Calculate the distance between A and B to one decimal place.
   (b) Calculate the bearing of B from A to one decimal place.

Further Practice

W Use the diagram to work out the following.

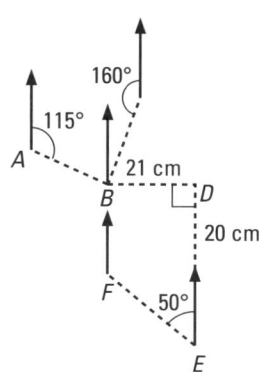

1 The bearing of A from B.

2 The bearing of C from B.

3 The bearing of E from B.

4 The distance from E to B.

5 What is the bearing of E from F?

F is directly below B.

6 How far below B is F?

6 Trigonometric Ratios of Special Angles

Learn About It

Some angles have trigonometric ratios that
we can calculate exactly, rather than to a certain
number of decimal places.

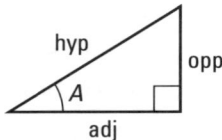

$$\sin A = \frac{\text{opp}}{\text{hyp}} \quad \cos A = \frac{\text{adj}}{\text{hyp}} \quad \tan A = \frac{\text{opp}}{\text{adj}}$$

For example, if A = 0°, then the length of the opposite must be 0 and the
length of the adjacent must be equal to the length of the hypotenuse.

So $\quad \sin 0° = \dfrac{0}{\text{hyp}} = 0$

$\qquad \cos 0° = \dfrac{\text{hyp}}{\text{hyp}} = 1$

$\qquad \tan 0° = \dfrac{0}{\text{adj}} = 0.$

Also if A = 90° then the length of the adjacent is 0 and the length of the
opposite is the same as the length of the hypotenuse.

So $\quad \sin 90° = \dfrac{\text{hyp}}{\text{hyp}} = 1$

$\qquad \cos 90° = \dfrac{0}{\text{hyp}} = 0$

$\qquad \tan 90° = \dfrac{\text{hyp}}{0} = \text{undefined}.$

tan 90° requires you to divide by zero, so we say that it is undefined.

We can find the trigonometric ratios of 45° by
looking at an isosceles triangle with two sides
with length 1.

Then, using Pythagoras' theorem, the hypotenuse
has length √2 units.

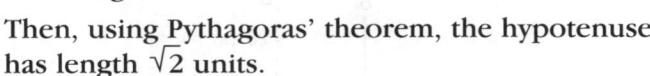

Also, since AC = BC, BÂC = AB̂C.
Angles in a triangle add up to 180°,
so BÂC + AB̂C = 90°.
Hence BÂC = AB̂C = 45°.

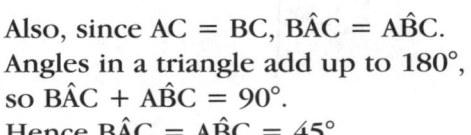
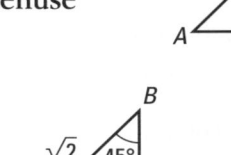

Using this special triangle we can see that:

$$\sin 45° = \frac{1}{\sqrt{2}}$$

$$\cos 45° = \frac{1}{\sqrt{2}}$$

$$\tan 45° = 1.$$

To find the trigonometric ratios of 30° and 60° we use another special triangle. This one is an equilateral triangle with sides of length 2 units, which is split in two.

$$\sin 30° = \frac{1}{2} \qquad \sin 60° = \frac{\sqrt{3}}{2}$$

$$\cos 30° = \frac{\sqrt{3}}{2} \qquad \cos 60° = \frac{1}{2}$$

$$\tan 30° = \frac{1}{\sqrt{3}} \qquad \tan 60° = \sqrt{3}$$

We can summarise these results in a table:

Angle	Sine	Cosine	Tangent
0°	0	1	0
30°	$\frac{1}{2}$	$\frac{\sqrt{3}}{2}$	$\frac{1}{\sqrt{3}}$
45°	$\frac{1}{\sqrt{2}}$	$\frac{1}{\sqrt{2}}$	1
60°	$\frac{\sqrt{3}}{2}$	$\frac{1}{2}$	$\sqrt{3}$
90°	1	0	Undefined

Practice

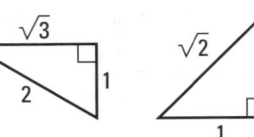

X The following triangles are similar to one or another of the special triangles. Use the special triangles to find the exact lengths of the marked sides.

1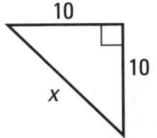

2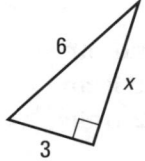

3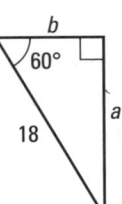

4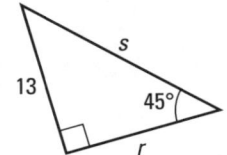

5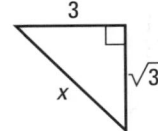

6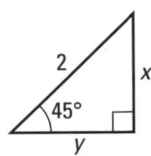

Finished Early?
➡ Go to page 454

7 Trigonometric Identities

Learn About It

There are several useful identities that we can use to manipulate trigonometric ratios and simplify equations that involve the trigonometric ratios.

Two of the most useful are:

$$\tan \theta = \frac{\sin \theta}{\cos \theta}$$

$$\sin^2 \theta + \cos^2 \theta = 1$$

$\sin^2 \theta$ means $(\sin \theta)^2$ and $\cos^2 \theta$ means $(\cos \theta)^2$.

These identities are true for any angle θ.

Practice

Y **1** Given that $\cos \theta = \frac{4}{5}$ and that $\sin \theta > 0$, find $\sin \theta$ without using a calculator.

2 Given that $\sin \theta = \frac{2}{3}$ and that $\cos \theta > 0$, find $\cos \theta$ without using a calculator.

3 Without using a calculator, find $\tan \theta$ given that $\sin \theta = \frac{5}{13}$ and $\cos \theta = \frac{12}{13}$.

4 Without using a calculator, find $\tan \theta$ given that $\cos \theta = \frac{15}{17}$ and $\sin \theta > 0$.

Learn More About It

Example   Prove that $\tan^2 \theta + 1 = \dfrac{1}{\cos^2 \theta}$.

Working

$$\tan^2 \theta + 1 = \frac{\sin^2 \theta}{\cos^2 \theta} + 1 \qquad\qquad \text{Using } \tan \theta = \frac{\sin \theta}{\cos \theta}$$

$$= \frac{\sin^2 \theta + \cos^2 \theta}{\cos^2 \theta}$$

$$= \frac{1}{\cos^2 \theta} \qquad\qquad \text{Using } \sin^2 \theta + \cos^2 \theta = 1$$

Practice

Z **1** Prove that $\dfrac{1}{\sin^2 \theta} + \dfrac{1}{\cos^2 \theta} = \dfrac{1}{\sin^2 \theta \cos^2 \theta}$.

2 Prove that $\tan^2 \theta = \dfrac{1 - \cos^2 \theta}{\cos^2 \theta}$.

3 Prove that $(1 - \sin^2 \theta)\tan^2 \theta + \cos^2 \theta = 1$.

4 Prove that $\tan^2 \theta - \dfrac{\cos^2 \theta}{\sin^2 \theta} = \dfrac{\sin^4 \theta - \cos^4 \theta}{\sin^2 \theta \cos^2 \theta}$.

5 Prove that $\dfrac{1}{\sin A} + \dfrac{\tan A}{\cos A} = \dfrac{1}{\sin A \cos^2 A}$.

13 Transformation Geometry

In this chapter you will learn about ...

① translations
② reflections
③ rotations
④ enlargements
⑤ distinguishing between transformations

① Translations

Remember?

A **transformation** can change a shape and alter its position. The shape before the transformation is called the **object**. The shape after the transformation is called the **image**.

Translations 'slide' a shape from its original position to its new position. A translation will change the position of a shape, but not its size or shape.

Translations are described using column vectors. The vector $\begin{pmatrix} -2 \\ 3 \end{pmatrix}$ moves each point of the shape 2 units left and 3 units up.

 Squared paper

Practice

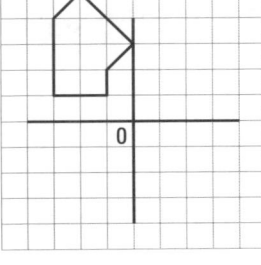

Ⓐ 1 Copy the diagram.

2 Translate the shape by $\begin{pmatrix} 4 \\ -3 \end{pmatrix}$.

3 Measure the lengths of the corresponding sides on the object and the image. What do you notice?

4 The point (–2, 5) on the object translates to which point of the image?

5 The point (4, 0) on the image is translated from which point of the object?

216

Learn About It

A transformation is a one-to-one mapping of the points in the plane (see Chapter 2, pages 21 and 22). This means that each point moves to one and only one point.

In a translation the lengths of the corresponding sides in the object and the image are the same. Also the sizes of corresponding angles are the same in the object and the image. This means that the object and image are **congruent**. If the object and the image are congruent, then we call the transformation a **congruency transformation**.

We usually use T to denote a translation.

> **Word Check**
>
> **congruent** objects whose corresponding sides and angles are the same size.

Practice

B For each of the following questions copy the diagram and find the image.

1 $\begin{pmatrix} 2 \\ 4 \end{pmatrix}$

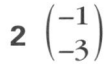

2 $\begin{pmatrix} -1 \\ -3 \end{pmatrix}$

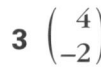

3 $\begin{pmatrix} 4 \\ -2 \end{pmatrix}$

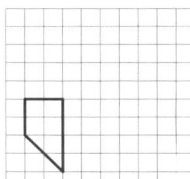
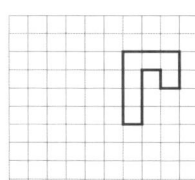
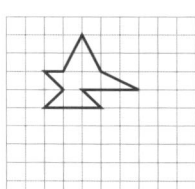

C Find the translation vector T for each of these translations.

1

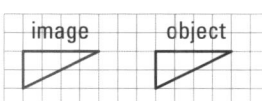

image   object

2

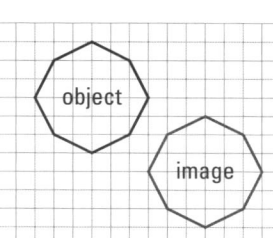

object

image

3

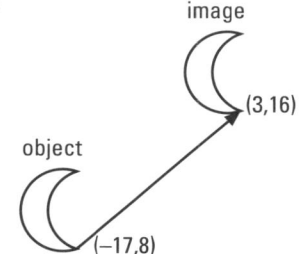

image

(3,16)

object

(−17,8)

4

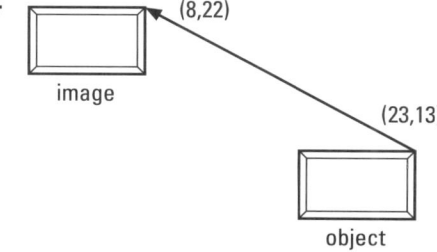

(8,22)

image

(23,13)

object

D 1 (a) Draw the graph of $y = x + 3$ on squared paper.

(b) Translate the line by $T = \begin{pmatrix} 0 \\ -3 \end{pmatrix}$.

(c) What is the equation of the image?

2 (a) On graph paper, construct a triangle ABC with sides AB = 5 cm, AC = 4 cm and angle BAC = 60°.

(b) Translate the triangle by $\begin{pmatrix} 3\,\text{cm} \\ -5\,\text{cm} \end{pmatrix}$.

3 A line of length 12 cm is translated by the vector $\begin{pmatrix} 5 \\ 2 \end{pmatrix}$. How long is its image?

4 The triangle ABC has corners A (−1, 0), B (2, −4) and C (−1, −4). It is translated through a vector $\begin{pmatrix} x \\ y \end{pmatrix}$. Write down the area of the image.

2 Reflections

Remember?

To describe a **reflection** you need to give the position of its **mirror line**. Given the object and image we can find the mirror line:

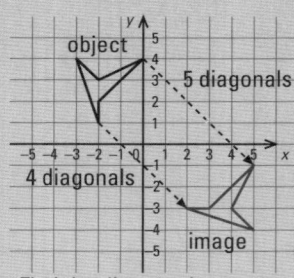 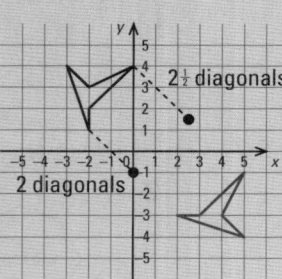 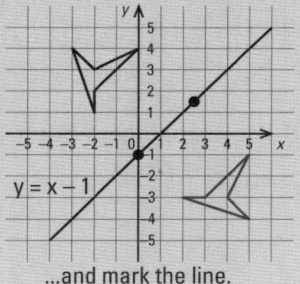

Find the distance between corresponding points... ...halve the distance to find a point on the line... ...and mark the line.

Given the object and a mirror line we can find the image. The object and image are equal distances from the mirror line.

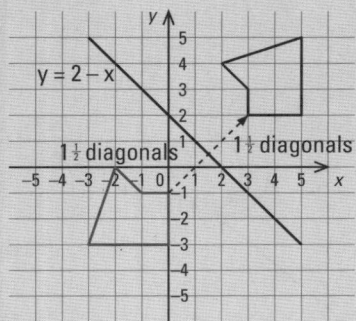

Just like translations, a reflection is a congruency transformation. The size and shape of the image is the same as the object.

Practice

E Use the diagram to copy and complete the table.

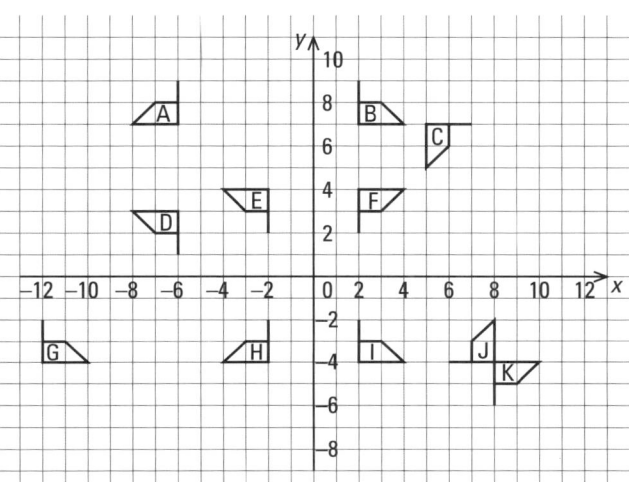

Object	Mirror line	Image
A		D
F	x-axis	
E	x = 0	
H		G
I		E
B		F
F	y = −x	
	x = −2	A
C		F
J		K

F On squared paper, draw coordinate axes, labelling the x- and y-axes from −5 to 5.

1 Plot and join the following points, in the given order:

$(-4, 2) \rightarrow (-2, 2) \rightarrow (0, 0) \rightarrow (-4, 0) \rightarrow (-4, 2)$

2 Reflect your answer to **1** in the line $y = x$.

3 Reflect the shapes in **1** and **2** in the y-axis.

G On squared paper, draw coordinate axes, labelling the *x*- and *y*-axes from −10 to 10. Plot and join the following points, in order:

$(4, 4) \rightarrow (7, 4) \rightarrow (7, 1) \rightarrow (6, 3) \rightarrow (4, 4)$

Reflect the object in each of the following lines.

1 The *x*-axis   **2** $x = 2$ **3** $y = -2$ **4** The *y*-axis

5 $y = x$ **6** $y = -x$ **7** $y = x - 3$

Finished Early?
➡ Go to page 454

③ Rotations

Remember?

In a rotation all points of the object are rotated through the same angle about the same **centre of rotation**.

To describe a rotation we need an **angle** of rotation, a **direction** of rotation (clockwise or anticlockwise) and the centre of rotation.

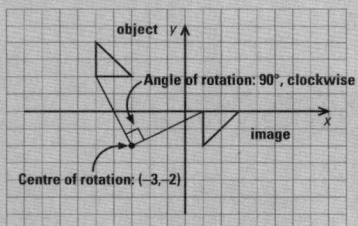

Once again, the sizes of corresponding sides and angles in the object and image are the same. So the object and image are congruent and rotations are also congruency transformations.

Practice

H Copy the diagram and find the images after these transformations.

1 180°, centre origin

2 90° clockwise, centre origin

3 90° anticlockwise, centre (2, 1)

4 180°, centre (5, −3)

5 270° anticlockwise, centre (1, −3)

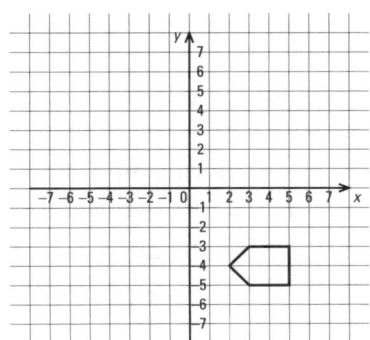

I For each image find the angle and centre of rotation.

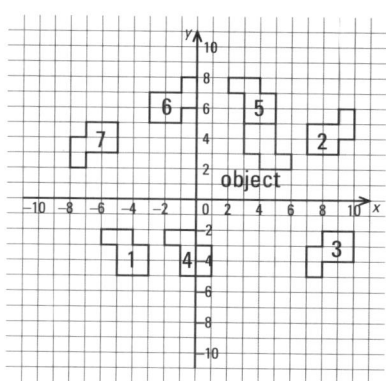

J On squared paper, draw coordinate axes, labelling the *x*- and *y*-axes from −8 to 8. Plot and join the following points, in order:
(−3, −1) → (−2, −2) → (−1, −2) → (−3, −4) → (−5, −2) → (−4, −2) → (−3, −1)
Find the image after these rotations.

1 180°, (0, −4)

2 90° anticlockwise, (0, −4)

3 90° clockwise, (−5, −2)

4 270° clockwise, (−5, 1)

5 90° clockwise, (5, −3)

6 180°, (−3, −3)

❹ Enlargements

Remember?

An **enlargement** is a transformation which changes the size but not the shape of the object. Enlargements are described by their **scale factor** and **centre of enlargement**.
Each side of the shape is multiplied by the scale factor. When the scale factor is larger than one, the image is bigger than the object. When it is equal to one, the image is the same size as the object.

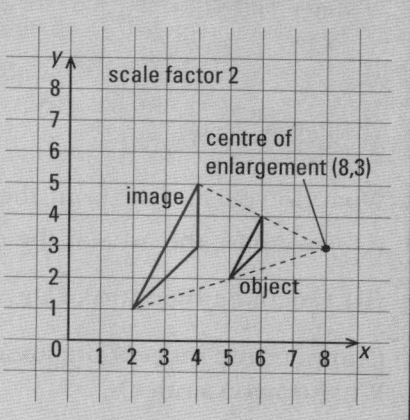

The centre of enlargement can be found by using rays.

Learn About It

Enlargements are not restricted to scale factors greater than one. The scale factor of an enlargement can be less than one or negative. If the scale factor is between zero and one, then the image is smaller than the object, and on the same side of the centre of enlargement.

If the scale factor is negative, then the image is inverted (upside-down) and on the other side of the centre of enlargement.

Practice

K The diagram shows the object R and two images R_1 and R_2 after two enlargements.

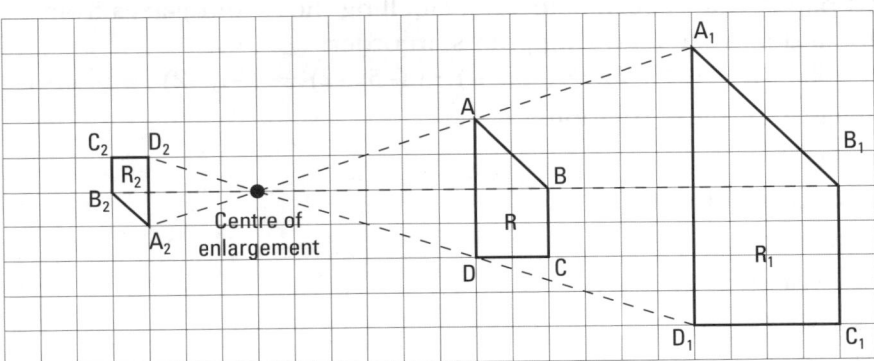

1 Using the diagram above copy and complete the table.

R	AD =	BC =	CD =
R_1	$A_1D_1 =$	$B_1C_1 =$	$C_1D_1 =$
Ratio of sides (R_1)	$\dfrac{A_1D_1}{AD} =$	$\dfrac{B_1C_1}{BC} =$	$\dfrac{C_1D_1}{CD} =$
R_2	$A_2D_2 =$	$B_2C_2 =$	$C_2D_2 =$
Ratio of sides (R_2)	$\dfrac{A_2D_2}{AD} =$	$\dfrac{B_2C_2}{BC} =$	$\dfrac{C_2D_2}{CD} =$

2 What do you notice about the ratios of the sides for each image?

3 **(i)** Calculate the area of the object R and its images R_1 and R_2.

(ii) Calculate the ratio of the areas: $\dfrac{\text{area of } R_1}{\text{area of } R}$ and $\dfrac{\text{area of } R_2}{\text{area of } R}$.

Compare the ratio of the areas with the ratio of the sides for each image. What do you notice?

Learn More About It

Remember that the scale factor of an enlargement is the factor by which a length is multiplied to get the corresponding length in the image. The ratio of the sides of R_1 to R is 2. So the enlargement R to R_1 has scale factor 2.

The enlargement R to R_2 inverts the image, so the scale factor is negative. The ratio of the sides is $\frac{1}{2}$ so the scale factor is $-\frac{1}{2}$.

Key Facts

scale factor > 1: image larger than object

scale factor = 1: image same size as object

0 < scale factor < 1: image smaller than object

−1 < scale factor < 0: image smaller than object and inverted

scale factor = −1: image same size as object and inverted

scale factor < −1: image larger than object and inverted

Try It Out

 Draw a simple object on graph paper.

1 (a) Enlarge the object by a scale factor of 1 centre O.
   (b) Compare the object with the image. What do you notice?

2 (a) Enlarge your object by a scale factor of −1 centre O.
   (b) Can you find another transformation that does the same thing?

Practice

For each question, draw axes labelled from −10 to 10. Copy the object and draw the image.

1

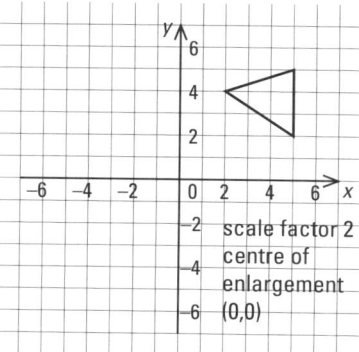

scale factor 2
centre of
enlargement
(0,0)

2

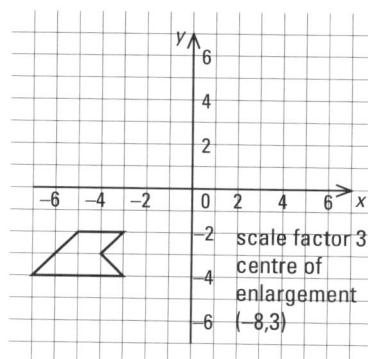

scale factor 3
centre of
enlargement
(−8,3)

3

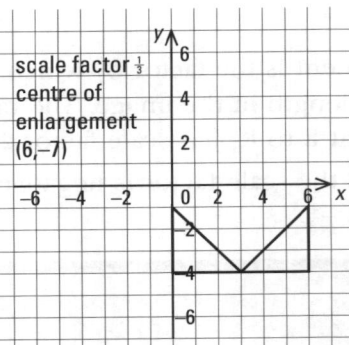

scale factor ⅓
centre of
enlargement
(6,−7)

4

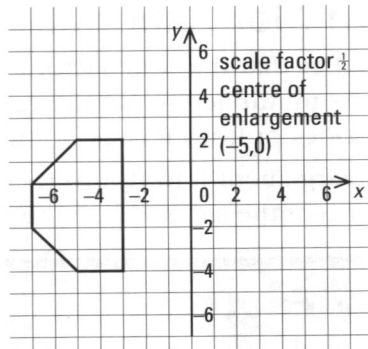

scale factor ½
centre of
enlargement
(−5,0)

5

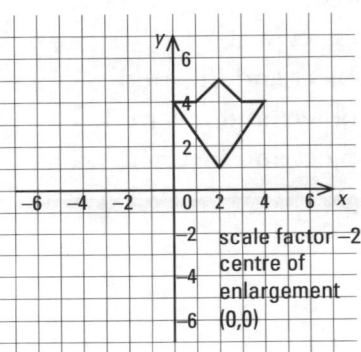

scale factor −2
centre of
enlargement
(0,0)

6

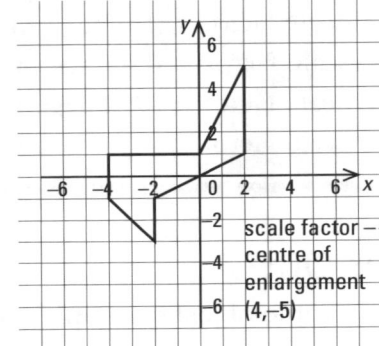

scale factor −½
centre of
enlargement
(4,−5)

N Identify the enlargement that transforms the object to the image.

1

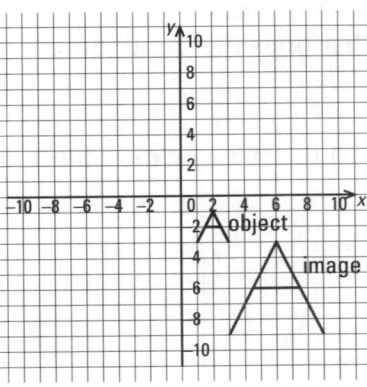

2

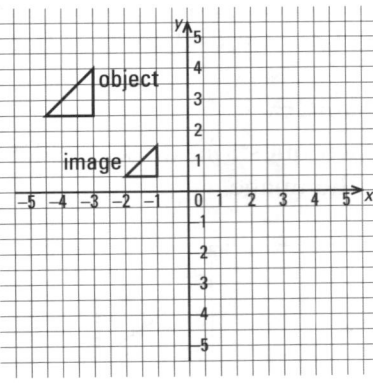

3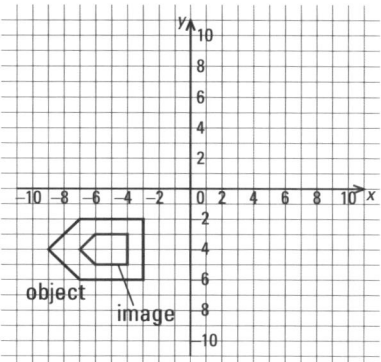

4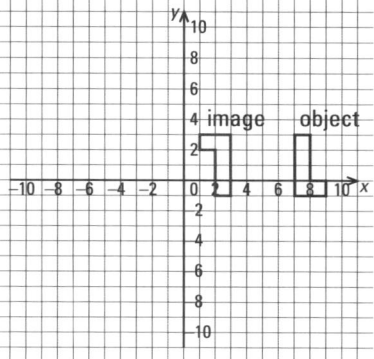

5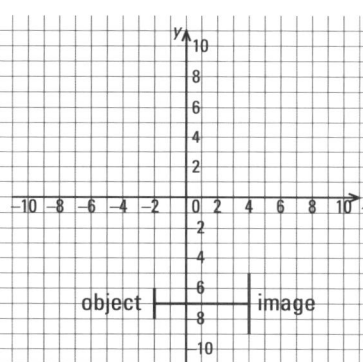

6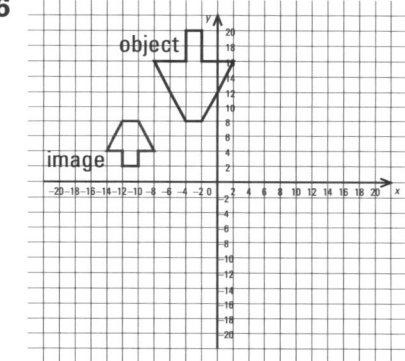

◎ **1** A triangle ABC has corners A (−1, 1), B (3, 1), C (3, −2). After an enlargement the image is A'B'C' and the points A and B have moved to A'(−3, 3) and B'(9, 3).

(a) Write down the scale factor of the enlargement.

(b) Calculate the area of A'B'C'.

(c) Find C'.

(d) Describe the transformation.

2 The rectangle PQRS has corners P (1, 3), Q (5, 3) and R (5, 1). After an enlargement the image has corners at P'(−2, 1½), Q'(−4, 1½) and R'(−4, 2½).

(a) Calculate the scale factor.

(b) Find the coordinates of S'.

(c) Describe the transformation.

Finished Early?

 Go to page 455

5 Distinguishing Between Transformations

In the previous sections we have revised translations, reflections, rotations and enlargements. The following exercise will give you practice at distinguishing between these transformations.

This table should help identify which transformation is which.

If the image:	then the transformation is:
is a different size to the object	an enlargement
has been 'flipped over'	a reflection
has a different orientation to the object	a rotation
is the same size and orientation as the object	a translation

Sometimes different transformations can result in the same image.

Practice

P For each diagram identify the transformation that moves the object to each of the images.

1

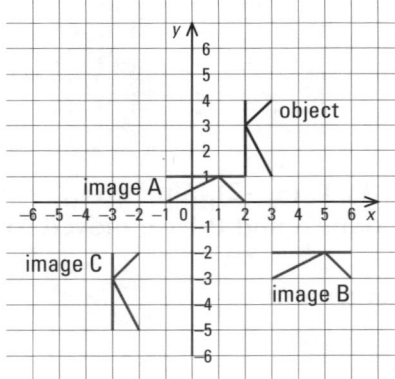

2

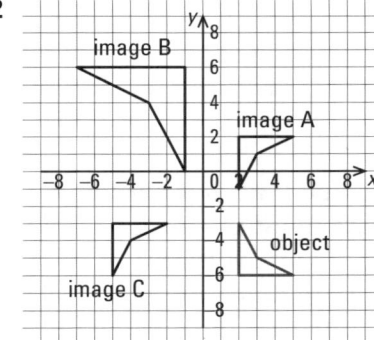

3

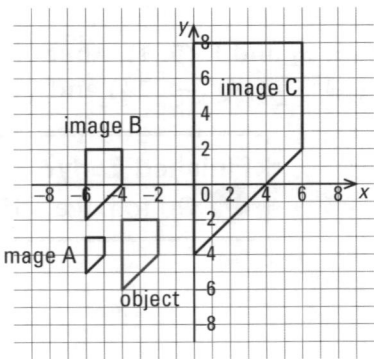

4 Each of these images can be made using two different transformations. Try to find both.

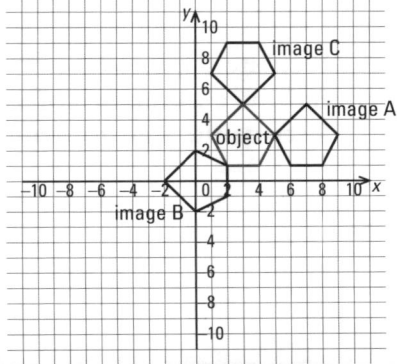

Q In the following questions, the image can be obtained from the object using more than one transformation. Identify them all.

1 Two transformations

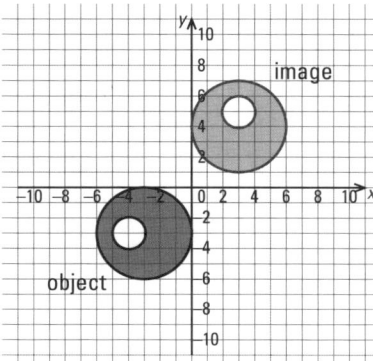

2 Four transformations

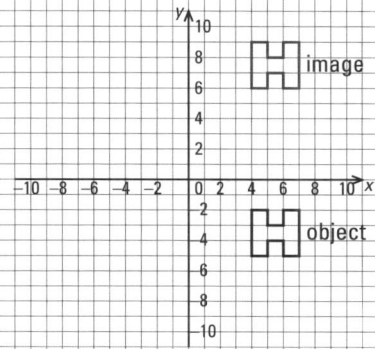

Practice

R Use the diagram to copy and complete the table.

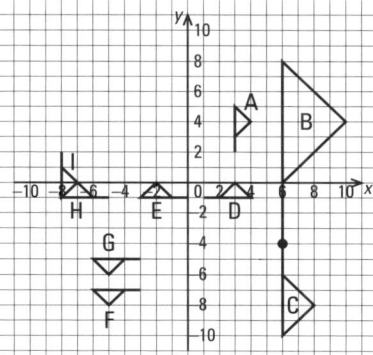

Object	Transformation	Image
A		B
A	rotation 90° clockwise centre (3, −1)	
H		G
A		J
J	translation through $\begin{pmatrix} -8 \\ 3 \end{pmatrix}$	
B		A
F	rotation 180° centre (−2, −4)	
H		I
I		H
B	enlargement centre (6, −4) s.f. $-\dfrac{1}{2}$	
G		I
D		J

14 Circle Geometry

In this chapter you will learn about ...
1. arcs, sectors and segments
2. angle properties of circles
3. cyclic quadrilaterals
4. tangents
5. proofs

1 Arcs, Sectors and Segments

Remember?

A circle of radius r has circumference $2\pi r$ and area πr^2.

π is 3.142 to three decimal places (or you can use your calculator key).

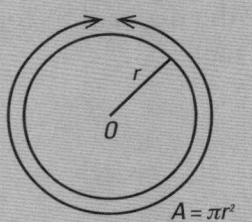

$A = \pi r^2$

Try It Out

A 1 Find the circumference and area of the circles with these radii.

    (a) 3 cm   **(b)** 52 mm   **(c)** $\frac{1}{2}$ m   **(d)** 8.2 m

2 Find the radii of these circles to two decimal places.

    (a) Circumference 35 cm   **(b)** Circumference 17 m
    (c) Area 154 m^2 **(d)** Area 66 000 mm^2

3 Two circles have the same centre.
One has radius 12 cm, the other radius 17 cm.
Calculate the area between the circles in terms of π.

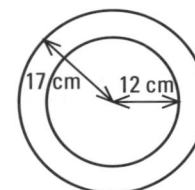

Find the areas of these shapes to the nearest cm².

(a)

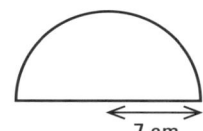

7 cm

(b)

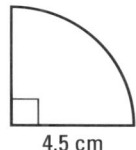

4.5 cm

(c)

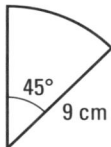

45°

9 cm

(d)

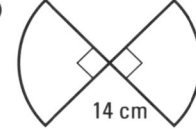

14 cm

(e)

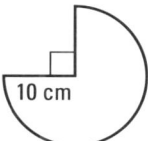

10 cm

Learn About It

An **arc** of a circle is part of the circumference of the circle.

A **sector** of a circle is a region bounded by two radii and an arc of the circle. It looks a bit like a slice of cake.

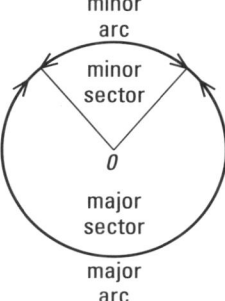

minor arc

minor sector

O

major sector

major arc

The two radii that form a sector divide the circle into two parts: a **major sector** and a **minor sector**. The arcs associated with these sectors are called the **major arc** and **minor arc** respectively.

An arc is said to **subtend** the angle at the centre of the circle. For example, in the diagram the arc AB subtends the angle AOB.

When an arc subtends an angle of 90°, what is the length of the arc? An angle of 360° is subtended by the entire circumference of the circle. So an angle of 90° is subtended by an arc of length:

$\dfrac{90}{360}$ or $\dfrac{1}{4}$ × the circumference of the circle.

Similarly the length of an arc that subtends an angle of 45° is:

$\dfrac{45}{360}$ or $\dfrac{1}{8}$ × the circumference of the circle.

We already know that the circumference of a circle with radius r is $2\pi r$.

So the length of the arc subtending an angle $x°$ at the centre of a circle is given by:

$$l = \dfrac{x}{360} \times 2\pi r$$

Try It Out

 Calculate the lengths of the following arcs.

1 Radius 14 cm, subtends angle 45°.

2 Radius 5.3 cm, subtends angle 74.2°.

3 Radius 7.8 m, subtends angle 307°.

We can work out the area of a sector using a similar method to the way we found the length of an arc. In fact, you have already worked out the areas of some sectors in **B**.

A sector with angle 360° is the entire circle, so it has area πr^2. A sector with angle 90° has area:

$$\frac{90}{360} \text{ or } \frac{1}{4} \times \text{area of the circle.}$$

So the area of a sector with angle x is given by:

$$A = \frac{x}{360} \times \pi r^2$$

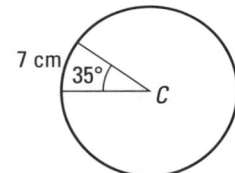

Example	An arc of a circle subtends an angle of 35°. The arc has length 7 cm.

An arc of a circle subtends an angle of 35°. The arc has length 7 cm.

(a) Find the radius of the circle to the nearest mm.

(b) Calculate the area of the sector to two decimal places.

Working Make a sketch of the problem.

(a) The length of an arc is given by

$$l = \frac{x}{360} \times 2\pi r$$

Rearranging gives

$$360l = x \times 2\pi r$$

$$r = \frac{360l}{2\pi x}$$

So the radius is given by

$$r = \frac{360 \times 7}{2\pi \times 35}$$

$$= 11.459... \text{ cm}$$

To the nearest mm the radius is 11.5 cm.

(b) The area of the sector is given by

$$A = \frac{x}{360} \times \pi r^2$$

$$= \frac{35}{360} \times \pi \times 11.459...^2$$

$$= 40.107... \text{ cm}^2$$

So to two decimal places the area of the sector is 40.11 cm².

Answer (a) 11.5 cm   (b) 40.11 cm²

Try It Out

D Calculate the areas of the following sectors.

1 Radius 3.3 cm, angle 56°.

2 Radius 78.6 mm, angle 175°.

3 Radius 14.9 cm, angle 207°.

Practice

E 1 (a) To two decimal places, what is the length of an arc of a circle of radius 8 cm that subtends an angle of 202°?

(b) Calculate the length of the minor arc to two decimal places.

2 A circle has radius 12 cm. A sector of the circle has angle 60°. Giving your answer in terms of π, find:

(a) the area of the minor sector

(b) the area of the major sector.

3 The length of an arc of a circle of radius 4 cm is 1.6πcm.

(a) Calculate the angle subtended by the arc.

(b) Find the area of the sector to three significant figures.

F 1 A workman is winding cable around a drum.
He turns the handle on the drum to wind up the cable.
The drum is 1.2 m in diameter, and there is 47 m of cable.

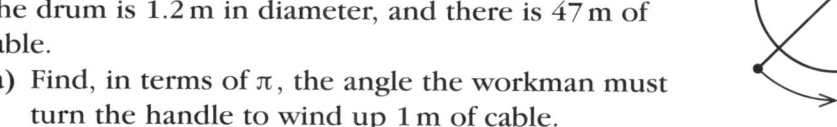

(a) Find, in terms of π, the angle the workman must turn the handle to wind up 1 m of cable.

(b) To the nearest centimetre, how much cable is wound up if the workman rotates the handle through one revolution?

(c) To the nearest quarter turn, how many turns of the handle are needed to wind-up all the cable.

2 Brian has a cake for his birthday. The cake is cylindrical with radius 12 cm, and is 7 cm deep. Brian cuts the cake into eight equal slices. What is the volume of each slice of cake, in terms of π?

(Assume Brian cuts the cake into sectors.)

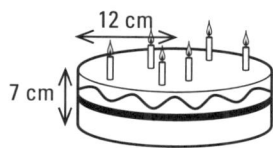

3 The diagram shows an athletics track. The total length of the track is 400 m, measured around the inside of the track. The two straights are exactly 100 m long. The bends are arcs of circles of radius r.

The track is 10 m wide.

(a) Find r in terms of π.

(b) Two runners compete in a 400 m race. One runner runs around the inside of the of the track, and one runs around the outside. To the nearest cm, what head-start should the runner on the outside get?

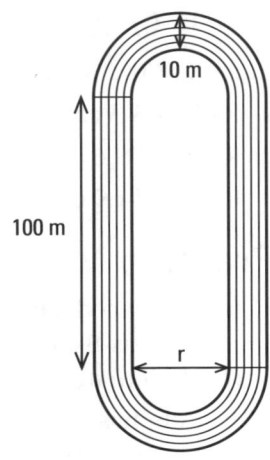

Learn More About It

A **chord** of a circle is a straight line joining any two points on the circumference.

A diameter is an example of a chord.

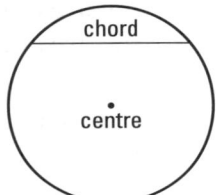

> ## Key Fact
> The line joining the centre of a circle to the mid-point of a chord is perpendicular to the chord.

Another way of thinking of this, is to say that the perpendicular bisector of a chord passes through the centre of the circle.

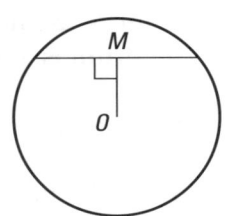

A chord divides a circle into two parts called a **major segment** and a **minor segment**.

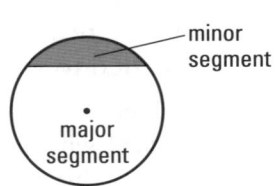

The area of the minor segment AOB can be found from the areas of the sector AOB and the triangle:

 area of segment AOB =
 area of sector AOB − area of triangle AOB

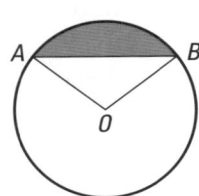

Example AOB is a sector of a circle with radius 12 cm.
The angle AOB is 68°.
Find the area of the segment AOB.

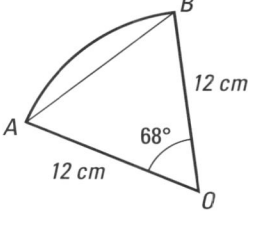

Working The area of the sector is

$$A_s = \frac{x}{360} \times \pi r^2$$

$$= \frac{68}{360} \times \pi \times 12^2$$

$$= 85.45\ldots \text{ cm}^2$$

The area of a triangle is $\frac{1}{2}bh$.

We know that the line joining the centre of the circle to the
mid-point of a chord is perpendicular to the chord.
So we can divide the triangle into
two identical right-angled triangles.

Using trigonometry:
    $h = 12 \cos 34°$ and $b = 2 \times 12 \sin 34°$
The area of the triangle is
    $\frac{1}{2} \times 24 \sin 34° \times 12 \cos 34° = 66.75\ldots \text{ cm}^2$.
So the area of the segment is
area of sector – area of triangle
$$= 85.45\ldots - 66.75\ldots$$
$$= 18.69 \text{ cm}^2 \text{ to two decimal places}$$

Answer The area of the segment is 18.69 cm² to two decimal places.

Try It Out

G Find the areas of the shaded segments.

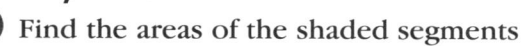

1

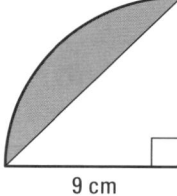

9 cm

2

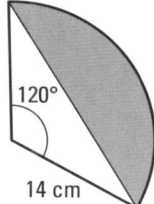

120°

14 cm

3

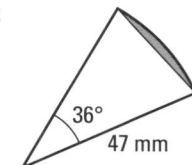

36°

47 mm

4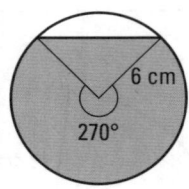

5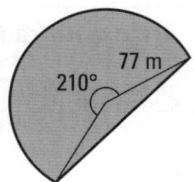

Practice

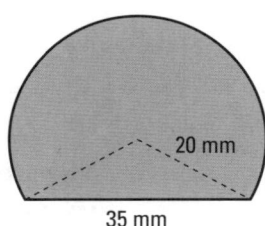

H **1** The diagram shows a cross-section of a chocolate bar. The top is formed from an arc of a circle. Calculate the area of the cross-section.

2 A doorway is formed by a rectangle with an arc of a circle at the top. Calculate the area of the doorway.

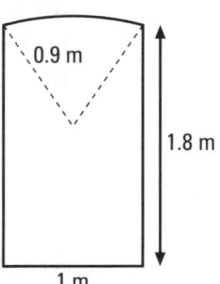

Further Practice

I Find the areas of the shaded parts of the following shapes to two decimal places.

1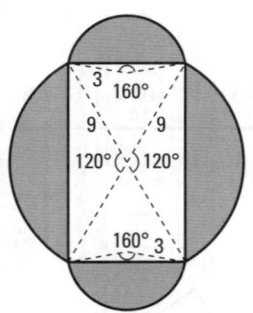

2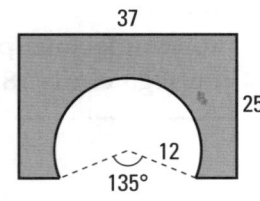

Finished Early?
➡ Go to page 455

❷ Angle Properties of Circles

🖩 If there is access to computer facilities, then your teacher may use the
computer to demonstrate some constructions using the *Angles in circles*
lesson from the CD-ROM.

📐 Compasses, ruler, protractor

Practice

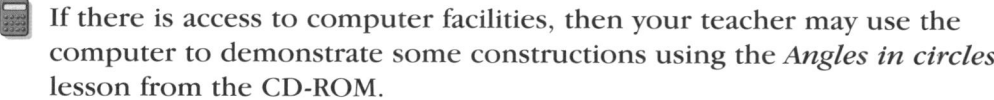

Ⓙ **1** With a pair of compasses, draw a large circle
and mark its centre O.

2 Choose two points A and B on the circumference
of the circle and draw the radii from the points
to the centre.

3 Choose another point on the circumference, C,
and draw straight lines joining it to A and B.

4 Using a protractor, measure the angles AOB and ACB.

Can you see relationship between the two angles?

You should have found that angle AOB is twice the size of angle ACB no
matter which points A, B and C you chose.

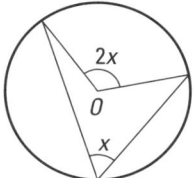 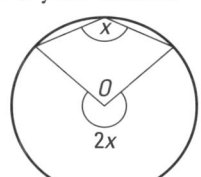 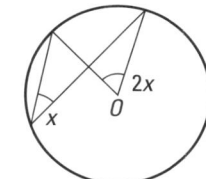

This leads us to the
first theorem of angles
in a circle.

When the centre of the
circle and two of the
chosen points on the
circumference form
a straight line, the
points lie on a

> ## Key Fact
>
> The angle which an arc of a circle subtends at
> the centre of a circle is twice the angle it
> subtends at any point on the remaining part
> of the circumference.
>
> We often shorten this to: the angle at the
> centre is twice the angle at the circumference.

diameter of the circle. Therefore, the angle at the centre is
180° and so the angle at the circumference is 90°. This
leads to a second theorem of angles in a circle.

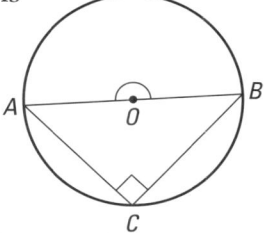

> ## Key Fact
>
> The angle in a semi-circle is a right-angle.

Try It Out

K Find the sizes of the angles marked by letters.

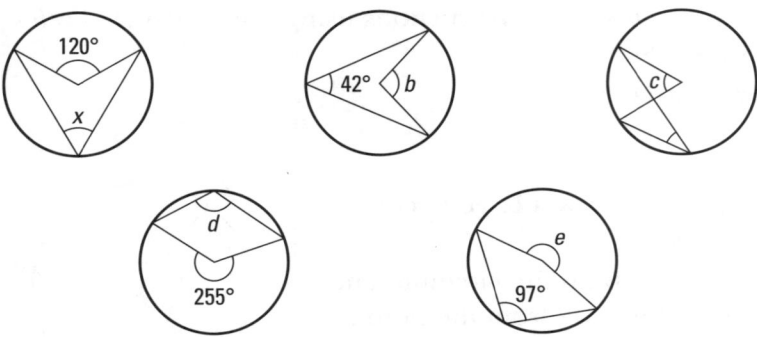

Practice

L Find the sizes of the angles marked by letters.

1

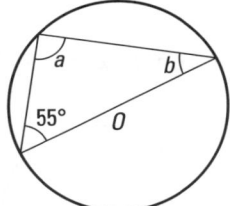

2

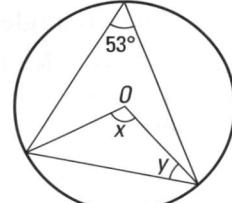

3

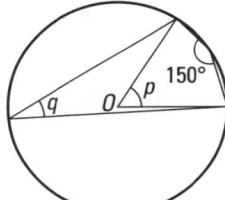

4

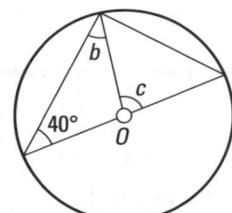

5

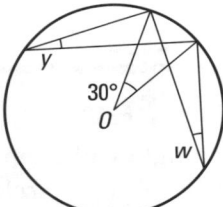

6

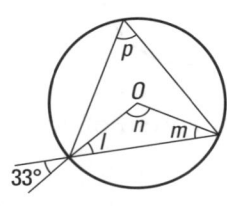

Learn About It

Suppose that angles a, b and c are all subtended by the same arc and are in the same segment.

Then using the theorem from the previous part, a, b and c must all be half the size of angle AOB.
So a, b and c must be the same.

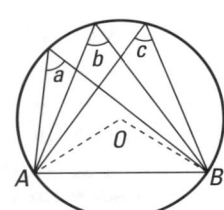

Key Fact

Angles in the same segment of a circle and subtended by the same arc are equal. We can usually shorten this to: angles in the same segment are equal.

Try It Out

 Find the sizes of the angles marked by letters.

1
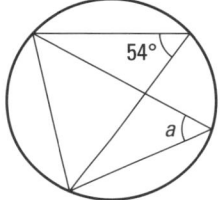
54°
a

2
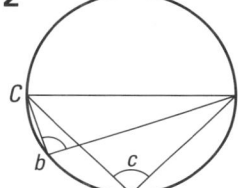
C
b
c

3
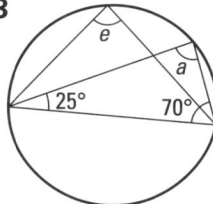
e
25°
a
70°

Practice

 In these questions, O is the centre of the circle. Find the sizes of the angles marked by letters.

1
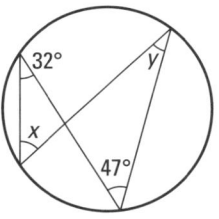
32°
y
x
47°

2
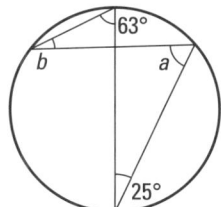
63°
b
a
25°

3
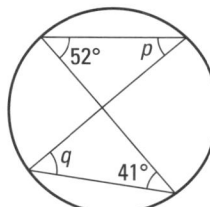
52°
p
q
41°

4
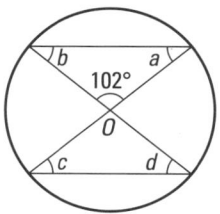
b
a
102°
O
c
d

5
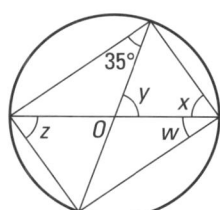
35°
y
x
z
O
w

6
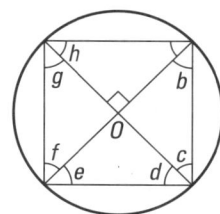
h
g
b
f
O
e
d
c

Further Practice

◉ Find the sizes of the angles marked by letters.

1

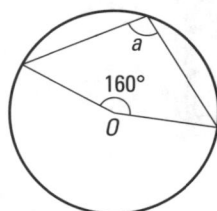

2

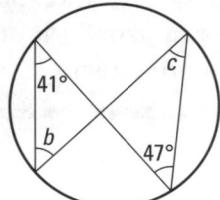

3

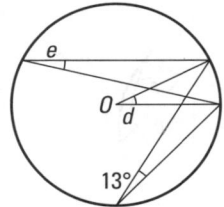

4

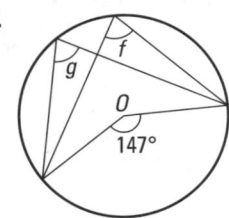

❸ Cyclic Quadrilaterals

Learn About It

A **cyclic quadrilateral** is a quadrilateral with all four vertices lying on the circumference of a circle.

Opposite angles of a cyclic quadrilateral are supplementary.

So in the diagram:
   angle DAB + angle BCD = 180°
   angle ABC + angle ADC = 180°

> **Key Fact**
>
> Opposite angles of a cyclic quadrilateral are supplementary.

Also, the exterior angle of a cyclic quadrilateral is equal to the interior opposite angle.

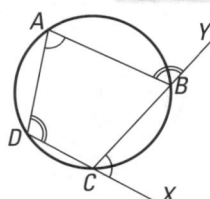

So in the diagram:
   angle BCX = angle BAD
   angle ABY = angle ADC

> **Key Fact**
>
> The exterior angle of a cyclic quadrilateral is equal to the interior opposite angle.

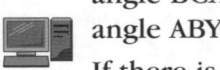

If there is access to computer facilities, then your teacher may use the computer to demonstrate some constructions using the *Angles in circles* lesson from the CD-ROM.

Try It Out

P Find the sizes of the angles marked by letters.

1
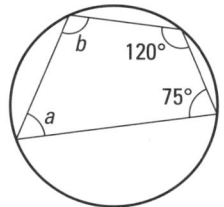

2
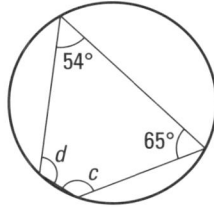

3
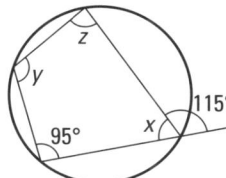

4
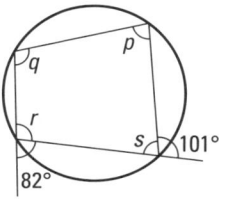

5
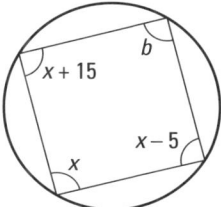

Practice

Q Find the sizes of the angles marked by letters.

1
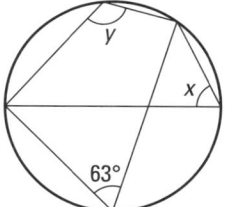

2
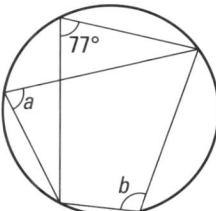

3
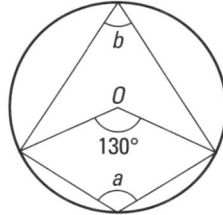

4
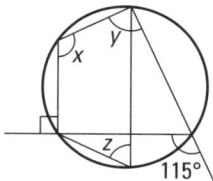

5
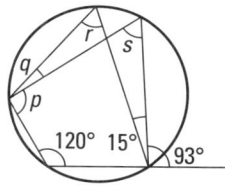

Further Practice

R Find the sizes of angles *a* to *h*.

1

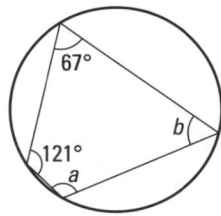

2

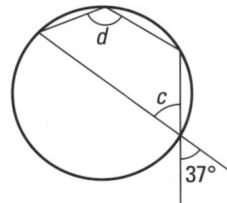

3

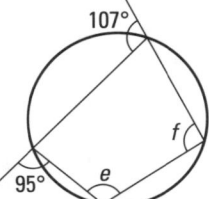

4

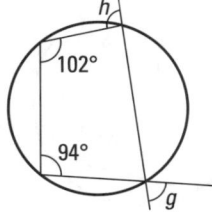

Finished Early?
➡ Go to page 455

4 Tangents

Learn About It

Normally a line that comes into contact
with a circle touches it at two places.

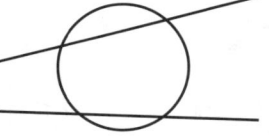

A **tangent** to a circle is a line that just
touches the circle at one point.

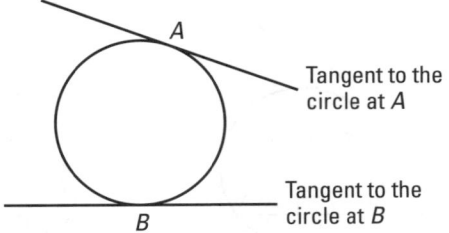

Tangent to the
circle at *A*

Tangent to the
circle at *B*

Key Fact

A tangent to a circle is perpendicular to the
radius of that circle at the point of contact.

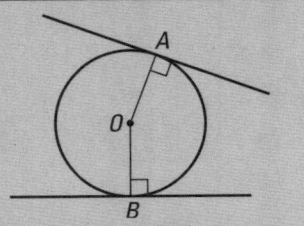

So the line perpendicular to the tangent passing through the point of contact also passes through the centre.

If we choose any point outside of the circle, then there are always two tangents to the circle that pass through the point.

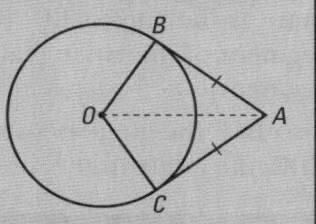

Key Fact

The lengths of two tangents from an external point to the points of contact on the circle are equal.

Also BÔA = CÔA and BÂO = CÂO (the line OA bisects angles BAC and BOC).

We can summarise these points in one diagram:

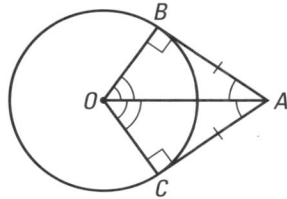

Try It Out

S Find the value of *x* in each diagram.

1

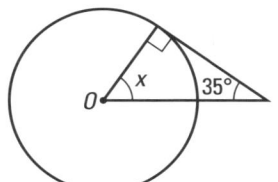

2

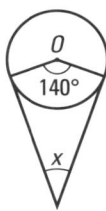

3

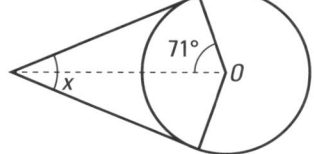

4

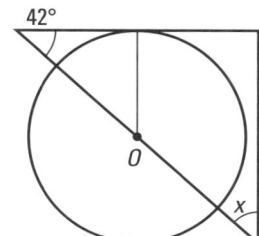

Learn More About It

Suppose we have a circle with a tangent AB that
touches the circle at C. We can add a chord, CD,
that also touches the circle at C. Then the angle
between the tangent and the chord, $A\hat{C}D$, is the
same as the angle $C\hat{E}D$, which is in the other
segment of the circle (called the alternate
segment).

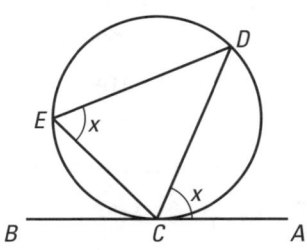

Also $B\hat{C}E$ the angle between the tangent and the chord CE, is the same as
$C\hat{D}E$, the angle in the alternate segment.

Key Fact

The **alternate segment theorem**:
The angle between a tangent to a circle and a
chord through the point of contact is equal to
the angle in the alternate segment.

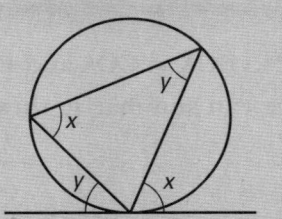

Try It Out

T Find the sizes of the angles marked by letters.

1

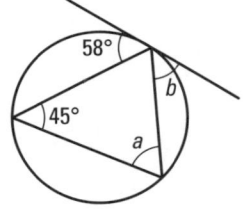

2

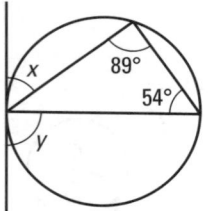

3

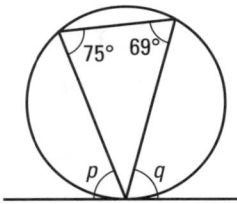

Practice

U Find the sizes of the angles marked by letters.

1

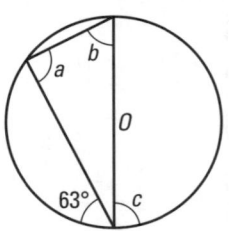

2

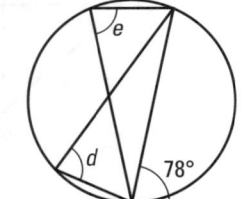

3

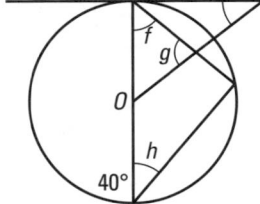

4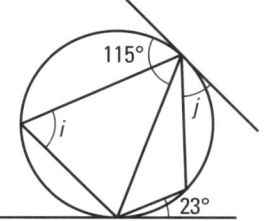

5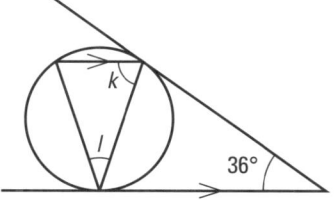

Further Practice

 Find the sizes of angles *a – e*.

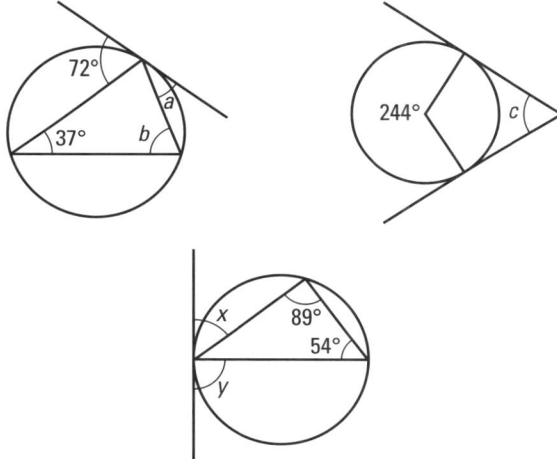

Finished Early?

 Go to page 456

5 Proofs

Learn About It

In this section, we will use the theorems we have already learnt to prove some new theorems.

To prove a theorem we start off with the facts we know, and use a sequence of logical statements to prove the theory.

Example Prove that the angle that an arc of a circle subtends at the centre of a circle is twice the angle it subtends at any point on the remaining part of the circumference.

Proof Let A, B and C be three points on the circumference of a circle centre O.

We want to show that $B\hat{O}C = 2B\hat{A}C$.

Let D be a point on AO (extended beyond O).

Let $O\hat{A}B = x$ and $O\hat{A}C = y$.

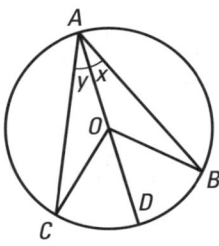

Then AOB and AOC are isosceles triangles with $O\hat{A}B = x$ and $O\hat{A}C = y$.

So $A\hat{O}B = 180° - 2x$ and $A\hat{O}C = 180° - 2y$.

Now $B\hat{O}D = 180° - A\hat{O}B$
$= 180° - (180° - 2x)$
$= 2x$

Similarly $C\hat{O}D = 2y$

So $B\hat{O}C = 2x + 2y = 2(x + y) = 2B\hat{A}C$ as required.

Practice

 1 A is a point outside a circle with centre O. The tangents from A touch the circle at B and C. Prove that the triangles ABO and ACO are congruent.

2 Show that $y = 90° - \frac{1}{2}x$.

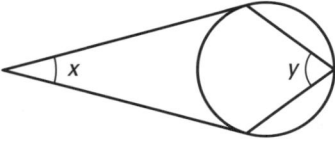

3 AC is a diameter of a circle and B is another point on the circumference. D is a point on AC such that BD is perpendicular to AC. Show that the triangles ABD, BCD and ABC are similar.

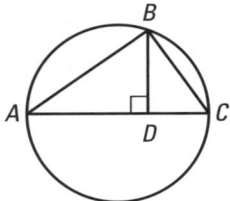

4 The lines AB, BC, CD and DA are tangents to the circle. Show that $AB + CD = AD + BC$.

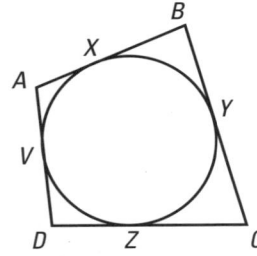

Finished Early?
➡ Go to page 456

Unit 6 *Geometry and Trigonometry 1*

Summary of Chapters 12, 13 and 14

Geometry and Trigonometry 1

- The **hypotenuse** is the longest side in a right-angled triangle.

- **Pythagoras' theorem** states that in a right-angled triangle $c^2 = a^2 + b^2$.

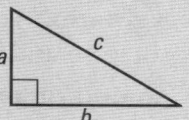

- $\sin A = \dfrac{\text{opp}}{\text{hyp}} \quad \cos A = \dfrac{\text{adj}}{\text{hyp}} \quad \tan A = \dfrac{\text{opp}}{\text{adj}}$

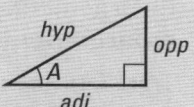

- We can use special triangles to find certain trigonometric ratios:

Angle	Sine	Cosine	Tangent
0°	0	1	0
30°	$\dfrac{1}{2}$	$\dfrac{\sqrt{3}}{2}$	$\dfrac{1}{\sqrt{3}}$
45°	$\dfrac{1}{\sqrt{2}}$	$\dfrac{1}{\sqrt{2}}$	1
60°	$\dfrac{\sqrt{3}}{2}$	$\dfrac{1}{2}$	$\sqrt{3}$
90°	1	0	Undefined

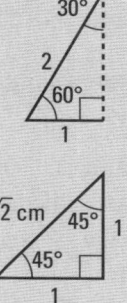

- The **angle of elevation** is the angle between the horizontal and a line of sight above the horizontal.

- The **angle of depression** is the angle between the horizontal and a line of sight below the horizontal.

- The **bearing** from a particular point is the angle measured clockwise from north. It is always written as a three-digit number.

- Some useful trigonometric identities are:

$$\tan \theta = \frac{\sin \theta}{\cos \theta}$$

$$\sin^2 \theta + \cos^2 \theta = 1$$

Transformation Geometry

- A **transformation** can change a shape and alter its position. The shape before the transformation is called the **object**. The shape after the transformation is called the **image**.

- **Translations** slide a shape from its original position to its new position. A translation will change the position of a shape, but not its size or shape.

- Translations are described using column vectors.

- **Reflections** are described using a mirror line.

- A **rotation** is described by giving a centre of rotation, direction of rotation and angle of rotation.

- An **enlargement** is a transformation which changes the size but not the shape of the object.

- Enlargements are described by their **scale factor** and **centre of enlargement**.

- Translations, reflections and rotations are **congruency transformations**. The image has the same side lengths and angles as the object.

- Enlargements are **similarity transformations**. The angles of the image are the same as the object.

- Given the object and its image after a transformation it is possible to identify the transformation by considering its effect on the object.

If the image:	then the transformation is:
is a different size to the object	an enlargement
has been 'flipped over'	a reflection
has a different orientation to the object	a rotation
is the same size and orientation as the object	a translation

Circle Geometry

- An **arc** of a circle is part of the circumference of the circle.

- A **sector** of a circle is a region bounded by two radii and an arc of the circle.

- The two radii that form a sector divide the circle into two parts: a **major sector** and a **minor sector**. The arcs associated with these sectors are called the **major arc** and **minor arc** respectively.

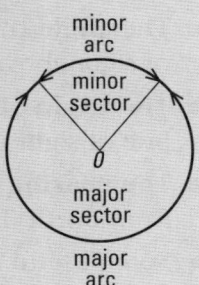

- The length of the arc of a circle, radius r, subtending an angle $x°$ is:

$$l = \frac{x}{360} \times 2\pi r$$

- The area of a sector of a circle, radius r, with angle $x°$ is given by

$$A = \frac{x}{360} \times \pi r^2$$

- A **chord** of a circle is a straight line joining any two points on the circumference.

- The line joining the centre of a circle to the mid-point of a chord is perpendicular to the chord.

- A chord divides a circle into two parts called a **major segment** and a **minor segment.**

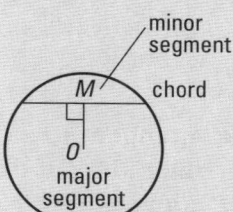

- The area of the minor segment AOB can be found by subtracting the area of the sector AOB from the area of the triangle AOB.

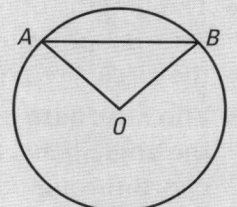

- The angle which an arc of a circle subtends at the centre of a circle is twice the angle it subtends at any point on the remaining part of the circumference.

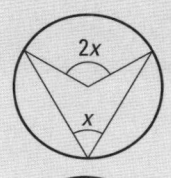

- The angle in a semi-circle is a right-angle.

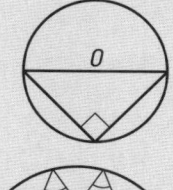

- Angles in the same segment of a circle and subtended by the same arc are equal.

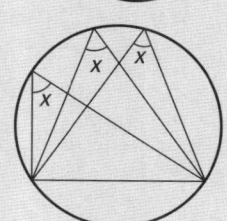

- Opposite angles of a cyclic quadrilateral are supplementary.
- The exterior angle of a cyclic quadrilateral is equal to the interior opposite angle.

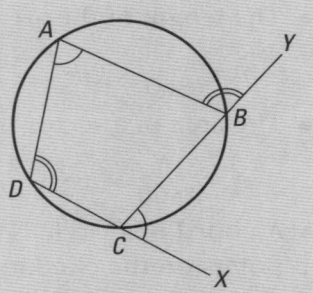

- A tangent to a circle is perpendicular to the radius of that circle at the point of contact.
- The lengths of two tangents from an external point to the points of contact on the circle are equal.

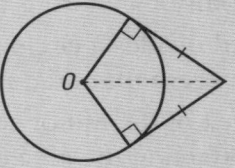

- The **alternate segment theorem** states that: the angle between a tangent to a circle and a chord through the point of contact is equal to the angle in the alternate segment.

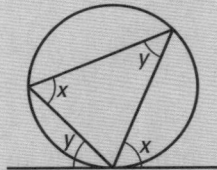

15 Straight-line Graphs

In this chapter you will learn about ...
1. gradient of a straight line
2. equation of a straight line
3. mid-point of a line
4. length of a line

1 Gradient of a Straight Line

Learn About It

On graph paper, draw axes for x-values from -4 to $+4$, and for y-values from -10 to $+10$.

For the set of ordered pairs, $\{(1,3), (2,6), (3,9), ...\}$, plot the points C $(1,3)$, B $(2,6)$, and A $(3,9)$, as in the diagram on the right.

Join the points, A, B and C. What do you notice?

ABC is a straight line.

On the same axes, plot the points D $(-1, -3)$ and F $(-3, -9)$ and join D and F.

What do you notice about the lines, ABC and DF?

ABC and DF form one straight line that passes through $(0, 0)$, the origin.

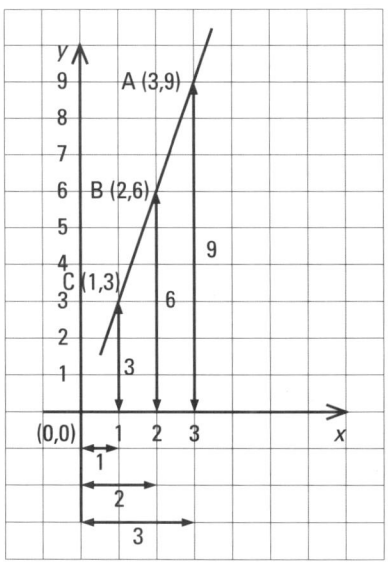

For each ordered pair, write the ratio of the y-value to the x-value so that we get

$$3 : 1 = 6 : 2 = 9 : 3.$$

All the ratios are equal to $3 : 1$.

Thus, for any point (x, y) on this straight line passing through the origin,

$$y : x = 3 : 1; \text{ that is, } \frac{y}{x} = 3.$$

Hence, if the ratio between the corresponding members of a set of ordered pairs is a constant, say m, then the graph of the function is a straight line passing through the origin $(0, 0)$, and m is called the **gradient** of the line.

From the diagram on the right,
the gradient of the

line AC = $\dfrac{FA}{CF}$ = $\dfrac{\text{increase in } y}{\text{increase in } x}$

$\qquad = \dfrac{2}{6} = \dfrac{1}{3}$

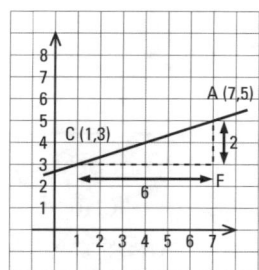

We can also calculate the gradient of the
straight line ABCDF by using the coordinates
of any two points on the line.

For the points A (3, 9) and B (2, 6), we find that

$\dfrac{9 - 6}{3 - 2} = \dfrac{3}{1} = 3$

If the points are F (−4, −12) and D (−1, −3),
we get

$\dfrac{-3 - (-12)}{-1 - (-4)} = \dfrac{9}{3} = 3$

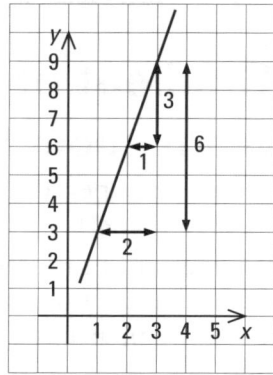

Therefore we see that for any two points M and N on the line,

$\dfrac{\text{difference of the } y\text{-coordinataes from N to M}}{\text{difference of the } x\text{-coordinates from N to M}}$ = gradient of the line

Note also that if θ is the positive angle between the
x-axis and the line, then

$\tan \theta = \dfrac{\text{difference of the } y\text{-coordinataes from O to P}}{\text{difference of the } x\text{-coordinates from O to P}}$

$\tan \theta$ = gradient of the line

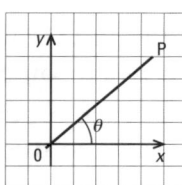

Key Fact

The gradient of a straight line is the
same at all points on the line.

Try It Out

A Find the gradient of the line joining each of the following pairs of points.

1 (3, 5) and (5, 9)   **2** (4, 2) and (7, 1)

3 (−3, 1) and (3, −2)   **4** (2, 3) and (−1, −1)

5 (2, 5) and (6, 5)   **6** (2, −1) and (2, 3)

We can express the gradient for any straight line in symbols.
For any two points (x_1, y_1) and (x_2, y_2) on a straight line, the gradient m is given by

$$m = \frac{y_2 - y_1}{x_2 - x_1}$$

Key Fact

The gradient of a line is the rate of change of y as x increases;

if y increases as x increases, the gradient is positive, and if y decreases as x increases, the gradient is negative.

Note also that

(i) if y increases as x increases, θ is an acute angle and $\tan \theta > 0$

(ii) if y decreases as x increases, θ is an obtuse angle and $\tan \theta < 0$.

(i)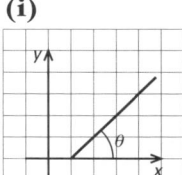

(ii)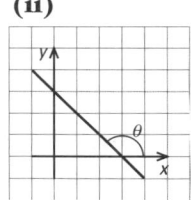

Practice

B Find the gradient of each of the lines joining the following pairs of points:

1 (8, 7) and (2, 5)   **2** (2, 5) and (4, −1)

3 (5, 3) and (1, −5)   **4** (6, 2) and (0, 4)

5 (4, 0) and (−3, 2)   **6** (0, 3) and (−3, 0)

C Write down the gradients of the lines represented by the sketches in the diagrams.

1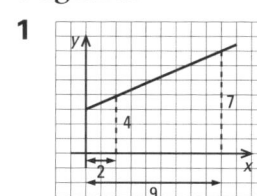

2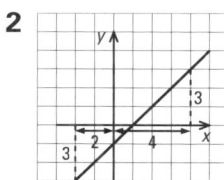

3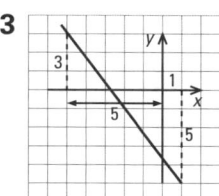

Finished Early?
➡ Go to page 456

Key Fact

The gradient of a line parallel to the *x*-axis is 0, since there is no change in *y* for any increase in *x*.

The gradient of a line parallel to the *y*-axis is undefined, since for any change in *y*, the increase in *x* is zero.

Note also that

(i) if the line is parallel to the *x*-axis, $\theta = 0°$ and $\tan \theta = 0$

(ii) if the line is parallel to the *y*-axis, $\theta = 90°$ and $\tan \theta$ is undefined.

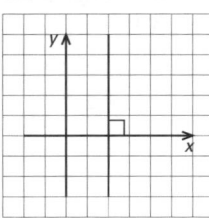

Further Practice

D Find the gradient of each of the lines joining the following pairs of points.

1 (2, –1) and (2, 1)

2 (3, 4) and (4, –2)

3 (0, 6) and (–2, –2)

4 (1, –2) and (0, 2)

5 (3, 3) and (–2, 3)

6 (4, –3) and (–2, –5)

E Write down the gradients of the lines represented by the sketches in the diagrams.

1

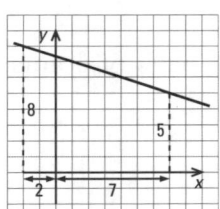

2

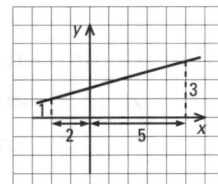

3

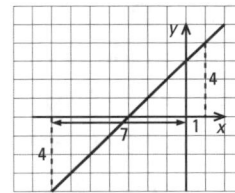

Finished Early?

 Go to page 456

Learn More About It

If a straight line passes through the origin, then $y = 0$ when $x = 0$.

If a straight line does *not* pass through the origin, then when $x = 0$, $y \neq 0$.

The *y*-coordinate of the point where the line intersects or cuts the *y*-axis is called the **intercept** on the *y*-axis, for example, if the point of intersection is at (0, 1), then the intercept is equal to 1.

The gradient of the line *l* passing through
A (3, 5) and B (6, 8) is given by

$$m = \frac{8-5}{6-3} = 1$$

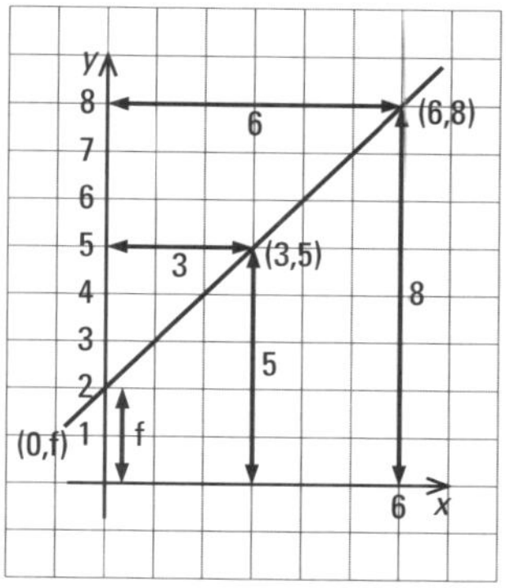

If the *y*-coordinate of F, the point of intersection
of the line *l* with the *y*-axis is *f*, then, using the
gradient of BF to find the value of *f*, we get

$$\frac{8-f}{6-0} = 1$$

then $8 - f = 6$

so that $f = 2$

Using A (3, 5) and F (0, *f*) for the gradient of *l*, we get

$$\frac{5-f}{3-0} = 1$$

and $5 - f = 3$

so that, again $f = 2$

Hence, the point of intersection of the line *l* on the *y*-axis is a fixed point,
(0, 2).

Try It Out

F (a) Show that the line passing through (1, 7) and (2, 10) has gradient equal
to 3.
(b) Find OP, the intercept on the *y*-axis of the line of gradient 3 that passes
through the point (1, 7).
(c) Show that the line of gradient 3 through (2, 10) intersects the *y*-axis at
the same point, P.

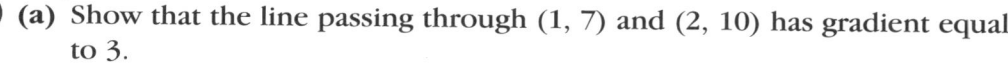

Word Check

intercept the *y*-coordinate of the point where
the line intersects the axis

intersection point where two or more lines
meet or cut one another

Learn More About It

Sketch, on the same axes, the graphs of the straight lines that have gradient 3 and pass through **(a)** (0, 0)   **(b)** (0, 1)   **(c)** (0, 3).

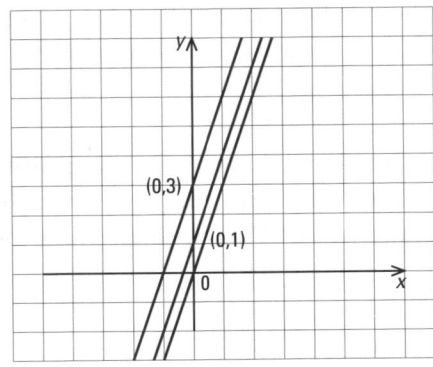

The graphs should look like the diagram on the right.

Since parallel lines can be defined as lines that are the same distance apart, the straight lines are all parallel.

Each parallel line passes through a constant point of intersection on the y-axis.

Try It Out

G **1** Sketch, on the same axes, the straight lines that pass through each of the following pairs of points.

    (a) (5, 3) and (1, –5)   **(b)** (2, 6) and (1, 4)   **(c)** (–2, –3) and (2, 5)

2 For each of the lines in question 1, find the point of intersection with the y-axis.

3 Calculate the gradient of the line joining each pair of points in question 1. What do you notice?

Key Fact

Lines that have the same gradient are parallel lines.

Learn More About It

Sketch the straight line passing through A (3,1) and B (6, 5) and the straight line through C (2, 8) and B (6, 5).

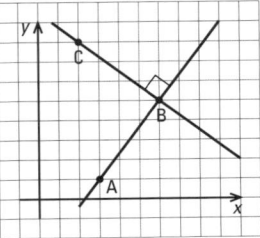

What do you notice about the angle between the lines?

The angle between the lines is 90°.

Find m_1 the gradient of AB and m_2 the gradient of CB.

Gradient of line AB $= m_1 = \frac{4}{3}$

Gradient of line CB $= m_2 = -\frac{3}{4}$

Then $m_1 m_2 = -\frac{4}{3} \times \frac{3}{4} = -1$

Try It Out

 **1** Sketch, on the same axes, each pair of straight lines passing through the following pairs of points.

(a) (5, 3) and (1, −5)   and   (0, 2) and (6, −1)
(b) (−1, −3) and (2, 6)   and   (4, 5) and (1, 6)

2 Calculate the gradient of the line joining each pair of points in question 1.

3 For each pair of lines in question 1, state the relation between the gradients of the two lines.

What do you notice about the angle between the two lines in each pair of lines?

Key Fact

When lines have equal gradients, the lines are parallel.
When the product of the gradients of two lines is −1, the lines are perpendicular.

Practice

Using the graph below, find for each line.

(i) the gradient by   (a) drawing   (b) calculation
(ii) the intercept on the *y*-axis.

Are there any parallel lines? perpendicular lines? Give a reason for your answer.

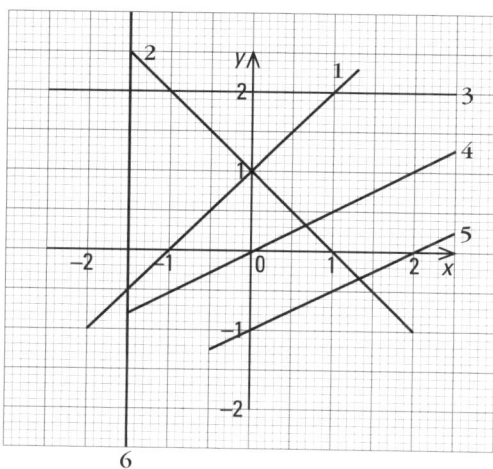

J **(a)** Draw x- and y-axes using a scale of 1 cm : 1 unit on each axis.
   (b) On the same axes, draw the line that passes through each of the following pairs of points.
   (c) For each line: **(i)** write the intercept on the y-axis
                         (ii) calculate the gradient.
   (d) What can you say about the lines?

   1 (–1, –1) and (3, 3)   **2** (3, 4) and (3, –1)   **3** (2, –1) and (4, 1)
   4 (1, 0) and (–2, 3)   **5** (–2, –4) and (4, –4)   **6** (0, 5) and (5, 0)

> ## Key Fact
>
> For any given straight line, the intercept on the y-axis is a constant value denoted by c.

Further Practice

K Using the graph below, find for each line:
   (i) the gradient by **(a)** drawing   **(b)** calculation
   (ii) the gradient on the y-axis.
   Are there any parallel lines? perpendicular lines? Give a reason for your answer.

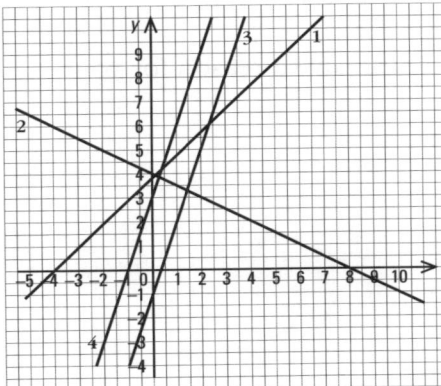

L **(a)** Draw x- and y-axes using a scale of 1 cm : 1 unit on each axis.
   (b) On the same axes draw the line that passes through each of the following pairs of points.
   (c) For each line   **(i)** write the intercept on the y-axis:
                           (ii) calculate the gradient.
   (d) What can you say about the lines?

1 (1, 3) and (–1, –3) **2** (–1, 4) and (–1, –1) **3** (0, 1) and (3, 0)
4 (2, –3) and (4, 3) **5** (–2, 0) and (4, 0) **6** (–1, 0) and (3, 0)

Finished Early?
 Go to page 456

2 Equation of a Straight Line

Learn About It

The equation of a line is the relationship between the coordinates, x and y, of any point on the line. Since only one straight line can be drawn through any two points, only two facts are required to find the equation of a line, for example:

I the gradient and the coordinates of one point

II the coordinates of any two points – particular examples are the coordinates of the intercepts on both axes

III the intercept on the y-axis and the gradient of the line, which may be found from a graph of the line.

I For the two points, take any point P (x, y) and a known point $P_1 (x_1, y_1)$. The gradient m of the line PP_1 is given by

$$m = \frac{y - y_1}{x - x_1}$$

Multiply both sides of the equation by $(x - x_1)$.
Then $y - y_1 = m (x - x_1)$ (1)

This gives the relation between x and y in terms of the coordinates of the given point (x_1, y_1) and the gradient m. Therefore, substituting the values for (x_1, y_1) and m gives the required equation of the line.

Example	Write the equation of the line passing through the point A (3, 5) and having gradient $m = 2$.
Working	Let P (x, y) be any point on the line. Substituting in $y - y_1 = m(x - x_1)$, $$y - 5 = 2(x - 3)$$ $$y = 2x - 6 + 5$$ $$y = 2x - 1$$
Answer	The equation of the line is $y = 2x - 1$.

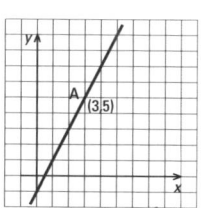

Try It Out

 Find the equation of the straight line:

(a) of gradient 3 and passing through
- (i) (2, 5) (ii) (–2, 6) (iii) (4, –1)

(b) of gradient –2 and passing through
- (i) (3, 1) (ii) (0, –3) (iii) (–1, 0).

Learn More About It

When the line passes through the origin, that is, when $(x_1, y_1) = (0, 0)$, the gradient becomes

$$m = \frac{y}{x}$$

and the equation of the line becomes $y = mx$.

Try It Out

 1 2 boxes of nails cost $26 and 5 boxes cost $65.

(a) Using 1 cm : 1 box of nails along the x-axis and 1 cm : $10 on the y-axis, draw a graph to represent this information.

(b) Find the gradient of the graph.

(c) State the equation of the graph.

(d) Use the graph to find:
- (i) the cost of 7 boxes of nails
- (ii) the number of boxes that cost $78.

2 B$10 is equivalent to F$4 and B$15 is equivalent to F$6.

(a) Using 1 cm to represent F$1 along the x-axis and 1 cm to represent B$1 on the y-axis, draw a graph to represent the data.

(b) Find the gradient of the graph.

(c) State the equation of the graph.

(d) Use the graph to find:
- (i) the number of F$ for B$20
- (ii) the number of B$ for F$3.

Learn More About It

II For any two given points P_1 (x_1, y_1) and P_2 (x_2, y_2), the gradient m is given by

$$m = \frac{y_2 - y_1}{x_2 - x_1}$$

Substituting for m in the equation $y - y_1 = m(x - x_1)$,

we get $y - y_1 = \dfrac{y_2 - y_1}{x_2 - x_1} (x - x_1)$ \hfill (2)

This gives the relation between x and y in terms of the coordinates of the given points (x_1, y_1) and (x_2, y_2). Therefore, substituting the given values of the coordinates gives the required equation of the line.

Key Fact
Any two points on a straight line define its gradient.

Example   Write the equation of the line passing through the points R (3, 5) and T (6, 8).

Working   Let P (x, y) be any point on the line.

$$\text{Gradient of the line} = \frac{8 - 5}{6 - 3}$$

$$= 1$$

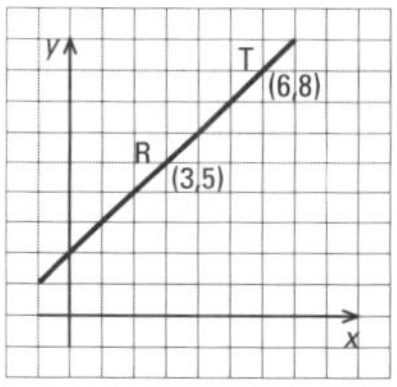

Substituting in $y - y_1 = m(x - x_1)$,

$$y - 5 = 1(x - 3)$$
$$y = x - 3 + 5$$
$$y = x + 2$$

Answer   The equation of the line is $y = x + 2$.

Note: Either of the given points can be used to substitute for (x_1, y_1).

Try It Out

Write the equation of the line passing through each of the following pairs of points.

1 (2, 5) and (−2, 6)   **2** (3, −2) and (−1, 1)

3 (4, −1) and (0, 2)   **4** (−1, 3) and (−2, −3)

Key Fact
The equation of the line is the relation between the coordinates, x and y, of every point on the line.

Learn More About It

III The equation of the straight line having a gradient m and passing through the origin is $y = mx$.
For each parallel line the y-coordinate of the point of intersection with the y-axis (that is when $x = 0$), has a constant value c called the intercept, as shown in the diagram.

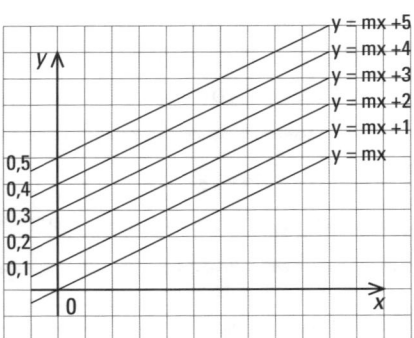

Using $y - y_1 = m(x - x_1)$ where (x_1, y_1) is the point $(0, c)$ the equation becomes

$y - c = m(x - 0)$

Simplifying, the general equation of a straight line may be written as

$y = mx + c$, where m is the gradient of the line
and c is the intercept on the y-axis.

What is the equation of the straight line passing through the point $(0, 5)$?

What is the intercept for the straight line through the point P $(0, -2)$?

Example For line I,
    (a) calculate the gradient
    (b) state the intercept
    (c) write the equation of the line.

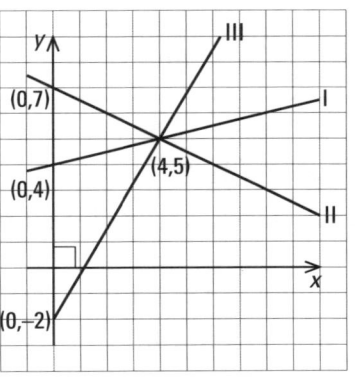

Working & Answer Let P (x, y) be any point on the line.

    (a) Gradient of the line $= \dfrac{5 - 4}{4 - 0}$

$= \dfrac{1}{4}$

    (b) Intercept, $c = 4$

    (c) Substituting in $y = mx + c$,
        the equation of the line is $y = \frac{1}{4}x + 4$

This equation may be simplified and written as $4y = x + 16$

Note that the gradient of the line is the coefficient of x only if the coefficient of y is 1.

Try It Out

P **1** For lines II and III in the previous example:

    (a) find the gradient

    (b) note the intercept

    (c) write the equation of the line.

2 In each of the given equations of the following lines, state:

    (a) the gradient   **(b)** the intercept on the y-axis.

    (i) $y = 2x + 3$ **(ii)** $y + 3x = 1$

    (iii) $y - 4x + 2 = 0$ **(iv)** $2y + x = 0$

    (v) $3y = 6x + 2$ **(vi)** $2x + 3y + 1 = 0$

    (vii) $4y - 1 = 3x$ **(viii)** $-2y + 5x = 1$

Key Fact

The equation of a line parallel to the y-axis is $x = a$,
where a is a constant. The equation of the y-axis is $x = 0$.
The equation of a line parallel to the x-axis is $y = b$,
where b is a constant. The equation of the x-axis is $y = 0$.

Practice

Q **1** Find the equation of the line which passes through the point:

    (a) $(4, 8)$ and has a gradient of 3

    (b) $(0, 0)$ and has a gradient of $2\frac{1}{2}$

    (c) $(-2, 6)$ and has a gradient of -1

    (d) $(0, -5)$ and has a gradient of -2.

2 Find the equation of the line which passes through the points:

    (a) $(0, 0)$ and $(3, 7)$

    (b) $(-4, -3)$ and $(3, -6)$

    (c) $(7, 2)$ and $(-9, 7)$.

3 The equation of the line l is $y = 6 - \frac{1}{2}x$.

    (a) Find: **(i)** the gradient of the line l

               (ii) the intercept on the y-axis.

    A line L passes through the point $(-\frac{1}{2}, 6)$ and is perpendicular to the
    line l.

    (b) Find the equation of the line L.

R For each of the following straight lines:
(a) write down the intercept on the *y*-axis
(b) find the gradient of the line
(c) draw on the same axes, the graph of the line.

1 $y = 2x$ **2** $y = 2x + 3$ **3** $2y = 4x - 3$
4 $2y + x = 0$ **5** $2y + x = 2$

> # Key Fact
> In the equation of a straight line *the coefficient of y must be* 1 for the coefficient of *x* to be equal to the gradient of the line.

Further Practice

S **1** A straight line passes through the points R (3, 5) and T (6, 8). Find the equation of the line.

2 Find the equation of the line which passes through the point:
(a) (3, –1) and has a gradient of 3
(b) (6, 0) and has a gradient of $-\frac{1}{2}$
(c) (–1, 2) and has a gradient of –2
(d) (0, 3) and has a gradient of –4.

3 Find the equation of the line which passes through the points:
(a) (0, 0) and (3, –7)
(b) (–1, 4) and (5, –2)
(c) (2, –11) and (–4, –4)

4 Write down the equations of the lines **1–6** in the diagram under **l** on page 255.

5 The line *l* passes through the points (0, 0) and (7, –2).
(a) Find the equation of the line *l*.
The line L is parallel to the line *l* and crosses the *y*-axis at (0, 8).
(b) Find: **(i)** the equation of the line L
(ii) the coordinates of the point where L crosses the *x*-axis.

Finished Early?
 Go to page 456

3 Mid-point of a Line

Name the coordinates of two points on the straight line P_1 (x_1, y_1) and P_2 (x_2, y_2).

Draw lines through P_1 and P_2 parallel to the x-axis and parallel to the y-axis.

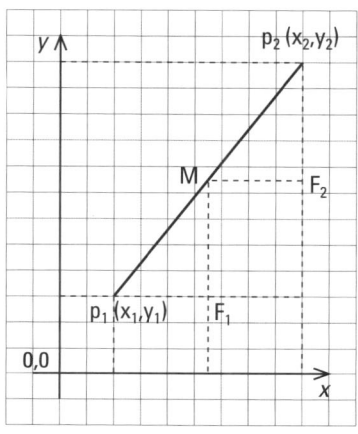

Name the point of intersection of these lines F_1 and F_2 as in the diagram.

Name the mid-point of the line M (X, Y).

Since P_2F_2 // MF_1 and MF_2 // P_1F_1,
and angle MF_2P_2 = angle P_1F_1M = 90°,
and since $P_2M = MP_1$,
triangles P_2MF_2 and MP_1F_1 are congruent.

Therefore, $P_2F_2 = MF_1$
$$(y_2 - Y) = (Y - y_1)$$

Simplifying, $y_2 + y_1 = 2Y$

and $Y = \frac{1}{2}(y_2 + y_1)$

And $MF_2 = P_1F_1$,
$$(x_2 - X) = (X - x_1)$$

Simplifying, $x_2 + x_1 = 2X$

and $X = \frac{1}{2}(x_2 + x_1)$

Therefore, the coordinates of the mid-point M are $(\frac{1}{2}(x_2 + x_1), \frac{1}{2}(y_2 + y_1))$.

Try It Out

T Find the coordinates of the mid-point of the line joining F (6, 5) and G (2, 7).

Practice

U **1** Find the coordinates of the mid-point of the line joining each of the following pairs of points.

    (i) (−1, 5) and (3, 3)   **(ii)** (3, 4) and (1, 2)   **(iii)** (2, 5) and (−3, 6)

    (iv) (0, 1) and (−2, 3)   **(v)** (−3, 4) and (−1, 2)   **(vi)** (0, 5) and (5, 0)

2 For each of the following lines, find the equation of the parallel line that passes through the mid-point of the line joining the points (2, 5) and (−4, −1).

    (a) $y = 2x + 3$ **(b)** $2y + 3 = 0$

    (c) $y - 4x + 2 = 0$ **(d)** $2x + 3y + 1 = 0$

3 For each of the following lines, find the equation of the perpendicular line that passes through the mid-point of the line joining the points (–3, 2) and (5, 4).

(a) $y + 3x = 1$ (b) $3y + 6x + 2$ (c) $-2y + 5x = 1$ (d) $4y - 1 = 3x$

Further Practice

V Find the coordinates of the mid-point of the line joining each of the following pairs of points.

1 (a) (2, 5) and (–2, 6)   (b) (3, –2) and (–1, 1)   (c) (4, –1) and (0, 2)

(d) (–1, 3) and (–2, –3)   (e) (–1, –3) and (2, 6)   (f) (4, 5) and (1, 6)

2 Find the equation of the line that passes through the midpoint of the line joining the points (–4, –2) and –6, 6)

(a) parallel to the line $3y + x - 2 = 0$

(b) perpendicular to the line $2y = 4x - 1$

Finished Early?

➦ Go to page 457

Key Fact

If the gradient of a line l is m, then the gradient of a line perpendicular to the line l is $-\dfrac{1}{m}$.

---

④ Length of a Line

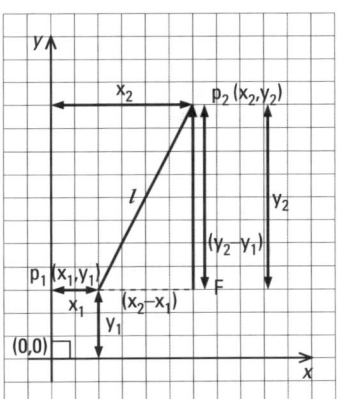

Name the coordinates of the end-points of the straight line P_1 (x_1, y_1) and P_2 (x_2, y_2).

Draw a line through P_1 parallel to the x-axis and a line through P_2 parallel to the y-axis.

Name the point of intersection of these lines F as in the diagram, where angle $P_1FP_2 = 90°$.

   Then $P_1F = (x_2 - x_1)$
   and $P_2F = (y_2 - y_1)$

Let the length of the line P_1P_2 be l (see diagram).

Using Pythagoras' theorem, in the right-angled triangle P_1P_2F,

$$(P_1P_2)^2 = (P_1F)^2 + (P_2F)^2$$

that is, $(l)^2 = (x_2 - x_1)^2 + (y_2 - y_1)^2$ and $l = \sqrt{(x_2 - x_1)^2 + (y_2 - y_1)^2}$

Example Find the length of the line joining the points, A (3, 5) and B (7, 8).

Working In the diagram on the right, using Pythagoras' theorem in the right-angled triangle AFB,

$$(AB)^2 = (7 - 3)^2 + (8 - 5)^2$$
$$= 4^2 + 3^2$$
$$= 25$$
$$AB = 5 \text{ units}$$

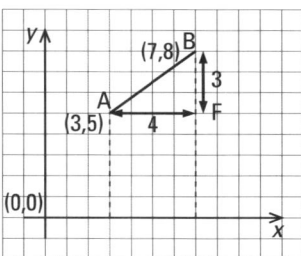

Answer The line is 5 units long.

Try It Out

W Find the distance between P (7, 5) and R (3, 2).

Practice

X Find the length of the line joining each of the following pairs of points.

1 (−1, −1) and (3, 3)   **2** (3, 4) and (3, −1)   **3** (2, −1) and (4, 1)
4 (1, 0) and (−2, 3)   **5** (−2, −4) and (4, −4)   **6** (0, 5) and (5, 0)

Y For the line joining each of the following pairs of points, calculate:
(a) the gradient of the line
(b) the equation of the line
(c) the coordinates of the mid-point
(d) the length of the line.

1 (−1, 4) and (3, −8)   **2** (−3, 4) and (4, −12)   **3** (−3, −2) and (−7, −4)

Further Practice

Z **(a)** Find the distance between each of the following pairs of points.

1 (2, 5) and (−2, 6)   **2** (3, −2) and (−1, 1)
3 (4, −1) and (0, 2)   **4** (−1, 3) and (−2, −3)

(b) For the line joining each of the following pairs of points, calculate:
(i) the gradient of the line
(ii) the equation of the line
(iii) the coordinates of the mid-point
(iv) the length of the line.

1 (8, 7) and (2, 5)   **2** (2, 5) and (4, −1)
3 (5, 3) and (1, −5)   **4** (6, 2) and (0, 4)
5 (4, 0) and (−3, 2)   **6** (0, 3) and (−3, 0)

Finished Early?
➡ Go to page 457

16 Linear Inequalities in Two Variables

In this chapter you will learn about ...
1. linear inequalities in two variables
2. linear programming

1 Linear Inequalities in Two Variables

Remember?

In a linear inequality in one variable, one of the inequality symbols connects either an algebraic expression and a numerical value or two algebraic expressions, for example, $2x + 3 > 7$ or $3x + 1 \leq x - 4$.

A number line is used to represent the solution of these inequalities. If the end-values of the range are included, then this is shown on the number line by a solid circle ●; if the end-values are *not* included, there is an open circle, ○; for example, if $x < 5$ is the solution set, the graph is shown in the diagram on the right.

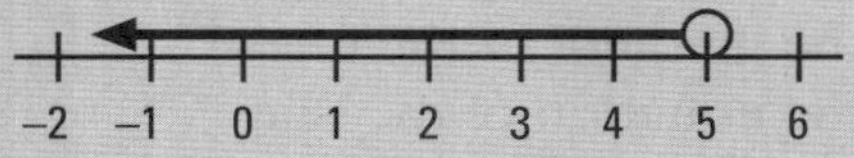

For simultaneous linear inequalities, the solution set is given by the intersection of the values in the solution set of each inequality. For example, if the solution of the inequalities are $x > -3$ and $x \leq 2$, then the solution set of the simultaneous inequalities is $-3 < x \leq 2$ (see the diagram on the right).

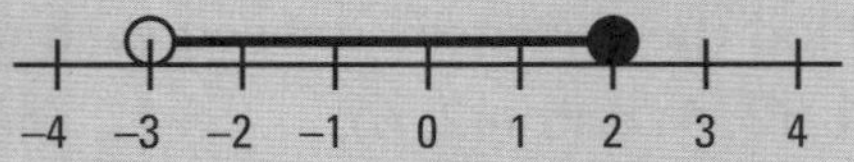

Practice

A 1 Solve each of the following inequalities.

(a) $3 - x \geq 1$

(b) $3x < 12$

(c) $8x - 5 > 6x + 7$

(d) $\dfrac{x}{2} + \dfrac{3}{4} \geq \dfrac{5x}{6} - \dfrac{7}{12}$

(e) $7x - (5x - 3) \geq 9$

(f) $\dfrac{7}{x + 2} > \dfrac{-2}{5 + 4x}$

2 Draw a number line to illustrate each of the following inequalities.
  (a) $-2 \leqslant x < 5$ **(b)** $3 < x \leqslant 11$ **(c)** $0 \leqslant x \leqslant 8$
  (d) $-7 < x < 4$ **(e)** $-4 < x \leqslant 0$ **(f)** $-9 \leqslant x < 6$

3 **(a)** Show the solution sets of $x \leqslant 5$ and $1 \leqslant x \leqslant 7$ on separate number lines.
  (b) Hence show the solution set of the simultaneous inequalities $x \leqslant 5$ and $1 \leqslant x \leqslant 7$ on a single number line.

4 Illustrate on a number line the set
  $\{-5 < x < 2\} \cap \{-3 \leqslant x \leqslant 3\}$.

Further Practice

B **1** Solve the following inequalities.
  (a) $x + 2 \leqslant 3$ **(b)** $4x + 20 < 0$ **(c)** $3x + 4(x - 3) > x - 6$
  (d) $2(x + 4) \geqslant 3(x - 1)$ **(e)** $-5x \leqslant 30$ **(f)** $\frac{1}{2}(3x - 2) \geqslant x - 6$

2 Sketch number lines to illustrate each of the inequalities in questions **A**1 and **B**1.

3 Use the number line to illustrate the solution set of the simultaneous inequalities $x \leqslant 1$ and $-3 < x < 5$.

> **Finished Early?**
> ⇨ Go to page 458

Learn About It

To find the set of points given by the inequality $\{(x, y) : x > 2 \text{ and } y \leqslant 5\}$ by a graphical method, draw x- and y-axes on graph paper. Then draw the lines given by the linear equations corresponding to the inequalities, that is, $x = 2$ and $y = 5$, as shown in the diagram on the right.

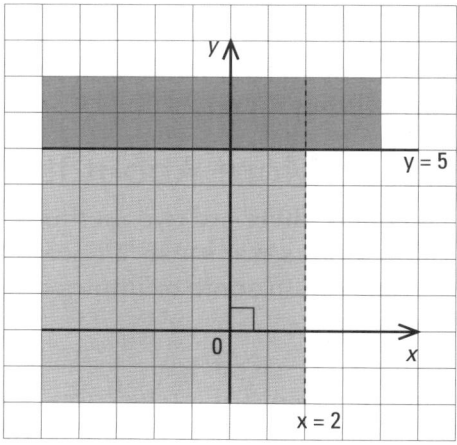

These lines are the **boundary lines** for the points satisfying the inequalities. Each line divides the Cartesian plane into two regions – a shaded region and an unshaded region. The boundary lines are either *broken* to show that the points on the line *are not* included in the solution, or *continuous* to show that the points on the line *are* included in the solution.

The broken line $x = 2$ is the boundary for the unshaded region where the x-value of every point in that region is greater than 2, that is, $x > 2$. The line $x = 2$ is broken to show that the points on the line, $x = 2$ are *not* included in the solution. The x-values of the points that lie in the shaded region are *not* members of the solution set of the inequality since the x-value of every point in that region is less than 2.

Similarly, the continuous line $y = 5$ is the boundary between an unshaded region below the line where the y-coordinates of the points are less than 5 and a shaded region above the line where the y-coordinates of the points are greater than 5. Also, the line is continuous to show that the points on the line $y = 5$ are included in the solution.

Key Fact

There is a choice between shading or not shading the region that satisfies an inequality. The convention in this text book uses shading for the region where the points do *not* satisfy the inequality. *It is therefore necessary to carefully check the instructions about the region to be shaded in every example that you do.*

Try It Out

C Show on a graph the region which contains the set of points
$\{(x, y) : x \geqslant -1, y < 1\}$.

[*Shade the region that contains the points that do **not** satisfy the inequality.*]

Learn More About It

Generally, there are two methods that can be used to decide the region of the points that satisfy a linear inequality in two variables, for example $y - 2x > 6$. In some examples one method may be easier to apply than the other.

Method 1
Find the points of intersection of the straight line given by the corresponding linear equation with the x-axis and the y-axis. Draw the line.

Check whether the coordinates of the origin, that is, $x = 0$ and $y = 0$, satisfy the inequality.

If the origin satisfies the inequality, then the origin lies in the required region, that is, the origin is on the same side of the boundary line as the points that satisfy the inequality.

If the origin does *not* satisfy the inequality, then the origin does not lie in the required region, that is, the origin is on the opposite side of the boundary line from the solution set and the region is shaded.

Method 2

First make y the subject of the inequality.

Write the corresponding linear equation, that is, the equation of the boundary line. Then check whether the required region is below or above the line.

Example Show on a graph the region which contains the set of points
$\{(x, y) : y + 2x \geq 3\}$

Working & Answer

Method 1

The line $y + 2x = 3$ ...... (1) is the boundary between the set of points that satisfy the inequality and the points that are not required.

In (1), when $x = 0$, $y = 3$; when $y = 0$, $x = \frac{3}{2}$.

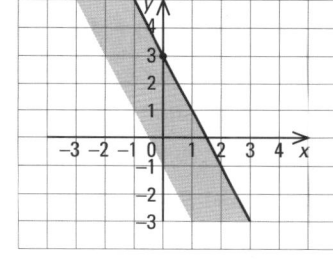

Since the points on the line are included, a continuous line AB is drawn.

Substituting $x = 0$ and $y = 0$ in $y + 2x \geq 3$,

gives $0 + 2(0) \geq 3 \rightarrow 0 \geq 3$.

Since this is not true, the origin and the set of points that satisfy the inequality are on opposite sides of the boundary and we shade the region containing $(0, 0)$. The unshaded region represents the set of points that satisfy the inequality.

Method 2

Writing y as the subject of the inequality: $y \geq -2x + 3$, the equation of the boundary line is $y = -2x + 3$.

Therefore, in order to satisfy the inequality, the set of points must lie in the unshaded region above the boundary line as shown in the diagram above.

Try It Out

D Show on a graph the region which contains the set of points
$\{(x, y) : x + 2y < 4\}$.

[*Shade the region where the points do **not** satisfy the inequality.*]

Key Fact

It is usually easier to draw a straight line by using the intercept on each axis since the coordinates of these points are calculated by putting $x = 0$, and then $y = 0$ in the equation of the line.

Word Check

boundary line between the region where the points meet stated conditions and the region where the points do not meet the conditions

cartesian plane flat surface defined by the x-axis and the y-axis

continuous unbroken, with no gaps

convention accepted method or usual practice based on general consent

integral indicating or involving only integers or whole numbers

simultaneous operating at the same time

Practice

E 1 For each of the following inequalities, draw a graph showing the region that contains the set of points.
   (a) $\{(x, y) : x \geqslant 3\}$ **(b)** $\{(x, y) : y < 4\}$
   (c) $\{(x, y) : 2y > 3\}$ **(d)** $\{(x, y) : 2x \leqslant 1\}$
   (e) $\{(x, y) : -3 < x < 2\}$ **(f)** $\{(x, y) : 2 \geqslant y \geqslant -1\}$

2 Draw graphs to show the solution set of the following.
   (a) $\{(x, y) : x > 0 \text{ and } y \geqslant -1\}$ **(b)** $\{(x, y) : x < 3 \text{ and } y \leqslant 2\}$
   (c) $\{(x, y) : y \geqslant 0 \text{ and } x > -2\}$ **(d)** $\{(x, y) : 2y \leqslant 1 \text{ and } x \leqslant 4\}$

3 Draw a graph to illustrate each of the following sets of points.
   (a) $\{(x, y) : y > 2x - 1\}$ **(b)** $\{(x, y) : 2y - x < 2\}$
   (c) $\{(x, y) : x + 2y \geqslant 2\}$ **(d)** $\{(x, y) : y + 2x < -2\}$

Practice

F In each of the following graphs
   (a) find the equation of the boundary line
   (b) write the solution set of the inequalities, where the unshaded area is the required region.

1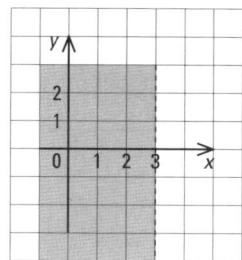

2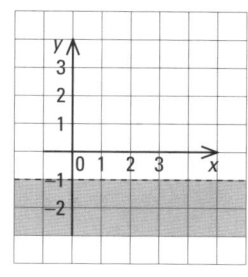

3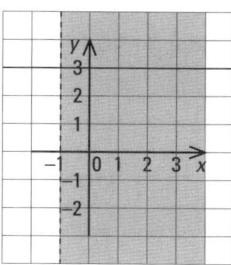

4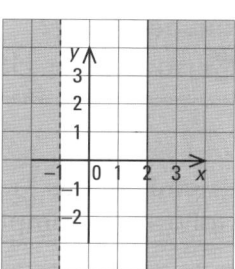

5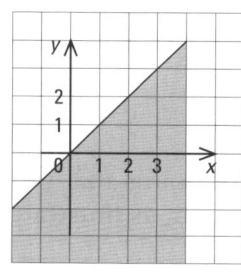

6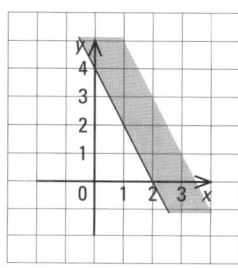

Further Practice

G For each of the following inequalities, draw a graph showing the region that contains the set of points.

1 $\{(x, y) : x < -2\}$

2 $\{(x, y) : 2x \geqslant -3\}$

3 $\{(x, y) : 1 > x \geqslant -4\}$

4 $\{(x, y) : 1 < y < 4\}$

5 $\{(x, y) : y > x - 3\}$

6 $\{(x, y) : 3x - y > 6\}$

Further Practice

H In each of the following graphs
(a) find the equation of the boundary line
(b) state the solution set of the inequalities, where the unshaded area is the required region.

1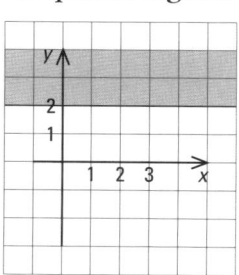

2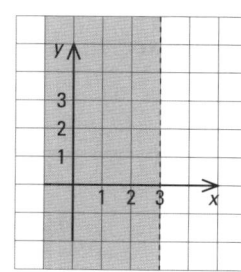

3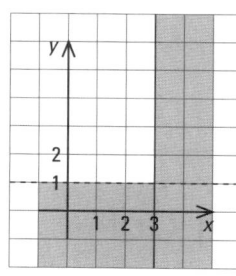

4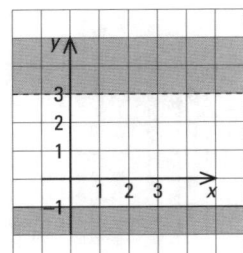

5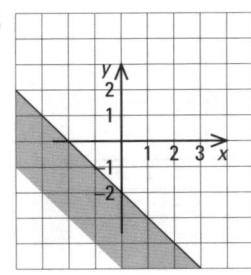

6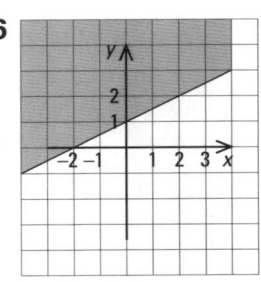

Finished Early?
➡ Go to page 458

Learn More About It

The region containing the set of points that satisfy three simultaneous
inequalities may be a closed region, as illustrated in the following examples.

Example   Solve graphically the simultaneous inequalities
$y \geqslant 0$, $x < 2$ and $y \leqslant 3x$,
for integral values of x.

Working   As shown in the diagram,
the corresponding
boundary lines are
   (i) for $y \geqslant 0$, $y = 0$, [the
      x-axis] and is a
      continuous line
  (ii) for $x < 2$, $x = 2$, and is
      a broken line
 (iii) $y \leqslant 3x$, $y = 3x$, and is
      a continuous line.

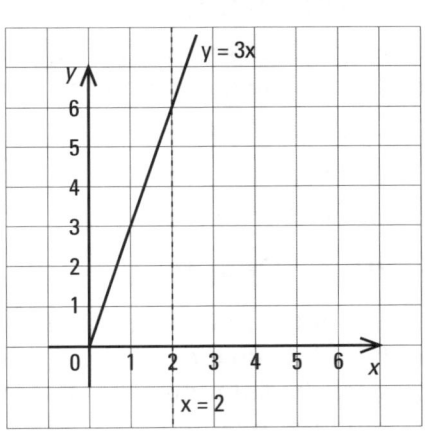

Answer   From the graph, the points
that satisfy the inequalities
for integral values of x are
$(0, 0)$, $(1, 0)$, $(1, 1)$,
$(1, 2)$, $(1, 3)$.

Try It Out

1 Solve graphically the simultaneous inequalities.
$x > 0$, $y \geqslant -1$ and $y + x < 3$, for integral values of x.

Example　(a) Find the equations of the boundary lines of the unshaded region labeled **R** in the diagram.

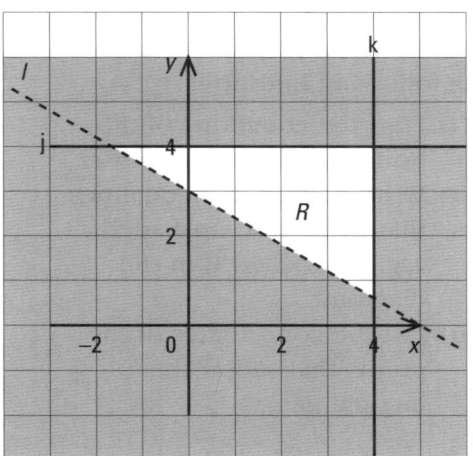

(b) Write down the inequalities that define **R**.

(c) List the solution set of the simultaneous inequalities, for integral values of x.

Working & Answer

(a) As shown in the diagram, name the boundary lines j, k and l.

The boundary line j is given by the equation $y = 4$.

Similarly, the boundary line k is given by the equation $x = 4$.

The boundary line l has a gradient of $-\frac{3}{5}$ and cuts the y-axis at $(0, 3)$ so that the equation of l is given by $y = -\frac{3}{5}x + 3$.

(b) The line j is a continuous line so that the points on the line are included in the solution set. Since the unshaded region is below the boundary line, the inequality is $y \leqslant 4$. The line k is a continuous line. Since the unshaded region is to the left of the boundary line, the inequality is $x \leqslant 4$. The line l is broken so that the points on the line are not included in the solution set. Since the unshaded region is above the boundary line, the inequality is $y > -\frac{3}{5}x + 3$.

Multiplying both sides of the inequality by 5:

$5y > -3x + 15$

Rearranging the terms: $5y + 3x > 15$

Therefore, the inequalities that define the unshaded region **R** are $x \leqslant 4$, $y \leqslant 4$ and $5y + 3x > 15$.

(c) From the diagram, the solution set is $\{(-1, 4), (0, 4), (1, 3), (1,4), (2, 2), (2, 3), (2, 4), (3, 2), (3, 3), (3, 4), (4, 1), (4, 2), (4, 3), (4, 4)\}$.

Try It Out

J Use the given diagram to answer the following questions.

(i) Find the equations of the boundary lines **a**, **b** and **c**.

(ii) Write down the inequalities that define the unshaded region labelled **R** in the diagram.

(iii) List the coordinates of the points that satisfy the inequalities.

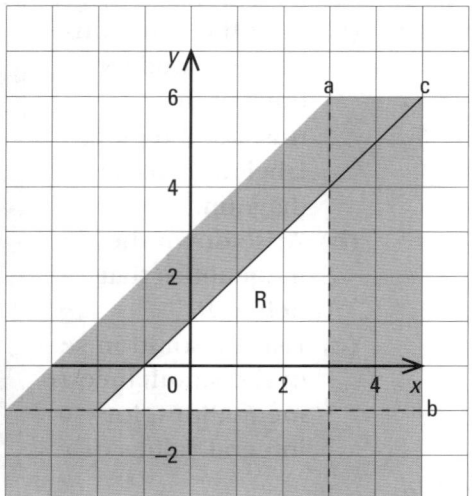

Example	Show on a graph the region S which contains the solution set of the simultaneous inequalities $2y + 3x < 6$, $y < x + 3$ and $y \geqslant -1$.

Working	Boundary line for the inequality $2y + 3x < 6$ is given by the line $2y + 3x = 6$ When $x = 0$, $y = 3$.
	                                                          When $y = 0$, $x = 2$.
	 Boundary line for the inequality $y < x + 3$ is given by the line $y = x + 3$ When $x = 0$, $y = 3$.
	                                                          When $y = 0$, $x = -3$.
	 Boundary line for the inequality $y \geqslant -1$ is given by the line $y = -1$.

Answer	

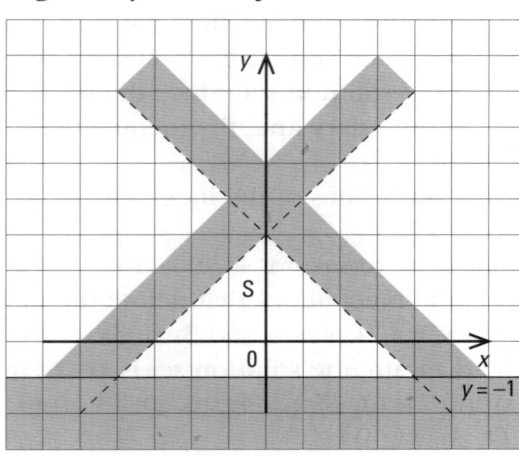

Try It Out

K Show on a graph the region **T** which contains the solution set of the simultaneous inequalities $x + y < 3$, $x - y < 1$ and $x \geqslant -1$.

Practice

L 1 Using graph paper, draw the regions defined by each of the following:
  (a) $y \geqslant 0$, $y < 3x$, $x + y \leqslant 4$ (b) $x \geqslant -3$, $y \leqslant 2$, $x - y < 2$
  (c) $y \leqslant 5$, $x - y \leqslant 1$, $4x + 3y \geqslant 12$ (d) $x \geqslant 0$, $y \geqslant 0$, $x + y < 6$, $y - x < 2$
  (e) $y < 3$, $x < 4$, $2x + y + 2 \geqslant 0$, $x - y - 2 \leqslant 0$

2 In the diagram, the broken line **b** passes through the origin and the point (2, 4); the continuous line **d** passes through (0, 5) and (5, 0).
  (a) Work out and find the boundary lines for the unshaded area **U**.
  (b) Write down the inequalities that define **U**.
  (c) List the solution set of the inequalities for integral values of *x*.

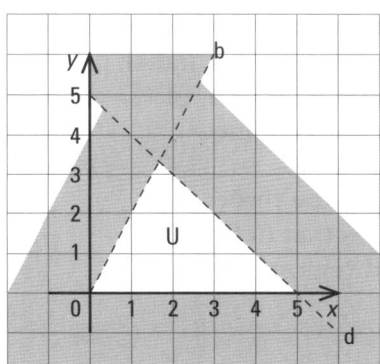

3 **T** is the set of points (x, y) which satisfies the four inequalities:
  $y - x \leqslant 1$, $2x \leqslant 5$, $5y > -4x$ and $y \leqslant 2$
  Show on a graph the region that represents **T**.

4 The equations of the two sloping lines in the diagram below are $x + y = 4$ and $x + 2y = 6$. Write down the four inequalities which define the region **R**.

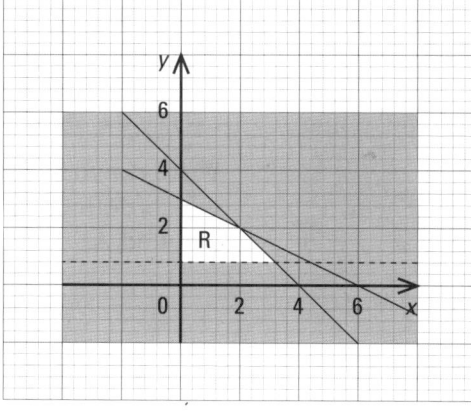

5 (a) Show on a graph the region which represents the set of inequalities
$y - x \leqslant 4$, $y \geqslant 6$ and $y \geqslant 2x - 6$

(b) Which of the following points lie within the region
P $(4, -2)$, Q $(8, 11)$, R $(4, 8)$, S $(4, 10)$?

Finished Early?
➡ Go to page 458

Further Practice

M 1 In the diagram on the right, the equation of the continuous line *a* is $x - y = 2$, of the broken line *b* parallel to the *y*-axis is $x = -4$, of the other broken line *c* is $x + y = -5$.
Write down the three inequalities that define the unshaded region labelled **A**.

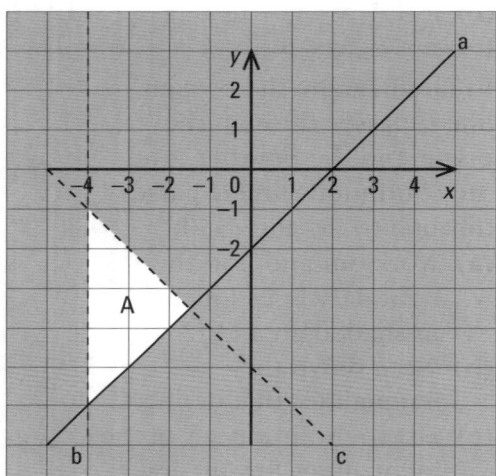

2 Work out the equations of the lines shown in the diagram on the right.

Hence, list the inequalities which define the unshaded area labelled **D**.

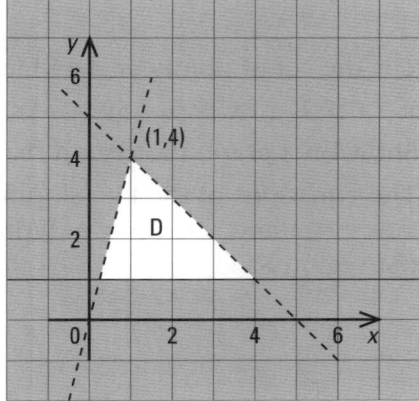

3

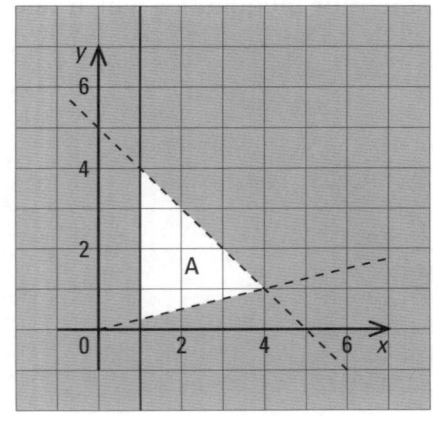

Write down the three inequalities which define the unshaded area labelled **A**.

② Linear Programming

Learn About It

Often in real-life there are quantities that have different values under varying conditions. These restrictions put limits on the values of the variable quantities. When there are two variable quantities in a problem and each condition in the problem can be stated as a linear inequality, then a graphical method may be used to solve the problem. By working out the solution set of each inequality and then finding the intersection of these sets, the values of the variables that meet all the stated conditions of the problem can be found. This method is called **linear programming**.

Example	A student has $50 to buy pens and notebooks. Pens cost $2 each and notebooks $5 each. She must buy at least five of each. She spends over $10 more on notebooks than on pens. Find the number of ways she can spend the money.
Working	Let the student buy p pens and n notebooks. Since she must buy at least 5 of each then $p \geqslant 5$ and $n \geqslant 5$. Money spent on pens is $2p$ and on notebooks $5n$. Since she spends over $10 more on notebooks than on pens, then $5n - 2p > 10$. Since she has $50 then $5n + 2p \leqslant 50$.

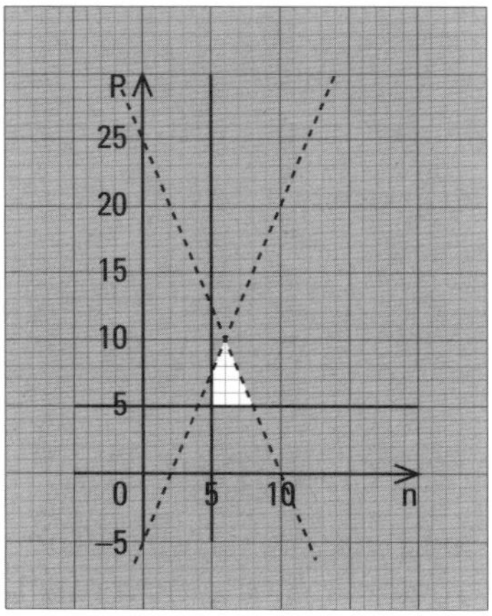

The corresponding linear equations are
$p = 5$, $n = 5$, $5n - 2p = 10$
and $5n + 2p = 50$.
These lines and the inequalities are shown in the diagram on the right.
The number of ways that she can buy the notebooks and pens is given by the ordered pairs in the unshaded area.
The first value in each ordered pair refers to the number of notebooks and the second value to the number of pens.

Answer	There are 12 ways. The values are $(5, 5)$, $(5, 6)$, $(5, 7)$, $(6, 5)$, $(6, 6)$, $(6, 7)$, $(6, 8)$, $(6, 9)$, $(7, 5)$, $(7, 6)$, $(7, 7)$, $(8, 5)$.

Try It Out

(N) The owner of a piece of land plans to divide it into not more than 36 plots and to build either a house or a shop on each plot. He decides that he will build at least 20 houses and that there will be at least twice as many houses as shops.

Taking h to represent the number of houses and s the number of shops, where $h > 0$ and $s > 0$,

(a) write the other three inequalities which satisfy the given conditions
(b) deduce the equations of the lines that define the limiting values
(c) use a scale of 1 cm : 2 houses and 1 cm : 2 shops to draw a graph to show the required region
(d) find the maximum number of shops in the possible combinations of houses and shops.

Word Check

deduce draw conclusions from known facts

determine state accurately

limiting values maximum or minimum values of the variables

maximum greatest

minimum least

restrictions conditions that determine the values that a variable can take

---

Learn More About It

It may also be necessary to find the maximum or minimum value of one quantity in relation to the other as the quantities vary under different restrictions. It is possible to use the graph of the inequalities to determine the maximum or minimum value. This value is usually a function of the variables for values at a point at a vertex of the required region. If the values of the variables must be integers and the coordinates of the vertex are not integers then the point may be near to a vertex.

Example	In the previous worked example (p.277), find the greatest number of **(a)** pens **(b)** notebooks that she can buy.
Working & Answer	From the listing of the members of the solution set, **(a)** the greatest number of pens is 9 [ordered pair: (6, 9)] and **(b)** the greatest number of notebooks is 8 [ordered pair: (8, 5)].

Example A manufacturer plans to buy new machines for his factory. The table below shows the cost and the floor space required for each machine.

Machine	Cost	Floor space
X	$6000	3 m^2
Y	$8000	$2\frac{1}{2} \text{ m}^2$

The total floor space available is 27 m^2 and he has $72\,000 to spend. According to the trade board rules, he must buy at least three of machine X and four of machine Y. Find the maximum number of machines he can buy.

Working Let the manufacturer buy x of machine X and y of machine Y.

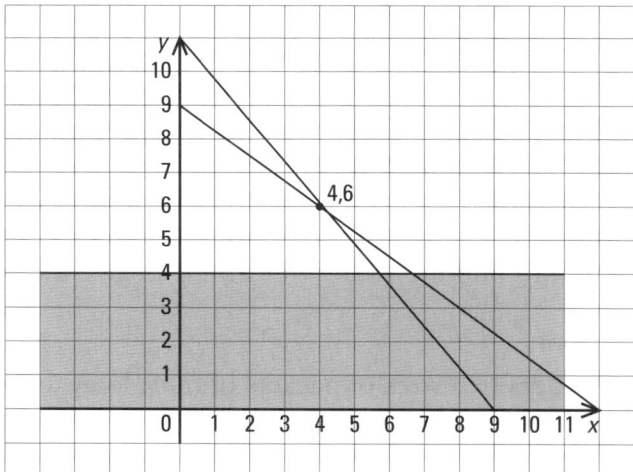

Trade conditions: $x \geqslant 3$ (1)
$y \geqslant 4$ (2)
Space conditions: $3x + 2\frac{1}{2}y \leqslant 27$
Simplifying $6x + 5y \leqslant 54$ (3)
Cost conditions: $6000x + 8000y \leqslant 72\,000$
Simplifying $3x + 4y \leqslant 36$ (4)
The lines defining the limiting values of the variables are
$x = 3$, $y = 4$, $6x + 5y = 54$ and $3x + 4y = 36$.
The values of the variables satisfying the conditions are
$(3, 4)$, $(3, 5)$, $(3, 6)$, $(4, 4)$, $(4, 5)$
$(4, 6)$, $(5, 4)$.

Answer The maximum number of machines is 10, 4 of X and 6 of Y.

Try It Out

○ A tailor uses 2 m of cloth to make a shirt and 3 m to make a dress. He must make at least 6 of each and has 36 m of cloth. He makes the same profit on a shirt as on a dress. Find the combination of shirts and dresses that gives the maximum profit.

Practice

P **1** In the example on machines on page 279 find the combination that
   (a) uses all the space available
   (b) is the most expensive.

2 Andrew has $840 and wishes to buy CDs at $120 and cassettes at $70. He has agreed to buy more than two but not more than five cassettes, and at least three CDs.
   (a) If c and d represent the number of cassettes and CDs respectively, write the inequalities that satisfy these conditions.
   (b) Using a scale of 1 cm to represent 1 unit on each axis, draw on the same axes a graph to show these inequalities. Shade the areas that do *not* satisfy the inequalities and label the region S where the points satisfy all the given conditions.
   The shop makes a profit of $30 on each CD and $14 on each cassette.
   (c) Write an algebraic expression to represent the total profit.
   (d) Use the graph to find the values of c and d to give the maximum profit.
   (e) Find this profit.

3 A shop-keeper orders two sizes of packets of nuts, large at $9 each and small at $4 each. She buys twice as many small packs as large ones with a minimum of 10 large and 20 small packs. She spends a maximum of $200.
   (a) Find the maximum number of packs that she can buy.
   The profit is 80 ¢ on a large pack and 40 ¢ on a small pack.
   (b) Find the combination that gives the largest profit.
   (c) Calculate that profit.

4 A bakery makes cakes and pies so that there are
   (i) 15 or more cakes
   (ii) more than 25 pies
   (iii) at least 45 but fewer than 60 cakes and pies altogether.
   Using p to represent the number of pies, and c to represent the number of cakes,
   (a) write the inequalities in p and c that satisfy these conditions
   (b) indicate, by a graphical method, the region containing the solution set of p and c (by shading the unwanted region).

5 The owner of a restaurant has to order olive oil and soya bean oil. Supplier A has the olive oil in 5-litre bottles and the soya oil in 3-litre bottles; supplier B has both the olive oil and the soya oil in 4-litre bottles. The owner decided to order at least 50 litres from Supplier A and at least 48 litres from Supplier B.
  (a) If x represents the number of bottles of olive oil and y the number of bottles of soya bean oil ordered from each store, write the two inequalities to express the above conditions.
  (b) Using the same axes and scales, draw the graph of the inequalities.
  (c) The owner wishes to spend the minimum amount of money. Find the number of bottles of each oil that the owner must order.

6 A distribution agent can carry 300 cartons of juice in his van. He has a standing order for 150 cartons of orange juice and 50 cartons of grapefruit juice and he knows that he never sells more than four times as much orange juice as grapefruit juice. If the profit on one carton of the orange juice is $3 and on one carton of the grapefruit juice is $4, calculate how many of each he should take each load for a maximum profit.

Finished Early?

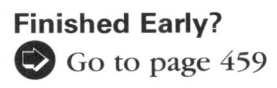 Go to page 459

Further Practice

1 A carpenter needs two types of nails, one costing $6 per box and the other $8 per box. He needs at least twice as many of the cheaper type as the other type and allows $600 to buy nails. He must get at least 50 boxes of the cheaper and 20 boxes of the other.
  (a) Use a graphical method to find the largest number of boxes of nails that he can buy, indicating the number of each type.
  (b) If he decides to get as many of the dearer ones as the restrictions allow, how many of each type can he get?

2 A school has to hire vehicles for an excursion to carry at least 900 kg of supplies and 60 persons. They planned to use two types of vehicles – vans and minibuses. Each van can carry 90 kg of supplies and 4 persons; each minibus can carry 50 kg of supplies and 6 persons.
  (a) If there were only 9 of each type of vehicle available;
    (i) list the possible arrangements
    (ii) find the smallest number of vehicles necessary for the trip, identifying the type of vehicles.
  (b) The charge for hiring one van is $300 and for one minibus is $400. Calculate the cost of the cheapest arrangement.

3 A vendor sells tomatoes at $32 per kg and carrots at $18 per kg. A customer decides that she will buy at least 1 kg of each but she cannot carry more than 6 kg altogether and she must not spend more than $144.

(a) Represent these conditions graphically on the same axes.

(b) The vendor makes a profit of $10 on 1 kg of tomatoes and $6 on 1 kg of carrots. Find how many kilograms of each the customer buys if the vendor makes the maximum profit.

(c) Calculate the maximum profit.

Finished Early?
➡ Go to page 459

Unit 7 *Functions and Graphs 1*

Summary of Chapters 15 and 16

Straight-line Graphs

- The graph of a **linear function in two variables**, $y = f(x)$, is a straight line and is called a **linear equation**.
- The **gradient** of the straight line is the ratio of *change in y* to *increase of x*; when the change is an increase, the gradient is positive, when the change is a decrease, the gradient is negative. The gradient of the line AB may also be defined as

$$m = \frac{\text{difference of the } y\text{-coordinates from B to A}}{\text{difference of the } x\text{-coordinates from B to A}}$$

  or $m = \tan \theta$, where θ is the positive angle between the x-axis and the line.
  Hence, the gradient of a line parallel to the x-axis is zero ($\theta = 0°$ and $\tan 0° = 0$).
  The gradient of a line parallel to the y-axis is undefined ($\theta = 90°$ and $\tan 90°$ is undefined).
  Parallel lines have equal gradients.
  The product of the gradients of perpendicular lines is -1.
- The equation of a straight line with gradient m is written as
  $y - y_1 = m(x - x_1)$, where (x_1, y_1) is a given point on the line or
  $y = mx + c$, where c is the **intercept** on the y-axis
  and $y = mx$ when $c = 0$, that is, the line passes through the origin.
- The coordinates of the mid-point of the line joining (x_1, y_1) and (x_2, y_2) is $(\frac{1}{2}(x_1 + x_2), \frac{1}{2}(y_1 + y_2))$.
  The length of the line joining (x_1, y_1) and (x_2, y_2) is
  $\sqrt{(x_2 + x_1)^2 + (y_2 + y_1)^2}$.

Linear Inequalities in Two Variables

- A **linear inequality in two variables** may be represented graphically on a Cartesian plane. An inequality separates the Cartesian plane into a region which contains the set of points that satisfy the inequality, and a region which contains the set of points that do not satisfy the inequality. The boundary between these regions is the line whose equation is found by replacing the symbol (one of $<, >, \leqslant, \geqslant, \neq$) in the inequality by the equals sign ($=$). When the symbol is $\leqslant$ or $\geqslant$, the line is continuous and the points on the line are included in the solution set; when the symbol is < or >, the line is *broken* and the points on the line are *not* included in the solution set. By convention (and in this text), the regions which are *not* included are shaded.

- When the methodology related to the graphical representation and solution of linear inequalities is applied to restrictions in real-world problems, the process is called **linear programming**. The unshaded area bounded by the straight lines represents the required region, which is the intersection of the solution sets of the inequalities defining the stated conditions. The maximum or minimum value of one quantity in relation to the varying values of other quantities under the stated conditions may also be determined from the graph as the vertices (or points near the vertices) of the unshaded area.

17 Quadratic Expressions

In this chapter you will learn about ...
1. expansion
2. factorisation
3. quadratic functions

1 Expansion

Learn About It

When we multiply two numbers, 7 and 4 for example, we can write

$$7 \times 4 = (2 + 5)(4) \qquad [2 \times 4 + 5 \times 4 = 28]$$
$$= (2 + 5)(1 + 3) = 2 \times (1 + 3) + 5 \times (1 + 3)$$
$$= (2)(1) + (2)(3) + (5)(1) + (5)(3)$$
$$= 2 + 6 + 5 + 15 = 28$$

We can compare this with the product of the two linear expressions $(x + 2)$ and $(y + 3)$ so that we get

$$(x + 2)(y + 3) = (x)(y + 3) + (2)(y + 3)$$
$$= (x)(y) + (x)(3) + (2)(y) + (2)(3)$$
$$= xy + 3x + 2y + 6$$

The final expression includes xy, a term made up of the product of the two variables, x and y.

Such an expression is called a **quadratic expression**.

Key Fact

When expanding algebraic expressions in two brackets, each term in one of the brackets must be multiplied by each term in the other bracket.

Similarly, $(x + 2)(x + 3) = (x)(x + 3) + (2)(x + 3)$
$$= (x)(x) + (x)(3) + (2)(x) + (2)(3)$$
$$= x^2 + 3x + 2x + 6$$

To simplify the result, we collect the like terms, $3x$ and $2x$, so that
$$(x + 2)(x + 3) = x^2 + 5x + 6$$
$x^2 + 5x + 6$ is called a **quadratic expression in x**.

Word Check

terms the parts of an expression that are added together

binomial expression an expression having two unlike terms

product the result of multiplying two numbers or two expressions

expand express a product as a sum of a number of terms

constant a numerical term that always has the same value

coefficient the factor that multiplies a variable

Let us work out the product of $(x + 2)$ and $(x - 3)$.

$$(x + 2)(x - 3) = (x)(x - 3) + (2)(x - 3)$$
$$= (x)(x) + (x)(-3) + (2)(x) + (2)(-3)$$
$$= x^2 - 3x + 2x - 6$$

Again, to simplify the result, we collect the like terms, $-3x$ and $+2x$:

$$(x + 2)(x - 3) = x^2 - x - 6$$

Work out the products of $(x - 2)(x + 3)$ and $(x - 2)(x - 3)$, paying careful attention to your signs. Check your working below.

$$(x - 2)(x + 3) = (x)(x + 3) + (-2)(x + 3)$$
$$= (x)(x) + (x)(3) + (-2)(x) + (-2)(3)$$
$$= x^2 + 3x - 2x - 6$$

We collect the like terms, $+3x$ and $-2x$, to simplify the result.

Then $(x - 2)(x + 3) = x^2 + x - 6$

$$(x - 2)(x - 3) = (x)(x - 3) + (-2)(x - 3)$$
$$= (x)(x) + (x)(-3) + (-2)(x) + (-2)(-3)$$
$$= x^2 - 3x - 2x + 6$$

We collect the like terms, $-3x$ and $-2x$, to simplify the result.

Then $(x - 2)(x - 3) = x^2 - 5x + 6$

Key Fact

The order of the brackets in an expansion does not matter; for example, $(x - 2)(x - 3)$ is the same as $(x - 3)(x - 2)$.

Try It Out

 Expand the following. Write out the product of each pair of terms as in the preceding examples. Simplify the quadratic expression where possible.

1 $(a + 4)(b + 3)$ **2** $(2x + 3)(y + 2)$ **3** $(c - 2)(d + 5)$

4 $(x - c)(y - d)$ **5** $(3k + n)(m + 4n)$ **6** $(2p + s)(p - 3s)$

After some practice, it will not be necessary to write down all the above steps in working through an expansion.

Practice

 1 Write five different examples of a binomial expression.

2 Write a quadratic expression that contains

     (a) one term   **(b)** two terms   **(c)** three terms.

Learn More About It

In the expansion of the product of the binomial expressions $(x + 2)$ and $(x + 3)$, that is, in $x^2 + 5x + 6$

(a) the first term, x^2, is the product of the first term in each bracket.

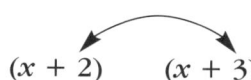

(b) the middle term, $+ 5x$, is the sum of two products – of the first term in the first bracket and the second term in the second bracket and of the second term in the first bracket and the first term in the second bracket.

(c) the last term, $+ 6$, is the product of the second term in each bracket.

Again in $(x + 2)(x - 3) = x^2 - x - 6$,

(a) the first term, x^2, is the product of the first term in each bracket.

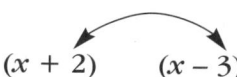

(b) the middle term, $-x$, is the sum of the products of the first term in the first bracket and the second term in the second bracket and of the second term in the first bracket and the first term in the second bracket.

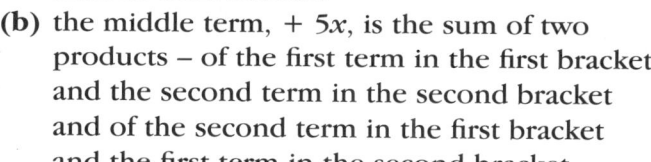

(c) the last term, $- 6$, is the product of the second terms in each bracket.

Example (a) Find the constant terms in the following expansions.

      1 $(x + 4)(x + 3)$ **2** $(2x + 3)(y - 2)$

      3 $(y - 2)(y + 5)$ **4** $(x - 2)(y - 4)$

   (b) In each of the following expansions,

      (i) write the coefficient of y^2

     (ii) work out the term in y.

      1 $(y + 4)(y + 3)$ **2** $(y - 3)(3y + 2)$

      3 $(3y - 2)(2y + 5)$ **4** $(2y - c)(y - d)$

Working and Answer

    (a) **1** $+12$ **2** -6 **3** -10 **4** $+8$

    (b) **(i) 1** 1   **2** 3   **3** 6   **4** 2

       (ii) 1 $3y + 4y = 7y$ **2** $2y - 9y = -7y$

            3 $15y - 4y = 11y$ **4** $-2dy - cy = -(2d + c)y$

Key Fact

A coefficient is usually a constant but may be an algebraic expression; for example, the coefficient of x in $3x$ is 3 and in $(2 + y)x$ the coefficient is $(2 + y)$.

Try It Out

C In the following expansions, find **(a)** the coefficient **(i)** of k^2 **(ii)** of k
                                    (b) the constant term.

1 $(k + 4)(k + 2)$ **2** $(4k + 3)(k + 1)$ **3** $(k - 2)(k + 2)$

4 $(k - 3)(k - 1)$ **5** $(3k + 1)(k - 3)$ **6** $(2k - 1)(k + 4)$

7 $(k + 5)(k + 5)$ **8** $(3k - 1)(k + 1)$ **9** $(k - 3)(k - 3)$

Key Fact

A **quadratic expression** is an expression in which the highest power of the variables in at least one term is 2; this includes terms such as xy, y^2 and x^2. Examples of quadratic expressions include $r^2 - 10r$, $2t^2 + 12tv$, $ab + 1$.

Learn More About It

In **C** question 7, $(k + 5)(k + 5) = (k)(k) + (k)(+5) + (+5)(k) + (+5)(+5)$
$$= k^2 \qquad + 2(5)(k) \qquad\qquad + (5)^2$$
$$= k^2 \qquad + 10k \qquad\qquad + 25$$

The expansion $k^2 + 10k + 25$ is an example of a **perfect square**.

In each factor of this product, the coefficient of the k-term is 1 and

$\qquad$ +5 is the constant term.

In the expansion, the coefficient of the k^2-term is 1

$\qquad$ the coefficient of the k-term, $+10$, is twice $+5$

and the constant term, $+25$, is the square of half the coefficient of the k-term,

$\qquad$ that is, $[\frac{1}{2}(+10)]^2$.

Similarly, in **C** question 9,

$$(k - 3)(k - 3) = (k)(k) + (k)(-3) + (-3)(k) + (-3)(-3)$$
$$= k^2 \qquad + 2(-3)k \qquad\qquad + (-3)^2$$
$$= k^2 \qquad - 6k \qquad\qquad + 9$$

The expansion $k^2 - 6k + 9$ is another example of a perfect square.

In each factor of this product, the coefficient of the k-term is 1 and

$\qquad$ −3 is the constant term.

In the expansion, the coefficient of the k^2-term is 1

$\qquad$ the coefficient of the k-term, −6, is twice −3

and the constant term, $+9$, is the square of half the coefficient of the k-term,

$\qquad$ that is, $[\frac{1}{2}(-6)]^2$.

Key Fact

In an expansion that is a perfect square, when the coefficient of the quadratic term is 1, the constant term is the square of half the coefficient of the linear term. Note therefore that the constant term in a perfect square is *always* positive.

Try It Out

D Expand the following.

1 $(f + 7)(f + 7)$	**2** $(x + 1)(x + 1)$	**3** $(h + 4)(h + 4)$
4 $(k - 5)(k - 5)$	**5** $(a - 4)(a - 4)$	**6** $(y + 2)(y + 2)$
7 $(x + 3)(x + 3)$	**8** $(j - 3)(j - 3)$	**9** $(y - 1)(y - 1)$

E In each of the following, add the term that will make the expression a perfect square.

1 $x^2 + 2x +$ ......   **2** $x^2 - 8x +$ ......   **3** $x^2 +$ ...... $+ 16$

4 ...... $+ 14x + 49$ **5** $x^2 + 6x +$ ......   **6** $x^2 - 6x +$ ......

Note that any quadratic expression can be written as a perfect square by replacing the constant term in the expression as the square of half of the coefficient of the x-term plus or minus a constant, for example,

$$a^2 - 6a + [5] = a^2 - 6a + [(\tfrac{1}{2} \times 6)^2 - 4] = (a^2 - 6a + 9) - 4 = (a - 3)^2 - 4$$
$$b^2 + 4b + [5] = b^2 + 4b + [\tfrac{1}{2} \times 4)^2 + 1] = (b^2 + 4b + 4) + 1 = (b + 2)^2 + 1$$

If the coefficient of the term in x^2 is negative, factor out -1 from all the terms in the quadratic expression and continue with the same method as above, for example,

$$-x^2 + 6x + [5] = -\{x^2 - 6x - [5]\} = -\{x^2 - 6x + [(\tfrac{1}{2} \times -6)^2 - 14]\}$$
$$= -\{(x^2 - 6x + 9) - 14\} = -\{(x - 3)^2 - 14\} = -(x - 3)^2 + 14$$

Try It Out

F In each of the following, write the quadratic expression as a perfect square.

1 $x^2 + 2x + 4$ **2** $x^2 - 8x + 1$ **3** $x^2 + 8x - 16$

4 $x^2 - 4x - 4$ **5** $-x^2 + 6x + 1$ **6** $-x^2 - 4x + 3$

Learn More About It

In C question 3, $(k - 2)(k + 2) = (k)(k) + (k)(+2) + (-2)(k) + (-2)(+2)$
$$= k^2 - 4 \quad \text{[note that the } k\text{-terms cancel]}$$

Again, $(2y - 3)(2y + 3) = (2y)(2y) + (2y)(+3) + (-3)(2y) + (-3)(+3)$
$$= 4y^2 - 9 \quad \text{[note that the } y\text{-terms cancel]}$$

In both examples, the linear terms cancel so that in these expansions, there is no *middle* term; there are only two terms and each one is a perfect square.

Hence, this type of expansion is called the **difference of two squares**.

What do you notice about the two expressions in the product?

Try It Out

G In each of the following expansions, find

(a) the term in x^2 **(b)** the x-term   **(c)** the constant term.

1 $(x + 3)(x - 3)$ **2** $(x + 5)(x - 5)$ **3** $(x - 3)(x + 3)$

4 $(2x - 3)(2x + 3)$ **5** $(4x + 1)(4x - 1)$ **6** $(2x - 1)(2x + 1)$

Practice

H Expand the following products.

1 $(x + 5)(x - 5)$ **2** $(x - 4)(x - 4)$ **3** $(x - 5)(x + 3)$

4 $(2x + 1)(3x + 2)$ **5** $(2x - 1)(2x + 1)$ **6** $(3x - 2)(x + 4)$

7 $(2x - 3)(2x - 5)$ **8** $(3x - 1)(x + 4)$ **9** $(2x + 3)(2x + 3)$

I Expand the following.

1 $(2m + 3)(2m + 3)$ **2** $(2y - 1)(2y + 1)$ **3** $(3b - 1)(3b - 1)$

4 $(2b + 5)(2b - 5)$ **5** $(2m + 1)(2m - 4)$ **6** $(3y - 2)(3y + 2)$

7 $(y + 3x)(y + 3x)$ **8** $(b - 3c)(b + 3c)$ **9** $(2y - x)(2y - x)$

J In each of the following expansions, find
(a) the coefficient **(i)** of y^2 **(ii)** of y
(b) the constant term.

1 $(2y + 5)(y - 3)$ **2** $(5y - 1)(y - 3)$ **3** $(y - 5)(3y + 1)$

4 $(3y - 2)(3y - 2)$ **5** $(2y - 1)(3y + 5)$ **6** $(y - 4)(y + 4)$

7 $(y - 4)(y + 5)$ **8** $(3y - 2)(3y + 2)$ **9** $(2y + 3)(2y + 3)$

> **Finished Early?**
> ➡ Go to page 459

Further Practice

K In each of the following expansions, write down the sign of
(a) the constant term   **(b)** the x-term.

1 $(3x + 1)(x - 1)$ **2** $(2x - 1)(x - 5)$ **3** $(x - 1)(3x + 1)$

4 $(2x - 5)(x - 3)$ **5** $(3x - 1)(x + 1)$ **6** $(x - 4)(5x + 7)$

7 $(x - 1)(3x - 2)$ **8** $(5x - 2)(x + 3)$ **9** $(3x + 1)(x + 7)$

L Write down the y-term in each of the following expansions.

1 $(4y + 3)(y - 3)$ **2** $(y - 3)(2y - 1)$ **3** $(y - 2)(y + 1)$

4 $(y - 3)(2y - 3)$ **5** $(3y + 1)(3y + 1)$ **6** $(2y - 3)(2y + 3)$

7 $(3y - 1)(3y - 1)$ **8** $(y - 4)(y + 1)$ **9** $(2y + 1)(y + 2)$

Key Fact

A quadratic expression in x may be expressed in the form $ax^2 + bx + c$ where a, b and c are constants. b and/or c may be 0.
Examples of quadratic equations are
$5x^2 + 2x - 3$; $5x^2 - 3$; $5x^2 + 2x$; $5x^2$.

> **Finished Early?**
> ➡ Go to page 459

② **Factorisation**

> ## Remember?
>
> To **factorise** an expression is to write it as a product of its factors, that is, to do the opposite of expansion. Common factors in an algebraic expression may be numbers, or variables, or may include both numbers and variables. For example,
>
> $$4x + 6y = 2(2x + 3y)$$
> $$15bh - 7bk = b(15h - 7k)$$
> $$12rl - 6rh = 6r(2l - h)$$
> $$6a^4b^2 + 3a^2b^5 = 3a^2b^2(2a^2 + b^3)$$
>
> The common factor may also be literal terms connected by plus or minus signs.
>
> For example, in the expression $15bh - 7bk$, if $b = (2a - c)$
> Then, the expression becomes $15(2a - c)h - 7(2a - c)k$
> $$= (2a - c)(15h - 7k)$$
> where the common factor is $(2a - c)$.

> ## Key Fact
>
> When you have factorised an expression, you should check your answer by working out the product of the factors.

Practice

 Factorise completely the following expressions.

1 $3a + 9b$ **2** $-20y - 15$ **3** $8rw - 12sw + 6tw$

4 $2xy^3 + 6x^2y$ **5** $10vw - 12uv$ **6** $9x^3 - 2xy^3$

7 $16d^2 - 8d + 6$ **8** $6m^3n + 12mn^3$ **9** $3ab + 7ac - 4ad$

10 $12a^3b + 9a^2b^5$ **11** $3(2x - y)x - 6(2x - y)^2$

12 $2g(h - 3k)j - 3(h - 3k)$ **13** $4lm + 3lm^2 + 6l^2m^2$

14 $(3a + b)(2a - b) - (3a + b)(3a - b) + (3a + b)(a + b)$

Further Practice

 Factorise completely the following expressions.

1 $21x + 3y$ **2** $8x^2 - 4x$ **3** $-12x - 6y - 3$

4 $5bd^2 - 3b^2 + 2bd$ **5** $15bh - 7bk$ **6** $5(m + 3) + (m + 3)n$

7 $x^2y - 10xy^2 + xy$ **8** $5d(d - 3)^2 - (d - 3)k$

9 $(h + 2k)(j - l) + (l + 6)(h + 2k)$ **10** $(1 + b^2)^2 - 3(1 + b^2)$

Word Check

inverse operation opposite of a given operation

reverse opposite sequence or order

Learn More About It

We know that when we expand $(a + b)(c + d)$, we get $ac + ad + bc + bd$. Since factorisation is the inverse of expansion, in order to factorise $ac + ad + bc + bd$, we have to do the inverse operations in the reverse order, as follows:

(i) group in pairs terms that have a common variable
$(ac + bc) + (ad + bd)$

(ii) take out the common variable in each group
$c(a + b) + d(a + b)$

(iii) take out the common factor, that is, $(a + b)$ in each product
$(a + b)(c + d)$

This method is called **factorisation by grouping**.

Note that by putting the terms in the following groups:
$(ac + ad) + (bc + bd)$, the product of the factors becomes $(c + d)(a + b)$.

Show that $(a + b)(c + d) = (c + d)(a + b)$.

What is the law that states that the final result is the same?

Try It Out

Factorise the following expressions.

1 $af + ag + bf + bg$ **2** $2ak - ch - 2ah + ck$

3 $2a^2 + axy - 2a - xy$ **4** $2jm - 2kn + 2km - 2jn$

Key Fact

The first step in factorising an expression is to take out any common factors in all the terms, for example, the factor '2' in **O** question 4.

Practice

P Factorise the following expressions.

1 $ac + bc + 2ad + 2bd$ **2** $3ux - 6uy - wx + 2wy$

3 $2rt + 3st - 2t^2 - 3rs$ **4** $6ab^2c - 2a^2b^2 - 3abc + a^2b$

5 $6acx + 4acy - 12adx - 8ady$ **6** $5y^2 - 10y - 3y + 6$

Further Practice

Q Factorise the following expressions.

1 $hm - 2km - 2hn + 4kn$ **2** $3sx + tx - 6sv - 2tv$

3 $6am - 3bm + 9bn - 18an$ **4** $x^2 + 5x - 3x - 15$

Word Check

quadratic term term in which the power of the variable is 2, or if there is more than one variable, the sum of their powers is 2 (e.g. a^2 or bc)

linear term term in which the power of the variable is 1

Learn More About It

In the same way that 7 and 4 are factors of 28, so are $(x + 2)$ and $(x + 3)$ the factors of $x^2 + 5x + 6$.

Therefore, in order to **factorise** a quadratic expression in which there are three terms, we have to find the two brackets that were multiplied, that is, to find the linear factors of the quadratic expression. Hence, we carry out the inverse operations of the expansion in the reverse order.

When the coefficient of the quadratic term is unity

for example in $x^2 + 5x + 6$, we consider:

(i) the factors of the quadratic term, x^2 : 'x and x', and we write $(x \quad)(x \quad)$

(ii) next, the factors of the constant term, $+6$, that is,
'$+1$ and $+6$', '-1 and -6', '-3 and -2' and '$+3$ and $+2$'

(iii) then, the pair of factors of '$+6$' which sum to the coefficient of the linear term, '$+5$', that is,

factors of $+6$	*sum of factors*
$+1$ and $+6$	$+7$
-1 and -6	-7
-3 and -2	-5
$+3$ and $+2$	$+5$ *

*Thus the pair of factors that will sum to '$+5$' is '$+3$ and $+2$'.

(iv) Hence, the factors of $x^2 + 5x + 6$ are $(x + 3)$ and $(x + 2)$,
that is, $x^2 + 5x + 6 = (x + 3)(x + 2)$.

Similarly, in the quadratic expression $y^2 - 3y - 4$, we consider

(i) the factors of the quadratic term, y^2: 'y and y', and we write $(y \quad)(y \quad)$

(ii) next, the factors of the constant term, ' -4', and the sum of each pair of factors

factors of -4	*sum of factors*
$+2$ and -2	0
-1 and $+4$	$+3$
$+1$ and -4	-3

(iii) The pair of factors that will sum to '-3', the coefficient of the linear term, is '$+1$ and -4'.

(iv) Hence, the factors of $y^2 - 3y - 4$ are $(y + 1)(y - 4)$,
that is, $y^2 - 3y - 4 = (y + 1)(y - 4)$.

Try It Out

(R) **1** Using the method in the examples above, work out and write down the factors of **(a)** $y^2 + 3y - 4$ **(b)** $x^2 - 5x + 6$.

2 In the quadratic expression $x^2 + cx + A$, A is the constant, and c is the coefficient of the linear term.
   (a) Copy and complete the following table for the *pairs of factors of A*.
   (b) For the given values of c, write the *required pair* of factors as shown in the first line.

A	pairs of factors of A		c	required
−8	−1 and +8; +1 and −8; −2 and +4; +2 and −4		−7	+1 and −8
+15			+8	
+4			−5	
−3			−2	
+12			+8	
−6			−5	
+10			−7	

Key Fact

In a quadratic expression, *when the coefficient of the quadratic term is* 1, and

- the *constant A is positive*, then both factors of A have the same sign.
  - ➤ When the linear term is negative, check only negative factors of A.
  - ➤ When the linear term is positive, check only positive factors of A.
- the *constant A is negative*, then the factors of A have opposite signs.
  - ➤ When the linear term is negative, the negative factor is numerically larger.
  - ➤ When the linear term is positive, the positive factor is numerically larger.

Practice

S Factorise each of the following expressions.

1 $a^2 + 3a - 4$ 2 $b^2 - 5b + 6$ 3 $c^2 + 5c + 6$

4 $f^2 + 4f - 12$ 5 $g^2 - 7g + 12$ 6 $j^2 + 8j + 12$

7 $3v^2 + 6v - 9$ 8 $2w^2 - 10w + 12$ 9 $4y^2 - 8y + 4$

Further Practice

T Factorise each of the following expressions.

1 $p^2 + 7p - 8$ 2 $r^2 - 12r + 20$ 3 $2t^2 - 7t + 6$

4 $d^2 + 6d + 5$ 5 $2b^2 - 10b + 12$ 6 $4h^2 - 12h - 16$

Learn More About It

Let the quadratic expression $x^2 + mx + n$ be a perfect square, where m and n are constants. Then, if the perfect square is $(x + D)^2$, where D is a constant, we know that $(x + D)^2 = x^2 + 2(D)x + (D)^2$ .... (1)

$$= x^2 + mx + n \qquad \text{.................................... (2)}$$

Comparing the x-terms in (1) and (2), we see that: $m = 2(D)$ .... (3)

and the constant terms in (1) and (2): $\qquad\qquad n = (D)^2$ .... (4)

From (3), $D = \frac{1}{2}m \rightarrow n = (\frac{1}{2}m)^2$

that is, *in a perfect square, when the coefficient of the x^2-term is 1, the constant term is the square of half the coefficient of the x-term.*

When $m > 0$, then the expression $x^2 + mx + n = (x + \frac{1}{2}m)^2$.

and the expression $x^2 - mx + n = (x - \frac{1}{2}m)^2$.

Try It Out

U Write the factors of the expansions found in **E** on page 290.

Practice

V Factorise each of the following expressions.

1 $p^2 + 8p + 16$ **2** $r^2 - 10r + 25$ **3** $2t^2 + 12t + 18$

4 $d^2 + 6df + 9f^2$ **5** $2b^2 - 8b + 8$ **6** $2ah^2 + 20ah + 50a$

Further Practice

W Factorise each of the following expressions.

1 $x^2 + 16x + 64$ **2** $m^2 - 12m + 36$ **3** $k^2 + 22k + 121$

4 $1 - 2y + y^2$ **5** $x^2 + 14xy + 49y^2$ **6** $81 + 18n + n^2$

Learn More About It

To factorise any quadratic expression, and in particular, *when the coefficient of the x^2-term is not unity*, for example, $3x^2 + 5x - 2$,

(i) find the product of the x^2-term and the constant term, that is,
$(3x^2) \times (-2)$

(ii) work out the factors of that product, $(-6x^2)$, and the pair of factors that sum to the coefficient of the x-term, $+5x$

factors of $-6x^2$	sum of factors
$+x$ and $-6x$	$-5x$
$-x$ and $+6x$	$+5x$ *
$-3x$ and $+2x$	$-x$
$+3x$ and $-2x$	$+x$

*Thus the pair of factors that will sum to '$+5x$' is '$-x$ and $+6x$'

(iii) replace '$+5x$' with '$-x$ and $+6x$' and write $3x^2 + 5x - 2$ as
$$3x^2 + 6x - x - 2$$

(iv) group in pairs the terms that have a common factor, that is,
$$(3x^2 + 6x) + (-x - 2)$$

Note that the common factor in the second group of terms is (-1).

(v) take out the common factor, $(x + 2)$, in each group, that is,
$$(x + 2)3x + (x + 2)(-1)$$

(vi) take out the common factor in each product, that is,
$$(x + 2)(3x - 1)$$

Hence, the factors of $3x^2 + 5x - 2$ are $(x + 2)$ and $(3x - 1)$,
that is, $3x^2 + 5x - 2 = (x + 2)(3x - 1)$.

Try It Out

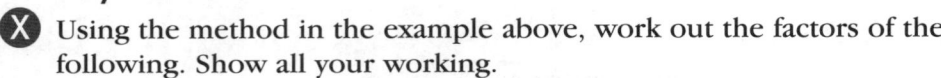 Using the method in the example above, work out the factors of the following. Show all your working.

1 $2y^2 + 7y + 3$ **2** $2y^2 + 5y - 3$ **3** $2y^2 - 5y - 3$

4 $4x^2 - 8xy + 3y^2$ **5** $4x^2 - xy - 3y^2$ **6** $4x^2 - 13xy + 3y^2$

Learn More About It

We may also use a method similar to the method used when the coefficient of the term in x^2 is 1. List the pairs of positive factors of the term in x^2 and the pairs of factors of the constant term. By finding the different products of these pairs, we can work out the x-term directly.

For example, in the expression $3x^2 + 5x - 2$, write

factors of $3x^2$	factors of -2	sum of factors
$+3x$ and $+x$	-2 and $+1$	$(+3x \times -2)$ and $(+x \times +1) = -5x$
$+3x$ and $+x$	$+1$ and -2	$(+3x \times +1)$ and $(+x \times -2) = +x$
$+x$ and $+3x$	-1 and $+2$	$(+x \times -1)$ and $(+3x \times +2) = +5x$ *
$+x$ and $+3x$	$+2$ and -1	$(+x \times +2)$ and $(+3x \times -1) = -x$

Note that we use only the positive factors of the term in x^2. but these factors have been reversed to multiply each pair of factors of the constant term in order to ensure that all possible products are obtained.

* Thus the pairs of factors that will sum to '$+5x$' are
'$+x$ and $+3x$'   and   '-1 and $+2$'.

Remember that, in order to get the x-term in the expansion, we have to multiply
(the first term in the first bracket × the second term in the second bracket)
and
(the second term in the first bracket × the first term in the second bracket).

Therefore, the factors of $3x^2 + 5x - 2$ are $(x + 2)$ and $(3x - 1)$,
that is, $3x^2 + 5x - 2 = (x + 2)(3x - 1)$.

Try It Out

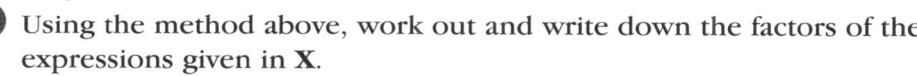 Using the method above, work out and write down the factors of the expressions given in **X**.

> # Key Fact
> The factors   of the perfect square, $x^2 + 2xy + y^2$ are $(x + y)^2$
>   of the perfect square, $x^2 - 2xy + y^2$ are $(x - y)^2$
>   of the difference of two squares, $x^2 - y^2$ are $(x + y)(x - y)$
> The expression $x^2 + y^2$ has no factors.

Practice

Z Factorise the following expressions.

1 $3y^2 + 10y + 3$ 2 $3y^2 + 6y + 3$ 3 $3y^2 - 6y - 3$

4 $3x^2 - 8x - 3$ 5 $6x^2 - 7x - 3$ 6 $6x^2 + 7x - 3$

7 $6m^2 - 6$ 8 $6m^2 - 12m + 6$ 9 $6m^2 - 13m + 6$

10 $2v^2 - 16vw + 32w^2$ 11 $12y^2 + 35yx + 18x^2$ 12 $8c^2 - 18d^2$

13 $(x - 3)^2 - 4y^2$ 14 $27x^2 - 12y^2$ 15 $x^2 - 15xy + 54y^2$

Further Practice

AA Factorise the following expressions.

1 $y^2 + 9y + 8$ **2** $2y^2 - 11y + 15$ **3** $9y^2 - 6y + 1$

4 $x^2 - 3x - 10$ **5** $3x^2 - 75$ **6** $4x^2 + 12x + 8$

7 $m^2 - 16n^2$ **8** $11m^2 - m(3m + 4)$ **9** $12 + 11m - 5m^2$

> **Finished Early?**
> Go to page 459

Key Fact

Factorisation can be used to simplify calculations, for example,

$$73 \times 59 + 27 \times 59 = 59(73 + 27) = 59 \times 100 = 5900$$

Remember to apply BODMAS when doing calculations.

Practice

AB Use factorisation to simplify the following.

1 $267 \times 4 + 267 \times 6$ **2** $67 \times 49 - 47 \times 49$

3 $73.41^2 - 26.59^2$

4 $\pi R^2 h - \pi r^2 h$, where $\pi = 3\frac{1}{7}$
and $R = 17\,\text{cm}$, $r = 11\,\text{cm}$, $h = 9\,\text{cm}$

Further Practice

AC Use factorisation to simplify the following.

1 $37 \times 53 - 17 \times 53$

2 $83 \times 34 + 83 \times 16$

3 $307^2 - 93^2$

> **Finished Early?**
> Go to page 459

3 Quadratic Functions

Learn About It

Consider the function $y = x^2$ for the domain $-3 \leqslant x < 4$, $x \in W$.

The table of values is given on the right.

x	-3	-2	-1	0	1	2	3
y	9	4	1	0	1	4	9

The set of ordered pairs for integral values in the given domain is

$\{(-3, 9), (-2, 4), (-1, 1), (0, 0), (1, 1), (2, 4), (3, 9)\}$

The arrow diagram is shown on the right.

Is this a one-to-one or a many-to-one function?

This is a many-to-one function since more than one object is mapped to the same image.

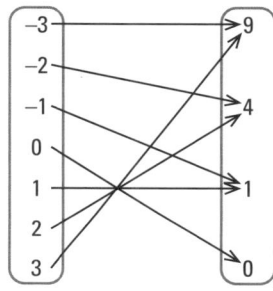

The function may be represented graphically by plotting the ordered pairs as the coordinates of points on x- and y-axes.

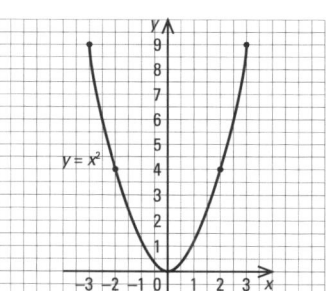

Key Fact

The quadratic function is the equation of the curve called a **parabola** that is either cup-shaped or cap-shaped. Hence, there exists a turning point on the curve, that is, either a minimum or a maximum value of the quadratic function.

Try It Out

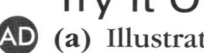 **(a)** Illustrate the function $y = x^2 - 2x - 3$, for $-3 < x \leqslant 4$, $x \in W$
  by means of **(i)** a table of values **(ii)** a set of ordered pairs
  (iii) an arrow diagram **(iv)** a Cartesian graph.
(b) On the graph identify:
  (i) the x-coordinate of the turning point of the function
  (ii) the maximum or minimum value of the function.

Learn More About It

We can find the maximum value or the minimum value of a quadratic function by writing the quadratic expression as a perfect square, that is,

(i) make the coefficient of the term in x^2 equal to 1
(ii) add the square of half the coefficient of the x-term
(iii) subtract the square of half the coefficient of the x-term (to keep the value of the expression the same).

We also use the fact that the square of any non-zero number – either positive or negative – is always positive, for example, $(+3)^2 = (-3)^2 = 9$. Note that $(0)^2 = 0$.

Given the function $y = x^2 - 4x + 1$
write the expression as $y = x^2 - 4x + (-\frac{4}{2})^2 + 1 - (-\frac{4}{2})^2$
$$y = (x - 2)^2 - 3$$

Since $(x - 2)^2 \geqslant 0$, $y \geqslant -3$, that is, the *minimum* value of y is –3. The minimum value of y occurs when $x - 2 = 0$, that is, when $x = 2$.

Try It Out

 Given the function $y = x^2 + 2x - 3$,
(a) write the function as a perfect square
(b) state whether the function has a minimum or a maximum value
(c) find this value.

Learn More About It

Remember that the general quadratic function is defined as $y = ax^2 + bx + c$, where y is a function of x, and a, b and c are positive or negative constants, $a \neq 0$.

To write the function as a perfect square,

divide all terms by a, the coefficient of x^2: $\frac{y}{a} = x^2 + \frac{b}{a}x + \frac{c}{a}$

add and subtract the square of half the coefficient of x:

$$\frac{y}{a} = x^2 + \frac{b}{a}x + \left(\frac{b}{2a}\right)^2 - \left(\frac{b}{2a}\right)^2 + \frac{c}{a}$$

write as a square and simplify: $\frac{y}{a} = \left(x + \frac{b}{2a}\right)^2 - \frac{b^2}{4a^2} + \frac{4ac}{4a^2}$

that is, $y = a\left(x + \frac{b}{2a}\right)^2 + \frac{4ac - b^2}{4a}$

A minimum or maximum value occurs when $x + \frac{b}{2a} = 0$

that is, when $x = -\frac{b}{2a}$

and the minimum or maximum value is equal to $y = \dfrac{4ac - b^2}{4a}$

> ## Key Fact
>
> When a > 0, the function has a minimum value;
> when a < 0 the function has a maximum value

Try It Out

 Given the function $y = 2x^2 - 7x + 6$,
  (a) state whether the function has a maximum or a minimum value
  (b) find this value and the corresponding x-coordinate.

Practice

 For each of the following functions
  (a) complete the square
  (b) state whether the function has a maximum or a minimum value
  (c) find this value.

1 $a^2 + 3a - 4$	**2** $b^2 - 5b + 6$	**3** $c^2 + 5c + 6$
4 $12 - f^2 - 4f$	**5** $g^2 - 7g + 12$	**6** $j^2 + 8j + 12$
7 $3v^2 + 6v - 9$	**8** $10w - 2w^2 - 12$	**9** $4y^2 - 8y + 4$
10 $-x^2 + 16x - 14$	**11** $m^2 - 12m + 25$	**12** $4c^2 - 9 - 6c$
13 $3y^2 + 10y + 2$	**14** $-2b^2 - 5b - 1$	**15** $h^2 + 1 - \dfrac{h+1}{2}$

Further Practice

 For each of the following functions

  (a) complete the square

  (b) state whether the function has a maximum or a minimum value

  (c) find this value.

1 $p^2 + 7p - 8$	**2** $12r - 20 - r^2$	**3** $2t^2 - 7t + 6$
4 $d^2 + 6d + 5$	**5** $2b^2 - 10b + 12$	**6** $16 - 4h^2 + 12h$
7 $1 - 2y - 2y^2$	**8** $x^2 + 11x - 14$	**9** $11 - 7n - n^2$

> **Finished Early?**
> Go to page 460

18 Quadratic Equations and Graphs

In this chapter you will learn about ...
1. algebraic solution
2. graphical solution
3. simultaneous linear and quadratic equations

1 Algebraic Solution

Learn About It

A **quadratic equation** is an equation in which 2 is the highest power of the variable in the algebraic expression, that is, an equation of the *second degree*. Examples of quadratic equations include

$$a^2 = 9; \quad ab + 3 = b; \quad b^2 - 3b = 0; \quad c^2 - 3c = 4$$

Key Fact

An equation is a statement that an algebraic expression is equal to another algebraic expression or to a numeric value.

To solve an equation is to find the values that satisfy the equation, that is, that make the equation true.

In order to solve a quadratic equation by an algebraic method, we use the fact that, if the product of two numeric values is zero, one or both of the values must be zero. For example,

$$5 \times 0 = 0; -3 \times 0 = 0; 0 \times 0 = 0.$$

If $p \times q = 0$, then p = 0 or $q = 0$.

Also, if $4pq = 0$, then $p = 0$ or $q = 0$, since $4 \neq 0$.

Again, if $p = (x + a) = 0$, then $x = -a$

and if $q = (x - b) = 0$, then $x = b$.

Therefore, to solve a quadratic equation we have to write the expression as a product of its factors and put the product equal to zero.

Before factorising the expression in a quadratic equation, the terms of the equation must be arranged so that the right-hand side (RHS) of the equation is zero.

For example, to solve the equation $x^2 + 3x + 4 = 2$, we write the equation as
$\quad x^2 + 3x + 2 = 0$.

Factorising the left-hand side (LHS) of the equation,

we get $\quad (x + 2)(x + 1) = 0$

so that $\quad (x + 2) = 0$ or $(x + 1) = 0$

and $\quad\quad x = -2$ or $x = -1$.

Therefore, the values of x that satisfy the quadratic equation are -2 and -1.

The solutions of a quadratic equation are called the **roots** of the equation.

Try It Out

A Solve the following equations.

1 $(x + 1)(x + 3) = 0$ **2** $x(x - 1) = 0$ **3** $(x + 2)^2 = 0$

4 $(x - 5)^2 = 0$ **5** $(4 + x)(x - 5) = 0$ **6** $x^2 - 3x = 10$

Key Fact

When the expression in a quadratic equation is a perfect square, we say that there is a repeated root, for example in $(x + 2)^2 = 0$, the roots are $x = -2$ twice.

Practice

B Solve the following equations.

1 $a^2 + 3a - 4 = 0$ **2** $b^2 = 5b - 6$ **3** $c^2 + 5c + 6 = 0$

4 $f^2 + 4f = 12$ **5** $g^2 - 7g + 12 = 0$ **6** $j^2 + 8j + 12 = 0$

7 $3v^2 + 6v - 9 = 0$ **8** $2w^2 = 10w - 12$ **9** $4y^2 - 8y + 4 = 0$

Further Practice

C Solve the following equations.

1 $p^2 + 7p = 8$ **2** $r^2 = 12r - 20$ **3** $2t^2 - 7t + 6 = 0$

4 $d^2 + 6d + 5 = 0$ **5** $2b^2 - 10b + 12 = 0$ **6** $4h^2 - 12h = 16$

Finished Early?

 Go to page 460

Learn More About It

In order to solve a quadratic equation, it can be useful to write the LHS as a perfect square, and rearrange the terms as follows.

Given the equation $x^2 + 4x - 5 = 0$

  (i) write the constant on the RHS of the equation
  $$x^2 + 4x = 5$$

  (ii) use the term in x^2 and the x-term to write a perfect square on the LHS, that is, add the square of half the coefficient of the x-term to both sides of the equation
  $$x^2 + 4x + (\tfrac{4}{2})^2 = 5 + 4$$

  Why do we add '4' to the RHS of the equation?

(iii) simplify both sides of the equation
  $$(x + 2)^2 = 9$$

 (iv) take square roots of both sides of the equation
  $$(x + 2) = \pm\sqrt{9}$$

  (v) write the equation with x only on the LHS and simplify the RHS
  $$x = -2 \pm 3$$

Then the roots of the equation are $(-2 + 3)$ and $(-2 - 3)$
that is, the roots are 1 and –5.

Note that in this example, the equation $x^2 + 4x - 5 = 0$ can be factorised directly to give the linear factors: $(x + 5)(x - 1) = 0$

Key Fact

When we take the square root of the constant on the RHS of the equation, we have to use both the positive and the negative values in order to get the two roots of the equation.

When the quadratic expression on the LHS cannot be factorised and the roots of the quadratic equation are non-rational, the above approach that rewrites the LHS of the equation as a perfect square is one method that we can apply. The roots of such equations are approximate and must be written to a given degree of accuracy.

For example, to solve the equation $x^2 + 6x - 2 = 0$, that cannot be factorised,

  (i) write the equation with the constant on the RHS
  $$x^2 + 6x = 2$$

(ii) use the term in x^2 and the x-term to write a perfect square on the LHS, that is, add the square of half the coefficient of the x-term to *both* sides of the equation

$$x^2 + 6x + \left(\tfrac{6}{2}\right)^2 = 2 + 9$$

(iii) simplify both sides of the equation

$$(x + 3)^2 = 11$$

(iv) take square roots of both sides of the equation

$$(x + 3) = \pm\sqrt{11}$$

(v) write only x on the LHS of the equation

$$x = -3 \pm \sqrt{11}$$

The roots of the equation are $(-3 + \sqrt{11})$ and $(-3 - \sqrt{11})$.

The above method of solving quadratic equations is called **completing the square**.

Word Check

surd square root of a number that is not a perfect square, for example, $\sqrt{3}$, $\sqrt{5}$, $\sqrt{11}$ and so on

Try It Out

D Use the method of completing the square to solve the following equations. If necessary, give your answers correct to 3 significant figures (s.f.).

1 $p^2 + p = 2$ **2** $r^2 = 2r + 5$ **3** $t^2 + 6t - 3 = 0$

4 $d^2 + 4d = 1$ **5** $b^2 - b + 8 = 9$ **6** $k^2 = 6k - 6$

Key Fact

Before completing the square, the coefficient of the term in x^2 in the quadratic expression must be made equal to 1, and the constant must be on the RHS of the equation.

Practice

E Use the method of completing the square to solve the following equations. Give your answers correct to 3 s.f.

1 $x^2 + 16x + 14 = 0$ **2** $m^2 = 12m - 25$ **3** $4c^2 - 9 = 6c$

4 $1 = 2y + 2y^2$ **5** $x^2 + 11x = 14$ **6** $11 = 7n + n^2$

7 $3y^2 + 10y + 2 = 0$ **8** $2b^2 + 5b + 1 = 0$ **9** $h^2 - 1 = \dfrac{h + 1}{2}$

Finished Early?
 Go to page 460

Further Practice

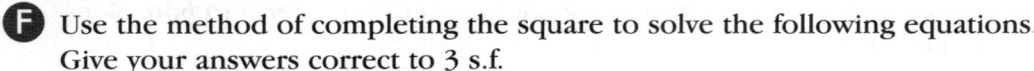

F Use the method of completing the square to solve the following equations. Give your answers correct to 3 s.f.

1 $y^2 + 4y = 6$ **2** $2y^2 + 5y - 20 = 0$ **3** $3y^2 = 6y - 1$

4 $x^2 - 3x + 1 = 0$ **5** $3x^2 - 7 = 2x$ **6** $x^2 + 2x = 7$

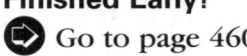

Finished Early?
➡ Go to page 460

Learn More About It

The general quadratic equation is $ax^2 + bx + c = 0$, where a, b and c are constants. The method of completing the square can be derived for the general quadratic equation, $ax^2 + bx + c = 0$, as follows:

  (i) make the coefficient of the term in x^2 equal to '1' by dividing *all the terms* by a, the coefficient of the term in x^2

$$x^2 + \frac{b}{a}x + \frac{c}{a} = 0$$

 (ii) put the constant term on the RHS of the equation

$$x^2 + \frac{b}{a}x = -\frac{c}{a}$$

(iii) use the term in x^2 and the x-term to write a perfect square on the LHS by adding the square of half the coefficient of the x-term to *both sides* of the equation

$$\left(x + \frac{b}{2a}\right)^2 = -\frac{c}{a} + \left(\frac{b}{2a}\right)^2$$

 (iv) take square roots of both sides of the equation

$$x + \frac{b}{2a} = \pm \sqrt{\frac{-4ac + b^2}{4a^2}}$$

  (v) write the equation with x only on the LHS and simplify the RHS

$$x = \frac{-b \pm \sqrt{b^2 - 4ac}}{2a}$$

This is *the formula* for solving any quadratic equation *but* neither the method of completing the square nor using the formula should be used when the quadratic equation can be factorised.

Try It Out

G Use the formula to solve the following equations. If necessary, give your answers correct to 3 s.f.

1 $p^2 + p = 2$ **2** $r^2 = 2r + 5$ **3** $t^2 + 6t - 3 = 0$

4 $d^2 + 4d = 1$ **5** $b^2 - b + 8 = 9$ **6** $k^2 = 6k - 6$

Practice

  Use the formula to solve the following equations.
Give your answers correct to 3 s.f.

1 $x^2 + 16x + 14 = 0$ **2** $m^2 = 12m - 25$ **3** $4c^2 - 9 = 6c$

4 $1 = 2y + 2y^2$ **5** $x^2 + 11x = 14$ **6** $11 = 7n + n^2$

7 $3y^2 + 10y + 2 = 0$ **8** $2b^2 + 5b + 1 = 0$ **9** $h^2 - 1 = \dfrac{h + 1}{2}$

Further Practice

Use the formula to solve the following equations.
Give your answers correct to 3 s.f.

1 $y^2 + 4y = 6$ **2** $2y^2 + 5y - 20 = 0$ **3** $3y^2 = 6y - 1$

4 $x^2 - 3x + 1 = 0$ **5** $3x^2 - 7 = 2x$ **6** $x^2 + 2x = 7$

> **Finished Early?**
> ➡ Go to page 460

② Graphical Solution

The general quadratic function is defined as $y = ax^2 + bx + c$, where y is a function of x, and a, b and c are positive or negative constants, $a \neq 0$.

When $y = 0$, the function becomes a quadratic equation.

Since $y = 0$ at the points where the graph of the function cuts the x-axis, the x-values at the points of intersection of the curve and the x-axis are the roots of the corresponding quadratic equation, $ax^2 + bx + c = 0$.

For a graph plotted on Cartesian axes, the curve is usually in one of three positions with respect to the x-axis, as shown in the following diagrams,

(i) intersecting the x-axis at 2 points (when $y = 0$, there are 2 distinct roots)

(ii) touching the x-axis at 1 point (when $y = 0$, there is 1 repeated root)

(iii) not intersecting or touching the x-axis (when $y = 0$, there are no real roots)

These curves are illustrated overleaf.

When $a > 0$, the curve is cup-shaped.

(i)

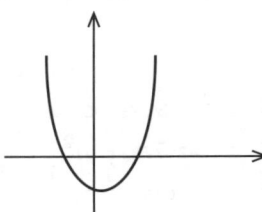

(ii)

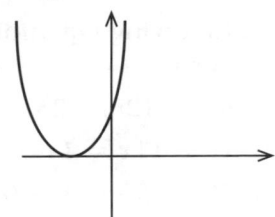

(iii)

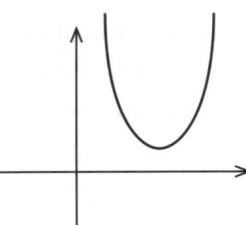

When a < 0, the curve is cap-shaped.

(i)

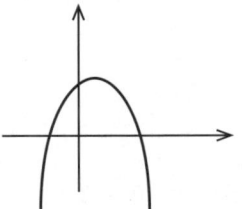

(ii)

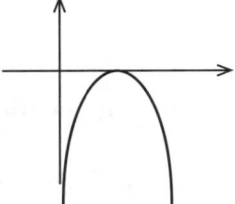

(iii)

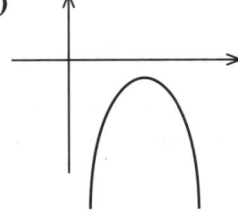

Try It Out

J Use this graph of the function
$y = x^2 + 2x - 3$ to write down:
  (a) the equation that can be solved
  (b) the roots of the equation.

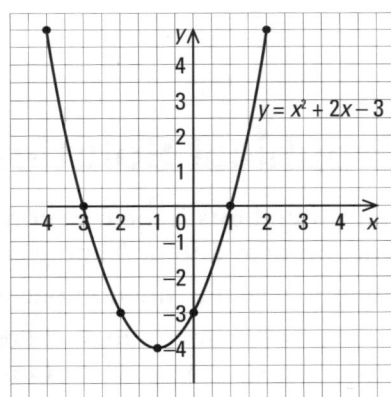

$y = x^2 + 2x - 3$

Key Fact

Note that the values of a quadratic
function for a given domain are
symmetrical about the **ordinate** at
the turning point of the function.

Example Given the quadratic function $y = f(x)$
where $y = x^2 - 4x + 1$ for the domain $-2 < x \leqslant 5, x \in W$
(a) draw up a table of values (b) list the set of ordered pairs
(c) draw the graph
(d) use the graph to find the roots of the equation
$x^2 - 4x + 1 = 0$, correct to 1 d.p.
(e) complete the square or use the formula to check your answers.

Working & Answer Consider the quadratic function
$y = x^2 - 4x + 1$, for the domain $-2 < x \leqslant 5$

(a) The table of values is given below.

x	−1	0	1	2	3	4	5
x^2	1	0	1	4	9	16	25
$-4x$	4	0	−4	−8	−12	−16	−20
$+1$	+1	+1	+1	+1	+1	+1	+1
y	6	1	−2	−3	−2	1	6

(b) $\{(-1, 6), (0, 1), (1, -2), (2, -3), (3, -2), (4, 1), (5, 6)\}$

(c)

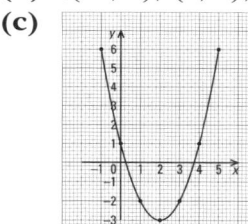

(d) From the graph, at the points of intersection of the curve and the x-axis, the roots of $x^2 - 4x + 1 = 0$
are $x = 0.3$ or 3.7

(e) **by completing the square**
Adding and subtracting $(-\frac{4}{2})^2$ to LHS: $(x - 2)^2 - 4 + 1 = 0$

Simplifying and writing the constant on RHS: $(x - 2)^2 = 3$
Taking the square root on both sides of the equation:
$x - 2 = \pm\sqrt{3}$
Writing only x on the LHS: $x = 2 \pm \sqrt{3}$
$x = 0.3$ or 3.7, correct to 1 d.p.

by formula
$$x = \frac{-b \pm \sqrt{b^2 - 4ac}}{2a}, \text{ where } a = 1, b = -4, c = 1$$

Substituting in the formula:
$$x = \frac{-(-4) \pm \sqrt{(-4)^2 - 4(1)(1)}}{2(1)} = \frac{4 \pm \sqrt{12}}{2}$$
$$= 2 \pm \sqrt{3} = 0.3 \text{ or } 3.7 \text{ to 1 d.p.}$$

Practice

1 For each of the following functions, find the range of the function:
   (a) $g : x \rightarrow 2x(x - 3)$ for the domain $-2, -1, 0, 1, 2, 3, 4$
   (b) $h : x \rightarrow 2x^2 - 3x - 5$, $x \in \{-2, 0, 2, 4, 6\}$

2 (a) Use this graph of the function
   $y = 2 - 3x - 2x^2$ to write down
   (i) the equation that can be solved
   (ii) the roots of the equation.
   (b) Check your answers by factorising the
   LHS of the corresponding equation.

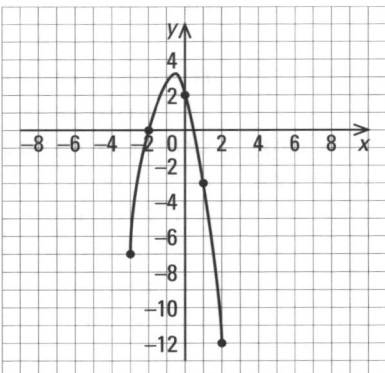

3 Below is a table of values for the function
   $y = x^2 + x - 8$ from $x = -4$ to $x = +3$.

x	−4	−3	−2	−1	0	1	2	3
y	4	−2	−6	−8	−8	−6	−2	4

Use the table to draw the graph of the function and solve graphically the
equation $x^2 + x - 8 = 0$.

4 Each curve in the figure
on the right represents
a quadratic function.

Find the roots of each of
the corresponding
equations where possible.

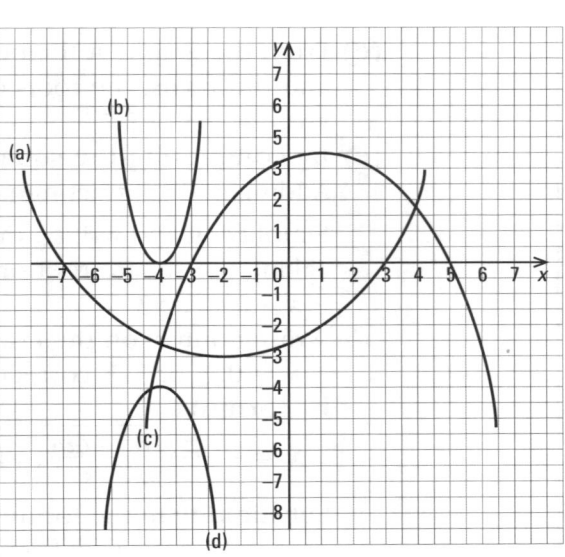

5 Given that
$$y = 4x^2 - 12x + 9$$
(a) copy and complete the table on the right
(b) draw a graph of the function
(c) find the roots of the equation
$$4x^2 - 12x + 9 = 0.$$

x	−1	0	1	2	3	4
4x²	4			16		64
−12x	12			−24		−48
9	9			9		9
y	25			1		25

6 (a) Draw a graph of the function $11 + 8x - 2x^2$ from $x = -2$ to $x = +6$.
(b) Hence, find the approximate roots of the equation
$$2x^2 - 8x - 11 = 0.$$

Key Fact

There are coincident roots (a repeated root) of an equation when the graph of the corresponding function *touches* the x–axis.

Further Practice

L 1 (a) Use the graph on the right of the function
$$y = 3x - x^2$$
to write down
(i) the equation that can be solved
(ii) the roots of the equation.
(b) Check your answers by factorising the equation.

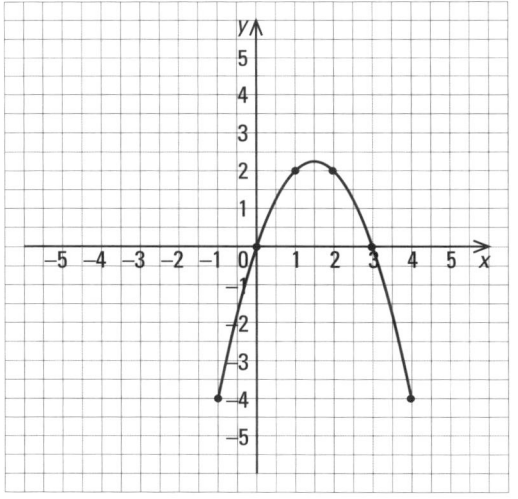

2 Below is a table of values for the function
$$y = 3x^2 + 10x + 6 \text{ from } x = -4 \text{ to } x = +1.$$

x	−4	−3	−2	−1	0	1
y	14	3	−2	−1	6	19

Use the table to draw the graph of the function and solve graphically the equation $3x^2 + 10x + 6 = 0$.

3 (a) Given that $y = x^2 + 3x - 2$, copy and complete the table below.

x	−5	−4	−3	−2	−1	0	1	2
x^2	25	16	9	4				
+3x	−15	−12	−9	−6				
−2	−2	−2	−2	−2				
y	8	2	−2	−4				

(b) Draw a graph of the function.

(c) Find the roots of the equation $x^2 + 3x - 2 = 0$.

4 (a) Draw a graph of the function $x^2 + 2x - 2$ from $x = -4$ to $x = +2$.

(b) Hence, find the approximate roots of the equation
$x^2 + 2x - 2 = 0$.

Finished Early?
➡ Go to page 461

Learn More About It

Some real-life problems may lead to quadratic equations that can then be solved to give the solution to the word problem.

Example	Andy and Annette walk to school. Andy walks at an average speed of v km/h. Annette walks the same distance at an average speed of $(v - 1)$ km/h. If the distance is 10 km and Andy takes 20 minutes less than Annette, find their speeds.
Working	Time taken by Andy $= \dfrac{10}{v}$ hours

Time taken by Annette $= \dfrac{10}{v - 1}$ hours

Since difference in times $= 20$ minutes,
$$\frac{10}{v - 1} - \frac{10}{v} = \frac{1}{3}$$

Multiplying by $3\,v(v - 1)$,
$$10 \times 3v - 10 \times 3\,(v - 1) = v(v - 1)$$
$$30v - 30v + 30 = v^2 - v$$
$$v^2 - v - 30 = 0$$
$$(v - 6)(v + 5) = 0$$
$$v = 6, \text{ since } v > 0$$

Answer	Andy's speed is 6 km/h.
	Annette's speed is 5 km/h.

Try It Out

 1 The sum of a number and its square is 90.

    (a) Write an equation to represent this information

    (b) If the number is greater than zero, find the number.

2 A fruit vendor sold n oranges at $(2n - 15)$ cents each and received $42.50. Write an equation to show this information and find the number of oranges the vendor sold.

3 Twice a whole number subtracted from 3 times the square of the number leaves 133. Find the number.

Practice

 1 When 12 times a number greater than zero is added to twice its square, the result is 270.

    (a) Write an equation to represent this information.

    (b) Find the number.

2 A cyclist travels from his home to his office 8 km away at x km/h and returns home along the same route at $(x - 3)$ km/h. If the total time of travel is 1 h 12 min, find his speeds.

3 The length of a plank is five times its width. When the width is reduced by 1 cm and the length is also reduced by 1 cm, the area is 352 cm². Find the original length and width of the plank.

4 The dimensions of a right-angled triangle are shown in the figure on the right.

    (a) Write and simplify an equation showing the relation between the lengths of the sides.

        (*Hint*: use Pythagoras' theorem.)

    (b) Find the length of each side.

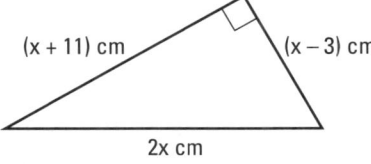

5 A path of uniform width runs along two sides of a rectangular garden that measures 16 m by 8 m, as shown in the diagram on the right.

If the total area of the garden and the path is 180 m², find the width of the path.

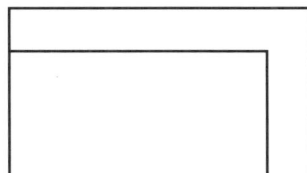

Further Practice

1 Divide 28 into two parts so that the product of the parts is 192.

2 The area of a rectangle is 180 cm². Its length is reduced by 5 cm and its breadth by 2 cm so that it becomes a square. Find the length of a side of the square.

3 The denominator of a fraction is 7 more than its numerator. If 6 is added to the numerator and 5 is added to the denominator, the fraction is doubled. Find the fraction.

4 Andy subtracted the same number from 15 and from 21. The product of his answers is 135. Find the number.

> **Finished Early?**
> Go to page 461

3 Simultaneous Linear and Quadratic Equations

Learn About It

It is often necessary to find the coordinates of the point where a straight line cuts a curve, that is, to solve simultaneous equations in two unknowns where one is a linear equation and the other is a quadratic equation. The most common algebraic method is the *substitution method*.

We use one of the equations (generally the linear equation) to write one of the unknowns in terms of the other. Substitute this expression in the other equation and solve the resulting equation in one unknown (generally a quadratic equation).

Example   Solve the pair of equations: $2x^2 - y^2 = -7$

$$x + y = 2$$

Working

$$2x^2 - y^2 = -7 \qquad\qquad\qquad (1)$$
$$x + y = 2 \qquad\qquad\qquad (2)$$

From (2) $y = 2 - x$ (3)

Substituting for y in (1) and simplifying

$$2x^2 - (2 - x)^2 = -7$$
$$2x^2 - 4 + 4x - x^2 + 7 = 0$$
$$x^2 + 4x + 3 = 0$$
$$(x + 1)(x + 3) = 0$$
$$x = -1 \text{ or } -3$$

Substituting for x in (3) and simplifying

$$y = 2 - (-1) \text{ or } 2 - (-3)$$
$$y = 3 \text{ or } 5$$

Answer   The solutions are: $x = -1$ and $y = 3$

$$x = -3 \text{ and } y = 5$$

Key Fact

The solutions of simultaneous linear and quadratic equations in two unknowns may be written as ordered pairs. In the above example, we may write the solutions as $(-1, 3)$ and $(-3, 5)$.

Try It Out

P Solve each of the following simultaneous equations.

1 $xy = 15$

    $4x - y = 7$

2 $x^2 - y^2 = -3$

    $x + y = 3$

Learn More About It

Simultaneous linear and quadratic equations may also be solved graphically.

Example (a) Draw up a table of values for $y = x^2 + x - 3$
for the domain $-4 \leqslant x \leqslant 3, x \in \mathbb{Q}$.
(b) Draw the graph of y, using a scale of 1 cm to 1 unit on
the y-axis and 2 cm to 1 unit on the x-axis.
From your graph,
(c) Find the roots of the equation $x^2 + x - 3 = 0$, to 1 d.p.
(d) Deduce the roots of the equation $x^2 + x - 5 = 0$
(e) State the minimum value of $x^2 + x - 3$.
(f) On the same axes, draw the graph of $y = 2(x - 1)$.
(g) Deduce the roots of the equation $x^2 + x - 3 = 2(x - 1)$.

Working $y = x^2 + x - 3$, for the domain $-4 \leqslant x \leqslant 3$
& Answer (a) The table of values for the given domain is

x	−4	−3	−2	−1	0	1	2	3
x^2	16	9	4	1	0	1	4	9
+x	−4	−3	−2	−1	0	1	2	3
−3	−3	−3	−3	−3	−3	−3	−3	−3
y	9	3	−1	−3	−3	−1	3	9

(b) and (f)

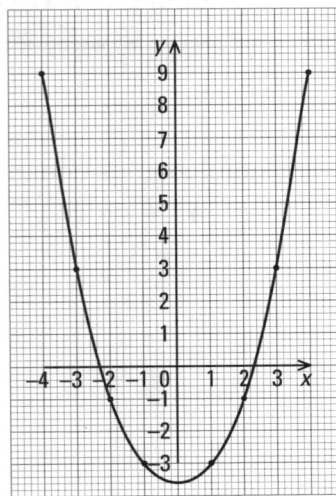

(c) From the graph, at $y = 0$, the roots of
$x^2 + x - 3 = 0$ are −2.3 and 1.3

(d) Minimum value of $x^2 + x - 3 = -3.3$

(e) Since $x^2 + x - 5 = x^2 + x - 3 - 2$,

$x^2 + x - 5 = 0 \rightarrow x^2 + x - 3 = 2$

From the graph, the roots of $x^2 + x - 5 = 0$ are at the points of intersection of the curve and $y = 2$, that is, the roots are $x = -2.8$ and 1.8

(g) Roots of $x^2 + x - 3 = 2(x - 1)$ are at the points of intersection of the curve and $y = 2(x - 1)$, that is, the roots are -0.6 and 1.6

Practice

1 Use the substitution method to solve each of the following simultaneous equations.

(a) $2x + y = 1$
$4x^2 + y^2 = 61$

(b) $2x^2 - y^2 = -2$
$3x + y = 1$

(c) $3x^2 - xy = 0$
$2y - 5x = 1$

(d) $x^2 - 3x = y$
$y = 2 - 2x$

(e) $xy + x = -8$
$x - y = 7$

(f) $x^2 - y^2 = -7$
$x + y = 2$

2 Use a graphical method to solve each pair of simultaneous equations.

(a) $x^2 - 3x = y$ and $y = 2 - 2x$

(b) $y = x^2 - 2x - 5$ and $y = 2x - 3$

3 The graph of the function

$y = 4x^2 - 9x - 1$

is shown in the diagram on the right. Use the graph to find the roots, correct to 1 d.p, of the following equations.

(a) $4x^2 - 9x - 1 = 7$

(b) $4x^2 - 9x + 3 = 0$

(c) $4x^2 - 9x - 1 = \frac{1}{4}(5x + 5)$

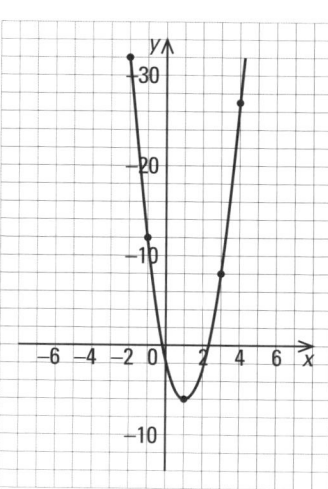

Further Practice

 1 Solve each of the following simultaneous equations algebraically.

(a) $x^2 + 2y^2 = 3$
$x - 3y = 2$

(b) $x^2 + y^2 = 25$
$2x + y = 5$

(c) $xy = 30$
$3x + y = 21$

(d) $x^2 + 2xy = 8$
$x + 2y = 2$

2 Write the equation in the form $ax^2 + bx + c = 0$, that is satisfied by the x-coordinates of the points of intersection of the following graphs.

(a) $y = x^2 - 3x - 6$ and $y = 3x - 2$
(b) $y = 3x^2 + 8x - 1$ and $y = 2(3x - 1)$
(c) $y = 5 - 3x - 4x^2$ and $3x + y - 7 = 0$

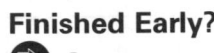

Finished Early?
➡ Go to page 462

Learn More About It

Some word problems may lead to more than one equation, one of which may be linear and the other quadratic.

Example	Find two numbers whose sum is 42 and whose product is 405.
Working	Let the numbers be m and n.

Then $\quad\quad\quad\quad m + n = 42 \quad\quad\quad$ (1)
and $\quad\quad\quad\quad\quad\; mn = 405 \quad\quad\quad$ (2)
From (1) $\quad\quad\quad m = 42 - n \quad\quad\;$ (3)
Substituting for m in (2)
$$(42 - n)n = 405$$
$$n^2 - 42n + 405 = 0$$
$$(n - 27)(n - 15) = 0$$
$$n = 27 \text{ or } 15$$
Substituting for n in (3),
$$m = 42 - 27 = 15$$
or $\quad\quad\quad\quad\quad m = 42 - 15 = 27$

Answer $\quad$ The numbers are 27 and 15.

Try It Out

(S) 1 The length, l, of a rectangular playing field is 12 m more than its width, w. The area of the field is 540 m². Find the dimensions of the field.

2 A girl is 24 years younger than her mother. The product of their ages is 180 years. Write the algebraic expressions to represent this information and calculate their ages.

3 The product of two numbers is 12. The sum of the larger number and twice the smaller number is 11. Find the two numbers.

Practice

(T) 1 The sum of the digits of a 2-digit number is 12. The tens digit is the square of its units digit. Write equations and solve them to find the 2-digit number.

2 Ann paid $480 for some tins of paint. If she had paid $8 less for each tin of paint, she could have bought 2 more tins of paint for the same amount of money. Find:
  (a) the number of tins of paint she bought
  (b) the cost of one tin.

3 A woman is x years old and her son is y years old. The sum of their ages is equal to twice the difference of their ages. The product of their ages is 432. Find their ages.

4 Two shelves have rectangular top surfaces. The length l cm of the Shelf A surface is $1\frac{1}{2}$ times its width, w cm. The length h cm of the Shelf B is 10 cm less than twice its width, b cm.

The surface area of Shelf A is 350 cm² greater than the surface area of Shelf B.
  (a) Write an algebraic equation in l and h to show this information.
  (b) If $h = l - 5$, find the values of l and h.
  (c) Discuss the results.

Further Practice

(U) 1 One number is seven more than twice a second number. The product of the numbers is 60. Find the two numbers.

2 The perimeter of a rectangle is 32 cm and the area is 63 cm². Find the dimensions of the rectangle.

Finished Early?
➥ Go to page 462

Unit 8 *Algebra 2*

Summary of Chapters 17 and 18

Quadratic Expressions

- Quadratic expressions derive from the expansion or product of two linear expressions.
  Quadratic expressions of special note are the **perfect squares**, for example,
  $x^2 + 2xy + y^2 = (x + y)^2$ and $x^2 - 2xy + y^2 = (x - y)^2$ and the
  difference of two squares, for example,
  $x^2 - y^2 = (x + y)(x - y)$.

- To **factorise** a quadratic expression is to write the expression as a product of its linear factors. Quadratic expressions that have four terms may be factorised by grouping in pairs, taking out the common variable in each pair of terms, and then taking out the factor common to each group.

- The general quadratic function is $ax^2 + bx + c$, where a, b and c are constants, and $a \neq 0$. The quadratic function is the equation of the curve called a **parabola** that is symmetrical about the ordinate (y-value) through the **turning point**.

- When the coefficient of the quadratic term is positive, the curve is 'cup-shaped' and the function has a **minimum** value; when the coefficient of the quadratic term is negative, the curve is 'cap-shaped' and the function has a **maximum** value.

- All quadratic expressions may not have linear factors – compare prime numbers in arithmetic. However, such an expression may be written as a perfect square plus or minus a constant term. This approach is useful in finding the maximum or minimum value of the expression.

Quadratic Equations and Graphs

- The general quadratic equation is $ax^2 + bx + c = 0$, in which the highest power of the variable is 2, that is, an equation of the second degree. The values of the variable that make the equation true are called the **roots** of the equation.

- When a quadratic expression can be factorised, then the factors of the corresponding equation can be written as the product of the two linear factors, each factor being equal to zero. The value of the variable in each of the two linear equations gives the two roots of the quadratic equation.

- When a quadratic expression cannot be factorised, other methods of solving the corresponding equation include

  completing the square from first principles

  applying the formula $x = \dfrac{-b \pm \sqrt{(b^2 - 4ac)}}{2a}$, that is derived

  from completing the square for the general quadratic equation.

  using a graphical method: writing the corresponding quadratic function, y, and finding on the graph of $y = f(x)$, the value(s) of x where $y = 0$.

- Simultaneous equations when one is a linear equation and the other a quadratic equation can be solved

  by substitution for one of the variables in terms of the other variable and solving the resulting equation in one variable; substituting that value in one of the given equations gives the solution for the second variable

  by a graphical method in which the points of intersection of the two graphs plotted give the values of the variables.

19 Inverse and Composite Functions

In this chapter you will learn about …

1 inverse functions

2 composite functions

1 Inverse Functions

Remember?

A **function** is a one-to-one or a many-to-one mapping and may be defined as:

(i) a relation between two sets when each member of the first set is connected to one and only one member of the second set; the first set is called the **domain** and each member is called an **object**; the second set is called the **range** and each member is called an **image**.

(ii) a set of ordered pairs if the first element appears only once in any ordered pair of the set.

The set of ordered pairs $\{(-1, 1), (0, 3), (1, 5), (2, 7), (3, 9)\}$ shows that for each x-value or object, the image is $2x + 3$ so that x is mapped onto $(2x + 3)$.

Functions are usually denoted by small letters such as f, g, and h. The function f may be written as

$f : x \to 2x + 3$ (read 'f is the function that maps x to $2x + 3$')

$f(x) = 2x + 3$ (f(x) is the image of each element x)

$y = f(x) = 2x + 3$ (y is a function of x)

In both a one-to-one mapping and a many-to-one mapping, all elements in the domain must be mapped onto an element in the range.

When an arrow diagram is used to represent a function, only one arrow leaves each element in the domain; furthermore, in a one-to-one mapping only one arrow goes to each image while in a many-to-one mapping there is at least one image to which more than one arrow goes.

Functions may also be represented in a table of values of the object and the corresponding images as well as illustrated graphically using each ordered pair as the coordinates of a point referred to Cartesian axes.

Key Fact

The order of the numbers in an ordered pair is significant.

Example For each of the following functions,

(a) draw up a table of values

(b) list the set of ordered pairs for integral values of x in the domain $-2 < x \leqslant 3$

(c) draw an arrow diagram to illustrate your answer

(d) state whether the function is a one-to-one or a many-to-one mapping

(i) $f(x) = 3x - 2$ (ii) $y = x^2 + 3$

Working & Answer

(i) $f(x) = 3x - 2$

(a)

x	−1	0	1	2	3
$3x$	−3	0	3	6	9
−2	−2	−2	−2	−2	−2
$f(x)$	−5	−2	1	4	7

(b) $\{(-1, -5), (0, -2), (1, 1), (2, 4), (3, 7)\}$

(c)
```
−1 ───────→ −5
 0 ───────→ −2
 1 ───────→  1
 2 ───────→  4
 3 ───────→  7
```

(d) a one-to-one mapping

(ii) $y = x^2 + 3$

(a)

x	−1	0	1	2	3
x^2	1	0	1	4	9
+3	+3	+3	+3	+3	+3
y	4	3	4	7	12

(b) $\{(-1, 4), (0, 3), (1, 4), (2, 7), (3, 12)\}$

(c)
```
−1 ╲
 0 ──────→  3
 1 ──────→  4
 2 ──────→  7
 3 ──────→ 12
```

(d) a many-to-one mapping

Practice

(A) 1 A function is defined by $f(x) = 3x - \dfrac{2}{x}$. Evaluate

  (i) $f(5)$ **(ii)** $f(0)$ **(iii)** $f(2x)$ **(iv)** $f(-x)$

2 If $h(x) = \dfrac{2x + 1}{x - 3}$, find x when $h(x)$ is

  (i) -2 **(ii)** -1 **(iii)** 3 **(iv)** x

(B) For each of the following functions
  (a) draw up a table of values
  (b) list the set of ordered pairs for integral values of x in the domain
      $-5 < x \leqslant 2$
  (c) draw an arrow diagram to illustrate your answer
  (d) state whether the function is a one-to-one or a many-to-one mapping.

1 $y = x^2 + 3x - 1$ **2** $f(x) = \dfrac{2x - 3}{x - 2}$

Further Practice

(C) 1 When the function $g(x)$ is given by $g(x) = 3x - 7$,
  (a) evaluate   **(i)** $g(5)$ **(ii)** $g(5) - g(2)$
  (b) find x if   **(i)** $g(x) = 0$ **(ii)** $g(x) = x$
  (c) list the set of ordered pairs in the domain $-2 \leqslant x < 3, x \in Z$.

2 If $h : x \rightarrow (x - 2)^2$,
  (a) evaluate   **(i)** $h(1)$ **(ii)** $h(-1)$ **(iii)** $-h(w)$
  (b) find x when   **(i)** $h(x) = 0$ **(ii)** $h(x) = x$ **(iii)** $h(x) = 2x^2 - 5$

3 The function g is defined by $g : x \rightarrow -\tfrac{1}{2}x + 1$.
  (a) Calculate the values of g when x is $-2, -1, 0, 1, 2, 3$.
  (b) List the set of ordered pairs for integral values of x in the domain
      $-2 < x \leqslant 3$.
  (c) Draw an arrow diagram to illustrate your answer.

> **Finished Early?**
> 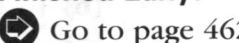 Go to page 462

Learn About It

The function $h(x) = 2x$, gives the set of ordered pairs
  $\{(-2, -4), (-1, -2), (0, 0), (1, 2), (2, 4), (3, 6)\}$.

Each object in the domain of h has one and *only one* image in the range so
that this is a one-to-one mapping.

Then, the set of ordered pairs

   {(−4, −2), (−2, −1), (0, 0), (2, 1), (4, 2), (6, 3)},

is also a one-to-one mapping and therefore defines a function, say k(x).

Since the range of h(x) is the domain of k(x) and the domain of h(x) is the range of k(x), the function k(x) is defined as the **inverse of the function** h(x).

The inverse of the function h(x) is written as $h^{-1}(x)$.

Key Fact

A flow chart is useful in identifying the operations in a function and the order in which they are done.

Try It Out

D Given the following functions,

(a) state whether an inverse function exists. Give reasons for your answer.

(b) if the inverse function exists, describe it.

1 'is a town in'

2 'is the capital city of'

3 'is 5 more than'

Learn More About It

The function $F(x) = x^2$ gives the set of ordered pairs

   {(−3, 9) (−2, 4), (−1, 1), (0, 0), (1, 1), (2, 4), (3, 9)}.

Each of the following pairs of objects has the same image

      '−3 and 3' → '9',
      '−2 and 2' → '4',

and   '−1 and 1' → '1'.

so that this is a many-to-one mapping.

The set of ordered pairs

   {(9, −3) (4, −2), (1, −1), (0, 0), (1, 1), (4, 2), (9, 3)},

is a one-to-many relation since each of the elements '9' '4', and '1' in the domain is mapped onto more than one element in the range.

Hence, there is no inverse of the function F(x).

This is true for all many-to-one functions.

Hence, *only one-to-one functions have inverses*.

Try It Out

E Given the following functions,

(a) state whether an inverse function exists. Give reasons for your answer.

(b) if the inverse function exists, describe it.

1 'is a street in'   **2** 'is 3 times'

3 'is 2 less than'   **4** 'is the square of'

Key Fact

The conditions for any functions, f and g to be inverse functions are

- each of the functions, f and g, must be a one-to-one mapping
- the range of f must be the domain of g and the range of g must be the domain of f
- *all* the elements in the domain of f must be mapped onto all the elements in the domain of g

---

Example   State, giving reasons, which of the following functions have inverse functions.

(a) 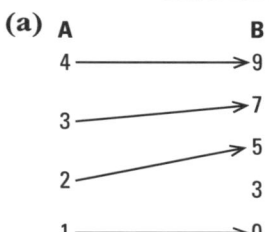   (b) 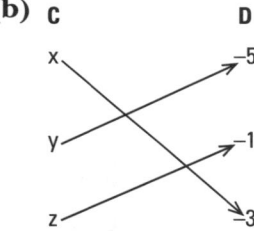   (c)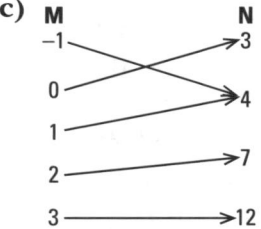

Working & Answer

(a) Function maps all the elements in A onto elements in B; but there is an element '3' in the set B that cannot be mapped onto a corresponding element in A. Since in the reverse process all the elements in B cannot be mapped onto the set A, there is no inverse function.

(b) Function maps C onto D so that each element of C is mapped onto one, and only one, corresponding element of D so that the inverse of the function exists.

(c) Function maps M onto N so that only one arrow leaves each element in the set M, that is, the mapping is a function. However, in the mapping from N onto M, the element '4' is mapped onto two elements '−1' and '1' in the set M so that this mapping is not a function. Thus there is no inverse of the function.

Learn More About It

We use an algebraic expression to denote a function by defining those operations that map an object onto its image. In order to describe the inverse of the function by an algebraic expression, we have to define the inverse operations in the reverse order. In finding the inverse of the function $y = x^2$, for example, it is necessary to take the square root so that the inverse of the function $y = x^2$ is $y = \pm\sqrt{x}$.

Note that in this example, since the inverse is a one-to-many relation, the inverse is not a function.

To find the inverse of the function, there are two methods that we may use.

Method I

In the function $f(x) = 2x + 3$, for example, x is first multiplied by 2 and then 3 is added.

The inverse operations in the reverse order are first subtract 3, and then divide by 2.

Hence, the inverse function is $f^{-1}(x) = \dfrac{x - 3}{2}$.

This example is illustrated graphically by flow charts. Remember in a flow chart the operations are put in boxes that are linked by arrows. The arrows indicate the sequence or order of the operations.

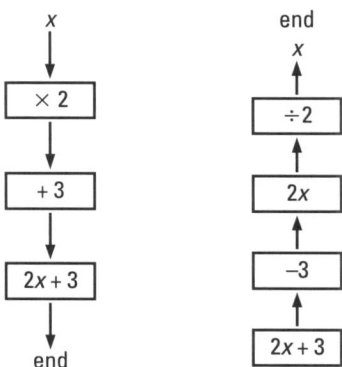

Method II

Write the function in terms of another variable, say y, that is,

$$y = 2x + 3$$

Interchange the variables so that the equation becomes

$$x = 2y + 3$$

and then write the equation in terms of the 'new' y, so that

$$2y = x - 3 \text{ and } y = \dfrac{x - 3}{2}$$

that is, $f^{-1}(x) = \dfrac{x - 3}{2}$

We can verify the inverse function by substituting the image of a given object in the inverse and checking whether the result is the original value of the object.

For example, using the fact that in $f(x) = 2x + 3$, $f(4) = 11$,

and substituting 11 in $f^{-1}(x) = \dfrac{x - 3}{2}$, we get

$$f^{-1}(11) = \tfrac{1}{2}(11 - 3) = 4$$

Key Fact

If an equation is given by $f(x) = n$, and $f^{-1}(n) = X$, then X is the value of x that satisfies the equation $f(x) = n$.
Hence, the inverse of a function can be used to solve an equation.

Try It Out

1 Use a flow chart to illustrate the operations that define:
  (a) the function $y = g(x)$, where $2y - 3x = 4$
  (b) the inverse of the function y.
2 (a) By interchanging the variables in the function $y = \dfrac{2x - 5}{x + 3}$, derive the inverse of the function.
  (b) State any value(s) of x for which the function is undefined.
  (c) Use the inverse function to find the solution of the equation $\dfrac{2x - 5}{x + 3} = 1$.

Key Fact

An inverse function of x is a function in which x, or a function of x, is in the denominator of the function, for example, $\dfrac{4}{3x}$, $\dfrac{5}{x + 3}$.

Note that the function is $\dfrac{2x - 3}{x - 2}$ undefined when $x = 2$, since the denominator, $x - 2 = 0$.

Practice

G For each of the following functions,
    (a) state a suitable domain and range
    (b) if the inverse function exists, find an expression and verify it.

1 $f(x) = 4x$ **2** $f(x) = \frac{1}{3}x - 1$

3 $f(x) = \dfrac{3x - 1}{4}$ **4** $f(x) = (2x + \frac{1}{2})^2$

5 $f(x) = \dfrac{x + 1}{x + 2}$ **6** $f(x) = \dfrac{2x + 1}{x}$

H **1** For the function defined by $f(x) = \dfrac{5x - 3}{x + 4}$,

    (a) derive an expression for $f^{-1}(x)$
    (b) find the value of $f^{-1}(-2)$
    (c) state the value of x for which the function is undefined.

2 By finding the inverse of $f(x) = \dfrac{3x + 2}{x + 2}$, solve the equation
$\dfrac{3x + 2}{x + 2} = 2$.

3 If $f(x) = x^2 - 8x + 5$, find:
    (a) **(i)** $f(4)$ **(ii)** $f(-3)$
    (b) x if   **(i)** $f(x) = 14$ **(ii)** $f(x) = 8$.

Further Practice

I For each of the following functions
    (a) find the value for integral values of x in the domain $-2 < x < 4$
    (b) derive the inverse function
    (c) state the value of x, if any, for which the function is undefined.

1 $f(x) = = -2x + 5$ **2** $f(x) = 2x^2 - x - 2$

3 $f(x) = = -x^2 - 3x - 1$ **4** $f(x) = \dfrac{-x + 2}{2x + 3}$

Finished Early?
➡ Go to page 462

② Composite Functions

Learn About It

Suppose there are two functions f and g such that f maps the element x in the domain P onto w in the range Q, and the function g maps the element w in the domain Q onto y in the range R.

Thus we can define a function that maps the element x in the domain P onto y in the range R. This defined function is written as $gf(x) = y$ and is called a **composite function**.

Note how the composite function is written. Since the first function is applied directly to the element and the second function to be applied may be considered to be a function of the first function, we write $g(f(x))$.

This is represented graphically in the following diagram:

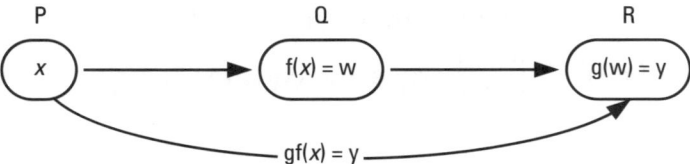

Key Fact

The elements in the domain of $gf(x)$ are the elements that are in both the domain and range of f.

Learn More About It

The composite function $gf(x)$ means apply the function f first and then apply the function g to the result.

What does the composite function $fg(x)$ mean?

Try It Out

J Consider the function $f(x) = x^2$
and the function $\quad g(x) = 2x + 3$
Then $\quad fg(x) = f(g(x)) = f(2x + 3)$
$$= (2x + 3)^2$$
and $\quad gf(x) = g(f(x)) = g(x^2)$
$$= 2x^2 + 3$$
thus, $\quad fg(x) \neq gf(x)$

Hence, the composites of these two functions f and g are not the same, that is, the composite functions are not *commutative*.

Practice

K **1** Given the two functions $f(x)$ and $g(x)$ where
$$f(x) = 4x$$
and $g(x) = x + 1$
find $gf(x)$ and $fg(x)$.

2 The arrow diagram below shows the domain and range for the functions f and g.

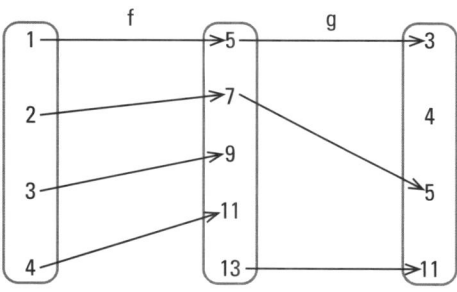

(a) Find gf (1), gf (2), gf (3).
(b) State the domain and range of gf.

3 Given the two functions $f(x)$ and $g(x)$ where
$$f(x) = x - 3 \text{ and } g(x) = x^2 + 1$$
find gf (x) and fg (x).

4 f, g and h are functions defined by the expressions
$$f : x \rightarrow 3x, \ g : x \rightarrow \tfrac{1}{4}x + 1, \ h : x \rightarrow x^2$$
(a) Find the expressions for
    (i) f^{-1} **(ii)** g^{-1} **(iii)** h^{-1} **(iv)** fg
    (v) gf   **(vi)** fh   **(vii)** $(hf)^{-1}$ **(viii)** $(gh)^{-1}$
(b) Show that **(i)** $(hf)^{-1} = f^{-1}h^{-1}$ **(ii)** $h^{-1}g^{-1} = (gh)^{-1}$

5 $f : x \rightarrow x + 5$

    (a) Find $f(3)$ and $ff(3)$ and express $ff(x)$ in its simplest form.

    (b) Find $f^{-1}(x)$ and the value of $f^{-1}(3)$ and $f^{-1}f^{-1}(3)$.

    (c) Express $f^{-1}f^{-1}(x)$ in its simplest form.

6 **(a)** Find two simple functions f and g such that $gf : x \rightarrow x^2 + 5$.

    (b) Find $fg(x)$ and the value of $gf(2)$ and $fg(2)$.

> **Finished Early?**
> ➡ Go to page 463

Further Practice

L **1** Given the two functions $f(x)$ and $g(x)$ where

    $f(x) = 2x + 3$ and $g(x) = x - 2$

    find $gf(x)$ and $fg(x)$.

2 f and g are functions on the set of integers defined by the expressions

    $f(x) = x + 2$ and $g(x) = 3x - 1$

    (a) Copy and complete the table on the right.

    (b) Show that $gf(x) = 3x + 5$.

    (c) Draw an arrow diagram to show the domain and range of $gf(x)$.

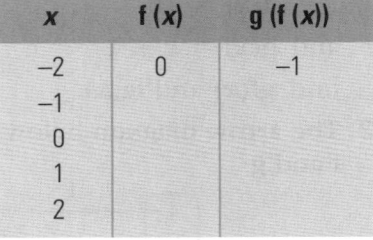

x	f (x)	g (f (x))
-2	0	-1
-1		
0		
1		
2		

3 Given the two functions $f(x)$ and $g(x)$ where

    $f(x) = x^2$ and $g(x) = x + 3$

    find $gf(x)$ and $fg(x)$.

4 **(a)** Find the inverses f^{-1} and g^{-1} of the functions

      $f : x \rightarrow 1 - 2x$ and $g : x \rightarrow 3x$

    (b) Find the expressions for

      (i) gf **(ii)** $f^{-1}g^{-1}$ **(iii)** $(gf)^{-1}$

5 $f(x) = 2x - 5$

    (a) Express $f^{-1}(x)$ in terms of x.

    (b) Find $f(7)$, $f^{-1}(7)$, $f^{-1}f(7)$, $ff^{-1}(7)$ and $f^{-1}f^{-1}(7)$

    (c) Express $f^{-1}f(x)$ and $ff^{-1}(x)$ in their simplest forms. Comment on the answers.

6 $f(x) = 2x + 1$ and $g(x) = x^2 - 1$.

    (a) Find two values of x such that $fg(x) = 17$.

    (b) Find two values of x such that $gf(x) = 8$.

> **Finished Early?**
> ➡ Go to page 463

Non-linear Graphs

In this chapter you will learn about …
1. gradient of a curve
2. area under a graph
3. cubic graphs
4. exponential graphs
5. inverse variation

1 Gradient of a Curve

Learn About It

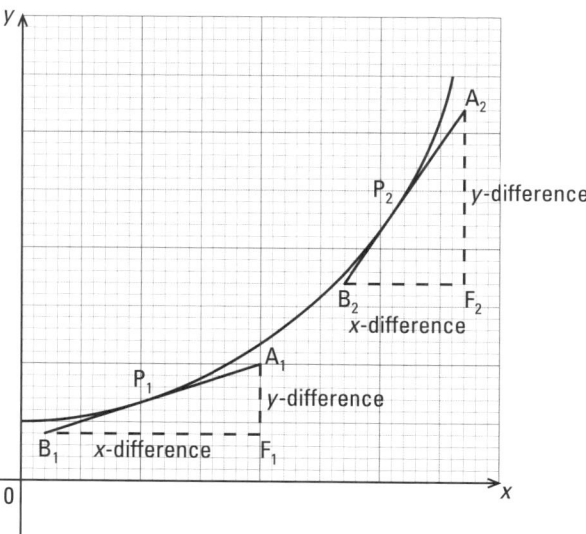

On graph paper, draw x- and y-axes and sketch a curve as in the diagram on the right.

Draw a line A_1B_1 that touches the curve at only one point. Name this point P_1.

From the diagram on the right, the gradient of the line B_1A_1

$$\frac{F_1A_1}{B_1F_1} = \frac{y\text{-difference}}{x\text{-difference}}$$

Repeat for another line A_2B_2 that touches the curve at P_2.

The gradient of the line B_2A_2

$$\frac{F_2A_2}{B_2F_2} = \frac{y\text{-difference}}{x\text{-difference}}$$

As the point P moves along the curve the gradient of the line BA changes since the lengths of FA and of BF change.

The gradient of a curve at a particular point P is defined as the gradient of the straight line that touches the curve at the point P.

Word Check

adjacent nearby, in the neighbourhood

gradient rate at which the y-value of a point changes as the x-value increases

tangent straight line that *touches* a curve at only one point

initially at the beginning

Key Fact

The gradient of a straight line is the same at all points on the line. The gradient of a curve is *not* constant but varies at different points on the curve.

Try It Out

 (a) Complete the table below for the function $y = \frac{1}{2}x^2$.

x	−4	−3	−2	−1	0	1	2	3	4
x²	16	9							
y	8	4.5							

(b) Using scales of 2 cm : 1 unit on each axis, draw the graph of the function $y = \frac{1}{2}x^2$ for $-4 \leqslant x \leqslant 4$.

(c) Draw tangents to the curve at
    (i) $x = -3$,   **(ii)** $x = -1$,   **(iii)** $x = 0$,   **(iv)** $x = 2$,   **(v)** $x = 3$.

(d) Use the tangents to find the gradient of the curve at
    (i) $x = -3$,   **(ii)** $x = -1$,   **(iii)** $x = 0$,   **(iv)** $x = 2$,   **(v)** $x = 3$.

Learn More About It

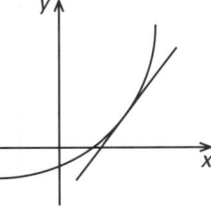

When the y-value increases as the x-value increases, then the gradient of the curve at the point is positive.

When the y-value decreases as the x-value increases, then the gradient of the curve at the point is negative.

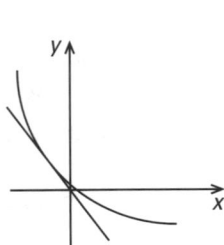

When the tangent at a point on the curve is parallel to the x-axis, there is no change in the y-value at the point for an increase in the x-value and the gradient of the tangent and of the curve at such a point is zero. Such a point on the curve is called a **turning point**.

When the value of the tangent is negative and then zero before being positive, the turning-point is a **minimum** as shown in the diagram (**i**).

When the value of the tangent is positive and then zero before being negative, the turning-point is a **maximum**, as shown in the diagram (**ii**).

(**i**) 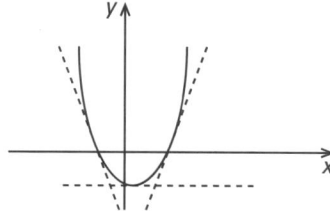   (**ii**)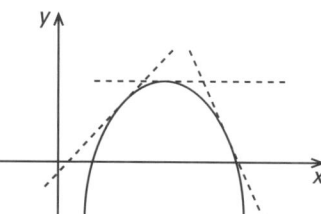

Key Fact

It is the gradient of the curve at a point which determines whether it is a turning point. Looking at the gradients of the curve on either side of a turning point shows whether it is a maximum or a minimum.

Try It Out

B (a) Copy the graphs and draw the tangents to the curves at each of the named points.

(b) Find the gradients of the curves at those points, indicating any turning points.

1 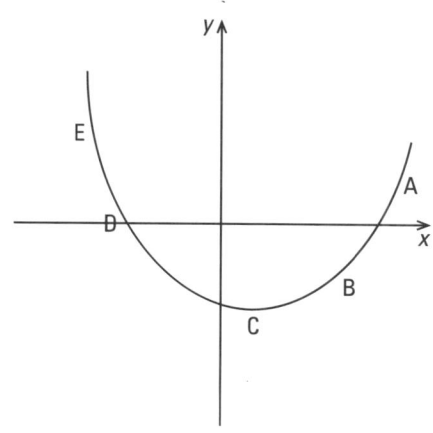   **2**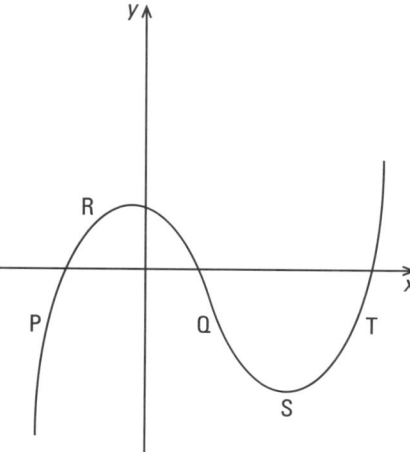

Remember?

In real-life problems, graphs are used to show the rate of change of the value of one quantity as the value of another quantity changes.

If y varies directly as x, that is, if $y \propto x$, then $y = kx$, where k is a constant. Hence, the graph is a straight line passing through the origin. The gradient of the line gives the value of k.

If y varies directly as x^2, that is, if $y \propto x^2$, then $y = Kx^2$, where K is a constant. The graph is a quadratic curve passing through the origin.

Key Fact

The line of symmetry of a quadratic curve passes through the maximum or minimum point on the curve.

Practice

1 The diagram on the right is the graph of $y = 3 - 2x - x^2$.

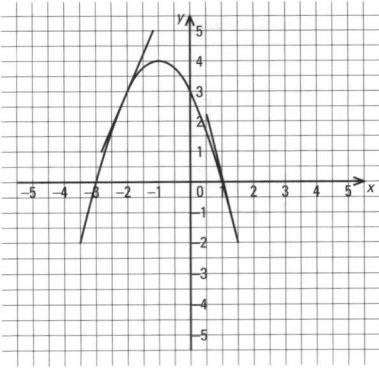

    (a) Use the tangents drawn to estimate the gradient of the curve at
        (i) $x = 1$ (ii) $x = -2$

    (b) By drawing a suitable tangent, find the coordinates of the turning point on the curve and state whether it is a maximum or a minimum point.

    (c) Write down the equation of the line of symmetry of the curve.

2 (a) Copy and complete the table below for $y = x^2 - 4x + 1$.

x	-2	-1	0	1	2	3	4	5
x^2		1	0	1		9		
$-4x$		+4				-12		
$+1$		+1				+1		
y		6				-2		

    (b) Using scales of
        1 cm : 1 unit on the x-axis and 2 cm : 5 units on the y-axis,
        draw the graph of the function $y = x^2 - 4x + 1$ for $-3 < x \leqslant 5$.
    (c) Use the graph to find the roots of the equation $x^2 - 4x + 1 = 0$
    (d) Draw tangents to the curve at
        (i) $x = -1$,   **(ii)** $x = 0$,   **(iii)** $x = 2$,   **(iv)** $x = 4$.
    (e) Use the tangents to estimate the gradient of the curve at
        (i) $x = -1$,   **(ii)** $x = 0$,   **(iii)** $x = 2$,   **(iv)** $x = 4$.
    (f) Find the turning point of the curve. State whether the turning pcint
        is a maximum or a minimum, giving your reason.

3 (a) Copy and complete
      the table on the right for
      $y = 3x - x^2$.

x	−1	0	1	2	3	4
$3x$	−3		3			
$-x^2$	−1		−1			
y	−4		2			

    (b) Using a scale of 2 cm to
        1 unit on both axes, draw
        the graph of $y = 3x - x^2$
        from $x = -1$ to $x = 4$.
    (c) Use the graph to find the roots of the equation $3x - x^2 = 0$.
    (d) Use tangents to estimate the gradient of the curve at
        (i) $x = -1$,   **(ii)** $x = 0$,   **(iii)** $x = 2$.
    (e) Find the equation of the line of symmetry of the curve.
    (f) Write down the turning point of the curve, stating whether the
        turning point is a maximum or a minimum, giving your reason.

Further Practice

D 1 (a) Draw up a table of integral values for $y = x^2 - 4x$ for $-1 \leqslant x \leqslant 5$.
    (b) Use a scale of 2 cm to 1 unit on both axes, and draw the graph of the
        function $y = x^2 - 4x$ for $-1 \leqslant x \leqslant 5$.
    (c) Use the graph to find the roots of the equation $x^2 - 4x = 0$.
    (d) Draw tangents to the curve at
        (i) $x = -1$,   **(ii)** $x = 0$,   **(iii)** $x = 2$,   **(iv)** $x = 4$.
    (e) Use the tangents to identify the turning point of the curve and find
        the maximum or minimum of the function.

2 (a) Copy and complete the table on the right for $y = 5x - 2x^2$.

x	−1	0	1	2	3	4
5x	−5		5			
−2x²	−2		−2			
y	−7		3			

(b) Using a scale of 2 cm to 1 unit on the x-axis and of 1 cm to 1 unit on the y-axis, draw the graph of $y = 5x - 2x^2$ from $x = -1$ to $x = 4$.

(c) Find the gradient of the curve at **(i)** $x = 0$, **(ii)** $x = 1$, **(iii)** $x = 3$.

(d) Write down the equation of the line of symmetry of the curve.

> **Finished Early?**
> Go to page 463

② Area Under a Graph

Learn About It

The area under a graph is defined as the area between the curve and the x-axis. This area may be found by a number of methods.

Method 1

The simplest method is to count the squares when using graph paper. The result can be as accurate as more complex methods but the process of counting and adding the pieces can be tedious.

Method 2

Approximate the area under the curve to a single trapezium formed by joining the ordinates at the limits of the given domain.

Method 3

Divide the area under the graph within the given domain into a number of trapezia, in which the ordinates are the parallel sides and all trapezia have equal widths. Find the area of each trapezium and sum all the areas. This is called the **trapezium rule** for finding the area under a curve.

Example

(a) Draw a table of values for the function $y = x^2 + 2$ for integral values of x in the domain $0 \leqslant x < 3$.

(b) Plot the graph of the function.

(c) Find the area under the graph.

Working & Answer

(a)

x	0	1	2	3
x^2	0	1	4	9
+2	+2	+2	+2	+2
y	2	3	6	11

(b) and (c) *Method 1: Count the squares under the curve*

Each square = (2×0.5) = 1 sq. unit

Counting the squares under the curve, the total number
= the number of whole squares + parts of squares
= $(12 + 3.5)$ squares

Area under the graph = 15.5 sq. units

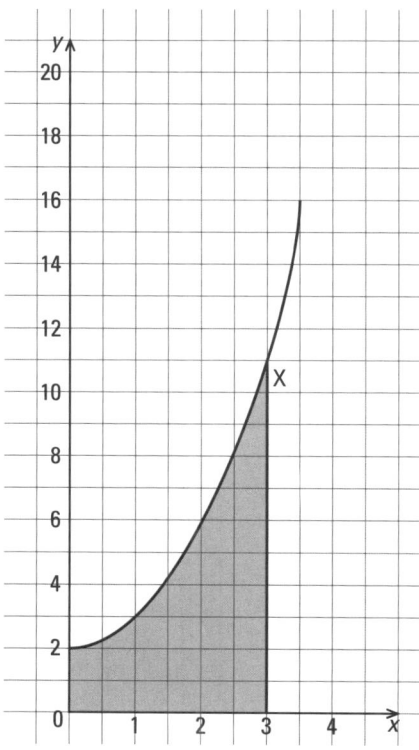

Method 2: Area of the approximate trapezium

When $x = 0$, $y = 2$; when $x = 3$, $y = 11$.

Area of trapezium $= \frac{1}{2}(2 + 11)3$

$= 39 \div 2 = 19.5$ sq. units

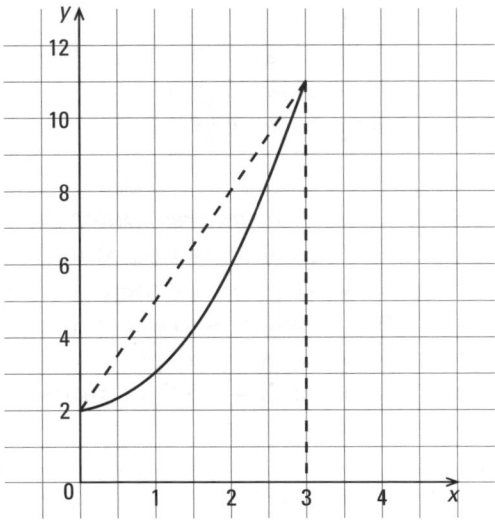

Method 3: Trapezium rule

Area under curve $= \frac{1}{2}(2 + 3) + \frac{1}{2}(3 + 6) + \frac{1}{2}(6 + 11)$

$= \frac{1}{2}(5 + 9 + 17)$

$= 31 \div 2$

$= 15.5$ sq. units

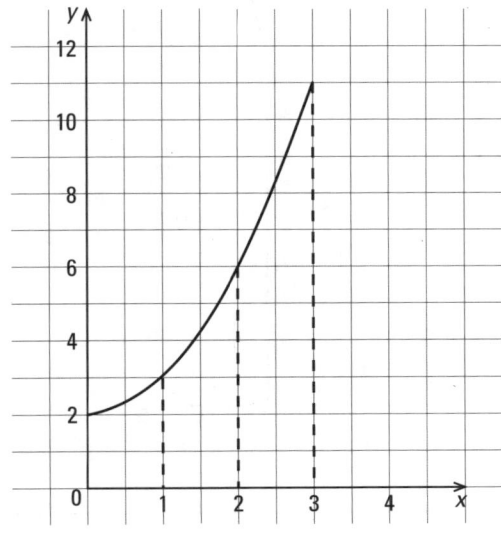

Learn More About It

Graphs representing journeys in a specified time are very widely used to get information about the distance moved, the speed and the acceleration of the moving objects (distance–time and speed–time graphs).

If the graph represents distance as a function of time, then at a given instant

- the value of the function gives the distance moved at that time
- the gradient of the graph is the rate of change of the distance with time, that is, the speed at that time.

If the graph represents speed as a function of time, then at a given instant

- the value of the function gives the speed at that time
- the gradient of the graph is the rate of change of the speed with time, that is, the acceleration at that time
- the area under the curve is the distance moved in the time interval.

Example A cyclist travelled the first 20 km in the first hour and the next 30 km in 3 hours.

   (a) Using a scale of 2 cm : 1 hour on the horizontal time axis and 1 cm : 10 km on the vertical distance axis, draw a graph to represent the data.

   (b) Find

     (i) the time when he was 40 km from his starting point

    (ii) his average speed (1) during the last 2 hours

              (2) for the 4 hours

Working (a)
& Answer

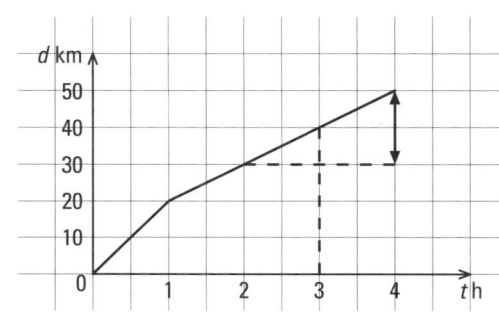

   (b) (i) 3 hours after he started

     (ii) Average speed (1) = (50 − 30) ÷ 2

             = 10 km/h

      Average speed (2) = 50 ÷ 4 = $12\frac{1}{2}$ km/h

Key Fact

In travel graphs, *time* is usually plotted along the horizontal axis.

Example The graph on the right shows the speed of a particle as a function of time. The distance moved in 8 sec was 40 m.

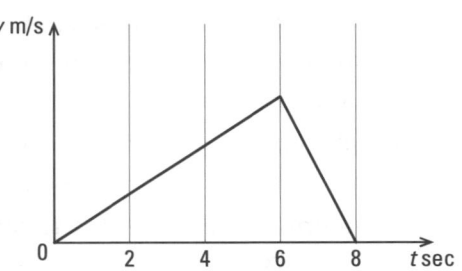

(a) Find the maximum speed V m/s.

If the time taken to reach V was 6 sec, find

(b) the acceleration in the first 6 sec

(c) the acceleration in the last 2 sec.

Working (a) Distance moved = area under the graph

that is, $40 = \frac{1}{2}V \times 8$

$$V = 10 \text{ m/s}$$

Acceleration = gradient of graph

(b) Acceleration $= \frac{10}{6} = \frac{5}{3}$ m/s^2

(c) Acceleration $= -\frac{10}{2} = -5$ m/s^2

Answer (a) 10 m/s   (b) $\frac{5}{3}$ m/s^2 (c) -5 m/s^2

Key Fact

The accuracy of the answers obtained from graphs can be improved by using the largest scale possible on each axis.

Try It Out

E **1** The graph on the right shows the journey of a cyclist. The vertical axis shows d, the distance covered in kilometres and the horizontal axis gives t, the time in minutes.

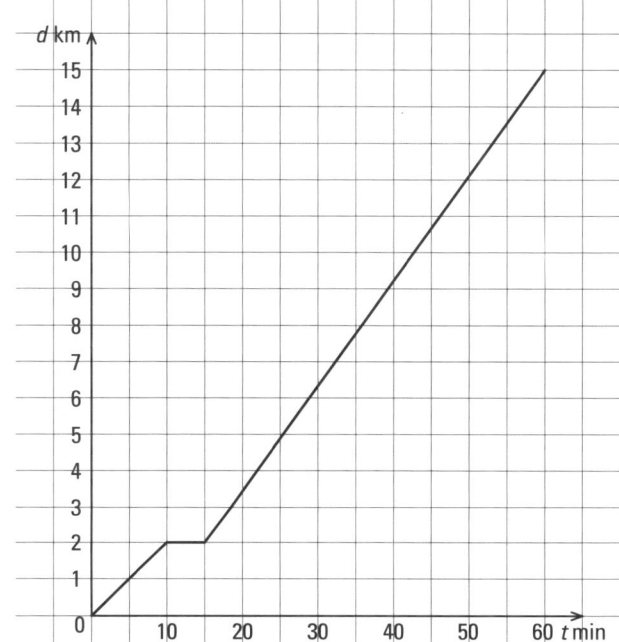

(a) How far did the cyclist go?

(b) What is the time needed for the journey?

(c) How long did the cyclist stop?

(d) What distance had he travelled after 30 min?

(e) What was the average speed

- before his stop

- after his stop

- for the whole journey?

2 Describe in your own words the journeys shown in the speed–time graphs below. *Do not work out any calculations.*

(i)
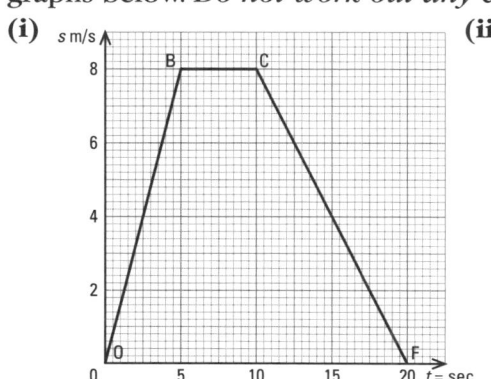

(ii)
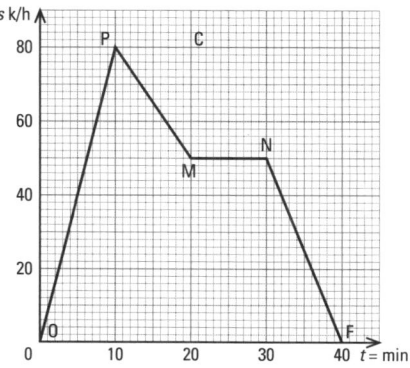

Practice

F **1** **(a)** Using scales of 2 cm : 10 sec on the horizontal axis, and 2 cm : 50 m on the vertical axis, draw on the same axes the graphs of the following sprint records from 1984:

distance (m)	time (s)
100	9.8
200	19.3
400	43.2

(b) Which record represents the fastest speed? Give reasons for your answer.

2 A bus travels between two towns, D and R, that are 12 km apart. The bus leaves D at 09:00. The bus covers a distance of 8 km in 12 min and then stops for 6 min. The bus arrives at R at 09:23.

(a) Using a scale of 1 cm to represent 2 min on the horizontal (time) axis and 1 cm to represent 1 km on the vertical (distance) axis, draw a graph to show this journey.

(b) From your graph, calculate the speed of the bus
  (i) before the stop   **(ii)** after the stop.

3 In each of the speed–time graphs OBCF and OPMNF in **Try It Out E**, find
  (a) the maximum speed
  (b) the acceleration along each part of the graph
  (c) the total distance in km, correct to 2 s.f.

4 At 09:00 a boy leaves home to walk to a shop 8 km away. He walks at 6 km/h. He remains at the shop for 15 min and then returns home cycling at 16 km/h.
  (a) Draw a distance–time graph to show this journey.
  (b) Use the graph to find the time when he **(i)** arrives at the shop
                                    (ii) gets home again.

5 The graph on the right, not drawn to scale, shows the graph of the motion of a car that starts from rest in 1st gear and then, after 4 sec, changes up to 2nd gear.
  (a) If the speed is given in m/s and the time in sec, find
      (i) the acceleration in 1st gear
      (ii) the distance moved in 1st gear.
  (b) If the car travels 54 m in 2nd gear, find
      (i) the value of V
      (ii) the acceleration in 2nd gear.

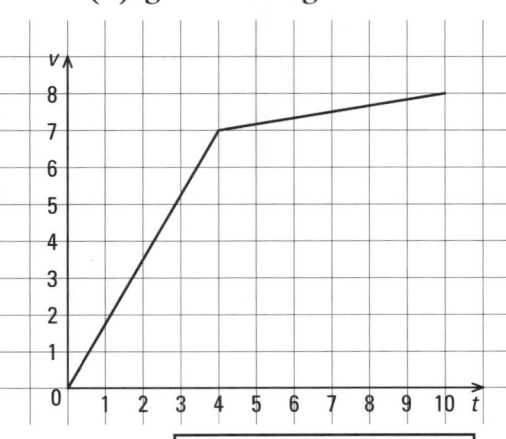

Finished Early?
→ Go to page 465

Further Practice

 1

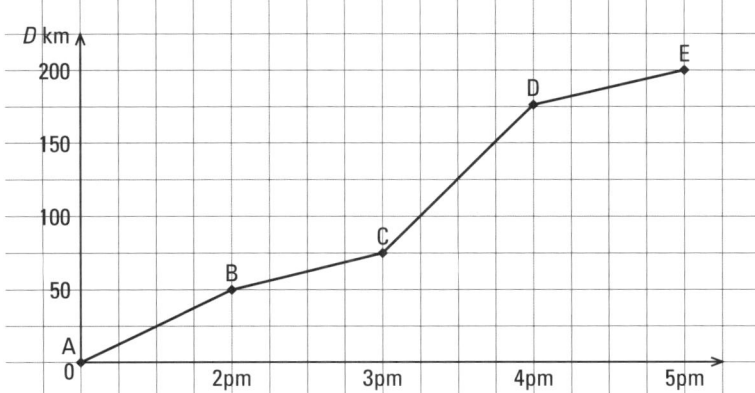

The distance–time graph above shows the journey of a motorist.
(a) Did the motorist stop at any time? Give the reason for your answer.
(b) At what time had the motorist travelled 25 km?
(c) What distance had the motorist travelled after 2 hours?
(d) What was the average speed for the whole journey?
(e) What was the speed between stage A and stage B of the journey?
(f) What was the speed between stage B and stage C of the journey?
(g) What was the speed between stage C and stage D of the journey?
(h) What was the speed between stage D and stage E of the journey?

2 The following graph represents the journeys of a pedestrian X, who walks steadily, and a motorist Y.

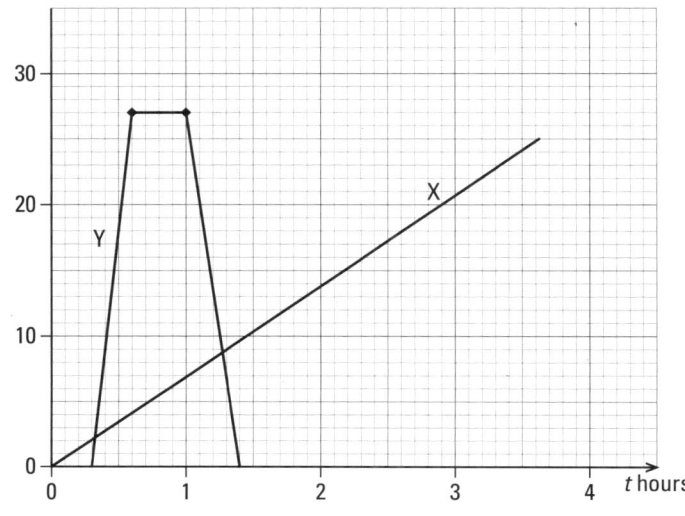

(a) Find X's average walking speed.

(b) Find the duration of Y's stop on his journey.

(c) Calculate Y's speed on his return.

(d) Find the distance that X walked between the times that Y passed him.

3 A car is moving at an average speed of 70 km/h.

(a) Using scales of 2 cm : 10 min and 2 cm : 10 km, draw a distance–time graph from 0 to 30 min.

(b) Read off the distance covered in (i) 11 min (ii) 25 min.

(c) Read off the time taken to travel (i) 10 km (ii) 26 km.

4 The table on the right gives the speeds v m/s of an object at 10-second intervals.

t sec	0	10	20	30	40
v m/s	9	16	23	30	37

Find (a) the acceleration

(b) the distance in km travelled throughout the 40 seconds.

5 The graph on the right shows the speed–time graph of a moving object. Calculate

(a) the deceleration during the last 3 seconds

(b) the speed of the object after 6 seconds

(c) the total distance travelled during the 8 seconds

(d) the average speed of the object during the 8 seconds.

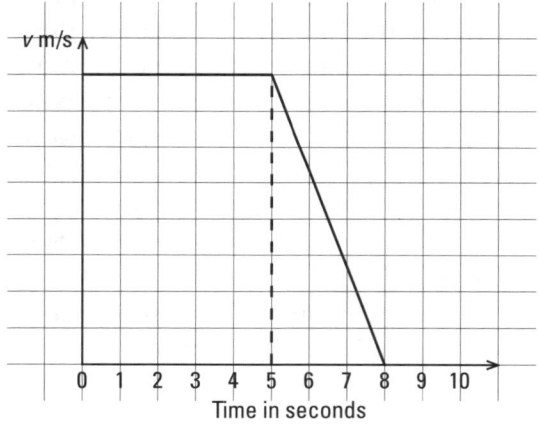

Time in seconds

Finished Early?

➮ Go to page 465

3 # Cubic Graphs

Learn About It

A table of values is given on the right.

x	−3	−2	−1	0	1	2	3	4
y	−27	−8	−1	0	1	8	27	64

The set of ordered pairs is $\{(-3, -27), (-2, -8), (-1, -1), (0, 0), (1, 1), (2, 8), (3, 27), (4, 64), \ldots (x, x^3), \ldots\}$ and defines the function $y = x^3$.

When the highest power of the x-variable in the algebraic expression is 3, the function is called a **cubic function**.

Ⓗ Try It Out

Using scales of 2 cm : 1 unit on the x-axis and 1 cm : 5 units on the y-axis, plot the ordered pairs given for $y = x^3$ and draw the graph.

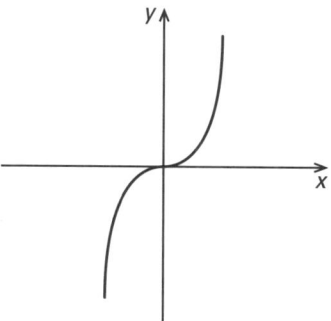

The curve should have the shape shown on the right.

Note that in a cubic function there may also be a quadratic term (when the power of the variable is 2); a linear term (when the power of the variable is 1); or a constant.

When the graph of a cubic function of the form $y = ax^3$ (where a is a constant) is drawn for corresponding values of x and y, the curve has the general shape shown above.

Learn More About It

On the graph of the function $y = x^3$, draw the tangent at each of the following points: **(i)** $x = -2$ **(ii)** $x = 0$ **(iii)** $x = 2$ **(iv)** $x = 3$

The gradient of each tangent gives the gradient of the curve at that point.

The results indicate that

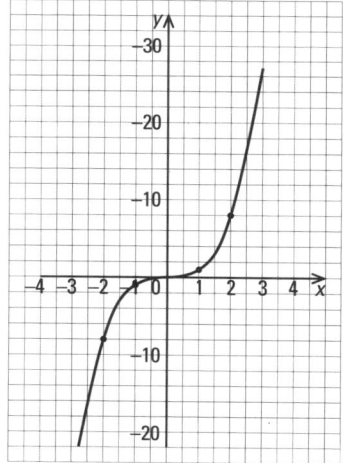

- the gradient of the curve is always positive or zero
- as x increases from numerically large negative values, the gradients of the tangents decrease.
- when $x = 0$, the gradient is zero
- as x increases from zero to positive values, the gradients of the tangents increase.

Try It Out

Ⓘ Draw up a table of values for the function $y = 2x^3$ for integral values of x, where $-3 < x < 4$.

Plot the ordered pairs and, using suitable scales, draw the graph of the function.

Practice

J On the graph of the function $y = 2x^3$,
    (a) draw the tangent at each of the following points:
        (i) $x = -2$ **(ii)** $x = 0$ **(iii)** $x = 2$ **(iv)** $x = 3$
    (b) find the gradient of the curve at these points
    (c) solve the equation $2x^3 = 18$.

Further Practice

K **(a)** Draw up a table of values for the function $y = \frac{1}{2}x^3$ for integral values
        of x, where $-5 < x < 6$.
    (b) Plot the ordered pairs and, using suitable scales, draw the graph of the
        function.
    (c) On the graph of the function $y = \frac{1}{2}x^3$, draw the tangent at each of the
        following points:
        (i) $x = -2$ **(ii)** $x = 0$ **(iii)** $x = 2$ **(iv)** $x = 3$
    (d) Find the gradient of the curve at these points.
    (e) Solve the equation $\frac{1}{2}x^3 = 20$.

> **Finished Early?**
> ➡ Go to page 466

4 Exponential Graphs

Learn About It

When the x-variable is in the
index or **exponent** of a function,
the function is called an
exponential function, for
example,

$$y = 2^x, y = 3^x, y = 4^x$$

When the graphs of these
functions are plotted for
corresponding values of x and y,
we get the curves in the diagram
on the right.

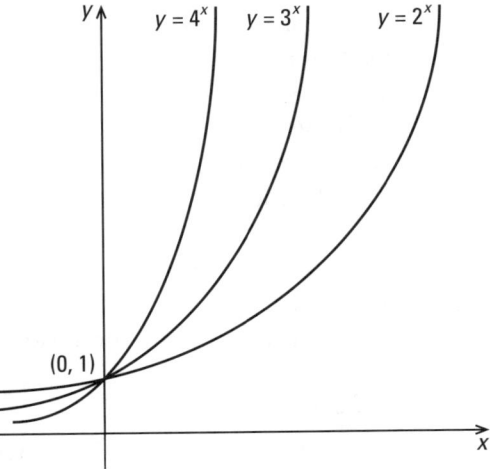

Notice that for every graph
plotted, the curves pass through
$(0, 1)$ since in each example, when $x = 0$, $y = 1$.

For all values of x, $x \in R$, $y > 0$, for example, when $x = -2$ in $y = 3^x$

$$y = 3^{-2} = \tfrac{1}{3}^2 = 0.111\,11\ldots\ldots$$

Try It Out

L (a) Given the function $y = 2^x$, draw up a table of corresponding values of x and y for $-3 \leqslant x \leqslant 3$.

(b) Using scales of 2 cm : 1 unit on each axis, plot the points and draw the curve.

(c) Find the gradient of the curve at (i) $x = 0$ (ii) $x = 2$ (iii) $x = 3$.

Learn More About It

When a bank pays interest on savings or charges interest on loans, the interest is generally calculated at regular specified periods, for example, daily, weekly, monthly or quarterly, and the interest is added to the original sum of money. For the next period, the interest is calculated on the new amount. This interest is called **compound interest** and the formula used to calculate the amount with the interest added is an exponential function.

Other examples of real-life problems that may be shown by exponential graphs include the increase of world population and the growth of bacteria.

> ### Word Check
> **formula** rule in mathematics for working out the value of a variable

Try It Out

M The amount earned on an investment of $20 000 over a 5-year period is given in the table on the right.

x	0	1	2	3	4	5
A	20.0	22.4	25.1	28.1	31.5	35.3

Using a scale of 2 cm : 1 year on the x-axis and 1 cm : $1000 on the A-axis for $20\,000 \leqslant A \leqslant 40\,000$, draw a graph to show the rate of increase of A.

Practice

N 1 Given the function $y = 3^x$,

(a) draw up a table of corresponding values of x and y for $-2 \leqslant x < 4$.

(b) Using scales of 2 cm : 1 unit on the x-axis and 2 cm : 3 units on the y-axis, plot the points and draw the curve.

(c) Find the gradient of the curve at (i) $x = 0$ (ii) $x = 2$.

2 Using the graph drawn for **Try It Out M**, estimate

(a) the value of the investment after $2\frac{1}{2}$ years, giving your answer correct to the nearest hundred dollars

(b) the time to the nearest half-year when the investment is worth $30\,000$.

3 The increase in the population of a town over 5-year periods is given in the table on the right.

x	1985	1990	1995	2000	2005
P	8000	8280	8570	8870	9180

Using a scale of 2 cm : 5-year periods on the x-axis, starting at the year 1985, and 1 cm : 100 persons on the vertical population axis for $8000 \leqslant P \leqslant 10000$,

  (a) draw a graph to show the relation between the year and the population P

  (b) from your graph, estimate, correct to 3 significant figures, the population in 2010.

4 The table below gives the returns on two investments of $3000 at different rates of interest.

x	0	1	2	3	4	5
A_1	3000	3180	3370	3575	3790	4015
A_2	3000	3360	3765	4215	4720	5290

Using a scale of 2 cm : 1 year on the horizontal axis, and 1 cm : $100 on the vertical axis for $3000 \leqslant A \leqslant 5300$,

  (a) draw a graph to show the relation between the number of years and the amount invested at each rate.

  (b) From your curves, estimate, correct to the nearest half-year, the period before A_1 will equal the value of A_2 had at the end of year 4.

Further Practice

1 Given the function $y = 4^x$,

x	−1	−0.5	0	0.5	1	1.5	2	2.5
y		0.5	1					

  (a) Copy and complete the table of corresponding values of x and y for $-1 \leqslant x < 3$

  (b) Using scales of 2 cm : 1 unit on the x-axis and 2 cm : 5 units on the y-axis, plot the points and draw the curve.

  (c) Find the gradient of the curve at **(i)** $x = 0$ **(ii)** $x = 2$.

2 The amount to the nearest dollar due on a loan of $1000 at the end of four one-month periods is given in the table on the right.

x	0	1	2	3	4
A	1000	1020	1040	1061	1082

(a) Using a scale of 2 cm : 1 month on the x-axis and 1 cm : $10 on the y-axis for $1000 \leqslant A \leqslant 1120$, draw a graph to show this relation.

(b) Estimate the amount due to the nearest $at the end of 5 months.

Finished Early?
➡ Go to page 467

---

⑤ Inverse Variation

Learn About It

In inverse variation, y varies as the inverse of x, that is, $y \propto \dfrac{1}{x} \rightarrow y = \dfrac{k}{x}$.

Hence, as one of the quantities increases, the other decreases. For example, in a rectangle of constant area, as the length increases, the width decreases; and vice versa.

Example   Draw the graph of the function $y = \dfrac{2}{x}$ for values of x where $-4 \leqslant x \leqslant 4$.

Working & Answer

x	−4	−3	−2	−1	0	1	2	3	4	±1½	±½
y	−½	−⅔	−1	−2		2	1	⅔	½	±1⅓	±4

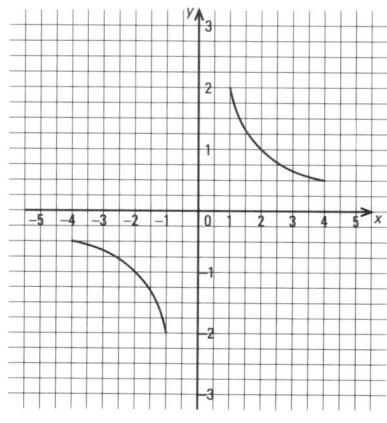

Key Fact

Note that the graph of $y = \dfrac{2}{x}$ is in two branches that are separated by the axes. When $x = 0$, y is undefined. As x increases towards 0, y decreases in value; as x decreases towards 0, y increases in value.

Try It Out

P **(a)** Complete the following table of values for the function $y = -\dfrac{3}{x}$.

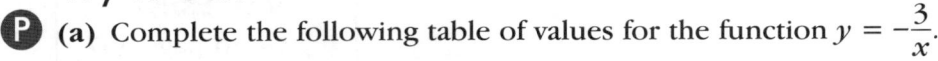

x	−6	−3	−2	−1	−$\frac{1}{2}$	0	$\frac{1}{2}$	1	2	3	6
y	$\frac{1}{2}$		$\frac{2}{3}$	3						−1	

(b) Using a scale of 1 cm : 1 unit on the *x*-axis and 2 cm : 1 unit on the *y*-axis, draw the graph of the function $y = -\dfrac{3}{x}$ for the given domain, $x \, \varepsilon \, R$.

Note that for the function $y = -\dfrac{3}{x}$, when $x = 0$, y is undefined; when $x < 0$, $y > 0$; when $x > 0$, $y < 0$.

As x increases from negative values towards 0, y increases; as x decreases from positive values towards 0, y decreases. Hence, the graph is not continuous.

Learn More About It

In inverse variation, y may also vary as the inverse of x^2, that is,

$$y \propto \frac{1}{x^2} \rightarrow y = \frac{k}{x^2}.$$

Example   Draw the graph of $y = \dfrac{3}{x^2}$ for values of x in the domain $-4 \leqslant x \leqslant 4$.

Working & Answer

x	−4	−3	−2	−1	0	1	2	3	4	$\pm\frac{1}{2}$
x^2	16	9	4	1	0	1	4	9	16	$\frac{1}{4}$
y	$\frac{3}{16}$	$\frac{1}{3}$	$\frac{3}{4}$	3		3	$\frac{3}{4}$	$\frac{1}{3}$	$\frac{3}{16}$	12

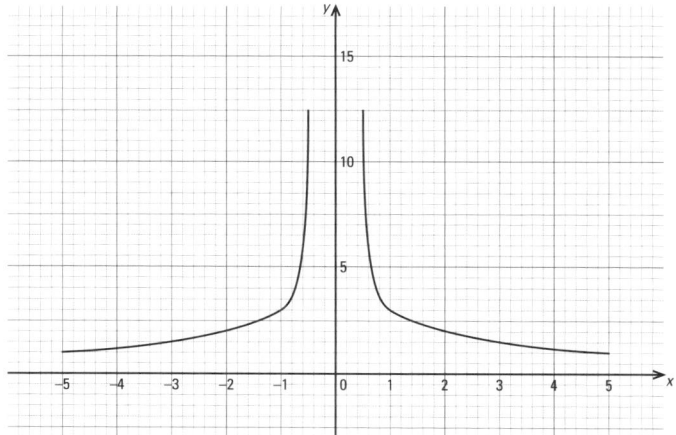

Key Facts

Notice that

- the graph of $y = \dfrac{3}{x^2}$ is in two branches that are separated by the y-axis

- the graph is symmetrical about the y-axis
- there are no negative values of y.

The graph of the function $y = -\dfrac{3}{x^2}$ may be obtained by reflection in the x-axis of the graph of $y = \dfrac{3}{x^2}$.

Try It Out

Q (a) Draw up a table of values for the function $y = -\dfrac{2}{x^2}$ for values
of x in the domain $-4 \leqslant x \leqslant 4$.

(b) Sketch the graph of $y = -\dfrac{2}{x^2}$ for values of x where $x \in R$.

> ### Word Check
>
> **interpolation** using a continuous graph (straight line or smooth curve)
> to find unknown values within a given domain and range
>
> **extrapolation** finding unknown values by the use of a graph when the
> values lie beyond the limiting values of the domain

Practice

R For each of the following functions
(a) complete a table of values for the domain $-3 \leqslant x \leqslant 5, x \in R$.
(b) using suitable scales along each axis, sketch the graph of the function.

1 $y = \dfrac{1}{x}$ **2** $y = -\dfrac{6}{x}$ **3** $y = -\dfrac{4}{x^2}$ **4** $y = \dfrac{1}{x^2}$

Further Practice

S For each of the following functions
(a) complete a table of values for $-3 \leqslant x \leqslant 5, x \in R$.
(b) using suitable scales along each axis, sketch the graph of the function.

1 $y = \dfrac{4}{x}$ **2** $y = -\dfrac{4}{x}$ **3** $y = -\dfrac{3}{x^2}$ **4** $y = \dfrac{2}{x^2}$

> **Finished Early?**
> Go to page 467

Unit 9 *Functions and Graphs 2*
Summary of Chapters 19 and 20

Inverse and Composite Functions

- If f(x) : A → B, and F(x) : B → A, that is, when the **range** of a function f(x) is the **domain** of another function F(x), and the domain of the function f(x) is the range of the function F(x), then f(x) is defined as the **inverse** of the function F(x) and is written as $F^{-1}(x)$ and F(x) is defined as the inverse of the function f(x) and is written as $f^{-1}(x)$. Hence, *only one-to-one functions can have inverse functions*.

- To find an inverse function, we may use flow charts, or an algebraic method in which the variables x and y are interchanged.

- If a function f maps the element x in the domain A onto the element w in the range B, and the function h maps the element w in the domain B onto the element y in the range C, then, a function can be defined that maps x in the domain A onto y in the range C. This function is written as hf(x) = y and is called a **composite function**.
  The elements in the domain of the composite function are those elements that are both in the domain and range of f.
  Generally, hf(x) ≠ fh(x).

Non-linear Graphs

- The **gradient of a curve** at a point (x, y) is the gradient of the tangent, that is, the gradient of the line touching the curve at that point. The gradient shows how y is changing as x increases, that is, the rate of change of y with respect to x.

- In speed–time and distance–time graphs, time is always plotted on the horizontal axis. In a distance–time graph, the slope of a tangent to the graph gives the speed at that time; in a speed–time graph, constant speed is indicated by a line parallel to the time axis.

- In a speed–time graph, a line parallel to the x-axis means constant speed, that is, zero acceleration. The slope of the tangent to the graph gives the acceleration at that time. Deceleration is negative acceleration so that the slope of the tangent is negative.

- The area under a graph can be found by counting squares on a grid or by finding the area of trapezia which approximate to the area. In speed–time graphs, the total distance travelled is given by the area under the curve.

- The cubic graph represents an equation of the third degree, that is, $y = kx^3$, where k is a constant. The graph is symmetrical about the origin.

- An **exponential graph** represents the relation in which x is an index or exponent, and is of the form $y = k^x$, where k is a constant. No matter how small the value of x, $x \in R$, the graph never meets the x-axis. For all values of k, the curve passes through the point $(0, 1)$.

- Graphs of inverse variation represent relations in which one variable is inversely proportional to a second variable, for example, $y \propto \dfrac{k}{x}$, that is, $y = \dfrac{k}{x}$, where k is a constant. The curve is symmetrical about the origin; there are two 'branches' since y is undefined when $x = 0$. As x approaches zero, y increases to very large values (numerically positive or negative). Since there are large differences in the values of y as x gets closer to zero, it is useful in plotting the graph to use additional values of x such as $\pm\frac{1}{2}$, $\pm 1\frac{1}{2}$. As x becomes very large, y becomes very small and the graph is very near to the x-axis.

- When $y \propto \dfrac{k}{x^2}$, then $y = \dfrac{k}{x^2}$, where k is a constant. As for $y = \dfrac{k}{x}$, there are two 'branches' since y is undefined when $x = 0$ but there are no negative values of y. The curve is symmetrical about the y-axis.

21 Matrix Algebra

In this chapter you will learn about ...
1. matrices
2. adding and subtracting matrices
3. scalar multiplication of matrices
4. matrix multiplication
5. inverting matrices
6. algebra problems

1 Matrices

Learn About It

The table below shows the results of a cricket competition between four teams:

	Won	Drawn	Lost
Trinity	4	2	0
Findlay C.C.	2	3	1
Liberty	2	1	3
Basiltown	0	2	4

This information can also be represented as a **matrix**:

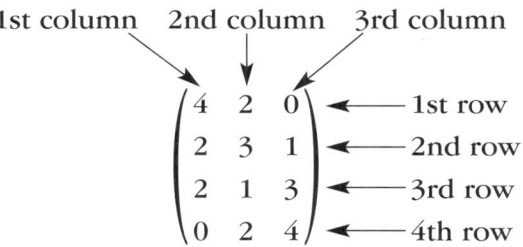

1st column   2nd column   3rd column

$$\begin{pmatrix} 4 & 2 & 0 \\ 2 & 3 & 1 \\ 2 & 1 & 3 \\ 0 & 2 & 4 \end{pmatrix}$$

← 1st row
← 2nd row
← 3rd row
← 4th row

The numbers in the matrix are called elements. All the elements in a horizontal line of the matrix make up a **row** of the matrix. The elements in a vertical line are a **column** of the matrix. So the matrix above has 4 rows and 3 columns. The **order** of a matrix is the number of rows × the number of columns, so our matrix has order 4 × 3.

Word Check

matrix a collection of numbers arranged into a rectangle

row horizontal line of elements

column vertical line of elements

order number of rows × number of columns

Key Fact

In the order of a matrix the number of rows is always written first.

Try It Out

 1 For the matrices below, write down the number of rows and the number of columns. What is the order of each matrix?

(a) $\begin{pmatrix} 1 & -2 \\ 4 & 0 \\ 0 & 1 \end{pmatrix}$ **(b)** $(-1 \ 0 \ 1 \ 0)$ **(c)** $\begin{pmatrix} 1 & 0 \\ 0 & 1 \end{pmatrix}$ **(d)** $\begin{pmatrix} \frac{1}{2} & -1 & \frac{3}{4} \\ 2 & -3 & \frac{5}{2} \end{pmatrix}$

(e) (-4) **(f)** $\begin{pmatrix} 3 \\ 1 \end{pmatrix}$

2 For the following problems write the information as
(i) a table **(ii)** a matrix.

(a) Mr Hinds and Mrs Johnson both sell gardening equipment. Mr Hinds has 19 spades, 22 forks and 12 hosepipes. Mrs Johnson has 19 forks, 12 spades and 17 hosepipes.

(b) All students at Holding's High School do exams in Maths, English and Spanish. In Maths Lacena got 28 marks, Wilbert got 17 and Clova got 20. Lacena also got 28 in English, but only 11 in Spanish. Clova and Wilbert both got 15 in English. In Spanish Wilbert got 21 and Clova got 17.

Finished Early?
 Go to page 468

❷ Adding and Subtracting Matrices

Imagine that our cricket teams play another round of matches and the results are:

	Won	Drawn	Lost
Trinity	2	2	2
Findlay C.C.	1	1	4
Liberty	3	2	1
Basiltown	3	1	2

Again the information can be written as a matrix:

$$\begin{pmatrix} 2 & 2 & 2 \\ 1 & 1 & 4 \\ 3 & 2 & 1 \\ 3 & 1 & 2 \end{pmatrix}$$

We can summarise the results between the teams after both rounds by adding the results in the tables:

	Won	Drawn	Lost
Trinity	4 + 2	2 + 2	0 + 2
Findlay C.C.	2 + 1	3 + 1	1 + 4
Liberty	2 + 3	1 + 2	3 + 1
Basiltown	0 + 3	2 + 1	4 + 2

Then the final results are:

	Won	Drawn	Lost
Trinity	6	4	2
Findlay C.C.	3	4	5
Liberty	5	3	4
Basiltown	3	3	6

You can also find the final results by adding the matrices for the two rounds:

$$\begin{pmatrix} 4 & 2 & 0 \\ 2 & 3 & 1 \\ 2 & 1 & 3 \\ 0 & 2 & 4 \end{pmatrix} + \begin{pmatrix} 2 & 2 & 2 \\ 1 & 1 & 4 \\ 3 & 2 & 1 \\ 3 & 1 & 2 \end{pmatrix} = \begin{pmatrix} 4+2 & 2+2 & 0+2 \\ 2+1 & 3+1 & 1+4 \\ 2+3 & 1+2 & 3+1 \\ 0+3 & 2+1 & 4+2 \end{pmatrix} = \begin{pmatrix} 6 & 4 & 2 \\ 3 & 4 & 5 \\ 5 & 3 & 4 \\ 3 & 3 & 6 \end{pmatrix}$$

Key Fact

To add matrices, add corresponding elements. You can only add matrices if they have the same order and the result will also have the same order.

We usually use capital letters to denote matrices so that we don't have to keep writing all the numbers out.

Example   If $A = \begin{pmatrix} 2 & 1 & -1 \\ 0 & 4 & 3 \end{pmatrix}$, $B = \begin{pmatrix} 0 & 2 & 1 \\ -3 & 1 & 3 \end{pmatrix}$ and $C = \begin{pmatrix} 1 & -3 & -2 \\ 1 & 1 & 1 \end{pmatrix}$

find $A + B + C$.

Working $A + B + C = \begin{pmatrix} 2 + 0 + 1 & 1 + 2 + (-3) & -1 + 1 + (-2) \\ 0 + (-3) + 1 & 4 + 1 + 1 & 3 + 3 + 1 \end{pmatrix}$

$= \begin{pmatrix} 3 & 0 & -2 \\ -2 & 6 & 7 \end{pmatrix}$

Answer $\begin{pmatrix} 3 & 0 & -2 \\ -2 & 6 & 7 \end{pmatrix}$

Try It Out

B Evaluate these sums, if possible.

1 $\begin{pmatrix} 3 & 0 \\ -2 & 1 \end{pmatrix} + \begin{pmatrix} 1 & -2 \\ -1 & 6 \end{pmatrix}$ **2** $(1\ \ 1\ \ 1) + (4\ \ -1\ \ 2) + (-5\ \ 0\ \ -3)$

3 $\begin{pmatrix} -3 & -1 \\ 0 & -2 \\ -4 & 2 \end{pmatrix} + \begin{pmatrix} 1 & -1 & 3 \\ 4 & -2 & -2 \end{pmatrix}$ **4** $(12) + (0) + (-5)$ **5** $\begin{pmatrix} 1 \\ -3 \end{pmatrix} + (2\ \ 1) + \begin{pmatrix} 0 \\ 0 \end{pmatrix}$

6 $\begin{pmatrix} 1 & -1 \\ -1 & 0 \\ 2 & 3 \end{pmatrix} + \begin{pmatrix} -7 & 13 \\ 9 & 22 \\ -14 & 3 \end{pmatrix}$ **7** $\begin{pmatrix} 2.5 \\ -1.3 \end{pmatrix} + \begin{pmatrix} 1.3 \\ 0.7 \end{pmatrix}$

Learn More About It

We can also subtract matrices, but we must be very careful with signs.

Example Evaluate $\begin{pmatrix} 13 & 1 & -8 \\ -2 & 0 & 0 \\ -5 & 3 & -6 \end{pmatrix} - \begin{pmatrix} 2 & -7 & -3 \\ 2 & 11 & -5 \\ 0 & -9 & -1 \end{pmatrix}$

Working $\begin{pmatrix} 13 & 1 & -8 \\ -2 & 0 & 0 \\ -5 & 3 & -6 \end{pmatrix} - \begin{pmatrix} 2 & -7 & -3 \\ 2 & 11 & -5 \\ 0 & -9 & -1 \end{pmatrix} = \begin{pmatrix} 13-2 & 1-(-7) & -8-(-3) \\ -2-2 & 0-11 & 0-(-5) \\ -5-0 & 3-(-9) & -6-(-1) \end{pmatrix}$

$$= \begin{pmatrix} 11 & 8 & -5 \\ -4 & -11 & 5 \\ -5 & 12 & -5 \end{pmatrix}$$

Answer $\begin{pmatrix} 11 & 8 & -5 \\ -4 & -11 & 5 \\ -5 & 12 & -5 \end{pmatrix}$

Key Fact

To subtract matrices, subtract corresponding elements. You can only subtract matrices if they have the same order and the result will also have the same order.

Try It Out

Ⓒ Evaluate these differences, if possible.

1 $\begin{pmatrix} 5 & 7 & 1 \\ -2 & 3 & 1 \end{pmatrix} - \begin{pmatrix} 2 & 6 & 4 \\ 3 & 1 & 1 \end{pmatrix}$ **2** $(-4 \ -2 \ -7 \ -1) - (2 \ 5 \ -1 \ 2)$

3 $\begin{pmatrix} 0 & 0 \\ 0 & 0 \end{pmatrix} - \begin{pmatrix} 0 \\ 0 \end{pmatrix}$ **4** $\begin{pmatrix} 2 & -9 & 15 \\ 18 & -13 & 7 \\ -4 & -4 & 0 \end{pmatrix} - \begin{pmatrix} 2 & -9 & 5 \\ 13 & -4 & 12 \\ -4 & 4 & 8 \end{pmatrix}$ **5** $(13) - (-21 \ 5)$

6 $\begin{pmatrix} 10 & 3 \\ -5 & 1 \\ 2 & -1 \\ 9 & -13 \end{pmatrix} - \begin{pmatrix} 1 & 3 \\ -1 & 1 \\ 3 & -2 \\ 5 & 2 \end{pmatrix}$ **7** $\begin{pmatrix} 1.2 \\ -3.4 \\ 0.6 \end{pmatrix} - \begin{pmatrix} 0.8 \\ 0.2 \\ 1.1 \end{pmatrix}$

Practice

D **1** If $A = \begin{pmatrix} 15 & -4 \\ 3 & -21 \end{pmatrix}$, $B = \begin{pmatrix} -12 & -7 \\ -5 & 13 \end{pmatrix}$, $C = \begin{pmatrix} 17 & -25 \\ -9 & 12 \end{pmatrix}$ find:

(a) $A + B$ (b) $A - C$ (c) $B + C - A$

2 $P = (9 \ -3 \ 5)$, $Q = (-2 \ 5 \ 7)$, $R = (0 \ 0 \ 0)$

Calculate:

(a) $Q + P$ (b) $Q - P$ (c) $P - Q$ (d) $R - Q$ (e) $P - R - Q$

3 Evaluate the following, if possible.

(a) $\begin{pmatrix} 7 & 8 \\ -4 & 0 \end{pmatrix} - \begin{pmatrix} -5 & 3 \\ 4 & -9 \end{pmatrix} + \begin{pmatrix} 6 & 8 \\ -2 & 10 \end{pmatrix}$ (b) $\begin{pmatrix} -8 & 1 & 6 \\ 4 & 2 & -5 \\ 11 & -8 & 2 \end{pmatrix} + \begin{pmatrix} -4 & 2 \\ 6 & 10 \\ -1 & -7 \end{pmatrix}$

(c) $\begin{pmatrix} -9 & 2 \\ 5 & -1 \\ -4 & -8 \\ 2 & 5 \end{pmatrix} + \begin{pmatrix} 5 & 4 \\ -7 & 1 \\ -2 & 5 \\ 7 & -1 \end{pmatrix} - \begin{pmatrix} 5 & -2 \\ -2 & 0 \\ 3 & 4 \\ -1 & 4 \end{pmatrix}$

(d) $\begin{pmatrix} 17 & -8 \\ 4 & 0 \end{pmatrix} - \begin{pmatrix} 9 & -5 \\ -2 & 7 \end{pmatrix} + \begin{pmatrix} -8 & 3 \\ -6 & 7 \end{pmatrix}$

4 At Holding's High School Eric, Arif and Petula study Physics and Biology. For each subject they do an exam at Christmas and another in the summer, and their results for the two exams are added to give a final mark for the subject. At Christmas Eric got 34 and 29, Arif 28 and 39 and Petula 30 and 22 in Physics and Biology respectively. In the summer the Physics results were 41 for Arif, 35 for Petula and 25 for Eric. The Biology results were 31 for Petula, 30 for Arif and 28 for Eric.

(a) Write the results in two matrices, one of Christmas results and one for the summer.

(b) Add the matrices to find the final marks.

(c) Write the final marks in a table.

> **Finished Early?**
> 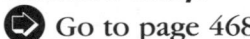 Go to page 468

● Scalar Multiplication of Matrices

Learn About It

Let's go back to our cricket teams. What would the final results have been if the results in the second round of matches had been the same as those in the first?

After the second round each team would have twice as many wins, draws and loses as they had after the first, so the final results would be:

$$\begin{pmatrix} 2 \times 4 & 2 \times 2 & 2 \times 0 \\ 2 \times 2 & 2 \times 3 & 2 \times 1 \\ 2 \times 2 & 2 \times 1 & 2 \times 3 \\ 2 \times 0 & 2 \times 2 & 2 \times 4 \end{pmatrix} = \begin{pmatrix} 8 & 4 & 0 \\ 4 & 6 & 2 \\ 4 & 2 & 6 \\ 0 & 4 & 8 \end{pmatrix}$$

But this is a bit unwieldy, so we write the matrix on the left as $2\begin{pmatrix} 4 & 2 & 0 \\ 2 & 3 & 1 \\ 2 & 1 & 3 \\ 0 & 2 & 4 \end{pmatrix}$.

This is called scalar multiplication.

Key Fact

To multiply a matrix by a scalar, multiply every element of the matrix by the scalar.

Example If $A = \begin{pmatrix} 2 & -3 \\ -1 & -6 \end{pmatrix}$ and $B = \begin{pmatrix} -4 & 3 \\ 5 & 2 \end{pmatrix}$ calculate $2A - 3B$.

Working $2A = 2\begin{pmatrix} 2 & -3 \\ -1 & -6 \end{pmatrix} = \begin{pmatrix} 2 \times 2 & 2 \times (-3) \\ 2 \times (-1) & 2 \times (-6) \end{pmatrix} = \begin{pmatrix} 4 & -6 \\ -2 & -12 \end{pmatrix}$

$3B = 3\begin{pmatrix} -4 & 3 \\ 5 & 2 \end{pmatrix} = \begin{pmatrix} 3 \times (-4) & 3 \times 3 \\ 3 \times 5 & 3 \times 2 \end{pmatrix} = \begin{pmatrix} -12 & 9 \\ 15 & 6 \end{pmatrix}$

$2A - 3B = \begin{pmatrix} 4 & -6 \\ -2 & -12 \end{pmatrix} - \begin{pmatrix} -12 & 9 \\ 15 & 6 \end{pmatrix} = \begin{pmatrix} 16 & -15 \\ -17 & -18 \end{pmatrix}$

Answer $\begin{pmatrix} 16 & -15 \\ -17 & -18 \end{pmatrix}$

Try It Out

E **1** If $A = \begin{pmatrix} -3 & 1 \\ 5 & -5 \end{pmatrix}$ and $B = \begin{pmatrix} 2 & 6 \\ -9 & 0 \end{pmatrix}$ find

(a) $3A$ (b) $-4B$ (c) $-B$ (*Hint*: $-B = -1 \times B$)   (d) $-2A + 3B$

Practice

F **1** Evaluate

(a) $\begin{pmatrix} -1 & 6 \\ 9 & -2 \end{pmatrix} + 3\begin{pmatrix} 2 & -2 \\ 1 & 1 \end{pmatrix}$

(b) $4\begin{pmatrix} -4 \\ 2 \\ -3 \end{pmatrix} - \begin{pmatrix} -5 \\ 2 \\ 1 \end{pmatrix}$

(c) $2\begin{pmatrix} 5 & -2 & 1 \\ -3 & -6 & 3 \\ 2 & 2 & 0 \end{pmatrix} - 3\begin{pmatrix} 3 & -2 & 1 \\ 4 & -4 & 1 \\ 3 & -1 & 2 \end{pmatrix}$

(d) $-2\begin{pmatrix} 3 & 1 \\ -4 & 7 \end{pmatrix} + \begin{pmatrix} 3 & -2 \\ 2 & -3 \end{pmatrix}$

2 If $P = \begin{pmatrix} 3 & -3 \\ 5 & 2 \end{pmatrix}$, $Q = \begin{pmatrix} -4 & 7 \\ 1 & 2 \end{pmatrix}$, $R = \begin{pmatrix} 1 & -4 \\ -6 & -4 \end{pmatrix}$ find:

(a) $3P + 2Q$ (b) $-P - 2R$ (c) $P + 2Q - 3R$

> **Finished Early?**
> ➡ Go to page 468

④ Matrix Multiplication

Learn About It

Think back to our cricket teams. The matrix representing the total results is:

Wins   Draw   Losses

$$\begin{pmatrix} 6 & 4 & 2 \\ 3 & 4 & 5 \\ 5 & 3 & 4 \\ 3 & 3 & 6 \end{pmatrix}$$

where the first column represents the number of wins for each team, the second column represents the draws and the third the number of losses. Suppose that each team is given 4 points for a win, 2 for a draw and none for a loss. We can represent this by another matrix $\begin{pmatrix} 4 \\ 2 \\ 0 \end{pmatrix}$.

Then to work out the final score for each team we can multiply the number of wins by the points for a win, the number of draws by the points for a draw and the number of losses by the points for a loss, and then add them together. So we get:

$$\begin{pmatrix} 6 \times 4 & 4 \times 2 & 2 \times 0 \\ 3 \times 4 & 4 \times 2 & 5 \times 0 \\ 5 \times 4 & 3 \times 2 & 4 \times 0 \\ 3 \times 4 & 3 \times 2 & 6 \times 0 \end{pmatrix} = \begin{pmatrix} 32 \\ 20 \\ 26 \\ 18 \end{pmatrix}$$

Number of wins ↓   Points for a win ↙   Total ↓

We can write this calculation in a shorter way as:

$$\begin{pmatrix} 6 & 4 & 2 \\ 3 & 4 & 5 \\ 5 & 3 & 4 \\ 3 & 3 & 6 \end{pmatrix} \times \begin{pmatrix} 4 \\ 2 \\ 0 \end{pmatrix} = \begin{pmatrix} 32 \\ 20 \\ 26 \\ 18 \end{pmatrix}$$

We call this matrix multiplication – we have multiplied two matrices together to get a third matrix.

Have a look at the order of the matrices in the product. We have multiplied a 4×3 matrix by a 3×1 matrix to get a 4×1 matrix.

[($4 \times \underline{\mathbf{3}}$ matrix) × ($\underline{\mathbf{3}} \times 1$ matrix) = (4×1 matrix)]

Notice that the underlined middle numbers on the left-hand side are the same. This means that the number of columns in the first matrix is the same as the number of rows in the second matrix. We can *never* multiply matrices if this isn't true.

Key Fact

You can only multiply matrices if the number of columns in the first matrix is the same as the number of rows in the second matrix.

Also the bold outer numbers make up the order of the final matrix. This means that the final matrix has the same number of rows as the first matrix and the same number of columns as the second matrix.

Key Fact

When you multiply matrices the final matrix has the same number of rows as the first matrix and the same number of columns as the second matrix.

Try It Out

G **1** Can these matrices be multiplied? *You don't need to solve them unless you want to.*

(a) $\begin{pmatrix} 2 & 3 \\ -1 & 0 \end{pmatrix} \begin{pmatrix} -5 & 4 \\ 1 & 1 \end{pmatrix}$ **(b)** $(4 \ -8 \ 1) \begin{pmatrix} 2 \\ 3 \\ -1 \end{pmatrix}$ **(c)** $(-8 \ -6)(4 \ -12)$

(d) $\begin{pmatrix} -6 & 3 & 9 \\ 2 & -8 & -1 \end{pmatrix} \begin{pmatrix} 1 & -1 \\ 0 & 5 \\ -4 & 9 \end{pmatrix}$ **(e)** $\begin{pmatrix} 1 & -1 \\ 0 & 5 \\ -4 & 9 \end{pmatrix} \begin{pmatrix} -6 & 3 & 9 \\ 2 & -8 & -1 \end{pmatrix}$

(f) $\begin{pmatrix} 5 & -5 \\ 9 & 1 \\ 0 & -13 \\ 7 & -3 \end{pmatrix} \begin{pmatrix} 5 & -5 \\ 9 & 1 \\ 0 & -13 \\ 7 & -3 \end{pmatrix}$

2 For these products work out the order of the resulting matrix.

(a) $\begin{pmatrix} -3 & 9 \\ 11 & 4 \end{pmatrix} \begin{pmatrix} -1 & 0 \\ -4 & 8 \end{pmatrix}$ **(b)** $(-3 \ 10 \ 4) \begin{pmatrix} 2 \\ 17 \\ -5 \end{pmatrix}$

(c) $\begin{pmatrix} 10 & -13 & 7 & -2 \\ -4 & -9 & -3 & -1 \end{pmatrix} \begin{pmatrix} -6 & 1 & 4 \\ 8 & -14 & 7 \\ -2 & 5 & 1 \\ 0 & -1 & 1 \end{pmatrix}$ **(d)** $\begin{pmatrix} -8 & 4 & 1 \\ 0 & 0 & 0 \\ 3 & -2 & 7 \end{pmatrix} \begin{pmatrix} -8 & 4 & 1 \\ 0 & 0 & 0 \\ 3 & -2 & 7 \end{pmatrix}$

(e) $\begin{pmatrix} 4 \\ 5 \end{pmatrix} (-2 \ 3)$ **(f)** (a 4 × 3 matrix) × (a 3 × 3 matrix)

(g) (a 4 × 94 matrix) × (a 94 × 3 matrix)

Learn More About It

So we know when you can multiply matrices and the type of matrix you should get, but how do you multiply matrices?

Example Evaluate $\begin{pmatrix} 2 & 3 & 4 \\ -1 & 5 & 3 \end{pmatrix} \begin{pmatrix} -2 \\ 1 \\ 6 \end{pmatrix}$

Working

$\begin{pmatrix} 2 & 3 & 4 \\ -1 & 5 & 3 \end{pmatrix} \begin{pmatrix} -2 \\ 1 \\ 6 \end{pmatrix} = \begin{pmatrix} 2 \times (-2) + 3 \times 1 + 4 \times 6 \\ (-1) \times (-2) + 5 \times 1 + 3 \times 6 \end{pmatrix} = \begin{pmatrix} -4 + 3 + 24 \\ 2 + 5 + 18 \end{pmatrix} = \begin{pmatrix} 23 \\ 25 \end{pmatrix}$

Answer $\begin{pmatrix} 23 \\ 25 \end{pmatrix}$

Let's take a look at what we have done. The first element of the answer was formed by multiplying the elements of the first row of the first matrix by the elements of the column matrix, and adding:

$$\begin{pmatrix} 2 & 3 & 4 \\ * & * & * \end{pmatrix} \begin{pmatrix} -2 \\ 1 \\ 6 \end{pmatrix} = \begin{pmatrix} 2 \times (-2) + 3 \times 1 + 4 \times 6 \\ * \end{pmatrix} = \begin{pmatrix} 23 \\ * \end{pmatrix}$$

The last element of the answer was formed by multiplying the elements of the last row of the first matrix by the elements of the column matrix, and adding:

$$\begin{pmatrix} * & * & * \\ -1 & 5 & 3 \end{pmatrix} \begin{pmatrix} -2 \\ 1 \\ 6 \end{pmatrix} = \begin{pmatrix} * \\ (-1) \times (-2) + 5 \times 1 + 3 \times 6 \end{pmatrix} = \begin{pmatrix} * \\ 25 \end{pmatrix}$$

Example Evaluate $\begin{pmatrix} 2 & 3 & 4 \\ -1 & 5 & 3 \end{pmatrix} \begin{pmatrix} -2 & 3 \\ 1 & 7 \\ 6 & -4 \end{pmatrix}$

Working $\begin{pmatrix} 2 & 3 & 4 \\ -1 & 5 & 3 \end{pmatrix} \begin{pmatrix} -2 & 3 \\ 1 & 7 \\ 6 & -4 \end{pmatrix}$

$$= \begin{pmatrix} 2 \times (-2) + 3 \times 1 + 4 \times 6 & 2 \times 3 + 3 \times 7 + 4 \times (-4) \\ (-1) \times (-2) + 5 \times 1 + 3 \times 6 & (-1) \times 3 + 5 \times 7 + 3 \times (-4) \end{pmatrix}$$

$$= \begin{pmatrix} 23 & 11 \\ 25 & 20 \end{pmatrix}$$

Answer $\begin{pmatrix} 23 & 11 \\ 25 & 20 \end{pmatrix}$

The table below shows how the elements in the solution matrix are calculated from the two matrices.

First matrix		Second matrix		Element in solution	
1st row	×	1st column	to get	1st row	1st column
1st row	×	2nd column	to get	1st row	2nd column
2nd row	×	1st column	to get	2nd row	1st column
2nd row	×	2nd column	to get	2nd row	2nd column

In general, multiply the elements in the mth row of the first matrix by those in the nth column of the second matrix to get the element in the mth row and nth column of the answer.

Try It Out

H **1** Find the following matrix products.

(a) $(3\ 1)\begin{pmatrix} 2 \\ 7 \end{pmatrix}$
(b) $(-4\ 2\ 1)\begin{pmatrix} -1 \\ 2 \\ -5 \end{pmatrix}$
(c) $(1\ 4)\begin{pmatrix} -2 & 1 \\ 6 & 5 \end{pmatrix}$

(d) $\begin{pmatrix} 6 & 0 \\ 5 & 7 \end{pmatrix}\begin{pmatrix} 3 \\ 4 \end{pmatrix}$
(e) $\begin{pmatrix} -2 & 6 & 1 \\ 0 & 4 & 5 \end{pmatrix}\begin{pmatrix} -5 \\ 2 \\ 1 \end{pmatrix}$
(f) $(1\ 0\ 1\ 0)\begin{pmatrix} 1 & 2 & 3 & 4 \\ 2 & 1 & 2 & 3 \\ 3 & 2 & 1 & 2 \\ 4 & 3 & 2 & 1 \end{pmatrix}$

2 Find the following matrix products.

(a) $\begin{pmatrix} 5 & 2 \\ 4 & 1 \end{pmatrix}\begin{pmatrix} 3 \\ 2 \end{pmatrix}$
(b) $\begin{pmatrix} 7 & 1 \\ -4 & 2 \end{pmatrix}\begin{pmatrix} -2 \\ 4 \end{pmatrix}$
(c) $\begin{pmatrix} 2 & 0 \\ 4 & 5 \end{pmatrix}\begin{pmatrix} 3 & 2 \\ 1 & 1 \end{pmatrix}$

(d) $\begin{pmatrix} 7 & -3 \\ 4 & -6 \\ 5 & 2 \end{pmatrix}\begin{pmatrix} -4 & 2 \\ 5 & 3 \end{pmatrix}$
(e) $\begin{pmatrix} -4 & 9 \\ 7 & 4 \end{pmatrix}\begin{pmatrix} 1 & 3 \\ 2 & -6 \end{pmatrix}$
(f) $(5\ 1\ -6)\begin{pmatrix} 1 & 2 \\ 3 & 4 \\ 5 & 6 \end{pmatrix}$

Practice

I **1** Evaluate these products.

(a) $\begin{pmatrix} 5 & 4 \\ 6 & 11 \end{pmatrix}\begin{pmatrix} -4 & 2 \\ 9 & -1 \end{pmatrix}$
(b) $\begin{pmatrix} -5 & 2 \\ 4 & 2 \end{pmatrix}\begin{pmatrix} 13 & -15 \\ 8 & 5 \end{pmatrix}$

(c) $\begin{pmatrix} 1 & 0 \\ 0 & 1 \end{pmatrix}\begin{pmatrix} -19 & 43 \\ 17 & 2 \end{pmatrix}$
(d) $\begin{pmatrix} 3 & -1 \\ 0 & 2 \end{pmatrix}\begin{pmatrix} \frac{1}{3} & \frac{1}{6} \\ 0 & \frac{1}{2} \end{pmatrix}$
(e) $\begin{pmatrix} -4 & 2 & 3 \\ 1 & 0 & 0 \end{pmatrix}\begin{pmatrix} 5 & 2 \\ -8 & 1 \\ -5 & 3 \end{pmatrix}$

(f) $\begin{pmatrix} 7 & -2 \\ -5 & -4 \end{pmatrix}\begin{pmatrix} 1 & 0 \\ 0 & 1 \end{pmatrix}$
(g) $\begin{pmatrix} -2 & 1 & 4 \\ 3 & -1 & 0 \\ 6 & 3 & 1 \end{pmatrix}\begin{pmatrix} 7 & -3 & 1 \\ 0 & 0 & 1 \\ -4 & -3 & 1 \end{pmatrix}$

2 If $A = \begin{pmatrix} 5 & -3 \\ -7 & 3 \end{pmatrix}$ and $B = \begin{pmatrix} -2 & 7 \\ 4 & 5 \end{pmatrix}$, show that $AB \neq BA$.

Key Fact
In general matrix multiplication is not commutative, so $AB \neq BA$.

3 If $A = \begin{pmatrix} 5 & 4 & 1 \\ 2 & -5 & 3 \end{pmatrix}$, $B = \begin{pmatrix} 3 & 2 \\ 1 & 1 \\ 2 & 3 \end{pmatrix}$, $P = \begin{pmatrix} -4 & 3 \\ 0 & 6 \end{pmatrix}$, $Q = \begin{pmatrix} -2 & 4 & 2 \\ 5 & 1 & -3 \\ 2 & 4 & -1 \end{pmatrix}$ calculate:

    (a) AB **(b)** BA **(c)** BP **(d)** AQ

    (e) QB **(f)** $P^2 \ (=P \times P)$ **(g)** P^3

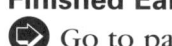

Finished Early?

➡️ Go to page 468

⑤ Inverting Matrices

Learn About It

If we multiply any number by 1 the number doesn't change. For example, $1 \times 10 = 10 \times 1 = 10$. We call 1 the identity when multiplying numbers.

Similarly, when we multiply any matrix by the **identity matrix** the matrix is unchanged. The symbol for the identity matrix is I and the 2×2 identity matrix is $\begin{pmatrix} 1 & 0 \\ 0 & 1 \end{pmatrix}$.

So and $\begin{pmatrix} a & b \\ c & d \end{pmatrix}\begin{pmatrix} 1 & 0 \\ 0 & 1 \end{pmatrix} = \begin{pmatrix} a & b \\ c & d \end{pmatrix}$ and $\begin{pmatrix} 1 & 0 \\ 0 & 1 \end{pmatrix}\begin{pmatrix} a \\ b \end{pmatrix} = \begin{pmatrix} a \\ b \end{pmatrix}$.

Numbers have inverses. The inverse of 10, for example, is the number that we multiply 10 by to get the identity (1). $10 \times \frac{1}{10} = 1$ so the inverse of 10 is $\frac{1}{10}$.

Matrices also have inverses. If

$$\begin{pmatrix} a & b \\ c & d \end{pmatrix}\begin{pmatrix} p & q \\ r & s \end{pmatrix} = \begin{pmatrix} 1 & 0 \\ 0 & 1 \end{pmatrix} = \begin{pmatrix} p & q \\ r & s \end{pmatrix}\begin{pmatrix} a & b \\ c & d \end{pmatrix}$$

> **Word Check**
>
> **pre-multiply** a matrix A is pre-multiplied by B if we calculate BA
>
> **post-multiply** a matrix A is post-multiplied by B if we calculate AB

then $\begin{pmatrix} p & q \\ r & s \end{pmatrix}$ is the **inverse** of $\begin{pmatrix} a & b \\ c & d \end{pmatrix}$.

The inverse of the matrix A is written as A^{-1}.

But how do we find the inverse of a matrix? The inverse of the matrix $\begin{pmatrix} a & b \\ c & d \end{pmatrix}$ is $\dfrac{1}{ad - bc}\begin{pmatrix} d & -b \\ -c & a \end{pmatrix}$

$ad - bc$ is called the **determinant** of the matrix. The determinant of a matrix A is written $|A|$.

So to find the inverse of a 2 × 2 matrix:

(i) swap the top-left and bottom-right elements $\begin{pmatrix} a & b \\ c & d \end{pmatrix}$

(ii) multiply the other elements by –1 $\begin{pmatrix} d & -b \\ -c & a \end{pmatrix}$

(iii) divide by the determinant of the original matrix $\dfrac{1}{ad - bc} \begin{pmatrix} d & -b \\ -c & a \end{pmatrix}$

Example   Find the inverse of $\begin{pmatrix} 3 & 2 \\ 5 & 4 \end{pmatrix}$.

Working   The determinant of $\begin{pmatrix} 3 & 2 \\ 5 & 4 \end{pmatrix}$ is $3 \times 4 - 2 \times 5 = 2$.

Swap top-left and bottom-right and multiply the others by –1: $\begin{pmatrix} 4 & -2 \\ -5 & 3 \end{pmatrix}$

So the inverse is $\dfrac{1}{2} \begin{pmatrix} 4 & -2 \\ -5 & 3 \end{pmatrix}$

Check: $\dfrac{1}{2} \begin{pmatrix} 4 & -2 \\ -5 & 3 \end{pmatrix} \begin{pmatrix} 3 & 2 \\ 5 & 4 \end{pmatrix} = \dfrac{1}{2} \begin{pmatrix} 2 & 0 \\ 0 & 2 \end{pmatrix} = \begin{pmatrix} 1 & 0 \\ 0 & 1 \end{pmatrix}$

Answer $\dfrac{1}{2} \begin{pmatrix} 4 & -2 \\ -5 & 3 \end{pmatrix}$

In this example we could also have written the answer as $\begin{pmatrix} 2 & -1 \\ -\frac{5}{2} & \frac{3}{2} \end{pmatrix}$ by using scalar multiplication.

Example   Find the inverse of $\begin{pmatrix} 2 & -6 \\ 3 & -9 \end{pmatrix}$.

Working   The determinant is $2 \times (-9) - (-6) \times 3 = -18 - (-18) = 0$.
So to find the inverse we need to divide by zero, which can't be done. So the matrix has no inverse.

Answer   No inverse.

In this example we had a matrix which had determinant zero, and so has no inverse. These matrices are called **singular** matrices.

Word Check

singular matrix a matrix with determinant zero

Try It Out

J **1** Find the determinants of these matrices.

(a) $\begin{pmatrix} 7 & 3 \\ 2 & 1 \end{pmatrix}$ (b) $\begin{pmatrix} 2 & 5 \\ 3 & 4 \end{pmatrix}$ (c) $\begin{pmatrix} -4 & 6 \\ 1 & -5 \end{pmatrix}$ (d) $\begin{pmatrix} -6 & -3 \\ -4 & -2 \end{pmatrix}$

(e) $\begin{pmatrix} -7 & 5 \\ -4 & 3 \end{pmatrix}$ (f) $\begin{pmatrix} 5 & 4 \\ 4 & 5 \end{pmatrix}$

2 Find the inverses of these matrices, if possible.

(a) $\begin{pmatrix} 1 & 3 \\ -1 & 1 \end{pmatrix}$ (b) $\begin{pmatrix} 2 & 3 \\ 3 & 5 \end{pmatrix}$ (c) $\begin{pmatrix} -6 & 12 \\ 2 & -4 \end{pmatrix}$ (d) $\begin{pmatrix} -4 & 6 \\ -2 & 5 \end{pmatrix}$

(e) $\begin{pmatrix} 1 & 0 \\ 0 & 1 \end{pmatrix}$ (f) $\begin{pmatrix} 3 & 1 \\ -2 & \frac{2}{3} \end{pmatrix}$

Practice

K **1** Let $A = \begin{pmatrix} 6 & -4 \\ -5 & 5 \end{pmatrix}$.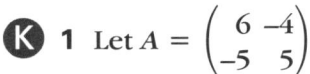

(a) Calculate $|A|$.
(b) Find A^{-1}.
(c) Calculate $|A^{-1}|$, the determinant of the inverse.
(d) Compare $|A^{-1}|$ with $|A|$. What do you notice?
(e) Show that the inverse of A^{-1} is A, that is $(A^{-1})^{-1} = A$.

2 Let $P = \begin{pmatrix} -6 & a \\ 9 & 3 \end{pmatrix}$ be a singular matrix. Find a.

3 Let B be the matrix $\begin{pmatrix} k+1 & -k-1 \\ k-2 & k-1 \end{pmatrix}$.

For which values of k is B singular?

> **Finished Early?**
> Go to page 469

6 Algebra Problems

Learn About It

We have already looked at matrix products such as $\begin{pmatrix} 3 & -1 \\ 4 & 2 \end{pmatrix}\begin{pmatrix} 2 \\ 3 \end{pmatrix} = \begin{pmatrix} ? \\ ? \end{pmatrix}$. But

what happens when we don't know one of the other matrices? For example,

how do we find x and y in $\begin{pmatrix} 3 & -1 \\ 4 & 2 \end{pmatrix}\begin{pmatrix} x \\ y \end{pmatrix} = \begin{pmatrix} 3 \\ 14 \end{pmatrix}$?

If we multiply the matrices we get:

$$3 \times x + (-1) \times y = 3 \qquad \text{so} \qquad 3x - y = 3$$
$$4 \times x + 2 \times y = 14 \qquad \text{so} \qquad 4x + 2y = 14$$

This should look familiar. It is an example of a pair of simultaneous equations, a subject we met in Chapter 9.

So we can write $3x + (-1)y = 3$
$$4x + 2y = 14$$

as a matrix equation: $\begin{pmatrix} 3 & -1 \\ 4 & 2 \end{pmatrix} \begin{pmatrix} x \\ y \end{pmatrix} = \begin{pmatrix} 3 \\ 14 \end{pmatrix}$

The inverse of $\begin{pmatrix} 3 & -1 \\ 4 & 2 \end{pmatrix}$ is $\frac{1}{10} \begin{pmatrix} 2 & 1 \\ -4 & 3 \end{pmatrix}$, so we can pre-multiply both sides by

the inverse to get:

$$\frac{1}{10} \begin{pmatrix} 2 & 1 \\ -4 & 3 \end{pmatrix} \begin{pmatrix} 3 & -1 \\ 4 & 2 \end{pmatrix} \begin{pmatrix} x \\ y \end{pmatrix} = \frac{1}{10} \begin{pmatrix} 2 & 1 \\ -4 & 3 \end{pmatrix} \begin{pmatrix} 3 \\ 14 \end{pmatrix}$$

$$I \begin{pmatrix} x \\ y \end{pmatrix} = \frac{1}{10} \begin{pmatrix} 20 \\ 30 \end{pmatrix} \begin{pmatrix} x \\ y \end{pmatrix} = \begin{pmatrix} 2 \\ 3 \end{pmatrix}$$

So the solution of the simultaneous equations $\begin{matrix} 3x - y = 3 \\ 4x + 2y = 14 \end{matrix}$

is $x = 2$, $y = 3$.

Example   Solve $2x + y = 23$
$$x - y = 1$$

Working   Write the left-hand side as a matrix equation:

$$\begin{pmatrix} 2 & 1 \\ 1 & -1 \end{pmatrix} \begin{pmatrix} x \\ y \end{pmatrix} = \begin{pmatrix} 23 \\ 1 \end{pmatrix} \qquad [1]$$

The inverse of $\begin{pmatrix} 2 & 1 \\ 1 & -1 \end{pmatrix}$ is $-\frac{1}{3} \begin{pmatrix} -1 & -1 \\ -1 & 2 \end{pmatrix} = \frac{1}{3} \begin{pmatrix} 1 & 1 \\ 1 & -2 \end{pmatrix}$.

Pre-multiply both sides of [1] by the inverse:

$$\frac{1}{3} \begin{pmatrix} 1 & 1 \\ 1 & -2 \end{pmatrix} \begin{pmatrix} 2 & 1 \\ 1 & -1 \end{pmatrix} \begin{pmatrix} x \\ y \end{pmatrix} = \frac{1}{3} \begin{pmatrix} 1 & 1 \\ 1 & -2 \end{pmatrix} \begin{pmatrix} 23 \\ 1 \end{pmatrix}$$

$$\frac{1}{3} \begin{pmatrix} 3 & 0 \\ 0 & 3 \end{pmatrix} \begin{pmatrix} x \\ y \end{pmatrix} = \frac{1}{3} \begin{pmatrix} 24 \\ 21 \end{pmatrix}$$

$$\begin{pmatrix} 1 & 0 \\ 0 & 1 \end{pmatrix} \begin{pmatrix} x \\ y \end{pmatrix} = \begin{pmatrix} 8 \\ 7 \end{pmatrix}$$

$$\begin{pmatrix} x \\ y \end{pmatrix} = \begin{pmatrix} 8 \\ 7 \end{pmatrix}$$

So $x = 8$ and $y = 7$.

Check $2 \times 8 + 7 = 23$ ✓
$$8 - 7 = 1 \qquad ✓$$

Answer $x = 8$, $y = 7$

Try It Out

 **1** Convert these simultaneous equations into matrix equations.

(a) $3x + 2y = 3$	**(b)** $x + 3y = 7$	**(c)** $4x - 3y = 0$
$x + 5y = 14$	$2x + 3y = 11$	$x + y = 7$
(d) $c - 2d = -2$	**(e)** $-5x + 4y = 1$	
$-c + 6d = 2$	$4x - 5y = 1$	

2 Solve the equations in question 1 by using inverse matrices.

Practice

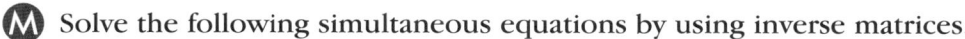 Solve the following simultaneous equations by using inverse matrices.

1 $2x + 3y = 10$
$-2x - y = -6$

2 $p + q = 10$
$p - q = 2$

3 $-2a - b = 5$
$a + 2b = -7$

4 $x - 6y = 1$
$3x + 2y = 13$

Mr Phillips and Mrs Ryan went to the shops.
Mr Phillips bought 2 loaves of bread and 1 pint of milk.
Mrs Ryan bought 1 loaf of bread and 3 pints of milk.

(a) Copy and complete the table:

	Loaves of bread	Pints of milk
Mr Phillips		
Mrs Ryan		

(b) Put the information in the table into a matrix.

Both Mr Phillips and Mrs Ryan paid a total of $5 for their shopping.

(c) Put this information into a matrix.

(d) If a loaf of bread costs x and a pint of milk costs y form a matrix equation to find x and y.

(e) Solve the equation to find the cost of a loaf of bread and the cost of a pint of milk.

> **Finished Early?**
> Go to page 469

22 Vectors

1 Vectors

Learn About It

Imagine you are trying to find the post office and you ask someone how to get there. They might say something like: 'Go towards the centre of town. It is about 300 m away.' They have told you which direction to go in, and how far to go. This is an example of a **vector**.

A vector is a quantity that has both a size and a direction. The size of a vector is called the **magnitude**. In the example above, the direction is 'towards the centre of town' and the magnitude is 'about 300 m'.

Velocity is a vector. It has a magnitude (the speed, for example 30 km/h) and a direction (e.g. due north). The translations that we used in Chapter 13 were also vectors; they move the object through a certain distance in a particular direction.

A **scalar** is a quantity that has a magnitude but no direction. Temperature is a scalar because it has a magnitude (e.g. 100 °F), but no direction.

> **Word Check**
>
> **vector** a quantity with both a magnitude and a direction
>
> **scalar** a quantity with a magnitude and no direction

Suppose we walked from a point A to point B.

We represent the vector by a line segment with an arrow. The direction in which the arrow points is the direction of the vector; the length of the line segment represents the magnitude of the vector.

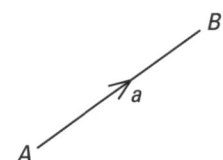

This vector can be written in a number of ways:
$\overline{AB}$, $\overrightarrow{AB}$, **AB**, $\underline{AB}$, $\overline{a}$, $\vec{a}$, **a**, $\underline{a}$.

If we walk from B back to A we walk the same distance but in the opposite direction. The vector with the same magnitude as $\overrightarrow{AB}$ but opposite direction is written $-\overrightarrow{AB}$ or $-\mathbf{a}$. If you look at the diagram this is the same as the vector $\overrightarrow{BA}$.

So $\overrightarrow{BA} = -\overrightarrow{AB}$.

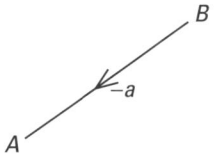

> # Key Fact
>
> For any two points A and B then
> $\overrightarrow{BA} = -\overrightarrow{AB}$.

Instead of returning to A, suppose we walked due east to a point C. We can represent this by adding another vector, written $\overrightarrow{BC}$ or $\mathbf{b}$.

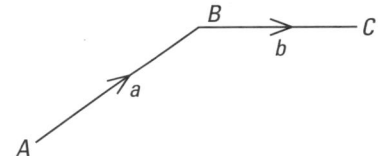

 Protractor

Ⓐ Try It Out

1 Ravi walks 100 m south. Draw a vector to represent his journey.

2 An aircraft takes off then flies 150 km due west, and then turns to the north-east and flies for another 200 km. Draw a vector diagram to represent the flight.

3 A cow walks 35 m in a south-westerly direction. She then turns through an angle of 120° clockwise and walks 12 m. Draw a vector diagram showing the cow's walk.

Two vectors are equal if they have the same direction and magnitude. In the diagram $\mathbf{r}$ and $\mathbf{s}$ have the same magnitude and direction so $\mathbf{r} = \mathbf{s}$.

Any two vectors that have the same direction are parallel. $\mathbf{a}$, $\mathbf{b}$ and $\mathbf{c}$ all have different magnitudes but the same direction, so they are all parallel.

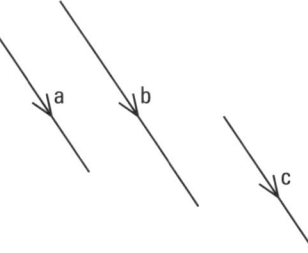

We can write a vector as a 2 × 1 column matrix.

In the diagram the vector $\overrightarrow{AB}$ represents a move of 2 units right and 3 units up, so it can be written $\binom{2}{3}$.

The vector $\overrightarrow{CD}$ represents a move of 4 units left and 1 down and so can be written $\binom{-4}{-1}$.

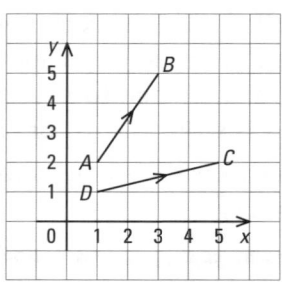

Practice

B **1** Use the diagram to write the following vectors as column matrices.

(a) $\overrightarrow{CD}$ (b) $\overrightarrow{BA}$ (c) $\overrightarrow{XY}$

(d) $\overrightarrow{XZ}$ (e) $\overrightarrow{GH}$ (f) $\overrightarrow{VU}$

(g) **a** (h) **p** (i) **q**

(j) **r**

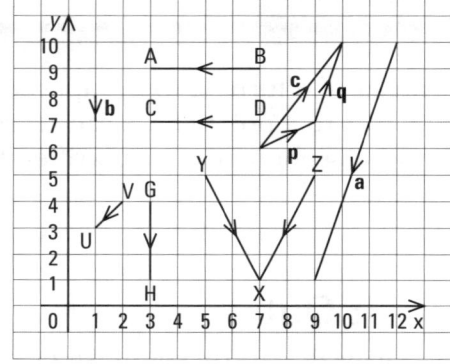

2 Which pairs of these vectors are parallel?

Learn More About It

If A is the point (1, 1) and B the point (5, 4) then the vector $\overrightarrow{AB} = \binom{4}{3}$.

The magnitude of $\overrightarrow{AB}$ is written $|\overrightarrow{AB}|$.

It can be found using Pythagoras' theorem:

$$|\overrightarrow{AB}| = \sqrt{4^2 + 3^2}$$
$$= \sqrt{16 + 9}$$
$$= \sqrt{25}$$
$$= 5 \text{ units}$$

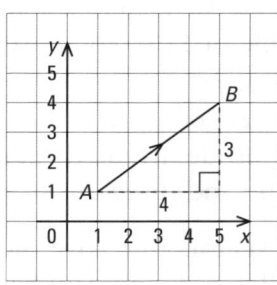

In general, a vector $\mathbf{a} = \binom{x}{y}$ has magnitude given by

$$|\mathbf{a}| = \sqrt{x^2 + y^2}$$

A vector that has a magnitude of 1 is called a **unit vector**.

Word Check

unit vector a vector with magnitude 1

The vectors **a**, 2**a** and $\frac{1}{3}$**a** have the same direction (so they are parallel), but different magnitudes. The magnitude of the vector 2**a** is twice the magnitude of **a**. The magnitude of $\frac{1}{3}$**a** is $\frac{1}{3}$ the magnitude of **a**.

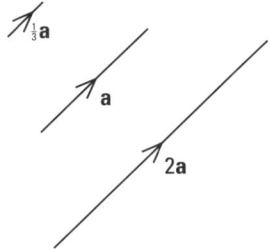

In general, for $k > 0$, the vector k**a** has the same direction as **a** and has magnitude k times the magnitude of **a**.

The vectors –**a** and –2**a** are parallel to **a** but they point in the opposite direction. –**a** has the same magnitude as **a**. –2**a** has twice the magnitude of **a**. In general, for $k < 0$, the vector k**a** points in the opposite direction to **a** and has magnitude k times the magnitude of **a**.

Example	Point R is (0, –1) and point S is (3, 1).
	(a) Write $\overrightarrow{RS}$ as a column vector.
	(b) Find the magnitude of $\overrightarrow{RS}$.
	(c) $\overrightarrow{AB}$ has the same direction as $\overrightarrow{RS}$ but has three times the magnitude. Write $\overrightarrow{AB}$ in terms of $\overrightarrow{RS}$.
	(d) Write the vector $\overrightarrow{AB}$ in the form $\begin{pmatrix} x \\ y \end{pmatrix}$.
Working	**(a)** $\overrightarrow{RS} = \begin{pmatrix} 3 - 0 \\ 1 - (-1) \end{pmatrix} = \begin{pmatrix} 3 \\ 2 \end{pmatrix}$
	(b) The magnitude of $\overrightarrow{RS}$ is $|\overrightarrow{RS}|$ and $$\begin{aligned} |\overrightarrow{RS}| &= \sqrt{3^2 + 2^2} \\ &= \sqrt{9 + 4} \\ &= \sqrt{13} \text{ units.} \end{aligned}$$
	(c) $\overrightarrow{AB} = 3\overrightarrow{RS}$
	(d) From **(c)** $\overrightarrow{AB} = 3\overrightarrow{RS}$ and from **(a)** $\overrightarrow{RS} = \begin{pmatrix} 3 \\ 2 \end{pmatrix}$ so $$\begin{aligned} \overrightarrow{AB} &= 3\overrightarrow{RS} \\ &= 3 \times \begin{pmatrix} 3 \\ 2 \end{pmatrix} \\ &= \begin{pmatrix} 9 \\ 6 \end{pmatrix} \end{aligned}$$
Answer	**(a)** $\begin{pmatrix} 3 \\ 2 \end{pmatrix}$ **(b)** $\sqrt{13}$ units **(c)** $\overrightarrow{AB} = 3\overrightarrow{RS}$ **(d)** $\begin{pmatrix} 9 \\ 6 \end{pmatrix}$

Practice

C Find the magnitudes of the vectors in question **B1**.

D Given that $\mathbf{a} = \begin{pmatrix} 1 \\ 4 \end{pmatrix}$, $\mathbf{b} = \begin{pmatrix} -6 \\ 3 \end{pmatrix}$, on squared paper draw vectors representing:

(a) $2\mathbf{a}$ (b) $3\mathbf{a}$ (c) $\frac{1}{2}\mathbf{b}$ (d) $-\mathbf{a}$ (e) $-\frac{1}{3}\mathbf{b}$

E If $\mathbf{a} = \begin{pmatrix} 4 \\ -6 \end{pmatrix}$, $\mathbf{b} = \begin{pmatrix} 8 \\ -12 \end{pmatrix}$, $\mathbf{c} = \begin{pmatrix} 2 \\ -3 \end{pmatrix}$, $\mathbf{d} = \begin{pmatrix} -2 \\ 3 \end{pmatrix}$ and $\mathbf{e} = \begin{pmatrix} -1 \\ \frac{3}{2} \end{pmatrix}$.

(i) Write **b**, **c**, **d** and **e** in terms of **a**.

(ii) Write **e** in terms of **c**, and **c** in terms of **e**.

> **Finished Early?**
> ➡ Go to page 469

❷ Vector Arithmetic

Learn About It

Petula is walking to her friend's house. She starts at her house, A, and walks to the shops, B. She then goes to her friend's house, C.

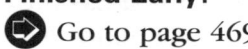

The diagram shows a vector representation of her journey. Petula walks along $\overrightarrow{AB}$ and then $\overrightarrow{BC}$. This is equivalent to walking along $\overrightarrow{AC}$.

In general if a vector $\overrightarrow{AB}$ is followed by a vector $\overrightarrow{BC}$ then this is equivalent to a vector $\overrightarrow{AC}$. We can write this as:

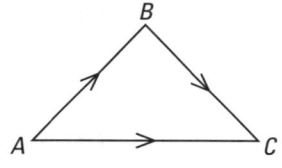

$$\overrightarrow{AC} = \overrightarrow{AB} + \overrightarrow{BC}$$

or $\mathbf{r} = \mathbf{p} + \mathbf{q}$

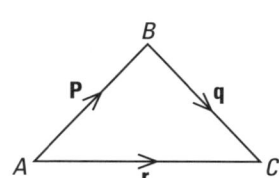

This is the **triangle law** of vector addition.

$\overrightarrow{AC}$ is called the **resultant vector**.

If the vectors $\overrightarrow{AB}$ and $\overrightarrow{BC}$ are written as column vectors then we can find $\overrightarrow{AC}$ using matrix addition. Suppose $\overrightarrow{AB} = \begin{pmatrix} 3 \\ 2 \end{pmatrix}$ and $\overrightarrow{BC} = \begin{pmatrix} 3 \\ -4 \end{pmatrix}$ then

$$\overrightarrow{AC} = \overrightarrow{AB} + \overrightarrow{BC}$$

$$= \begin{pmatrix} 3 \\ 2 \end{pmatrix} + \begin{pmatrix} 3 \\ -4 \end{pmatrix}$$

$$= \begin{pmatrix} 3 + 3 \\ 2 + (-4) \end{pmatrix}$$

$$= \begin{pmatrix} 6 \\ -2 \end{pmatrix}$$

Remember that the vector **–b** has the same magnitude as **b** but the opposite direction.
a – **b** = **a** + (**–b**). So subtracting **b** from **a** is the same as adding **–b** to **a**.

In terms of column vectors, if $\mathbf{a} = \begin{pmatrix} 3 \\ 2 \end{pmatrix}$ and $\mathbf{b} = \begin{pmatrix} 3 \\ -4 \end{pmatrix}$ then

$$\mathbf{a} - \mathbf{b} = \begin{pmatrix} 3 \\ 2 \end{pmatrix} - \begin{pmatrix} 3 \\ -4 \end{pmatrix}$$

$$= \begin{pmatrix} 3 - 3 \\ 2 - (-4) \end{pmatrix}$$

$$= \begin{pmatrix} 0 \\ 6 \end{pmatrix}$$

Try It Out

Squared paper, ruler

F **a**, **b** and **c** are shown in the diagram.

For each of the following vectors

 (i) draw a representation of the vector on squared paper

(ii) write the vector as a column vector.

1 **a** + **b**   **2** **a** + 2**c**   **3** 3**b** + 2**c** + **a**

4 **c** – **b**   **5** **a** + **b** – **c**   **6** –2**a** + **c** – **b**

Finished Early?
➡ Go to page 469

Learn More About It

Remember?

The opposite sides of a parallelogram are parallel and have the same length.
AB = DC and AD = BC.

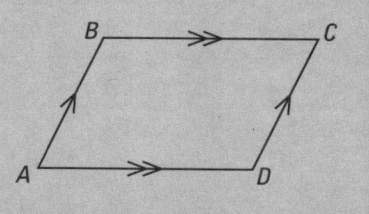

ABCD is a parallelogram. This means that CD is parallel to AB and has the same length.
So $\overrightarrow{AB} = \overrightarrow{DC} = \mathbf{a}$

Also BC is parallel to AD and has the same length.
So $\overrightarrow{AD} = \overrightarrow{BC} = \mathbf{b}$

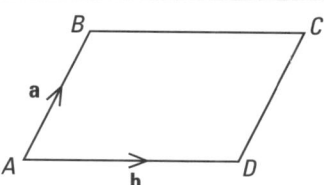

Looking at triangle ABC, the vector $\overrightarrow{AC}$ is the resultant of $\overrightarrow{AB}$ and $\overrightarrow{BC}$ so

$\overrightarrow{AC} = \overrightarrow{AB} + \overrightarrow{BC} = \mathbf{a} + \mathbf{b}$

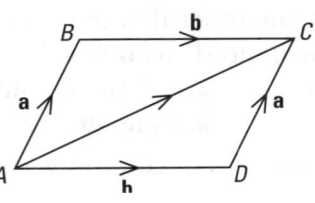

Looking at triangle ADC, the vector $\overrightarrow{AC}$ is the resultant of $\overrightarrow{AD}$ and $\overrightarrow{DC}$ so

$\overrightarrow{AC} = \overrightarrow{AD} + \overrightarrow{DC} = \mathbf{b} + \mathbf{a}$

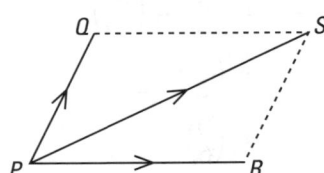

This tells us that vector addition is commutative: $\mathbf{a} + \mathbf{b} = \mathbf{b} + \mathbf{a}$

Given two vectors $\overrightarrow{PQ}$ and $\overrightarrow{PR}$ we can complete a parallelogram PQRS to find $\overrightarrow{PS}$, the resultant of $\overrightarrow{PQ}$ and $\overrightarrow{PR}$,

$\overrightarrow{PS} = \overrightarrow{PQ} + \overrightarrow{PR}$

This is the **parallelogram law** of vector addition.

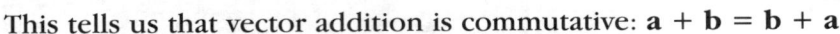

Example

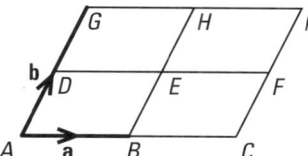

The small parallelograms in the diagram are congruent.
$\overrightarrow{AB} = \mathbf{a}$ and $\overrightarrow{AG} = \mathbf{b}$

(a) Write the following vectors in terms of $\mathbf{a}$ and $\mathbf{b}$.

    (i) $\overrightarrow{AD}$ (ii) $\overrightarrow{AE}$ (iii) $\overrightarrow{HF}$

(b) If $\mathbf{a} = \begin{pmatrix} 3 \\ 0 \end{pmatrix}$ and $\mathbf{b} = \begin{pmatrix} 1 \\ 4 \end{pmatrix}$ write $\overrightarrow{AE}$ as a column vector.

Working

(a) (i) D is halfway between A and G so $\overrightarrow{AD}$ has the same direction as $\overrightarrow{AG}$ but half the length.

    So $\overrightarrow{AD} = \frac{1}{2}\overrightarrow{AG} = \frac{1}{2}\mathbf{b}$

  (ii) By the parallelogram law $\overrightarrow{AE} = \overrightarrow{AD} + \overrightarrow{DE}$

    From (i) $\overrightarrow{AD} = \frac{1}{2}\mathbf{b}$. $\overrightarrow{DE}$ is parallel to and the same length as $\overrightarrow{AB}$, so $\overrightarrow{DE} = \mathbf{a}$.

    Hence $\overrightarrow{AE} = \frac{1}{2}\mathbf{b} + \mathbf{a}$.

  (iii) Using the parallelogram law $\overrightarrow{HF} = \overrightarrow{HI} + \overrightarrow{IF}$.

    $\overrightarrow{HI}$ is parallel to and the same length as $\overrightarrow{AB}$, so $\overrightarrow{HI} = \mathbf{a}$.

    $\overrightarrow{IF}$ is parallel to, and has the same length as $\overrightarrow{AD}$, but it points in the opposite direction so $\overrightarrow{IF} = -\overrightarrow{AD} = -\frac{1}{2}\mathbf{b}$.

    Hence $\overrightarrow{HF} = \overrightarrow{HI} + \overrightarrow{IF} = \mathbf{a} - \frac{1}{2}\mathbf{b}$.

(b) From (a)(ii) $\overrightarrow{AE} = \frac{1}{2}\mathbf{b} + \mathbf{a}$ so

$$\overrightarrow{AE} = \frac{1}{2}\begin{pmatrix} 1 \\ 4 \end{pmatrix} + \begin{pmatrix} 3 \\ 0 \end{pmatrix}$$

$$= \begin{pmatrix} \frac{1}{2} \\ 2 \end{pmatrix} + \begin{pmatrix} 3 \\ 0 \end{pmatrix}$$

$$= \begin{pmatrix} 3\frac{1}{2} \\ 2 \end{pmatrix}$$

Answer

(a) (i) $\frac{1}{2}\mathbf{b}$ (ii) $\frac{1}{2}\mathbf{b} + \mathbf{a}$ (iii) $\mathbf{a} - \frac{1}{2}\mathbf{b}$

(b) $\begin{pmatrix} 3\frac{1}{2} \\ 2 \end{pmatrix}$

The vectors we have met so far are called **free vectors**. Any two free vectors with the same magnitude and direction are equal. It doesn't matter where the vector starts from or finishes.

Consider a point P (x, y). The vector **p** gives the position of P relative to the origin O, so we call **p** the **position vector** of P. **p** is also called the **displacement** of P from O.

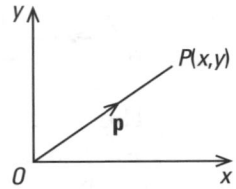

Word Check

position vector a vector drawn from the origin

free vector a vector that doesn't depend on its starting point

In general, the position vector of the point (x, y) is $\begin{pmatrix} x \\ y \end{pmatrix}$.

If A is the point $(2, 5)$ and B is $(4, 3)$, then the position vector of A is $\mathbf{a} = \begin{pmatrix} 2 \\ 5 \end{pmatrix}$ and the position of B is $\mathbf{b} = \begin{pmatrix} 4 \\ 3 \end{pmatrix}$.

Using position vectors we can find $\overrightarrow{AB}$, the displacement vector of B from A.

$\overrightarrow{OA} + \overrightarrow{AB} = \overrightarrow{OB}$

So $\overrightarrow{AB} = \overrightarrow{OB} - \overrightarrow{OA}$

$$= \mathbf{b} - \mathbf{a}$$
$$= \begin{pmatrix} 4 \\ 3 \end{pmatrix} - \begin{pmatrix} 2 \\ 5 \end{pmatrix}$$
$$= \begin{pmatrix} 2 \\ -2 \end{pmatrix}$$

The distance between A and B is given by the magnitude of $\overrightarrow{AB}$. Hence:

distance from A to B $= |\overrightarrow{AB}|$
$$= \sqrt{2^2 + (-2)^2}$$
$$= \sqrt{8} \text{ units}$$

Practice

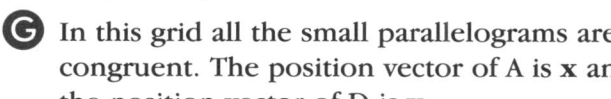

G In this grid all the small parallelograms are congruent. The position vector of A is **x** and the position vector of D is **y**.

1 Write down three other vectors that are equivalent to **x**.

2 Find the position vectors of the following points in terms of **x** and **y**.

    (a) E   **(b)** J   **(c)** H   **(d)** M   **(e)** I

3 Identify the points with the following position vectors.

    (a) **y**   **(b)** $3\mathbf{x} + \mathbf{y}$ **(c)** $2\mathbf{y} + 2\mathbf{x}$ **(d)** $4\mathbf{x} + 3\mathbf{y} - \mathbf{x}$

4 Find the following vectors in terms of **x** and **y**.

    (a) $\overrightarrow{EK}$ **(b)** $\overrightarrow{PM}$ **(c)** $\overrightarrow{HC}$ **(d)** $\overrightarrow{PE}$

5 There are two vectors equivalent to $\overrightarrow{BM}$. Name them.

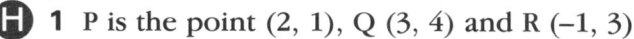

H 1 P is the point (2, 1), Q (3, 4) and R (−1, 3).

    (a) Write down **p**, **q** and **r**, the position vectors of P, Q and R.

    (b) Find the vectors $\overrightarrow{PQ}$, $\overrightarrow{QR}$ and $\overrightarrow{RP}$.

    (c) Calculate the distance of Q from P, R from Q and P from R.

2 A is the point (−2, −3) and B is the point (−5, 0).

    (a) Calculate $\overrightarrow{AB}$. Hence find the distance between A and B.

    The point C is the mid-point of A and B.

    (b) Write down $\overrightarrow{AC}$ in terms of $\overrightarrow{AB}$.

    (c) Calculate $\overrightarrow{AC}$.

    (d) Find the position vector of C. Give your answer as a column vector.

③ Vector Geometry

Learn About It

This section uses what you already know about vectors to solve geometry problems.

Example OAB is a triangle.
The position vector of A is **a** and the position vector of B is **b**.
The ratio OC : CA = 1 : 2 and the ratio OD : DB = 1 : 2.

1 Express, in terms of **a** and **b**:
  (a) $\overrightarrow{AB}$ **(b)** $\overrightarrow{CD}$ **(c)** $\overrightarrow{BC}$

2 Show that CD is parallel to AB.

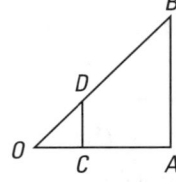

Working & Answer

1 (a) From the diagram
$$\overrightarrow{OA} + \overrightarrow{AB} = \overrightarrow{OB}$$
$$\text{So } \overrightarrow{AB} = \overrightarrow{OB} + \overrightarrow{OA}$$
$$= \mathbf{b} - \mathbf{a}$$

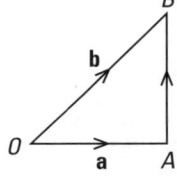

(b) OC : CA = 1 : 2
$$\text{So } \overrightarrow{OC} = \tfrac{1}{3}\overrightarrow{OA} = \tfrac{1}{3}\mathbf{a} \text{ and}$$
$$\overrightarrow{CA} = \tfrac{2}{3}\overrightarrow{OA} = \tfrac{2}{3}\mathbf{a}$$
Similarly $\overrightarrow{OD} = \tfrac{1}{3}\overrightarrow{OB} = \tfrac{1}{3}\mathbf{b}$.
$$\overrightarrow{OC} + \overrightarrow{CD} = \overrightarrow{OD}$$
$$\text{Hence } \overrightarrow{CD} = \overrightarrow{OD} - \overrightarrow{OC}$$
$$= \tfrac{1}{3}\mathbf{b} - \tfrac{1}{3}\mathbf{a}$$
$$= \tfrac{1}{3}(\mathbf{b} - \mathbf{a})$$

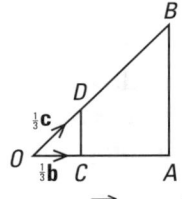

(c) Remember that for any points R and S: $\overrightarrow{RS} = -\overrightarrow{SR}$
$$\overrightarrow{BC} = \overrightarrow{BA} + \overrightarrow{AC}$$
$$= -\overrightarrow{AB} - \overrightarrow{CA}$$
$$= -(\mathbf{b} - \mathbf{a}) - \tfrac{2}{3}\mathbf{a}$$
$$= \tfrac{1}{3}\mathbf{a} - \mathbf{b}$$

2 From **1(a)** we know that $\overrightarrow{AB} = \mathbf{b} - \mathbf{a}$.
From **1(b)** we know that $\overrightarrow{CD} = -\tfrac{1}{3}(\mathbf{b} - \mathbf{a})$.
$\overrightarrow{CD}$ is a multiple of $\overrightarrow{AB}$ and so $\overrightarrow{CD}$ is parallel to $\overrightarrow{AB}$.
Hence CD is parallel to AB.

Example PQRSTU is a regular hexagon, with $\vec{PQ} = \mathbf{p}$, $\vec{QR} = \mathbf{q}$
and $\vec{RS} = \mathbf{r}$.

Prove that

(a) $\vec{PS} = \mathbf{p} + \mathbf{q} + \mathbf{r}$

(b) $\vec{SU} = -\mathbf{p} - \mathbf{q}$

(c) $\vec{UR} = \mathbf{p} + \mathbf{q} - \mathbf{r}$

Working   **(a)** $\vec{PS}$ is the resultant of $\vec{PQ}$, $\vec{QR}$
& Answer   and $\vec{RS}$.
$$\text{So } \vec{PS} = \vec{PQ} + \vec{QR} + \vec{RS}$$
$$= \mathbf{p} + \mathbf{q} + \mathbf{r}$$

(b) $\vec{SU} = \vec{ST} + \vec{TU}$

Because PQRSTU is a regular hexagon, $\vec{ST}$ is the same
length as $\vec{PQ}$, and parallel to $\vec{PQ}$, but in the opposite
direction.

So $\vec{ST} = -\vec{PQ} = -\mathbf{p}$.

Similarly, $\vec{TU} = -\vec{QR} = -\mathbf{q}$.

So $\vec{SU} = \vec{ST} + \vec{TU} = -\mathbf{p} - \mathbf{q}$.

(c) $\vec{UR} = \vec{UP} + \vec{PQ} + \vec{QR}$

$\vec{UP}$ is the same length as, and parallel to $\vec{RS}$. But it points
in the opposite direction, so $\vec{UP} = -\vec{RS} = -\mathbf{r}$.

$\vec{PQ} = \mathbf{p}$ and $\vec{QR} = \mathbf{q}$

So $\vec{UR} = -\mathbf{r} + \mathbf{p} + \mathbf{q}$
$$= \mathbf{p} + \mathbf{q} - \mathbf{r}$$

Try it out

1 For each question express the vectors in terms of $\mathbf{x}$
and $\mathbf{y}$.

1 ABCD is a rectangle.
  (a) $\vec{DA}$ **(b)** $\vec{DC}$ **(c)** $\vec{CB}$ **(d)** $\vec{AC}$

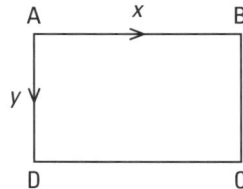

2 VWXYZ is a rhombus.
  (a) $\vec{ZY}$ **(b)** $\vec{WY}$ **(c)** $\vec{XZ}$ **(d)** $\vec{WV}$

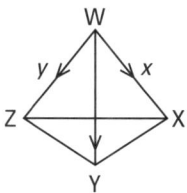

Practice

J 1 ABCD is a trapezium.

$\vec{AB} = \mathbf{p}$, $\vec{AD} = \mathbf{r}$, $\vec{BC} = \mathbf{q}$ and $\vec{DC} = 2\vec{AB}$.

Find, in terms of $\mathbf{p}$ and $\mathbf{q}$:

(a) $\vec{AC}$ (b) $\vec{BD}$ (c) $\vec{DC}$

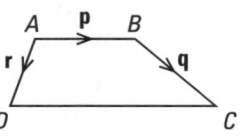

2 OAB is a triangle, with $\vec{OA} = \mathbf{a}$ and $\vec{OB} = \mathbf{b}$. M is the mid-point of AB.

Find:

(a) $\vec{AB}$ (b) $\vec{OM}$

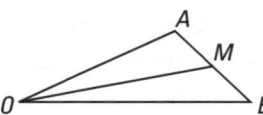

3 OABC is a parallelogram. M and N are the midpoints of OA and OC respectively.

$\vec{OM} = \mathbf{m}$, and $\vec{ON} = \mathbf{n}$.

Find, in terms of $\mathbf{m}$ and $\mathbf{n}$:

(a) $\vec{OA}$ (b) $\vec{OB}$ (c) $\vec{NM}$

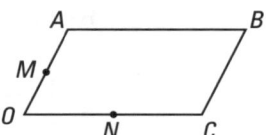

K 1 PQRS is a parallelogram. $\vec{PQ} = \mathbf{p}$ and $\vec{PS} = \mathbf{s}$. T is a point on QR such that $\vec{QT} = \frac{1}{3}\vec{QR}$, and U is a point on RS such that $\vec{RU} = \frac{1}{3}\vec{QS}$.

Find the following in terms of $\mathbf{p}$ and $\mathbf{s}$:

(a) $\vec{PT}$ (b) $\vec{TS}$ (c) $\vec{TU}$

2 OCD is a triangle. A is a point on OC such that OC : AB = 1 : 3 and similarly B is a point on OD such that OB : BD = 1 : 3.

$\vec{OA} = \mathbf{a}$, and $\vec{OB} = \mathbf{b}$.

(a) Show that $\vec{CD} = 4(\mathbf{b} - \mathbf{a})$.

(b) Hence show that CD is parallel to AB.

3 ABCD is a trapezium. AB and CD are parallel. $\vec{AB} = 3\mathbf{a}$, $\vec{AC} = 4\mathbf{q} + 2\mathbf{b}$ and $\vec{AD} = 2\mathbf{a} + 2\mathbf{b}$.

Find, in terms of $\mathbf{a}$ and $\mathbf{b}$:

(a) $\vec{BC}$ (b) $\vec{CD}$

> **Finished Early?**
> ➡ Go to page 470

Unit 10 *Matrices and Vectors*

Summary of Chapters 21 and 22

Matrix Algebra

- A **matrix** is a collection of numbers arranged into a rectangle.
- A **row** of a matrix is a horizontal line of elements. A **column** of a matrix is a vertical line of elements.
- The **order** of a matrix is the number of rows × number of columns.
- To **add** or **subtract** matrices, add or subtract corresponding elements.
- You can only add or subtract matrices if they have the same order. The result will also have the same order.
- To **multiply** a matrix by a scalar, multiply every element of the matrix by the scalar.
- To **multiply** two matrices, multiply the elements in a row of the first matrix with the corresponding elements of a column in the second matrix, and add them together.
- If A is a matrix with order $m \times n$ and B is a matrix with order $p \times q$, then the matrices can only be multiplied if $n = p$. The resulting matrix has order $m \times q$.
- In general, matrix multiplication is not commutative, so $AB \neq BA$.
- The **determinant** of a matrix $\begin{pmatrix} a & b \\ c & d \end{pmatrix}$ is $ad - bc$.
- The **inverse** of a matrix $\begin{pmatrix} a & b \\ c & d \end{pmatrix}$ is $\dfrac{1}{ad - bc} \begin{pmatrix} d & -b \\ -c & a \end{pmatrix}$.
- A **singular matrix** is a matrix with determinant zero.

Vectors

- A **vector** has a magnitude and a direction.
- A **scalar** is a quantity with a magnitude but no direction.
- Two vectors are **equal** if they have the same magnitude and direction.
- A vector $\mathbf{a} = \begin{pmatrix} x \\ y \end{pmatrix}$ has magnitude given by $|\mathbf{a}| = \sqrt{x^2 + y^2}$.
- A vector that has a magnitude of 1 is called a **unit vector**.

- The **triangle law of vector addition** states that if a vector $\overrightarrow{AB}$ is followed by a vector $\overrightarrow{BC}$ then this is equivalent to a vector $\overrightarrow{AC}$. We write this as $\overrightarrow{AC} = \overrightarrow{AB} + \overrightarrow{BC}$.

- $\overrightarrow{AC}$ is called the **resultant vector**.

- The **parallelogram law of vector addition** states that given two vectors $\overrightarrow{PQ}$ and $\overrightarrow{PR}$ we can complete a parallelogram PQRS to find $\overrightarrow{PS} = \overrightarrow{PQ} + \overrightarrow{PR}$.

- Vector addition is commutative.

- The **position vector**, p, of a point P is the vector from the origin to P.

- If P has coordinates (x, y) then the position vector, p, of P is $\begin{pmatrix} x \\ y \end{pmatrix}$.

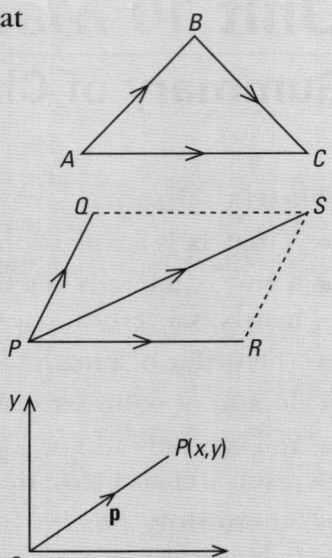

23 Transformations

1 Combining Transformations

Remember?

Translations 'slide' the object to the image. They are described by giving a translation vector.

Reflections reflect the object in a mirror line.

Rotations rotate the shape through an angle about a centre of rotation.

Enlargements change the size of the object by a scale factor from a centre of enlargement.

In translations, reflections and rotations the object and image are **congruent**. In enlargements the object and image are **similar**.

 If there is access to computer facilities, your teacher may use the computer to demonstrate some transformations using the *Translation and Reflection*, *Rotation* or *Enlargement* lesson from the CD-ROM.

Learn About It

In Chapter 13 we learnt about transforming an object using a single transformation. There is nothing stopping us from performing several transformations, one after another.

Example ABCD is a parallelogram with vertices at A (3, –1), B (6, –1), C (5, –3) and D (2, –3). The parallelogram is translated by $\begin{pmatrix} 0 \\ 4 \end{pmatrix}$ to get a new parallelogram A'B'C'D', and then reflected in the line $x = 1$ to give A"B"C"D".

(a) Find the coordinates of A'B'C'D' and A"B"C"D", and draw the image of ABCD following both the transformations.

(b) What is the image if the parallelogram is first reflected in the mirror line and then translated by $\begin{pmatrix} 0 \\ 4 \end{pmatrix}$?

Working (a) The translation $\begin{pmatrix} 0 \\ 4 \end{pmatrix}$ moves all the points of ABCD up

4 units. So the coordinates of A'B'C'D' are A'(3, 3), B'(6, 3), C'(5, 1) and D'(2, 1).

This parallelogram is then reflected in the line $x = 1$. So the coordinates of A"B"C"D" are A" (–1, 3), B" (–4, 3), C" (–3, 1) and D" (0, 1).

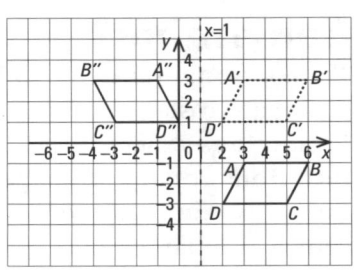

(b) Performing the reflection first and then translating the parallelogram results in the same image: A"B"C"D".

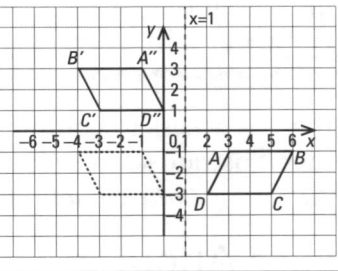

The combined translation in the previous example is an example of a **glide reflection**. A glide reflection is defined by the magnitude and direction of the translation and the mirror line, called the **glide axis**.

The position of your feet when taking steps look like a glide reflection.

Word Check

glide reflection a translation parallel to a mirror line followed by a reflection in the mirror line, or vice versa

glide axis the mirror line for a glide reflection

In a glide reflection, G, an object is mapped to an image by a translation T parallel to a mirror line followed by a reflection M in the mirror line. We can write this as

G = MT

This means that T is performed first, *then* the reflection M is performed.

As we saw in the example, the same image is obtained if the object is reflected in the mirror line then translated parallel to the mirror line, so

G = TM

So G = TM = MT. Hence in a glide reflection the reflection and translation are commutative.

A glide reflection is just one example of a combination of transformations. We can combine any group of translations, reflections, rotations and enlargements.

In general, the image resulting from a combination of transformations is different depending upon the order in which the transformations occur. For example, a rotation followed by a reflection might not be the same as the reflection followed by a rotation. The transformations are NOT commutative.

Key Fact

The image resulting from a combination of transformations is dependent upon the order in which the transformations occur.

Practice

 1 The point P has coordinates $(1, 2)$. Find the image of P after the following combinations of transformations.

(a) Reflection in the x-axis, followed by a rotation through 180° about the origin.

(b) A glide reflection, with translation $\begin{pmatrix} 2 \\ 2 \end{pmatrix}$ and mirror line $y = x$.

(c) A reflection in the line $y = -x - 1$ followed by a rotation through 90° clockwise about the point $(-1, -2)$.

(d) A rotation through 90° clockwise about the point $(-1, -2)$ followed by a reflection in the line $y = -x - 1$.

2 ABC is a triangle with vertices A (2, –2), B (4, –2) and C (3, –4). Find the coordinates of its image after the following transformations.

(a) A glide reflection with translation $\begin{pmatrix} -3 \\ 3 \end{pmatrix}$ and mirror line $y = -x - 2$.

(b) An enlargement scale factor 2, centre (1, –1), followed by a clockwise rotation through 90° about (3, –3).

(c) A clockwise rotation through 90° about (3, –3) followed by an enlargement scale factor 2, centre (1, –1).

(d) A reflection in the line $y = 1$ followed by a rotation of 180° about (3, 1).

B 1 ABCD is a rectangle with vertices A (2, 5), B (5, 5), C (5, 3) and D (2, 3).

The image after a glide transformation with translation $\begin{pmatrix} -3 \\ -3 \end{pmatrix}$ and mirror line $y = x - 2$ is A'B'C'D'.

(a) Draw the image A'B'C'D' and state the coordinates of the vertices.

(b) A'B'C'D' is rotated through an angle of 90° about (–1, 1) to give an image A"B"C"D". Find the coordinates of A"B"C"D".

2 PQR is a triangle with vertices P (–5, 3), Q (–2, 3) and R (–2, 1).

(a) The triangle is transformed to P'Q'R' by a glide reflection with translation $\begin{pmatrix} -4 \\ 0 \end{pmatrix}$ and mirror line $x = -1$. Find the coordinates of P', Q' and R'.

(b) P'Q'R' is reflected in the y-axis giving P"Q"R". Find the single transformation that maps P"Q"R" back to PQR.

Finished Early?
 Go to page 470

2 Matrices and Transformations

Learn About It

In Chapter 13 we learned how to represent a translation as a matrix. A translation of 3 units left and 2 units up is written as the 2 × 1 matrix $\begin{pmatrix} -3 \\ 2 \end{pmatrix}$.

Each point of the object is translated by the vector $\begin{pmatrix} -3 \\ 2 \end{pmatrix}$ and we can find the equivalent points on the image by adding vectors.

Suppose the point A has position vector **a** and that we want to translate A through a vector **t**. Then the position vector of the image of A, **a'**, is given by

$$\mathbf{a'} = \mathbf{a} + \mathbf{t}$$

Example   The triangle ABC has vertices A (−1, 3), B (0, 1) and C (−2, 1). Find the coordinates of the vertices of the image A'B'C' following a translation $\begin{pmatrix} 4 \\ -1 \end{pmatrix}$.

Working   Consider each vertex separately.
A is the point (−1, 3) so its position vector is $\mathbf{a} = \begin{pmatrix} -1 \\ 3 \end{pmatrix}$.
The position vector of A' is

$$\mathbf{a}' = \mathbf{a} + \begin{pmatrix} 4 \\ -1 \end{pmatrix}$$

$$= \begin{pmatrix} -1 \\ 3 \end{pmatrix} + \begin{pmatrix} 4 \\ -1 \end{pmatrix}$$

$$= \begin{pmatrix} -1 + 4 \\ 3 - 1 \end{pmatrix}$$

$$= \begin{pmatrix} 3 \\ 2 \end{pmatrix}$$

So A' has position vector $\begin{pmatrix} 3 \\ 2 \end{pmatrix}$. Hence the coordinates of A' are (3, 2).

Similarly the position vector of B is $\mathbf{b} = \begin{pmatrix} 0 \\ 1 \end{pmatrix}$ and
$$\mathbf{b}' = \mathbf{b} + \begin{pmatrix} 4 \\ -1 \end{pmatrix} = \begin{pmatrix} 4 \\ 0 \end{pmatrix}$$

So B' has position vector $\begin{pmatrix} 4 \\ 0 \end{pmatrix}$ and so B' is the point (4, 0).

The position vector of C is $\mathbf{c} = \begin{pmatrix} -2 \\ 1 \end{pmatrix}$ so

$$\mathbf{c}' = \mathbf{c} + \begin{pmatrix} 4 \\ -1 \end{pmatrix} = \begin{pmatrix} 2 \\ 0 \end{pmatrix}$$

So the position vector of C' is $\begin{pmatrix} 2 \\ 0 \end{pmatrix}$. Hence the coordinates of C' are (2, 0).

Answer   A' (3, 2), B' (4, 0), C' (2, 0)

Try It Out

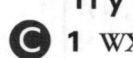

1 WXYZ is a rectangle with vertices W (2, 1), X (4, 1), Y (4, –2) and Z (2, –2). Use position vectors to find the image of the rectangle following these translations.

(a) $\begin{pmatrix} -1 \\ 2 \end{pmatrix}$ **(b)** $\begin{pmatrix} -4 \\ 1 \end{pmatrix}$ **(c)** $\begin{pmatrix} -2 \\ -3 \end{pmatrix}$

2 The triangle ABC has vertices A (0, 1), B (3, –3) and C (–1, –2). Following a translation its image is A'B'C' where A' (–3, 3), B' (0, –1), C' (–4, 0). Find the vector describing the translation.

We can represent the other transformations using matrices too. We begin by looking at reflections.

Consider the square in the diagram and its image after reflecting it in the x-axis.

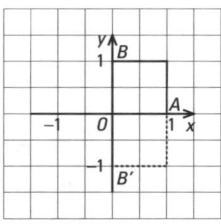

$$\overrightarrow{OA} = \begin{pmatrix} 1 \\ 0 \end{pmatrix}, \overrightarrow{O'A'} = \begin{pmatrix} 1 \\ 0 \end{pmatrix}$$

$$\overrightarrow{OB} = \begin{pmatrix} 1 \\ 0 \end{pmatrix}, \overrightarrow{O'B'} = \begin{pmatrix} 0 \\ -1 \end{pmatrix}$$

Suppose we can represent the reflection using a matrix M. We want to find M such that:

$$M(\overrightarrow{OA}) = \overrightarrow{O'A'}$$
$$M(\overrightarrow{OB}) = \overrightarrow{O'B'}$$

At the moment we don't know what M is, so we will write it as $\begin{pmatrix} a & b \\ c & d \end{pmatrix}$.

We need to find a, b, c and d. Using the previous equations we have:

$$\begin{pmatrix} a & b \\ c & d \end{pmatrix} \begin{pmatrix} 1 \\ 0 \end{pmatrix} = \begin{pmatrix} 1 \\ 0 \end{pmatrix}$$

$$\begin{pmatrix} a & b \\ c & d \end{pmatrix} \begin{pmatrix} 0 \\ 1 \end{pmatrix} = \begin{pmatrix} 0 \\ -1 \end{pmatrix}$$

Now we can multiply out these matrices to get simultaneous equations, and hence find a, b, c and d:

$a \times 1 + b \times 0 = 1$

$c \times 1 + d \times 0 = 0$

$a \times 0 + b \times 1 = 0$

$c \times 0 + d \times 1 = -1$

So $a = 1$, $b = 0$, $c = 0$ and $d = -1$.

Putting these values into the matrix M gives us:

$$M = \begin{pmatrix} 1 & 0 \\ 0 & -1 \end{pmatrix}$$

So the matrix that represents a reflection in the x-axis is $\begin{pmatrix} 1 & 0 \\ 0 & -1 \end{pmatrix}$.

The matrix representing reflection in the y-axis can be found in a similar way. It is $\begin{pmatrix} -1 & 0 \\ 0 & 1 \end{pmatrix}$.

Now consider the square and its image following a reflection in the line $y = -x$.

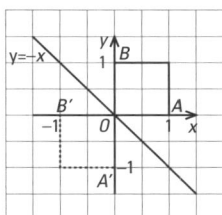

$$\overrightarrow{OA} = \begin{pmatrix} 1 \\ 0 \end{pmatrix}, \overrightarrow{O'A'} = \begin{pmatrix} 0 \\ -1 \end{pmatrix}$$

$$\overrightarrow{OB} = \begin{pmatrix} 0 \\ 1 \end{pmatrix}, \overrightarrow{O'B'} = \begin{pmatrix} -1 \\ 0 \end{pmatrix}$$

Again we can calculate the matrix M $= \begin{pmatrix} a & b \\ c & d \end{pmatrix}$ that represents a reflection in the line $y = -x$ by setting:

$$M(\overrightarrow{OA}) = \overrightarrow{O'A'}$$
$$M(\overrightarrow{OB}) = \overrightarrow{O'B'}$$

and finding the values of a, b, c and d by solving the simultaneous equations.

So the matrix representing a reflection in the line $y = -x$ is $\begin{pmatrix} 0 & -1 \\ -1 & 0 \end{pmatrix}$.

Similarly the matrix representing a reflection in the line $y = x$ is $\begin{pmatrix} 0 & 1 \\ 1 & 0 \end{pmatrix}$.

To summarise, the matrices representing reflections are:

Mirror line	Matrix
x-axis	$\begin{pmatrix} 1 & 0 \\ 0 & -1 \end{pmatrix}$
y-axis	$\begin{pmatrix} -1 & 0 \\ 0 & 1 \end{pmatrix}$
$y = x$	$\begin{pmatrix} 0 & 1 \\ 1 & 0 \end{pmatrix}$
$y = -x$	$\begin{pmatrix} 0 & -1 \\ -1 & 0 \end{pmatrix}$

We can use these matrices to find the images of points under these reflections.

Example The vertices of the triangle ABC are A (1, 1), B (4, 2) and C (2, 4).

(a) Find the image A'B'C' following reflections in the following mirror lines.

  (i) The x-axis.

  (ii) $y = x$

(b) If the image has vertices A' (−1, −1), B' (−2, −4), C' (−4, −2) identify the reflection that mapped ABC to A'B'C' .

Working (a) We can construct a 2 × 3 matrix that contains the coordinates of the points A, B and C.

$$\begin{array}{ccc} A & B & C \\ \begin{pmatrix} 1 & 4 & 2 \\ 1 & 2 & 4 \end{pmatrix} \end{array}$$

The image of the vertices of the triangle can be found by multiplying this by the appropriate reflection matrix.

(i) For a reflection in the x-axis the matrix is $\begin{pmatrix} 1 & 0 \\ 0 & -1 \end{pmatrix}$.

$$\begin{pmatrix} 1 & 0 \\ 0 & -1 \end{pmatrix} \begin{array}{ccc} A & B & C \\ \begin{pmatrix} 1 & 4 & 2 \\ 1 & 2 & 4 \end{pmatrix} \end{array} = \begin{array}{ccc} A' & B' & C' \\ \begin{pmatrix} 1 & 4 & 2 \\ -1 & -2 & -4 \end{pmatrix} \end{array}$$

So A' is (1, −1), B' (4, −2) and C' (2, −4).

(ii) For a reflection in $y = x$ the matrix is $\begin{pmatrix} 0 & 1 \\ 1 & 0 \end{pmatrix}$.

$$\begin{pmatrix} 0 & 1 \\ 1 & 0 \end{pmatrix} \begin{array}{ccc} A & B & C \\ \begin{pmatrix} 1 & 4 & 2 \\ 1 & 2 & 4 \end{pmatrix} \end{array} = \begin{array}{ccc} A' & B' & C' \\ \begin{pmatrix} 1 & 2 & 4 \\ 1 & 4 & 2 \end{pmatrix} \end{array}$$

So A' is (1, 1), B' (2, 4) and C' (4, 2).

(b) We don't know the transformation matrix to create this image, so we can write it as $\begin{pmatrix} p & q \\ r & s \end{pmatrix}$.

We do know the object and image matrices so we can use these to find the transformation matrix:

$$\begin{pmatrix} p & q \\ r & s \end{pmatrix} \begin{array}{ccc} A & B & C \\ \begin{pmatrix} 1 & 4 & 2 \\ 1 & 2 & 4 \end{pmatrix} \end{array} = \begin{array}{ccc} A' & B' & C' \\ \begin{pmatrix} -1 & -2 & -4 \\ -1 & -4 & -2 \end{pmatrix} \end{array}$$

$$\begin{pmatrix} p + q & 4p + 2q & 2p + 4q \\ r + s & 4r + 2s & 2r + 4s \end{pmatrix} = \begin{pmatrix} -1 & -2 & -4 \\ -1 & -4 & -2 \end{pmatrix}$$

So $p + q = -1$ and $r + s = -1$
    $4p + 2q = -2$ $4r + 2s = -4$

We can solve these simultaneous equations to find that $p = 0$, $q = -1$, $r = -1$, $s = 0$. We must check that these values work for the other equations in the matrix.

$2p + 4q = -4$ and $2r + 4s = -2$

So the transformation matrix is $\begin{pmatrix} 0 & -1 \\ -1 & 0 \end{pmatrix}$.

This is the matrix for a reflection in the line $y = -x$.

Answer   (a) (i) A' $(1, -1)$, B' $(4, -2)$, C' $(2, -4)$
    (ii) A' $(1, 1)$, B' $(2, 4)$, C' $(4, 2)$
    (b) Reflection in the line $y = -x$.

Practice

D **1** The triangle ABC has vertices A $(1, -2)$, B $(3, -1)$ and C $(3, -4)$. Using matrices, find the triangle's image after these transformations.
    (a) Reflection in the y-axis.
    (b) Reflection in $y = -x$.
    In both cases state clearly the matrix used.

2 PQRS is a parallelogram with vertices P $(1, 0)$, Q $(3, 1)$, R $(3, -2)$ and S $(1, -3)$.
    (a) Find its image P'Q'R'S' following a reflection in the x-axis.
    (b) Find P"Q"R"S", the reflection of P'Q'R'S' in the line $y = x$.

3 XYZ is a triangle with vertices X $(-2, -2)$, Y $(-1, -3)$ and Z $(-2, -3)$.

For each of the following images and transformations find the transformation matrix that maps XYZ to X'Y'Z' and describe the transformation in full.
    (a) Translation to X' $(2, 1)$, Y' $(3, 0)$, Z' $(2, 0)$.
    (b) Reflection to X' $(-2, 2)$, Y' $(-1, 3)$, Z' $(-2, 3)$.
    (c) Reflection to X' $(-2, -2)$, Y' $(-3, -1)$, Z' $(-3, -2)$.

Learn More About It

Let's go back to our square OAB.

Rotate it clockwise through an angle of 90° about the origin.

Then

$$\overrightarrow{OA} = \begin{pmatrix} 1 \\ 0 \end{pmatrix}, \overrightarrow{O'A'} = \begin{pmatrix} 0 \\ -1 \end{pmatrix}$$

$$\overrightarrow{OB} = \begin{pmatrix} 0 \\ 1 \end{pmatrix}, \overrightarrow{O'B'} = \begin{pmatrix} 1 \\ 0 \end{pmatrix}$$

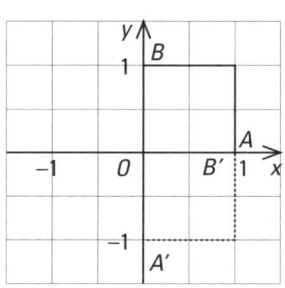

Just as we did for reflections we set

$M(\overrightarrow{OA}) = \overrightarrow{O'A'}$

$M(\overrightarrow{OB}) = \overrightarrow{O'B'}$

and solve simultaneous equations.

This gives the matrix representing a 90° clockwise rotation as $\begin{pmatrix} 0 & 1 \\ -1 & 0 \end{pmatrix}$.

A similar argument can be used to find the matrices for other rotations.

In general the matrix representing a clockwise rotation about the origin can be found using trigonometry. To obtain this matrix we can use a similar method to the one used for reflections.

Rotation	Matrix
90° clockwise about O	$\begin{pmatrix} 0 & 1 \\ -1 & 0 \end{pmatrix}$
180° clockwise about O	$\begin{pmatrix} -1 & 0 \\ 0 & -1 \end{pmatrix}$
270° clockwise about O	$\begin{pmatrix} 0 & -1 \\ 1 & 0 \end{pmatrix}$

Key Fact

A rotation through an angle θ clockwise about the origin is represented by the matrix

$$\begin{pmatrix} \cos\theta & \sin\theta \\ -\sin\theta & \cos\theta \end{pmatrix}$$

Example Find the image A'B'C'D' of the rectangle ABCD with vertices A (−3, 1), B (0, 1), C (0, −1) and D (−3, −1) after a rotation through 90° anticlockwise about the origin.

Working A rotation through 90° anticlockwise is equivalent to rotating the triangle through 270° clockwise.

So the image can be found from

$$\begin{pmatrix} \cos 270° & \sin 270° \\ -\sin 270° & \cos 270° \end{pmatrix} \overset{\text{A \ \ B \ \ C \ \ D}}{\begin{pmatrix} -3 & 0 & 0 & -3 \\ 1 & 1 & -1 & -1 \end{pmatrix}}$$

$$= \begin{pmatrix} 0 & -1 \\ 1 & 0 \end{pmatrix} \begin{pmatrix} -3 & 0 & 0 & -3 \\ 1 & 1 & -1 & -1 \end{pmatrix}$$

$$= \overset{\text{A' \ \ B' \ \ C' \ \ D'}}{\begin{pmatrix} -1 & -1 & 1 & 1 \\ -3 & 0 & 0 & -3 \end{pmatrix}}$$

Answer A' (−1, −3), B' (−1, 0), C' (1, 0), D' (1, −3)

Try It Out

E Find the matrices that represent the following rotations about the origin.
(a) 180° anticlockwise   (b) 30° clockwise   (c) −90° clockwise
(d) 45° anticlockwise   (e) 360° clockwise

So what happens to our square following an enlargement centre O, scale factor 2?

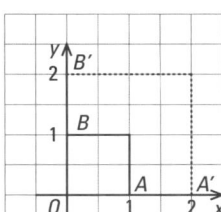

$$\vec{OA} = \begin{pmatrix} 1 \\ 0 \end{pmatrix}, \ \vec{O'A'} = \begin{pmatrix} 2 \\ 0 \end{pmatrix}$$

$$\vec{OB} = \begin{pmatrix} 0 \\ 1 \end{pmatrix}, \ \vec{O'B'} = \begin{pmatrix} 0 \\ 2 \end{pmatrix}$$

We can use the same method as the one used for reflections to find the matrix that represents the enlargement. Doing this gives the matrix that represents an enlargement centre O and scale factor 2.

It is: $\begin{pmatrix} 2 & 0 \\ 0 & 2 \end{pmatrix}$

Using the same method we can find the matrix that represents an enlargement centre O with a general scale factor k.

> ## Key Fact
> An enlargement with scale factor k, centre O is represented by the matrix $\begin{pmatrix} k & 0 \\ 0 & k \end{pmatrix}$.

Try It Out

F **1** Find the matrices that represent the following enlargements with centre O.
(a) Scale factor 3   (b) Scale factor −1   (c) Scale factor $\frac{1}{3}$

Practice

G **1** The parallelogram ABCD has vertices A $(1, -1)$, B $(3, -1)$, C $(4, -3)$ and D $(1, -3)$. Using matrices find the images after the following transformations.
(a) Rotation through −90° clockwise about the origin.
(b) Enlargement scale factor −4, centre origin.

In each case state clearly the matrix used.

2 PQR is a triangle with P $(-2, -1)$, Q $(0, 4)$ and R $(2, -2)$.
(a) Find its image P'Q'R' following a rotation through 180°.
(b) Find P"Q"R", the enlargement of P'Q'R' with centre O and scale factor $-\frac{1}{2}$.

3 XYZ is a triangle with vertices X (–4, 3), Y (–1, 3) and Z (–3, 0).

For each of the following images and transformations find the transformation matrix that maps XYZ to X'Y'Z' and describe the transformation in full.

(a) Rotation to X' (–3, –4), Y' (–3, –1), Z' (0, –3).

(b) Enlargement to X' (–12, 9), Y' (–3, 9), Z' (–9, 0).

(c) Enlargement to X' (4, –3), Y' (1, –3), Z' (3, 0).

Further Practice

H Use matrices to find the image of the line segment from A (3, –2) to B (1, 1) following these transformations.

1 Reflection in the *x*-axis.

2 Enlargement scale factor 3, centre the origin.

3 Rotation 270° anticlockwise about O.

4 Translation $\begin{pmatrix} -3 \\ 2 \end{pmatrix}$.

5 Reflection in $y = x$.

6 Enlargement scale factor –2, centre O.

Finished Early?

➡ Go to page 470

❸ Combining Transformations using Matrices

Learn About It

We already knew how to transform objects using translations, reflections, rotations and enlargements, so why do we need to use matrices?

Using matrices to represent transformations is particularly useful for combined transformations. If we combine any two reflections, rotations and enlargements we can multiply together the matrices representing the single transformations to get a matrix that represents the combined transformation.

For example, if we have a reflection represented by the matrix *M* and an enlargement represented by *E,* then the combined transformation of the reflection THEN the enlargement is *EM*.

Notice the order of the matrix multiplication, the second transformation goes on the left of the first. Remember matrix multiplication is not commutative, so usually *EM* ≠ *ME*.

Example PQR is a triangle with P (1, −3), Q (3, −1) and R (3, −3).
Find the image of PQR after the following combined
transformations:

(a) enlargement centre O scale factor 2 followed by a
rotation through 90° clockwise about O

(b) a glide reflection with translation $\begin{pmatrix} -4 \\ 4 \end{pmatrix}$ and mirror line
$y = -x$.

Working (a) The matrix representing an enlargement centre O with

scale factor 2 is $\begin{pmatrix} 2 & 0 \\ 0 & 2 \end{pmatrix}$. The matrix representing a

rotation of 90° clockwise about O is $\begin{pmatrix} 0 & 1 \\ -1 & 0 \end{pmatrix}$.

So the matrix representing the combined transformation
of the enlargement followed by the rotation is:

$$\begin{pmatrix} 0 & 1 \\ -1 & 0 \end{pmatrix}\begin{pmatrix} 2 & 0 \\ 0 & 2 \end{pmatrix} = \begin{pmatrix} 0 & 2 \\ -2 & 0 \end{pmatrix}$$

So the coordinates of the vertices of the image are

$$\begin{matrix} & P & Q & R & & P' & Q' & R' \end{matrix}$$
$$\begin{pmatrix} 0 & 2 \\ -2 & 0 \end{pmatrix}\begin{pmatrix} 1 & 3 & 3 \\ -3 & -1 & -3 \end{pmatrix} = \begin{pmatrix} -6 & -2 & -6 \\ -2 & -6 & -6 \end{pmatrix}$$

P' (−6, −2), Q' (−2, −6), R' (−6, −6)

(b) First apply the translation $\begin{pmatrix} -4 \\ 4 \end{pmatrix}$ to each point:

the position vector of P is $\begin{pmatrix} 1 \\ -3 \end{pmatrix}$ so the position vector of

P', after the translation, is $\begin{pmatrix} 1 \\ -3 \end{pmatrix} + \begin{pmatrix} -4 \\ 4 \end{pmatrix} = \begin{pmatrix} -3 \\ 1 \end{pmatrix}$.

Hence P' is (−3, 1). Similarly Q' is (−1, 3) and R' is (−1, 1).
Now reflect the triangle in the line $y = -x$.

The equivalent matrix is $\begin{pmatrix} 0 & -1 \\ -1 & 0 \end{pmatrix}$.

The image after the reflection is

$$\begin{matrix} & A & B & C & & A' & B' & C' \end{matrix}$$
$$\begin{pmatrix} 0 & -1 \\ -1 & 0 \end{pmatrix}\begin{pmatrix} -3 & -1 & -1 \\ 1 & 3 & 1 \end{pmatrix} = \begin{pmatrix} -1 & -3 & -1 \\ 3 & 1 & 1 \end{pmatrix}$$

So P'' (−1, 3), Q'' (−3, 1) and R'' (−1, 1).
Alternatively we could have done the reflection first followed
by the translation.

Answer (a) P' (−6, −2), Q' (−2, −6), R' (−6, −6)
(b) P'' (−1, 3), Q'' (−3, 1), R'' (−1, 1)

Try It Out

1 Find the single matrix that represents each of the following combined transformations.

1 Reflection in the y-axis then rotation 270° anticlockwise about O.

2 Enlargement centre O, scale factor –7 then reflection in $y = -x$.

3 Reflection in $y = -x$ then enlargement centre O, scale factor –7.

4 Rotation 180° about O then enlargement scale factor –1, centre O.

Practice

J **1** P (–3, –2), Q (–1, 2) and R (0, –1) are the vertices of a triangle. The triangle is reflected in the y-axis and then rotated through 90° clockwise about the origin.

(a) Write down the matrices representing the reflection and the rotation, and find the matrix representing the combined transformation.

(b) Find the image of PQR following the combined transformation.

(c) If the rotation had come before the reflection what would the image have been?

2 VXYZ is a parallelogram with vertices at V (–3, 6), X (–1, 4), Y (–1, 0).

(a) Find the coordinates of Z.

(b) Draw the image of the parallelogram following a glide reflection with glide axis $y = -x$ and translation $\begin{pmatrix} 5 \\ -5 \end{pmatrix}$.

3 Triangle ABC has vertices A (3, 0), B (5, –4) and C (1, –3).

The triangle is enlarged with scale factor –1, centre O and then reflected in the x-axis.

(a) Find a single matrix that represents the combined transformation.

(b) Use the matrix to find A'B'C'.

(c) Describe the single transformation that maps A'B'C' back to ABC.

4 The following matrix equation maps the point (a, b) to (a', b').

$$\begin{pmatrix} a' \\ b' \end{pmatrix} = \begin{pmatrix} -\frac{1}{2} & 0 \\ 0 & -\frac{1}{2} \end{pmatrix} \begin{pmatrix} a \\ b \end{pmatrix} + \begin{pmatrix} -2 \\ 4 \end{pmatrix}$$

Describe the transformation in words.

Further Practice

 The diagram shows two pentagons ABCDE and $A^1B^1C^1D^1E^1$.

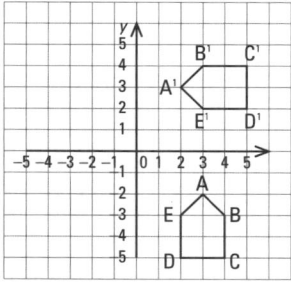

1 Describe the single transformation that maps ABCDE to $A^1B^1C^1D^1E^1$.

2 Write down the matrix that represents that transformation.

$A^1B^1C^1D^1E^1$ is mapped to $A^2B^2C^2D^2E^2$ with coordinates A^2 (−2, 3), B^2 (−3, 4), C^2 (−5, 4), D^2 (−5, 2) and E^2 (3, 2).

3 Describe the transformation that maps $A^1B^1C^1D^1E^1$ onto $A^2B^2C^2D^2E^2$.

4 Describe the single transformation from ABCDE to $A^2B^2C^2D^2E^2$ and find a matrix that represents it.

$A^1B^1C^1D^1E^1$ is mapped to $A^3B^3C^3D^3E^3$ by the matrix $\begin{pmatrix} 0 & 2 \\ -2 & 0 \end{pmatrix}$.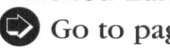

5 Describe the combined transformation.

Finished Early?
➡ Go to page 471

24 Trigonometry 2

In this chapter you will learn about ...
1. circular functions
2. the graphs of sine, cosine and tangent
3. the sine and cosine rules
4. area of a triangle
5. three-dimensional geometry
6. earth geometry

1 Circular Functions

Remember?

In a right-angled triangle:

$\sin \theta = \dfrac{\text{opp}}{\text{hyp}}$

$\cos \theta = \dfrac{\text{adj}}{\text{hyp}}$

$\tan \theta = \dfrac{\text{opp}}{\text{adj}}$

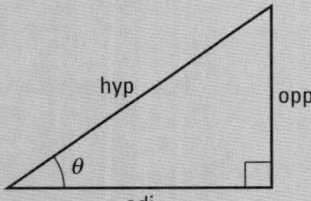

From the special triangles we can find the exact values of certain trigonometric ratios.

Angle	Sine	Cosine	Tangent
0°	0	1	0
30°	$\dfrac{1}{2}$	$\dfrac{\sqrt{3}}{2}$	$\dfrac{1}{\sqrt{3}}$
45°	$\dfrac{1}{\sqrt{2}}$	$\dfrac{1}{\sqrt{2}}$	1
60°	$\dfrac{\sqrt{3}}{2}$	$\dfrac{1}{2}$	$\sqrt{3}$
90°	1	0	Undefined

Learn About It

In Chapter 12 we learnt about the sine, cosine and tangent ratios for acute angles. The definitions of the sine, cosine and tangent ratios can be extended so that we can find the trigonometric ratios for all angles: acute, obtuse, reflex and negative.

From the diagram we can see that

$$\sin \theta = \frac{y\text{-coordinate of P}}{\text{OP}}$$

$$\cos \theta = \frac{x\text{-coordinate of P}}{\text{OP}}$$

$$\tan \theta = \frac{y\text{-coordinate of P}}{x\text{-coordinate of P}}$$

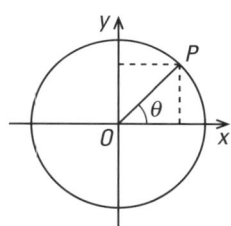

We use these definitions for the trigonometric ratios of all angles $-360° \leq \theta \leq 360°$.

θ obtuse θ reflex θ negative

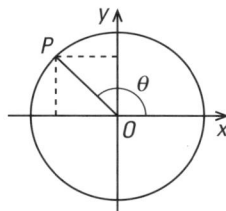 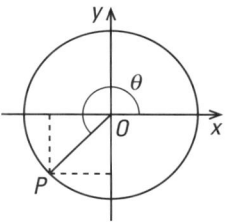 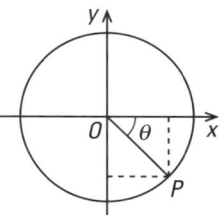

You can see from the diagrams above why the trigonometric ratios sine, cosine and tangent are called the **circular functions**.

Word Check

circular function sine, cosine or tangent

We can use these definitions of sine, cosine and tangent to derive some useful identities.

In the diagram P_1 has coordinates (x_1, y) and forms an angle θ with the positive x-axis.

P_2 has coordinates (x_2, y) and forms an angle $(180° - \theta)$ with the positive x-axis.

Notice that $x_2 = -x_1$.

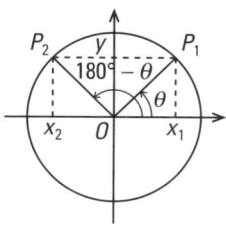

Then by definition:

$$\sin (180° - \theta) = \frac{y}{OP_2} = \frac{y}{OP_1} = \sin \theta$$

$$\cos (180° - \theta) = \frac{x_2}{OP_2} = \frac{-x_1}{OP_1} = -\cos \theta$$

$$\tan (180° - \theta) = \frac{y}{x_2} = \frac{y}{-x_1} = -\tan \theta$$

These identities give a relationship between the trigonometric ratio of an angle and the trigonometric ratio of its supplementary angle.

For example, $\cos (170°) = \cos (180° - 10°) = -\cos 10°$.

Key Facts

$$\sin (180° - \theta) = \sin \theta \qquad \cos (180° - \theta) = -\cos \theta \qquad \tan (180° - \theta) = -\tan \theta$$

Try It Out

 Write the following trigonometric ratios in terms of the ratios of their supplementary angles and evaluate them, giving exact values where possible.

1 $\sin 150°$ **2** $\cos 150°$ **3** $\tan 150°$ **4** $\tan 135°$

5 $\cos 120°$ **6** $\sin 168°$ **7** $\tan 90.2°$ **8** $\cos 137.4°$

Learn More About It

It is often useful to know for which angles each of the circular functions is positive and negative. To do this we can divide the plane into quadrants.

In the 1st quadrant $0 < \theta < 90°$ and $x > 0$ and $y > 0$ so from the definitions above $\sin \theta$, $\cos \theta$ and $\tan \theta$ are all positive.

	y
2nd quadrant $x < 0$ $y > 0$	1st quadrant $x > 0$ $y > 0$
3rd quadrant $x < 0$ $y < 0$	4th quadrant $x > 0$ $y < 0$

x

Quadrant	Angle	x	y	$\sin \theta$	$\cos \theta$	$\tan \theta$
1st	$0° < \theta < 90°$	+	+	+	+	+
2nd	$90° < \theta < 180°$	−	+	+	−	−
3rd	$180° < \theta < 270°$	−	−	−	−	+
4th	$270° < \theta < 360°$	+	−	−	+	−

These results can be seen more clearly in a diagram:

All the ratios are positive in the 1st quadrant.
Only sin is positive in the 2nd quadrant.
Only tan is positive in the 3rd quadrant.
Only cos is positive in the 4th quadrant.

Just remember **CAST**.

Sin	All
Tan	Cos

Try It Out

B Are the following trigonometric ratios positive or negative?

1 sin 75° **2** tan 137° **3** cos 271° **4** cos 269°

5 tan 354° **6** sin (−163°) **7** tan (−143.3°) **8** sin 1.43°

> **Finished Early?**
> ➡ Go to page 471

2 Graphs of Sine, Cosine and Tangent

Learn About It

We can put the sine ratios for the angles θ with $-360° \leq \theta \leq 360°$ in a table.
The table below shows just a few of the values.

θ	−360°	−330°	...	−30°	0°	30°	45°	...	360°
$\sin \theta$	0	0.5	...	−0.5	0	0.5	0.71	...	0

If we plot the values of θ against the values of $\sin \theta$ we get the **sine curve**:

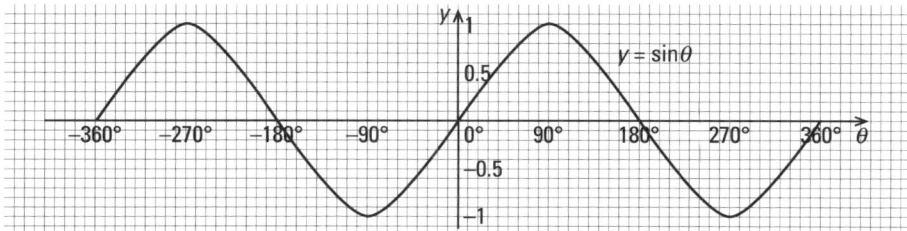

If you look carefully at the graph you can see that the graph repeats itself every 360°. We say that $y = \sin \theta$ is **periodic** and has **period** 360°.

So $\sin \theta = \sin (\theta + 360°) = \sin (\theta - 360°)$ for any value of θ.

So there are several values of θ that give a particular value of $\sin \theta$.

For example, in the range $-360° \leqslant \theta \leqslant 360°$ there are four values of θ that give $\sin \theta = 0.5$. We can clearly see this by drawing the line $\sin \theta = 0.5$ on the sine curve.

We already know that $\sin 30° = 0.5$, so $30°$ is a solution of $\sin \theta = 0.5$.

Also, using the identity
$\sin (180° - \theta) = \sin \theta$
we know that

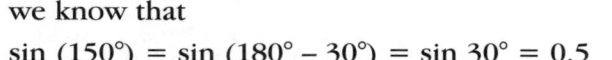

$\sin (150°) = \sin (180° - 30°) = \sin 30° = 0.5$

So $150°$ is another solution.

We can see from the graph that there are two other values of θ such that $\sin \theta = 0.5$. The sine curve is periodic with period $360°$, so $\sin \theta = \sin (\theta - 360°)$.

Hence $\sin 30° = \sin (30° - 360°) = \sin (-330°) = 0.5$

and $\quad \sin 150° = \sin (150° - 360°) = \sin (-210°) = 0.5$

So the solutions of the equation $\sin \theta = 0.5$ for $-360° \leqslant \theta \leqslant 360°$ are $\theta = 30°, 150°, -210°, -360°$.

Practice

! Do not use a calculator for these exercises.

C **1** Use the sine curve to find approximate values of
    (a) $\sin 130°$ **(b)** $\sin (-50°)$ **(c)** $\sin (-200°)$

2 Use the sine curve to find all the values of θ between $-360°$ and $360°$ such that:
    (a) $\sin \theta = 0$ **(b)** $\sin \theta = 1$ **(c)** $\sin \theta = -1$

3 Use the sine curve to approximate the values of θ such that
    (a) $\sin \theta = 0.75$ **(b)** $\sin \theta = -0.25$

D Use the sine curve given above to draw the following curves.

1 $y = \sin \theta + 1$

2 $y = -\sin \theta$

Learn More About It

The graphs of cosine and tangent can be plotted in the same way as the sine curve.

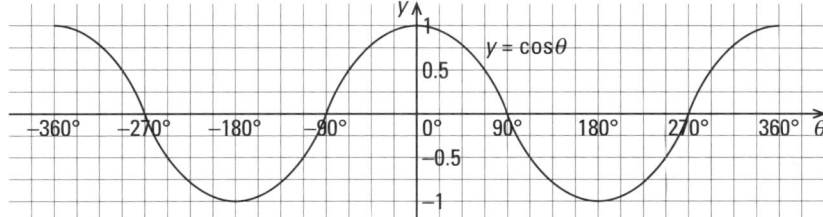

Like the sine curve, the cosine curve is also periodic with period 360°.

So $\cos \theta = \cos (\theta + 360°) = \cos (\theta - 360°)$ for any value of θ.

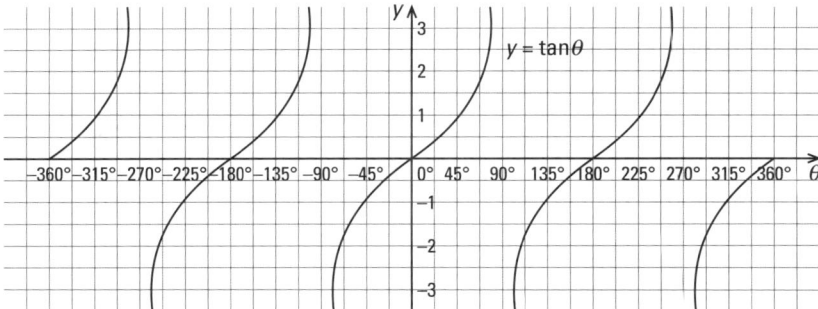

We can see from the diagram that the tangent curve is periodic with period 180°. So $\tan \theta = \tan (\theta + 180°) = \tan (\theta - 180°)$ for any value of θ.

Remember that $\tan 90°$ is undefined. We can see this on the graph. As θ increases, getting closer and closer to 90°, $\tan \theta$ gets bigger and bigger. $\tan \theta$ is undefined for $\theta = 90°$. For θ just larger than 90° $\tan \theta$ is suddenly very large and negative. The value of $\tan \theta$ 'jumps' when $\theta = 90°$.

Practice

 Do not use a calculator for these exercises.

 1 Use the curves to find approximate values of

(a) $\sin 22.5°$ (b) $\cos 22.5°$ (c) $\tan 22.5°$

(d) $\dfrac{\sin 112.5°}{\cos 112.5°}$ (e) $\sin^2 (-117°) + \cos^2 (-117°)$

(f) $\sqrt{1 - \sin^2 (-60°)}$

2 Use the curves to find all the values of θ between $-360°$ and $360°$ such that:

    (a) $\tan \theta = 0$ **(b)** $\cos \theta = -0.5$ **(c)** $\tan \theta = -1$

F Use the curves on page 411 to draw the following curves.

1 $y = \cos \theta - 1$

2 $y = -\tan \theta$

3 The Sine and Cosine Rules

Learn About It

In previous chapters we have used trigonometry to find angles and the lengths of sides in right-angled triangles. The sine and cosine rules can be used on any kind of triangle.

For a triangle ABC with sides of length a, b and c the **sine rule** says that

$$\frac{a}{\sin A} = \frac{b}{\sin B} = \frac{c}{\sin C}$$

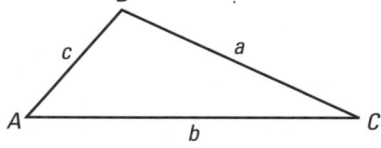

This can also be written

$$\frac{\sin A}{a} = \frac{\sin B}{b} = \frac{\sin C}{c}$$

> ## Key Fact
>
> The sine rule:
>
> For a triangle ABC with sides of length a, b and c
>
> $$\frac{a}{\sin A} = \frac{b}{\sin B} = \frac{c}{\sin C}$$

We can use the sine rule to find:

- the length of a side given two angles and a side, or
- an angle given two sides and an angle.

Example   The triangle ABC has AB = 5 cm, AC = 7 cm and $A\hat{B}C$ = 105°.
(a) Find $A\hat{C}B$ to the nearest degree.
(b) Find BC to one decimal place.

Working   First sketch the triangle.
(a) We have two sides and an
angle, and we want to find an
angle. So we use the sine rule.
Using the sine rule:

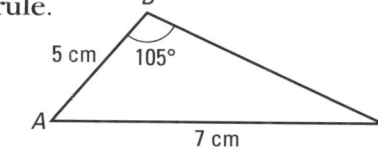

$$\frac{\sin A\hat{B}C}{AC} = \frac{\sin A\hat{C}B}{AB}$$

Putting in the known values:

$$\frac{\sin 105°}{7} = \frac{\sin A\hat{C}B}{5}$$

So $\sin A\hat{C}B = 5 \times \dfrac{\sin 105°}{7}$

$$= 0.6899...$$

Hence $A\hat{C}B = \sin^{-1} 0.6899... = 43.62...°$
To the nearest degree $A\hat{C}B$ = 44°.

(b) Using the sine rule:

$$\frac{BC}{\sin B\hat{A}C} = \frac{AC}{\sin A\hat{B}C}$$

AC = 7 cm, $A\hat{B}C$ = 105° and
$B\hat{A}C = 180° - (105° + 43.62...°) = 31.37...°$
Putting these into the sine rule:

$$\frac{BC}{\sin 31.37...°} = \frac{7}{\sin 105°}$$

Rearrange
$BC = \sin 31.27...° \times \dfrac{7}{\sin 105°}$

$$= 3.77 ... \text{ cm}$$

So to one decimal place BC = 3.8 cm.

Answer   (a) $A\hat{C}B$ = 44°   (b) *BC* = 3.8 cm

Try It Out

G For each triangle find the size of the angle or length of the side marked x.

1

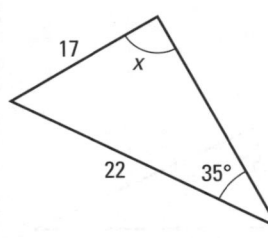

2

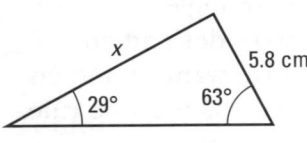

3

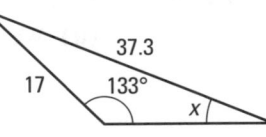

Practice

H

1 ABC is a triangle with AB = 19.5 cm, AC = 8.1 cm and $A\hat{C}B = 143°$.
Find angle $A\hat{B}C$.

2 Triangle PQR has QR = 9.3, $Q\hat{P}R = 67°$ and $P\hat{R}Q = 54°$.
Find PQ.

3 Triangle XYZ has ZX = 13.2 cm, $Z\hat{X}Y = 33°$ and ZY = 13.2°.
Find $X\hat{Y}Z$.

I

1 A ship leaves a harbour and travels 53 km at a bearing of 042°. It then
turns to a bearing of 300°. When it is due north of its starting point how
far has the boat travelled altogether?

[Hint: Draw a diagram and find the angles in the triangle.]

2 Until 1990 the Leaning Tower of Pisa in Italy
was leaning at an angle of 10° from the
vertical.

A surveyor stands 100 m from the base of the
tower and measures an angle of elevation of
32.6° to the top of the tower. How tall is the
tower to the nearest 10 cm?

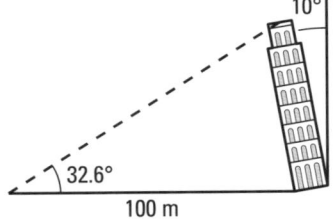

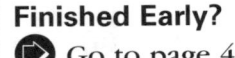

> **Finished Early?**
> ➡ Go to page 472

Learn More About It

The cosine rule is a generalisation of
Pythagoras' theorem.

For a triangle ABC the **cosine rule** can be
written as

$$a^2 = b^2 + c^2 - 2bc \cos A$$
or $$b^2 = c^2 + a^2 - 2ca \cos B$$
or $$c^2 = a^2 + b^2 - 2ab \cos C$$

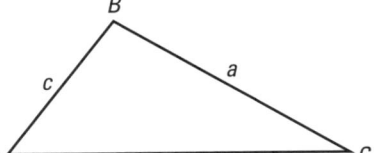

Key Fact

The cosine rule:

For a triangle ABC: $a^2 = b^2 + c^2 - 2bc \cos A$

We can use the cosine rule when:

- we want to find a side, given two sides and the included angle, or
- we want an angle given all three sides.

The 'included angle' is the angle between two sides. For example, for the pair of sides AB and AC the included angle is BÂC.

To find an angle given all the sides we want to rearrange the cosine rule. For example, rearranging $a^2 = b^2 + c^2 - 2bc \cos A$ gives:

$$\cos A = \frac{b^2 + c^2 - a^2}{2bc}$$

Example	A triangle ABC has sides AB = 6 m, BC = 10 m and AC = 13 m. Find all the angles of the triangle.
Working	First sketch the triangle. We know all three sides so we can find an angle using the cosine rule.

We will find the angle at A first.

Use $a^2 = b^2 + c^2 - 2bc \cos A$.

Putting in the known values gives:

$$10^2 = 13^2 + 6^2 - 2 \times 13 \times 6 \times \cos A$$

So $100 = 169 + 36 - 156 \cos A$

$$\cos A = \frac{169 + 36 - 100}{156}$$

$$= 0.67...$$

So $A = 47.69...°$.

Now we shall try to find B.

Use $b^2 = c^2 + a^2 - 2ca \cos B$

So $169 = 36 + 100 - 2 \times 6 \times 10 \times \cos B$

$$\cos B = \frac{36 + 100 - 169}{120}$$

$$= -0.275$$

So $B = 105.96...°$.

Finally $C = 180° - (47.69...° + 105.96...°) = 26.34...°$

Answer   A = 48°, B = 106°, C = 26° (to the nearest degree)

Try It Out

J Find the value of *x* in each of these triangles.

1

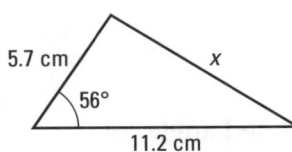

2

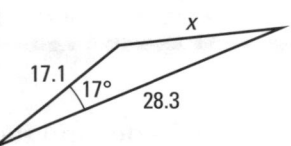

3

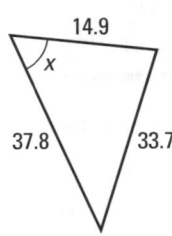

Practice

K **1** UVW is a triangle with UV = 137 mm, UW = 97 mm and VÛW = 64°. Find VW.

2 A triangle has sides 12.2, 18.7 and 15.5. Find the angles in the triangle.

3 A triangle has sides 1, $\sqrt{3}$ and 2. Find the angles in the triangle.

L **1** Two ships leave harbour. One travels 117 km on a bearing of 073°. The other travels 89 km on a bearing of 203°. What is the distance between the two ships, to the nearest kilometre?

2 Jearl leaves her house and cycles 16 km due east. She then changes direction and cycles another 7 km. Finally she cycles 12 km back to her house. At what bearing is she cycling for each of the three legs of her journey?

> **Finished Early?**
> ➡ Go to page 472

④ Area of a Triangle

> **Remember?**
> The area of a triangle is $\frac{1}{2}$ × base × height.
>
>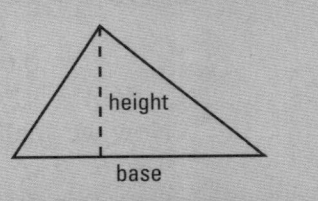

We already know that the area of triangle *ABC* is $\frac{1}{2}ah$.

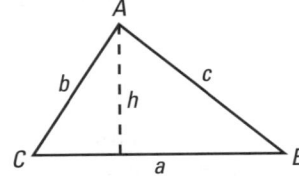

But using trigonometry:

$$\left[\sin C = \frac{h}{b} \Rightarrow h = b \sin C\right]$$

So area of triangle ABC $= \frac{1}{2}ab \sin C$.

> ## Key Fact
> Given the lengths of two sides of a triangle and the included angle we can find the area of the triangle using
>
> $$\text{area} = \frac{1}{2}ab \sin C$$

Example Find the area of triangle PQR.

Working To use the formula we need to know the lengths of two sides and the included angle.

We know the lengths of PR and QR, but we don't know the angle between the two, $P\hat{R}Q$. But we do know the other two angles.

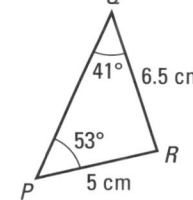

$$P\hat{R}Q = 180° - 53° - 41°$$
$$= 86°$$

Now use the formula:

$$\text{area of triangle PQR} = \frac{1}{2}ab \sin C$$
$$= \frac{1}{2} \times 5 \times 6.5 \times \sin 86°$$
$$= 16.2 \text{ cm}^2 \text{ to 1 decimal place}$$

Answer 16.2 cm² (to 1 decimal place)

Try It Out

 Find the area of each of these triangles.

1

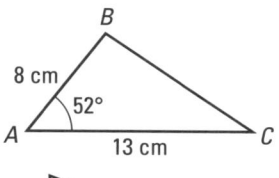

2

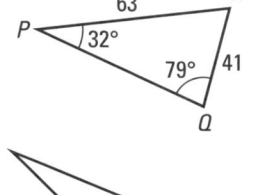

3

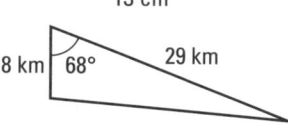

4

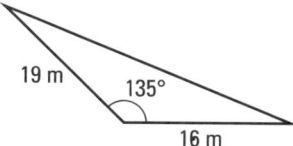

Practice

1 XYZ is a triangle with ZY = 13.9, XY = 21.1 and $X\hat{Y}Z$ = 143°.
Find the area of XYZ.

2 ABC is a triangle with AB = 16.3 cm, BC = 7.8 cm, $B\hat{A}C$ = 43° and
$A\hat{C}B$ = 66°. Find the area of ABC.

3 A triangle has sides of length 33.2 m and 16.0 m, and has area 152.3 m².
Calculate the size of the included angle to one decimal place.

4 A triangle DEF has $E\hat{D}F$ = 55°, $D\hat{F}E$ = 23° and EF = 18 cm.
Find the area of the triangle.
[*Hint*: Use the sine rule.]

5 A triangle KLM has a side of length LM = 17.1 cm and angles $L\hat{K}M$ = 41°
and $L\hat{M}K$ = 47°. Find the area of the triangle KLM.

Finished Early?
➡ Go to page 472

---

5 Three-dimensional Geometry

We've seen how to use trigonometry in two-dimensional shapes such as
triangles. We can also use trigonometry in three-dimensional shapes such as
pyramids.

Possibly the most difficult part of three-dimensional geometry is correctly
identifying angles.

The diagram shows a pyramid.
The sides ABC, ACD, ADE and ABE
are triangles and BCDE is a rectangle.
AZ is the vertical height of the pyramid.
AZ is perpendicular to the side BCDE.

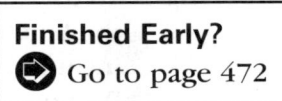

The angle between the side ADE and the base, BCDE, is $A\hat{Y}Z$.

The angle between the edge *AD* and the base is $A\hat{D}Z$.

Angles $A\hat{Y}Z$ and $A\hat{D}Z$ are NOT the same.

Notice that the dashed lines form right-angled triangles so the angles $A\hat{Y}Z$
and $A\hat{D}Z$ are just angles in right-angled triangles. We already know how to
find angles in right-angled triangles.

Try It Out

○ ABCDE is a pyramid with a square base with sides of length 8 cm and vertical height 3 cm. The vertex is directly above the centre of the base.

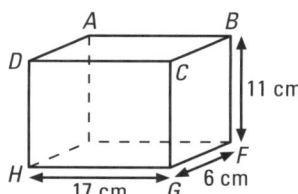

1 Write down the length YZ.

2 Find the length of AY and the angle between AY and the base BCDE.

3 Find the length DZ and the angle between YZ and DZ.

4 Find AD and the angle between AD and the base.

Practice

Ⓟ **1** The diagram shows a cuboid ABCDEFGH.
   (a) Calculate EG.
   (b) Calculate AG.
   (c) Find the angle between AG and the base EFGH.

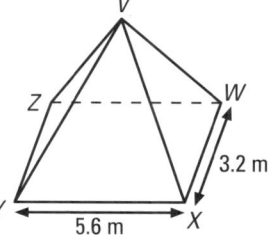

2 VWXYZ is a pyramid with vertical height 7.4 m and a rectangular base. The vertex V is directly above the centre of the base.

Calculate:
   (a) the length of VW
   (b) the angle between the edge VW and the base
   (c) the angle between the plane VWX and the base.

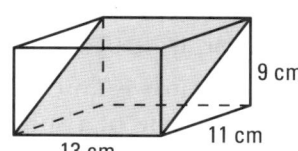

3 The diagram shows a cuboid.
Find the area of the shaded plane and the angle it makes it with the base.

Q **1** An aircraft takes off from the runway and flies 78 km south-east then 113 km south-west. At this point it is at an altitude of 13 000 m. How far is the aircraft from the runway?

2 The diagram shows a ski-slope. The slope is 800 m wide and the shortest distance from top to bottom is 3750 m. The slope makes an angle of 33° with the horizontal.

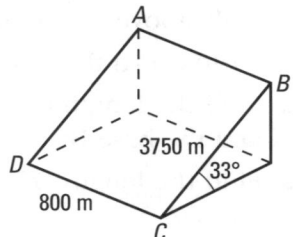

A skier starts at B and skis to D.

(a) To two significant figures, how far did the skier ski?

(b) Find the angle BD makes with the horizontal.

Further Practice

R VWXYZ is a pyramid with a rectangular base.

1 Find AV and the angle AV makes with the base.

2 Find VX and the angle it makes with the base.

3 Find VY and the angle it makes with the base.

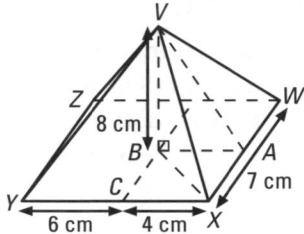

⑥ Earth Geometry

Learn About It

The Earth is a approximately a sphere. Its radius varies between 6357 km and 6378 km. It rotates about the **polar axis** – the line between the north and south poles.

The **Equator** is the circle midway between the north and south poles. The Earth's circumference, measured around the equator, is 40 075 km.

The Equator is an example of a **great circle**. A great circle of a sphere is formed by 'cutting' the sphere through the centre of the sphere.

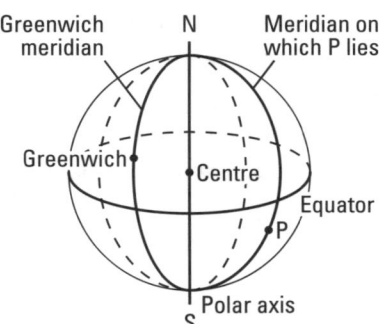

A **meridian** is formed by 'cutting' the Earth through the polar axis. It is half a great circle, running from the north to the south poles. The **prime meridian** or **Greenwich meridian** is the meridian that passes through Greenwich in London, Great Britain.

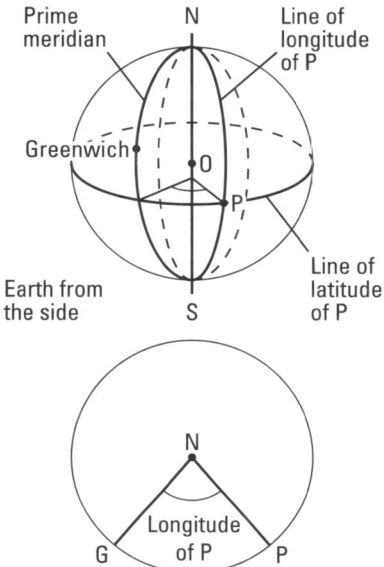

Earth from the side

Earth, looking down on the north pole

Word Check

great circle a circle formed by cutting a sphere through its centre

meridian half of a great circle formed by cutting through the polar axis

prime meridian the meridian through Greenwich, London

Suppose there is a town at P. Then we can identify the meridian it is on by measuring the angle from the prime meridian. This is called the **longitude** of P, it is measured in degrees east or west of the prime meridian. Lines of equal longitude run from north to south (or vice versa).

A circle on the Earth that is parallel to the Equator is called a **parallel of latitude**. The **latitude** of P is the angle between the Equator and the parallel of latitude P lies on. It is measured in degrees north or south of the equator. Lines of equal latitude run from east to west (or vice versa).

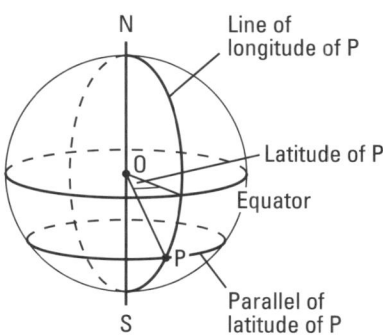

Word Check

longitude the angle a meridian makes with the prime meridian (east or west)

parallel of latitude a circle on the Earth parallel to the Equator

latitude the angle between a point on the Equator and a point on a parallel of latitude (north or south)

Example Kingston, Jamaica is about $18°$ north of the Equator and $77°$ west of the prime meridian.
(a) What is Kingston's latitude and longitude?
Johannesburg, South Africa is $44°$ south and $105°$ east of Kingston.
(b) What is the latitude and longitude of Johannesburg?

Working **(a)** Kingston is $18°$ north of the equator so its latitude is $18°$ north. It is $77°$ west of the prime meridian, so its longitude is $77°$ west.
The position of Kingston is $18°N$, $77°W$.

(b) Johannesburg is $44°$ south of Kingston. Measuring south from Kingston, we get to the Equator after $18°$ (the latitude of Kingston). We then measure another $(44 - 18)° = 26°$ south of the Equator to get to the latitude of Johannesburg. So its latitude is $26°$ south. Johannesburg is $105°$ east of Kingston. Measuring east from Kingston, we get to the prime meridian after $77°$ (the longitude of Kingston). We then measure another $(105 - 77)° = 28°$ east of the prime meridian to get to the longitude of Johannesburg. Its longitude is $28°$ east. The position of Johannesburg is $26°S$, $28°E$.

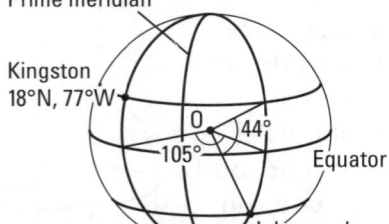

Answer **(a)** $18°N$, $77°W$ **(b)** $26°S$, $28°E$

Try It Out

 1 Use the diagram to find the latitude and longitude of A, B, C, D, E, F and G.

2 (a) How many degrees north of G is B?
  (b) How many degrees west of D is A?

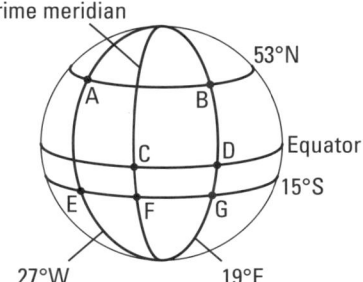

Learn More About It

Remember?

The length of an arc of a circle with radius r subtended by an angle of $\theta°$ is

$$l = \frac{\theta}{360} \times 2\pi r$$

There are 360 degrees in a circle and 60 minutes (60') in a degree.

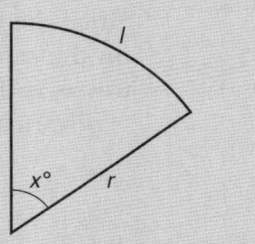

Remember a great circle is a circle formed by cutting the sphere through the centre of the sphere. We can find as many great circles on a sphere as we want, but we are only going to concern ourselves with distances on the Equator and the meridians.

We can calculate the distance along a great circle using the 'length of arc' formula from Chapter 14.

Example   The position of town A is 36°N, 51°W and town B is 15°S, 51°W. Calculate the distance from A to B in kilometres. Assume that the radius of the Earth R is 6370 km.

Working   The two towns are on the same line of longitude (51°W), so the angular difference between the two towns is $(36 + 15)° = 51°$.

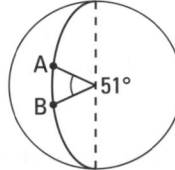
a

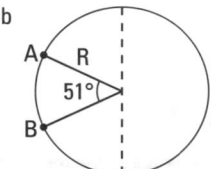
b

Since the towns are on the same line of longitude they are on the same great circle. So the distance between the two towns is the arc length subtended by an angle of 51°.

$$\text{distance} = \frac{\theta}{360} \times 2\pi \times R$$

$$= \frac{51}{360} \times 2\pi \times 6370$$

$$= 5670.05\ldots \text{ km}$$

Answer   Distance is 5670 km to the nearest kilometre.

The length of the arc of a great circle that subtends an angle of 1 minute on the surface of the Earth is called a **nautical mile** (written n.mi.). The nautical mile is the unit of distance that is often used in navigation; on ships for example.

There are 360 degrees in a circle and 60 minutes in a degree, so there are $360 \times 60 = 21\,600$ minutes in a circle. This means that the circumference of the Earth is 21 600 nautical miles.

Example   Calculate the distance between town A and town B in nautical miles.

Working   The towns lie on a great circle so the number of nautical miles between them is the same as the angular difference between them, measured in minutes. The angular difference between the two towns is $51° = 3060'$.
So the distance between the towns is 3060 nautical miles.

Answer   3060 n.mi.

Practice

T For the following questions take the radius of the Earth to be 6370 km.

1 How far is it in kilometres from Kingston, Jamaica (18°N, 77°W) to Cali, Columbia (3°N, 77°W)?

2 Quito, Ecuador and Kampala, Uganda both lie on the Equator. The longitude of Quito is 79°W and Kampala 32°E. How far is it from Quito to Kampala in nautical miles?

3 An aircraft takes off from Kiev (50°N, 31°E), in the Ukraine, and flies to Durban, South Africa (30°S, 31°E). The aircraft flies at an average speed of 750 km/h. How long does the journey take to the nearest hour?

4 A boat sets sail from Roseau in Dominica (15° 18'N, 61° 24'W) and sails due south for 78 nautical miles to reach Castries in St. Lucia. What is the latitude and longitude of Castries?

5 Town A has longitude 58°W and town B has longitude 112°E. They both lie on the Equator. It takes a plane 24 hours to fly from A to B. What is the plane's average speed in knots (nautical miles per hour)?

6 What is one nautical mile, measured in metres to the nearest metre?

We can use almost the same method to work out the distance along parallels of latitude (lines with the same latitude). Remember that a parallel of latitude is a circle on the surface of the Earth that is parallel to the Equator. So, if we can find the radius of the circle we can use the same method as for great circles.

Suppose we want to find the distance between two points X and Y on the same parallel of latitude θ. We first need to find the radius, r, of the circle on which they lie.

If C is the centre of this circle and A is the point on the equator with the same longitude as X, we can use trigonometry to find the radius. We know that OX = R. Also OA is parallel to CX, so $A\hat{O}X = \theta$ and $O\hat{X}C = \theta$. Using trigonometry:

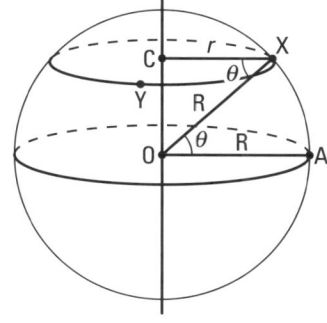

$$\cos \theta = \frac{\text{adjacent}}{\text{hypotenuse}}$$

$$= \frac{CX}{OX}$$

$$= \frac{r}{R}$$

So $r = R \cos \theta$.

So if we know the radius of the Earth (about 6370 km) and the latitude we can find the radius of the parallel of latitude.

Now to find the distance between X and Y we just do what we did to find distances on great circles.

Example	Boat A is at 24°N, 58°W and boat B is at 24°N, 36°W.

(a) Calculate the distance between them to the nearest kilometre.

(b) Calculate the distance between them to the nearest nautical mile.

Working (a) The boats both have the same latitude, so they are on the same parallel of latitude. To find the distance between them we must first find the radius of the parallel of latitude, r:

$r = R \cos \theta$

$\quad = 6370 \times \cos 24°$

$\quad = 5819.28...\text{km}$

The angular difference between the two boats is $(58 - 36)° = 22°$. So the distance between them is:

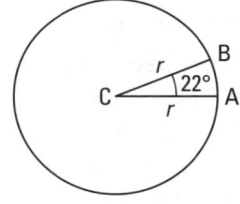

$\text{distance} = \dfrac{22}{360} \times 2\pi r$

$\qquad = \dfrac{11}{180} \times 2\pi \times 5819.28...$

$\qquad = 2234.44... \text{ km}$

So, to the nearest kilometre, the distance between the two boats is 2234 km.

(b) We know that the circumference of the Earth is

$2\pi R \text{ km} = 360 \times 60 \text{ n.mi.}$

So the distance in nautical miles is:

$\text{distance} = \dfrac{22}{360} \times 2\pi r$

$\qquad = \dfrac{22}{360} \times 2\pi \times R \cos \theta$

$\qquad = \dfrac{22}{360} \times 360 \times 60 \cos \theta$

$\qquad = 22 \times 60 \cos 24°$

$\qquad = 1205.88... \text{ n.mi.}$

Answer (a) 2234 km   (b) 1206 n.mi.

In part **(b)** of the previous example we found a simple formula for the distance between two points on a parallel of latitude θ with angular difference $x°$.

distance $= x \times 60 \times \cos \theta$

$\qquad = 60x \cos \theta$ nautical miles

Key Fact

The distance between two points on the same parallel of latitude is:

distance $= 60x \cos \theta$ nautical miles

Practice

Ⓤ In the questions that follow assume the radius of the Earth to be 6370 km.

1 Calculate the distance from Antigua (17°N, 62°W) to Belmopan, in Belize, at (17°N, 89°W) to three significant figures.

2 The Tropic of Cancer is the name of the parallel of latitude $23\frac{1}{2}°$N. Havana and Muscat (in Oman) both lie on the Tropic of Cancer. There longitudes are 82°W and 59°E respectively. Calculate the distance between them to:
(a) the nearest ten kilometres,
(b) the nearest five nautical miles.

3 A plane takes off from Chicago (41.9°N, 87.7°W) and flies to the Vatican City, Italy (41.9°N, 12.5°E). If the plane's average speed is 800 km/h, how long does the journey take to the nearest half an hour?

4 A ship is sailing in the Atlantic Ocean. It starts from Lisbon, Portugal (38°N, 9°W) and sails 804 nautical miles west to reach the Azores. What is the position of the Azores?

5 Two towns lie on the parallel of latitude 41° north. Town A lies on the prime meridian, town B is 5040 nautical miles east of A.
(a) Calculate the latitude and longitude of B to three significant figures.
(b) How far is B from A in kilometres (to the nearest kilometre)?

6 A plane flies 510 nautical miles around a parallel of latitude north of the Equator from A to B. The longitude of A is 10°E and the longitude of B is 27°E. What is the latitude of A and B?

Finished Early?

➡ Go to page 473

Further Practice

V The table shows the journeys flown by a plane. Use the diagram to complete the table, giving distances to the nearest nautical mile.

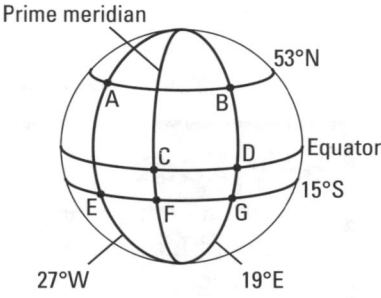

Prime meridian

Journey	Distance (in n.mi.)
C to F	
D to G	
C to D	
F to G	
A to B	
F to E to A	

Unit 11 *Geometry and Trigonometry 2*

Summary of Chapters 23 and 24

Transformations

- A **glide reflection** is a translation parallel to a mirror line followed by a reflection in the mirror line, or vice versa.

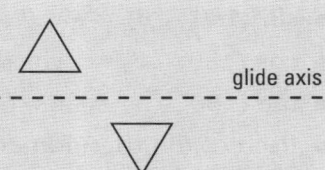
glide axis

- The **glide axis** is the mirror line for a glide reflection.

- The image resulting from a combination of transformations is usually dependent upon the order in which the transformations occur, that is the transformations are not usually commutative.

- Matrices can be used to represent transformations.

- A translation is represented by a column vector.

- Reflections, rotations and enlargements can be represented by 2 × 2 matrices.

- Reflections:

Mirror line	Matrix
x-axis	$\begin{pmatrix} 1 & 0 \\ 0 & -1 \end{pmatrix}$
y-axis	$\begin{pmatrix} -1 & 0 \\ 0 & 1 \end{pmatrix}$
y = *x*	$\begin{pmatrix} 0 & 1 \\ 1 & 0 \end{pmatrix}$
y = −*x*	$\begin{pmatrix} 0 & -1 \\ -1 & 0 \end{pmatrix}$

- A rotation through an angle θ clockwise about the origin is represented by the matrix

$$\begin{pmatrix} \cos\theta & \sin\theta \\ -\sin\theta & \cos\theta \end{pmatrix}$$

- The matrix representing an enlargement with scale factor *k*, centre O is

$$\begin{pmatrix} k & 0 \\ 0 & k \end{pmatrix}$$

- If *M* and *N* are matrices representing two transformations then the matrix representing the combined transformation of *M* first *then* *N* is *NM*.

Trigonometry 2

- A **circular function** is one of the trigonometric ratios: sine, cosine or tangent.
- $\sin(180° - \theta) = \sin\theta$
- $\cos(180° - \theta) = -\cos\theta$
- $\tan(180° - \theta) = -\tan\theta$
- Each of the trigonometric ratios is positive in just two quadrants. Remember **CAST**.

Sin	All
Tan	Cos

- The graph of $\sin\theta$ is:

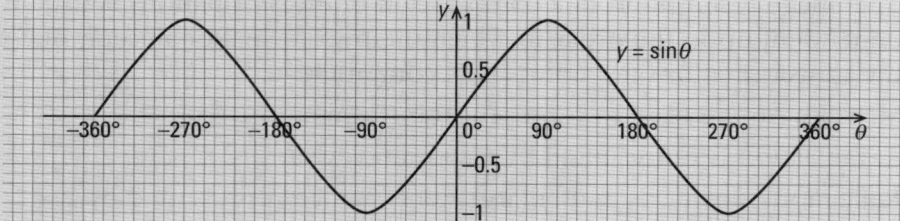

- The graph of $\cos\theta$ is:

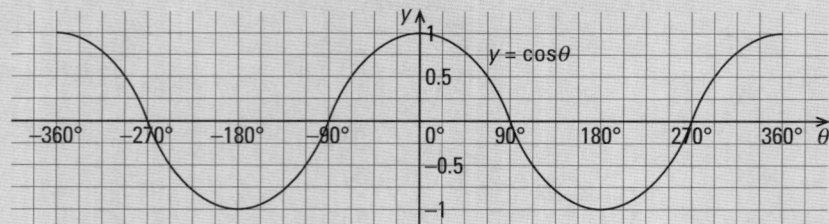

- The graph of $\tan\theta$ is:

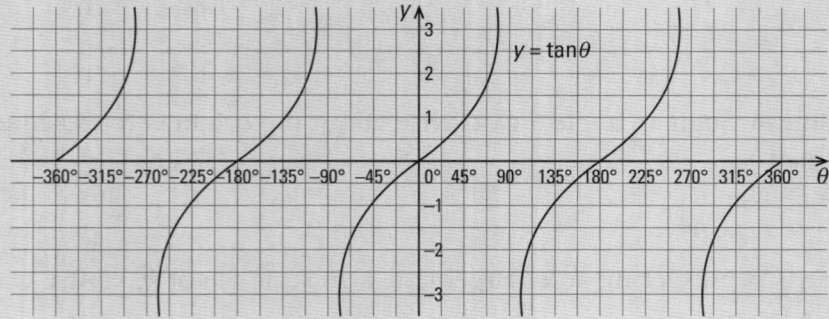

- For a triangle ABC with sides of length a, b and c the **sine rule** says that:

$$\frac{a}{\sin A} = \frac{b}{\sin B} = \frac{c}{\sin C}$$

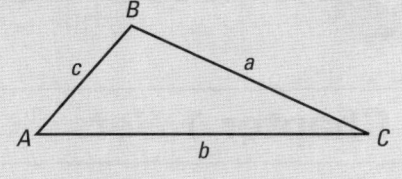

- For a triangle ABC the **cosine rule** says that:

$$a^2 = b^2 + c^2 - 2bc \cos A$$

- Given the length of two sides of a triangle and the included angle we can find the **area of the triangle** using area $= \frac{1}{2}ab \sin C$.

- To solve problems in three-dimensional geometry, break down the problem into right-angled triangles.

- The Earth rotates about the **polar axis**, which passes through the north and south poles.

- The **Equator** is the circle midway between the north and south poles.

- A **great circle** is a circle formed by cutting a sphere through its centre.

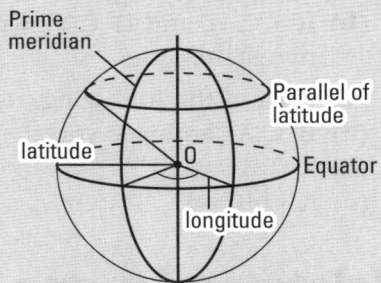

- A **meridian** is half of a great circle formed by cutting through the polar axis.

- The **prime meridian** is the meridian through Greenwich, London.

- The **longitude** of a point is the angle the meridian it lies on makes with the prime meridian (east or west).

- A **parallel of latitude** is a circle on the Earth parallel to the Equator.

- The **latitude** of a point is the angle between a point on the Equator and the point (north or south).

- A **nautical mile is** the length of the arc of a great circle that subtends an angle of 1 minute on the surface of the Earth.

- The distance (l) between two points on a great circle can be found using

$$l = \frac{x}{360} \times 2\pi R$$

where R is the radius of the earth and x the angular difference between the points.

- The distance between two points on a great circle is $60 \times x$ nautical miles.

- The **radius** (r) of a parallel of latitude θ is $r = R \cos \theta$.

- The distance between two points on a parallel of latitude is $60x \cos \theta$ nautical miles, where θ is the latitude and x is the angular difference.

Finished Early?

Chapter 1 *Sets*

❶ Symbols, Definitions and Operations

1 U = {all men}, Y = {young men}, S = {successful men}, and
H = {happy men}.
   (a) Write the symbols that represent each of the following.
      (i) {old men}   **(ii)** {unsuccessful men}
      (ii) {young happy men}   **(iv)** {unsuccessful old men}
   (b) If S' ⊂ H' and H' ⊂ Y', write in words the conclusion from the
   two statements.

2 For each of the following, use a Venn diagram to show that if A ⊂ B, then
   (a) B' ⊂ A'; and vice versa
   (b) A ∩ B' = Ø
   (c) A' ∪ B = U

❷ Relations Among Sets

1 List the elements of the following sets:
   (a) $\{t : t$ is a subject on your timetable$\}$
   (b) $\{f : f$ is a factor of both 27 and 36$\}$
   (c) $\{p : p$ is a prime factor of 42$\}$
   (d) $\{$integer $x : x > 8\}$
   (e) $\{$integer $y : y < -5\}$
   (f) $\{x : 3 < x < 5; x \in Z\}$
   (g) $\{x : 3 < x \leq 5; x \in Z\}$
   (h) $\{x : -2 < x < -1; x \in Z\}$

2 Using the inequality symbol <, write the following in set-builder
   notation.
   (a) $\{0, 1, 2, 3\}$ **(b)** $\{-1, 0, 1\}$
   (c) $\{-3, -2, -1, 0\}$ **(d)** $\{-9, -8, ..., 3, 4\}$
   (e) $\{9, 10\}$ **(f)** $\{-8, -7, ..., -1\}$

❸ Intersecting Sets

1 Let U = {multiples of 2}, F = {multiples of 4} and
   E = {multiples of 8}.

Draw a Venn diagram to show that all multiples of 4 are multiples of 2, and not all multiples of 4 are multiples of 8.

2 A survey was taken to find out the number of people who buy food from places outside the home. The results are shown in the Venn diagram on the right, where

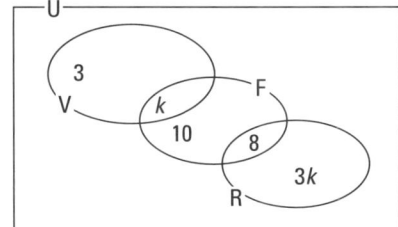

   V = {street vendors}
   F = {fast food outlets}
   R = {dine-in restaurants}.
   (a) If U = V ∪ F ∪ R and n(U) = 33,
      find **(i)** k **(ii)** n(V ∪ R)
           (iii) n(V ∩ R)   **(iv)** n(R' ∩ F)
   (b) What conclusions can you draw about the persons in the survey?

❹ Problem Solving

1 In the Venn diagram given on the right

U = {members of a Youth Club}
A = {group A of the Youth Club}
B = {group B of the Youth Club}

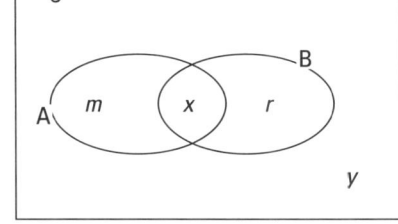

The letters m, r, x and y in the diagram represent the number of students in each subset.

If n(U) = 100, n(A) = 40, n(B) = 15,
(a) express m in terms of x
(b) find the smallest possible value of y
(c) find the largest possible value of x
(d) find the value of x, r, y if $m = 28$.

2 *Some students use computers.*
Some students are clever.
All clever students read.
(a) If U = {students}, draw the Venn diagrams that illustrate the above statements.
(b) Justify your arrangements of the sets.

3 U = {books}, M = {mathematics books},
G = {geometry Books}, P = {books with pictures}

For each of the following Venn diagrams,
(a) write down a statement using 'all', 'some', 'not all', 'not'
(b) write each statement using set notation.

(i)

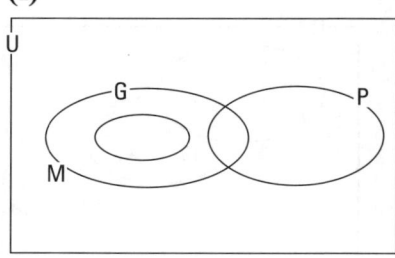

(ii)

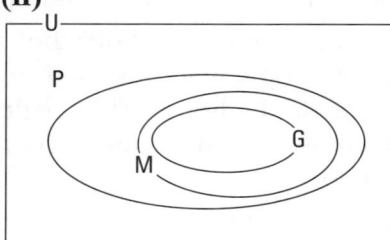

(iii)

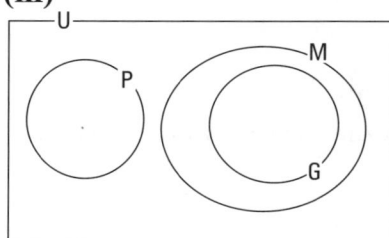

(iv)

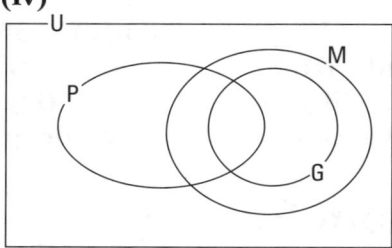

Chapter 2 *Relations and Functions*

❶ Relations

1 If the domain D = {1, 2, 3, 4} and the co-domain R = {1, 2, 4, 8, 16},
draw an arrow diagram to illustrate each of the following relations.
(**i**) Is greater than or equal to
(**ii**) Is the square root of
(**iii**) Is less than

2 For each relation in question 1,
(a) list the ordered pairs
(b) state the type of relation.

❷ Functions

1 Given R : $x \rightarrow y$ where R : $x + 3y = 18$ and $x \in \{3, 6, 9, 12, 15\}$,
   (a) find the range
   (b) write R as a set of ordered pairs
   (c) state whether the relation is a function, giving your reason.

2 N = $\{1, 2, 3, 4\}$ and L = $\{m, n\}$.
   A relation R maps each odd number to *m* and each even number to *n*.
   (a) List R as a set of ordered pairs.
   (b) Draw the arrow diagram.
   (c) Is R a function from N to L? Give a reason for your answer.

3 x and $y \in$ T, where T = $\{1, 2, 3, 4, 5, ..., 20\}$
   (a) If $x = 3y$, write down the set of ordered pairs.
   (b) Is this relation a function? Give reasons for your answer.

4 A = $\{1, 2, 3, ..., 8\}$ and $x \in$ A.
   f is a function such that if x is odd, $x \rightarrow 1$ and if x is even, $x \rightarrow \frac{1}{2}x$.
   (a) Express f as a set of ordered pairs.
   (b) Is this relation a function? Give reasons for your answer.

❸ Graphs

1 State, giving reasons, which of the following graphs does *not* represent a function for the domain $\{1, 2, 3, 4\}$.
   (a)

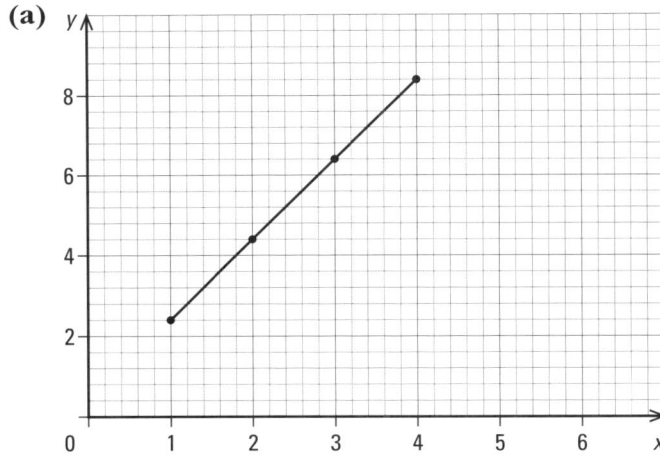

(b)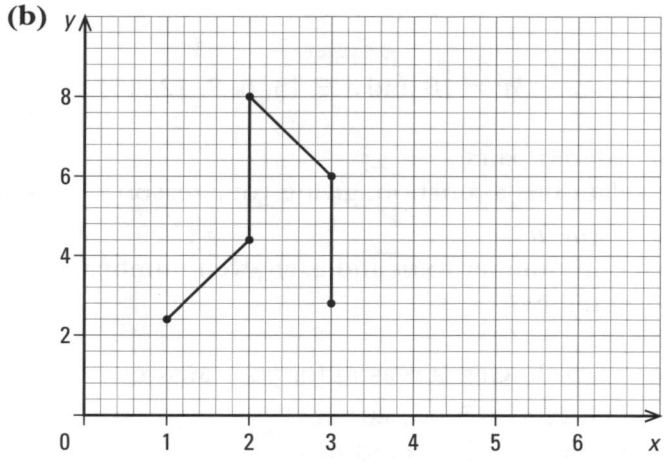

(c)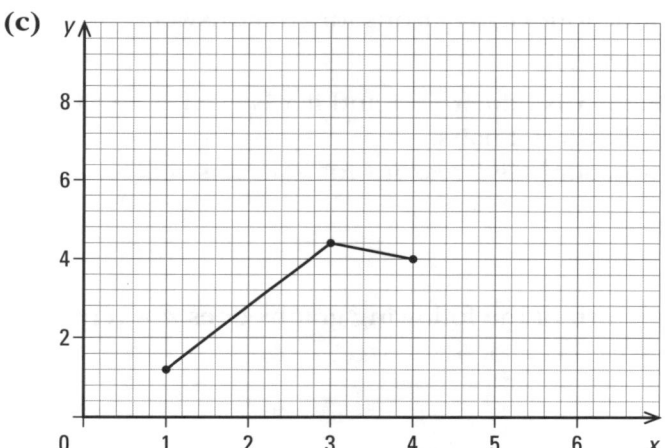

2 (a) State clearly the conditions that a relation must satisfy in order to be a function.

(Continued overleaf.)

(b) Discuss, giving reasons, why the graph of the relation $x \rightarrow y$ that is shown below would not represent a function.

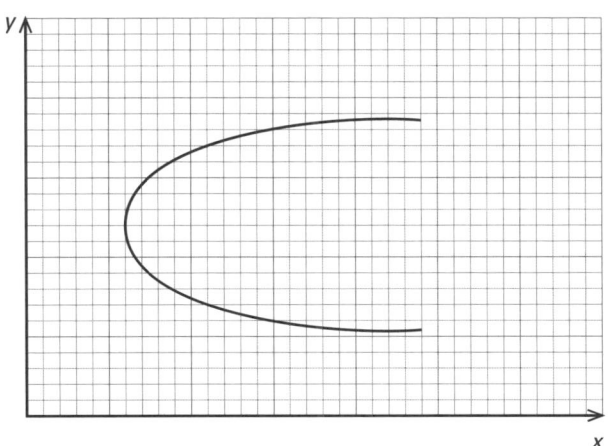

Chapter 3 *Number Theory*

❶ Number Systems

1 m and n are non-zero digits such that
$$mmm_{\text{four}} = nn_{\text{eight}}.$$
Find m and n.

2 Find the missing number if the addition is in base eight:

$$
\begin{array}{r}
1260 \\
362 \\
**** \\
\underline{124} \\
3011
\end{array}
$$

3 The figure on the right shows how a strip of graph paper may be used as a punch tape. The first two rows show how to space the 'holes'. The next row represents the first letter of a message. It shows the binary number 00011, equivalent to 3. This represents C, the 3rd letter of the alphabet.

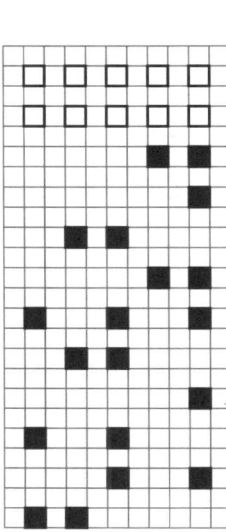

(a) What is the message in the given figure?

(b) Use a strip of graph paper to write the following messages in binary code:

   (i) APPROXIMATE

   (ii) COLLECT DATA.

❷ Sets of Numbers

1 For each of the following statements, say whether the answer is an even number or an odd number. Give examples to illustrate your answer.
  (a) An odd number is added to an odd number.
  (b) An odd number is added to an even number.
  (c) An odd number is multiplied by an odd number.
  (d) An odd number is multiplied by an even number.
  (e) An even number is multiplied by an even number.

2 Given the definition of a rational number as *a number which can be expressed in the form $\frac{p}{q}$, where p and q are integers*, define
  (a) integers **(b)** fractions **(c)** mixed numbers **(d)** zero.

❸ Fractional Parts

  (a) Show that 3.7979… is a rational number.
  Hint: call the number n, multiply the number by 10^2, find $10^2n - n$, and solve for n.
  (b) Use a similar method to show that the following are rational
    numbers: **(i)** 7.333…   [*multiply the number by 10^1*]
             (ii) 4.683 683…   [*multiply the number by 10^3*]
            (iii) 24.189 718 97…   [*multiply the number by 10^4*]
  (c) Hence, derive the rule for writing a recurring decimal as a fraction.

Chapter 4 *Computation*

---

❶ Operations and Laws

1 (a) Let $a \in Z$ and $b \in Z$, where $Z = \{\text{integers}\}$.
    Give examples and reasons for your answer to each of the following.
      (i) Is $a + b \in Z$ for all values of a and b?
      (ii) Is $a \times b \in Z$ for all values of a and b?
      (iii) Is $a - b \in Z$ for all values of a and b?
      (iv) Is $a \div b \in Z$ for all values of a and b?
  (b) What conclusions can you draw about the law of closure applied to the set of integers under the four basic arithmetic operations?

2 $x * y = x + y + xy$
   (a) Find the values of **(i)** $3 * 5$ **(ii)** $5 * 3$ **(iii)** $-2 * 3$ **(iv)** $3 * -2$.
   (b) Is the operation commutative?
   (c) Use an example of your own to investigate whether the operation obeys the associative law.
   (d) Solve the equation $x * 3 = 19$.
   (e) For what value of x is $x * 3 = x$?

❷ Calculating Fractions and Decimals

1 A jug is $\frac{5}{8}$ full. When 0.45 litres are poured in, the jug becomes $\frac{7}{8}$ full.
   (a) How many litres does the jug hold?
   (b) How many glasses each holding 0.13 litres can be filled from the jug?
   (c) How many litres are there left in the jug?

2 A 'light year' is defined as the distance light travels in one year (365 days). Given that the speed of light is 3×10^8 m/s, find the length of a light year in km in standard form.

3 **(a)** If $0.07 \times 6.9 = K \times 10^n$, where $1 \leqslant K < 10$ and n is an integer, work out the values of K and n.
   (b) If $b = 2.7 \times 10^3$, find **(i)** b^3 **(ii)** b^{-2}.

❸ Using Ratios and Rates

1 The height of a tree in a photograph is 4.4 cm. The photograph is enlarged in the ratio $7 : 2$.
   (a) Find the height of the tree in the new photograph.
   The length of a road is now 11.9 cm.
   (b) Find the length of the road in the original photograph.

2 A map has a scale of $1 : 20\,000$. This means that 1 cm on the map represents 20 000 cm or 200 m on the ground, that is 1 cm to 200 m. Note that this may also be written as 5 cm to 1 km.
   $\frac{1}{20\,000}$ is called the **representative fraction** (RF).

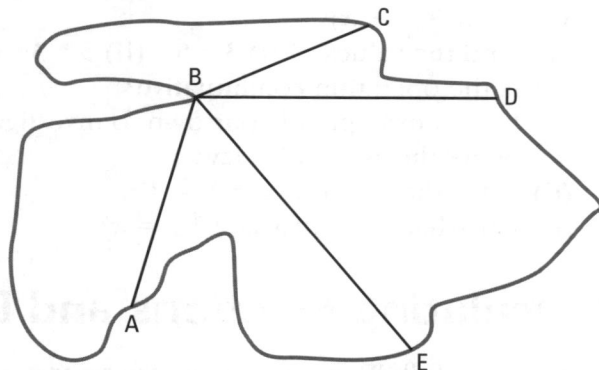

Scale 1 cm : 2 km

The diagram above is the plan of an island. On the island the shortest route between C and D by road is via B.

(a) Find the RF of the plan.

(b) On the diagram, measure the lengths CB and BD; and the length CD.

(c) Using the scale, find the actual distance from C to D
     (i) by road   **(ii)** by sea.

(d) What is the actual difference in the distances of A and E from B?

④ Approximation and Estimation

1 Explain the difference in meaning between '*30 kg to the nearest kg*' and '*30 kg to the nearest 10 kg*'.

2 Between what limits does each of the following lie:
  (a) 48 to the nearest whole number
  (b) 4600 to the nearest hundred
  (c) 0.07 to 2 decimal places
  (d) 50.7 to 3 significant figures?

3 A man estimates that he walks at 2 m/s. He leaves home at 10:13 to walk 1.8 km to catch a train that leaves at 10:30.
  (a) If the estimate of his speed is correct, work out how many minutes he will have to wait for the train.
  (b) If he really walks at $1\frac{1}{2}$ m/s, will he miss the train? If yes, by how many minutes?

4 Estimate to 2 s.f. the amount of money to be received weekly if an average of 230 items are sold for $ 6.70 each.

Chapter 5 *Consumer Arithmetic*

---

❶ Profit and Loss

1 Copy and complete the table. Calculate all monetary values to the nearest cent.

	Marked price	Selling price	Discount	VAT (17.5%)
(a)	$ 175	$ 155.75		
(b)	$ 1998		27%	
(c)		$ 110.98	8%	
(d)			14%	$ 89.60

2 *Comfy Clothes* sells shoes at a 25% discount. The selling price is $ 34.50. They make a 20% profit on the selling price. What percentage profit would they have made on the marked price?

❹ Interest

1 (a) Calculate the simple interest paid on a loan of $ 8000 with a rate of interest 10% over 5 years.

(b) Suppose that at the end of each year the interest is added to the principal.
How much interest is paid?

(c) How much more interest was paid in **(b)** than **(a)**?

2 Remember there is a formula for finding the simple interest paid on the principal:

$$I = \frac{PRT}{100}$$

where I is the interest, P is the principal, R is the rate of interest, T is the time in years.

The amount owed after T years is the principal + the interest, that is

$$\text{amount} = P + I$$

$$= P + \frac{PRT}{100}$$

There is a similar formula for the amount owed after T years when paying compound interest:

$$\text{amount} = P \times \left(1 + \frac{R}{100}\right)^{T}$$

where P, R, T are the same as before. This can be used instead of adding up the interest each year, as you did in the chapter.

(a) Use this formula to find the amount owed, to the nearest cent, in the following cases (remember BoMDAS):

    (i) principal \$ 2000, rate of interest 5% after 3 years

    (ii) principal \$ 750, rate of interest 7% after 2 years

    (iii) principal \$ 1800, rate of interest 3% after 3 years.

(b) Check the formula by calculating the answers to (a) using the method used in the chapter.

(c) You might ask why we need a formula when we already know a way to calculate the amount owed. Suppose Ameerah invested \$ 670 in a savings account giving a $3\frac{1}{2}$ % interest rate for 19 years.

    (i) Calculate the amount using the formula.

    (ii) Try it using the method used in the chapter. (You might get bored!)

Chapter 6 *Angles, solids and shapes*

---

❶ Angles and lines

1 Find the size of the angles marked x and y in the following diagram.

Give reasons for your answers.

(*Parallel lines are marked with arrows.*)

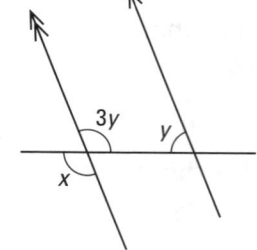

2 (a) Copy the diagram on the right and mark in any equal angles.

    (b) Explain how this diagram can be used to prove that the angles of a triangle add up to 180°.

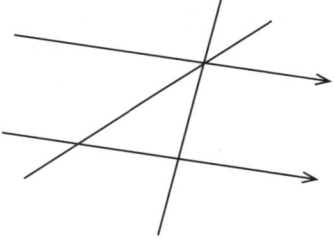

❷ Angles in triangles and quadrilaterals

(In questions 1 and 2, use centimetre-squared paper of sides 10 cm.)

1 Draw the following triangles
  (a) The largest possible isosceles triangle.
  (b) The largest possible obtuse-angled triangle.
  (c) The smallest possible acute-angled triangle.
  (d) The smallest possible right-angled, scalene triangle.

2 Change the position of the vertex C to obtain the following triangles.
  (a) Isosceles triangle with two sides of length 8.6 cm.
  (b) Isosceles triangle with two angles of 39°.
  (c) Right-angled triangle with a side of length 13.5 cm.
  (d) Scalene triangle with sides of length 10 cm, 13.0 cm and 7.1 cm.

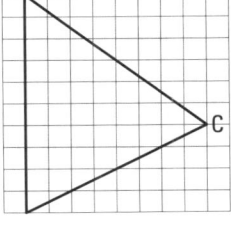

3 Each grid shows one diagonal of a quadrilateral.
For each one, draw in the sides of the named quadrilateral.

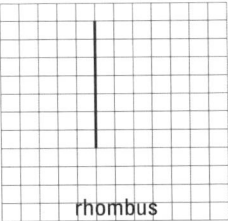

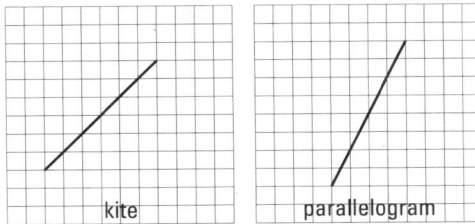

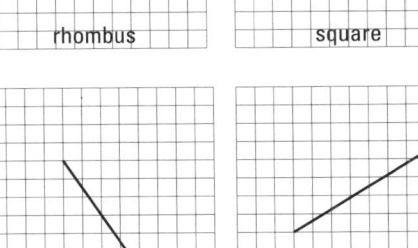

❸ Properties of polygons

1 (a) From any point *within* the following polygons, draw a line to *each* vertex and use the resulting figure to find the sum of its interior angles
    (i) quadrilateral   **(ii)** pentagon   **(iii)** hexagon   **(iv)** octagon.
  (b) Hence, derive the formula for the sum of the interior angles of an *n*-sided polygon.

2 A regular pentagon and a regular octagon have a common side as shown in the diagram at right. Find the size of angle *x*.

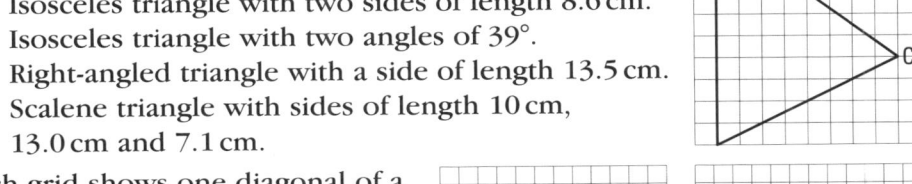

3 Sketch a hexagon which has rotational symmetry of order 2 and (a)2, (b)0 lines of symmetry.

❹ **Properties of solids**

1 A skeleton square-based pyramid is made from wire. All the edges are the same length. If the length of wire used is 40 cm, find the length of each edge of the pyramid.

2 On centimetre-squared paper draw a plan and side elevation of your classroom. State the scale you are using and indicate clearly the doors and windows.

3 Investigate and identify the five possible convex regular polyhedra. Draw diagrams to illustrate your answer.

Chapter 7 *Units of measurement*

---

❶ **Basic units of measurement**

1 Four bananas weigh approximately 640 g. and cost $3.60. A woman buys $2\frac{5}{8}$ kg of bananas.
  (a) Approximately how many bananas will she get?
  (b) Find how much she will have to pay.

2 A boy whirled a stone round at the end of a piece of string of length 63 cm The string made 120 revolutions per minute. Find the speed of the stone in centimeters per second, writing your answer in standard form.

3 The pages of a dictionary are numbered from 1 to 1632. The dictionary is 6.4 cm thick (excluding covers).
  (a) How many thicknesses of paper make 1632 numbered pages?
  (b) Estimate the thickness of one page, giving your answer in metres in standard form correct to 1 sig. fig.

4 The departure time of an airline is 13:40 for a journey that is scheduled to take 4h 40 min. The flight was delayed and left at 14:25 and arrived at its destination 35 min after the scheduled time of arrival. Work out:
  (a) The actual time taken for the journey.
  (b) The time of arrival.

❷ Perimeter and area

1 **(a)** A rope is wound 50 times round a cylinder of
radius 25 cm as in the diagram. Find the
approximate length of the rope.
(*Use the value 3.14 for π.*)
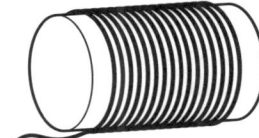
(b) Why is this an approximation?

2 A rectangular area, 8.55 m long by 5.89 m wide, is to be paved with the
largest possible square tiles which will fit in exactly.
(a) Calculate the length of the side of one tile.
(b) How many tiles will there be?

3 The cross-section of a chest is a square joined to a trapezium as shown in
the diagram at right.
(a) Calculate the outer surface
area of the chest.
(b) Find the cost of painting this
surface of the chest at $ 200
per square metre.

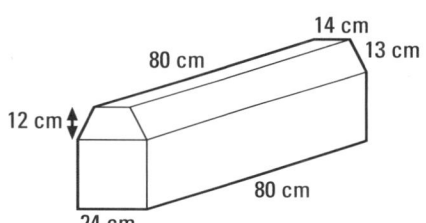

❸ Volume and capacity

1 A roll of paper is wound tightly onto a wooden cylinder 8 cm in diameter.
The roll of paper, as delivered to an office, is 60 cm in diameter. The
paper is 0.005 cm thick. Find the length of paper on the roll.
(*Hint: consider the area of the edge (cross-section) of the paper when on
the roll and when unrolled.*)

2 The base of a rectangular tin measures 9 cm by 7 cm internally. It contains
water to a depth of 4 cm. A solid iron cylindrical bar 8 cm long and 6 cm
in diameter is placed in the tin so that a circular face rests on the base.
Calculate the rise in the water level in the tin.

3 The diagram at right shows a cylinder of height
$2l$, and a sphere of diameter $2l$ that fits exactly into
the cylinder.
(a) Show that the surface area of the sphere is
equal to the curved surface area of the cylinder.
A cone has the same circular base and height as
the cylinder.
(b) Find the volume of:
    (i) The cylinder   **(ii)** The sphere   **(iii)** The cone.
(c) Work out and simplify the ratio of the volumes of the cone, cylinder
and sphere.

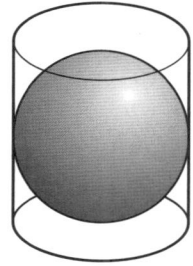

④ Accuracy in measurement

1 A rectangular picture has dimensions 8.2 cm and 10.3 cm. Measurements are taken to the nearest 0.1 cm. Between what limits do the following values lie:

(a) The total distance round the edges of the picture.

(b) The area of the picture.

2 A cyclist travels 82 m , measured to the nearest metre, in 15 seconds, to the nearest second. His average speed is calculated to 2 sig. fig.: Write down:

(a) The greatest and least possible distances.

(b) The greatest and least possible times.

Calculate to 2 sig. fig.:

(c) The greatest possible speed.

(d) The least possible speed.

3 On a map, the area representing a park is found to be 72 cm². On a second map, the same park is represented by an area of 200 cm².

(a) Find the ratio of:

  (i) The areas in its simplest form.

  (ii) The lengths of a path in the park.

The scale on the first map is 1 cm to 600 m.

(b) Calculate the scale of the second map.

Chapter 8 *Algebraic Processes*

---

① Algebraic Expressions

1 Simplify the following.

(a) $3x - y + 2y + x$ **(b)** $h - 2k + 3 - k + 2h - 1$

(c) $3(2a + b)d - ad$ **(d)** $(h - 2j)(h - 2) - 3h^2$

(e) $(3x - y)x - (2x + y)(x + y)$ **(f)** $(s - 2t + 3)s - (t + 2 + 2s)t$

(g) $(m - 2n)p + (p + n)m$ **(h)** $(h - 2k + 3)k - (k + 2h - 1)h$

2 Write the information in each of the following as an algebraic expression.

(a) The number of lengths of the pool that Gabby swims in m minutes if she swims one length of the pool in t seconds.

(b) The change Genna receives from $ 100 if she buys x CDs at $ c each and y DVDs at $ d each.

❷ Laws of Indices

1 Simplify
  (a) $4x^3 + 4x^3$ **(b)** $4x^3 - 4x^3$ **(c)** $4x^3 \times 4x^3$ **(d)** $4x^3 \div 4x^3$ **(e)** $(4x^3)^3$

2 (a) Express in the form x^n

  (i) $\dfrac{1}{x^5}$ **(ii)** $\sqrt[5]{x}$ **(iii)** $\dfrac{1}{\sqrt{x}}$ **(iv)** $(\sqrt{x})^5$ **(v)** $(\sqrt[5]{x})^3$

(b) Simplify
  (i) $(\tfrac{3}{8})^{-1}$ **(ii)** $a^{-3} \times c^0$ **(iii)** $(-3f^{-2})^3$ **(iv)** $\dfrac{(-x^3)^2}{-x^4}$

  (v) $x^3y^2 \times xy^{-1}$ **(vi)** $r^3 \div (4r)^{\frac{2}{3}}$ **(vii)** $(3h)^{\frac{1}{2}} \times h^{-\frac{1}{2}}$ **(viii)** $m^{\frac{1}{3}} \div m^{-\frac{3}{2}}$

❸ Substitution and Formulae

1 (a) A woman has \$ x in an account. She adds \$ d every week for n weeks. She then has \$ y in the account. Write the formula connecting y and x.
  (b) Use the formula to find n when $x = 560$, $d = 35$, and $y = 980$.

2 (a) Using $F = \dfrac{M}{8 + 2} + 2$ and $T = \dfrac{M}{4F}$, write T in terms of F only.

  (b) Make n the subject of the formula $p = \dfrac{2n - 3}{n + 5}$.

3 Two binary operations, ◉ and ☼ are defined as follows:

  ◉ is the remainder when the sum of two numbers is divided by 5.

  ☼ is the remainder when the product of two numbers is divided by 5.

  Evaluate
  (a) 4 ◉ 3 **(b)** 3 ☼ 4 **(c)** $(4$ ◉ $3)$ ☼ 4 **(d)** $(2$ ☼ $3)$ ☼ 4

❹ Expansion and Factorisation

1 In each of the following expand the brackets and collect like terms when possible.
  (a) $(x + 3)(2x + 7)$ **(b)** $3x(x - 1)$ **(c)** $(-x - 3)(2x - 1)$
  (d) $2(3x - 2)(2x + 3)$ **(e)** $(3x + 1)(3x + 1)$ **(f)** $(2x + 5)(2x - 5)$
  (g) $(2x + 1)^2 + (x - 3)^2$ **(h)** $(2x - y)^2 - (x + y)^2$ **(i)** $(x - y)^2 - (x + y)^2$
  (j) $(b - 4)(b - 3) - b(b - 7)$ **(k)** $c(c - 3) + (c - 1)(c - 2)$

2 Factorise each of the following expressions.

(a) $2x + 4y - 8w$ (b) $30c^2d + 42cd^2$ (c) $\dfrac{5a^3 - a^2}{2a}$

(d) $3f(g + h) - 2(g + h)$ (e) $\dfrac{6y - 4}{6y + 2}$ (f) $(R - h)^2 + 2(R - h)$

(g) $\dfrac{9xy - 6y}{3yx + 2y}$ (h) $(2n^2 - 3n) + (6mn - 9m)$ (i) $(x^2 + xy) + (xy + y^2)$

❺ Algebraic Fractions

Simplify the following fractions.

1 $\dfrac{x + 2}{2} + \dfrac{1 - x}{3}$ **2** $\dfrac{x - 4}{x + 2} - \dfrac{3}{5}$

3 $\dfrac{m - 3}{2m} - \dfrac{3n + 1}{6n}$ **4** $\dfrac{4}{y - 2} - \dfrac{3}{y + 3}$

5 $\dfrac{h - 4}{h + 3} - \dfrac{5}{6} + \dfrac{1 - h}{h + 1}$ **6** $\dfrac{3y - 1}{2y} - \dfrac{y}{6} + \dfrac{1 - 3y}{3}$

Chapter 9 *Linear Equations and Inequalities*

❶ Linear Equations

Solve the following equations.

1 (a) $3a - a + 2a + a = 1$ (b) $d - 2d + 1 = d + 2d - 1$

(c) $2(2w + 3) = \dfrac{3w}{2}$ (d) $-3(v - 2)(v + 2) + 3v^2 = 2v$

(e) $\dfrac{x + 2}{2} + \dfrac{1 - 3x}{3} = \dfrac{1}{3}$ (f) $\dfrac{x - 2}{x + 2} = \dfrac{3}{5}$

(g) $(b - 4)(b - 3) = b(b - 5)$ (h) $c(c - 5) + 6 = (c - 1)(c - 2)$

2 (a) A team played 20 matches. The team won 6 more matches than it lost. No match was drawn. Find the number of matches the team lost.

(b) One third of a number, n, is added to twice the number and then the total is subtracted from 20. If the final number is 6, find the original number, n.

❷ Identities

1 If $c(2x - 3) + 2d \equiv 4x + 2$, where c and d are constants, find c and d.

2 If $(x + p)^2 - (y + q)^2 \equiv (x + y + 1)(x - y - 3)$, where p and q are constants, find p and q.

❸ Linear Inequalities

1 Write the following inequalities using one of the inequality symbols.
  (a) −5 is less than −2.
  (b) h, the height of the cylinder, is greater than or equal to r, the radius of the base.
  (c) $(x + 2)$ is not equal to $(2x − 3)$.
  (d) w, the weight of the parcel, must not be greater than 5 kg.

2 State whether the *solution* of each of the following examples is correct or incorrect, giving the reason for your answer.

  (a) *Example* List three members of the solution set of
$$3x − (x + 1) > 7 \text{ , where } x \in \{integer\}.$$
  Working
$$2x + 1 > 7$$
$$2x > 7 + 1$$
$$x > 4$$
  Answer $\{5, 6, 7, \ldots\}$

  (b) *Example* Solve $\frac{3x}{4} − \frac{4x}{5} \leqslant −\frac{1}{2}$, where $x \in W$
  Working
$$\frac{15x}{20} − \frac{16x}{20} \leqslant −\frac{10}{20}$$
$$−\frac{x}{20} \leqslant −\frac{10}{20}x$$
  Answer $x \leqslant 10$

3 The traffic regulations state that the speed of vehicles along a certain road must not be more than 80 km/h but must be more than 40 km//h.
  (a) Express this rule using inequality symbols.
  (b) Show the range of values using a number line.

❹ Simultaneous Linear Equations

1 Solve the following simultaneous equations.

  (a)
$$\frac{m − 3}{2} = \frac{3n + 1}{3} − \frac{10}{3}$$
$$\frac{m − 4}{3} + \frac{3m + 4n}{6} = \frac{5}{6}$$

  (b)
$$\frac{6}{2x − 1} = \frac{3}{y + 1}$$
$$\frac{3y − 1}{2} − 6x = \frac{2x + y}{6}$$

2 When a student runs for 1 hour at u km/h and $\frac{1}{2}$ hour at v km/h, he travels a total distance of 13 km. When he runs for $\frac{1}{2}$ hour at u km/h and 1 hour at v km/h, he travels a total distance of 14 km. Find u and v.

3 A father is 28 years older than his son. In 4 years he will be twice as old as his son. Find their present ages.

Chapter 10 *Statistics*

❶ Types of Data

1 Choose a random page in this book.

(a) Choose ten lines at random and count the number of words on each line. Is this data discrete or continuous? Qualitative or quantitative?

(b) Use this to guess the number of words on that page.

(c) Do you think there are about the same number of words per line on this page as on any other in the book? What about the number of lines on a page?

(d) Estimate the percentage of the page that is text. How much is pictures, tables, graphs, etc.?

❷ Collecting Data

1 The table shows the distribution of top speeds for a selection of cars.

Top speed (km/h)	Frequency	Lower class boundary	Upper class boundary	Mid-point	Class interval
110–119	14	109.5			
120–124	17				
125–129	19				
130–134	13				
135–149	10		149.5		

(a) Copy and complete the table.

(b) **(i)** How many cars have a top speed less than 119.5 km/h?

(ii) How many have a top speed greater than 129.5 km/h?

(c) How many cars have a top speed of between 124.5 and 134.5 km/h?

❸ Presenting Data

1 The table shows the heights of 150 children at the ages of 12, 14 and 16.

Height (cm)	105–120	121–130	141–150	151–160	161–180
Age 12	54	48	36	12	0
Age 14	27	40	57	15	11
Age 16	15	23	42	38	32

(a) On the same axes, draw the frequency polygon for children aged 12, 14 and 16.

(b) Draw a histogram of the data for the 16-year-olds.

Hint: The class widths are not equeal so plot

$$\text{frequency density} = \frac{\text{frequency}}{\text{class width}} \text{ against the height.}$$

❹ Averages and Spread

1 A stationery shop sells paper clips in packs of 200. They open a few packs to check that there are enough inside.

Number	186–195	196–200	201–205	206–210	211–***
Frequency	12	16	26	22	11

(a) Given that the range of numbers of paper clips is 24, find the missing number ***.

(b) Find the mean of the data.

2 The table shows the sizes of cans of paint bought at a hardware store.

Size (ml)	250	500	1000	2000
Frequency	79	196	167	155

(a) Calculate the mean, median and mode.

(b) Imagine you are the shop-keeper, and you could only buy one size of tin. Which average would you use? Why?

❺ Cumulative Frequency and Percentiles

1 The two cumulative frequency curves show the times it takes a selection of men and women to complete the 400 m.

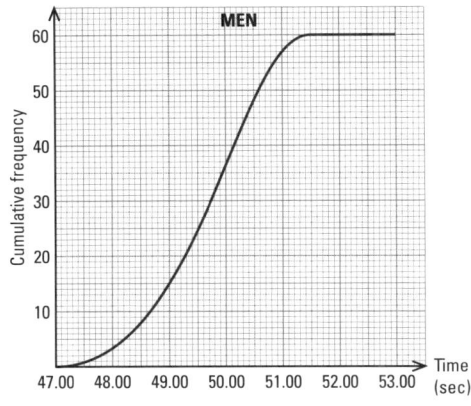

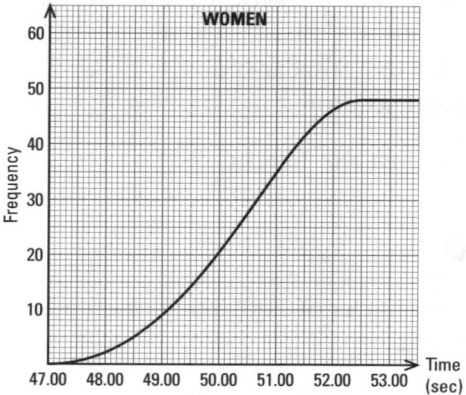

(a) How many men and how many women were timed?

(b) Find the medians and interquartile ranges for the men and women.

(c) What do these statistics tell you about the times for men and women?

(d) If they all started running at the same time, how many women would still be running when all the men had finished?

Chapter 11 *Probability*

❶ Theoretical and Experimental Probability

1 Start tossing a coin. Keep a count of the number of heads and the number of tosses. Plot a graph of $\dfrac{\text{number of heads}}{\text{number of tosses}}$ against the number of tosses.

What do you expect the graph to look like after you have tossed the coin a few times? What does the graph look like? Do you think the coin is fair?

❸ Expected Outcomes

1 Open up this book to a double-page spread that has lots of numbers on it.

(a) Work out the probability that a number on the page begins with a 1, and the probability that it begins with a 2.

There is a law (called Benford's law) that predicts that the probability of a number beginning with a 1 is 0.3, and that the probability of a number beginning with a 2 is 0.18.

(b) How well do your results for your chosen pages compare with this? If they don't agree, why do you think that is?

(c) Suppose there are 22 500 numbers in this book. According to Benford's law, how many of these do you expect to begin with a 1 and how many to begin with a 2?

❹ Possibility Spaces

1 When we toss two coins the possible combinations are {HH}, {HT}, {TH}, {TT}.

Suppose we toss three coins.
(a) Create a possibility space diagram.
(b) What is the probability of getting
    (i) three heads?   **(ii)** two heads and a tail?   **(iii)** more than one tail?
(c) How many possible combinations do you think there are when we toss four coins? What about five, six, seven, …? Is there a pattern?

Chapter 12 *Geometry and Trigonometry 1*

---

❶ Constructions

Ruler and compasses

1 (a) Draw a circle of radius 4 cm and draw any two chords in the circle.
(b) Construct the perpendicular bisectors of the chords.
(c) What do you notice about the bisectors?

❷ Pythagoras' Theorem

1 Pythagoras' theorem says:

'In a right-angled triangle, the square of the hypotenuse is equal to the sum of the squares of the other two sides.'

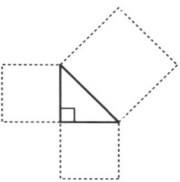

In other words, if you construct squares on the sides of a right-angled triangle the area of the square on the hypotenuse is equal to the sum of the areas of the squares on the other two sides.

You could also construct other shapes on the sides of a triangle. Investigate the relationship between the areas of semi-circles drawn on the sides.

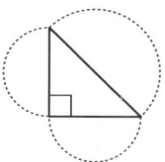

❸ Trigonometric Ratios

1 Remember that $\sin A = \dfrac{\text{opp}}{\text{hyp}}$, $\cos A = \dfrac{\text{adj}}{\text{hyp}}$ and $\tan A = \dfrac{\text{opp}}{\text{adj}}$.

Use this to prove that $\tan A = \dfrac{\sin A}{\cos A}$ for any angle A.

2 We could write Pythagoras' theorem as $(\text{hyp})^2 = (\text{adj})^2 + (\text{opp})^2$.

Use this and the trigonometric ratios to show that $(\sin A)^2 + (\cos A)^2 = 1$ for any angle A.

❻ Trigonometric Ratios of Special Angles

1 Earlier we used a special triangle to find exact values of $\sin 45°$, $\cos 45°$ and $\tan 45°$.

Use an equilateral triangle with sides of length 2 to find the exact values of $\sin 30°$, $\cos 30°$, $\tan 30°$, $\sin 60°$, $\cos 60°$ and $\tan 60°$,

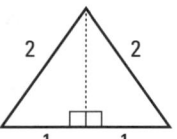

Chapter 13 *Transformation Geometry*

---

❷ Reflections

1 The **inverse** of a transformation is the transformation that moves the image back to the original object.

For example, if a triangle is translated

through $\begin{pmatrix} 1 \\ 4 \end{pmatrix}$. The inverse translation moves

the image back to the object.

So the inverse is $\begin{pmatrix} -1 \\ -4 \end{pmatrix}$.

Find the inverses of these transformations.

(a) Translation through $\begin{pmatrix} 1 \\ 4 \end{pmatrix}$ **(b)** Translation through $\begin{pmatrix} -3 \\ -2 \end{pmatrix}$

(c) Reflection in $y = 1$ **(d)** Reflection in $y = x$

2 Can you see a rule for finding the inverse of a translation? What about for reflections?

❹ Enlargements

1 The **identity** transformation is a transformation for which the image is the same as the object. It is a transformation that doesn't do anything! Try to find the identity translation.

2 Draw a triangle on a piece of squared paper. Try to find the identity rotation and identity enlargement.

3 We considered the inverses of translations and rotations in **Reflections** questions 1 and 2. Find the inverses of these transformations.
   (a) Rotation 90° clockwise, centre origin
   (b) Rotation 180°, centre (2, 1)
   (c) Enlargement, centre (−1, 2), scale factor 3
   (d) Enlargement, centre (0, 3), scale factor $\frac{1}{2}$

Chapter 14 *Circle Geometry*

---

❶ Arcs, Sectors and Segments

1 Find the areas of these shaded shapes in terms of x and π.

(a)

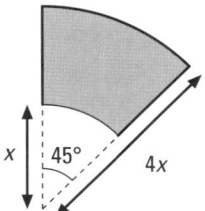

(b)

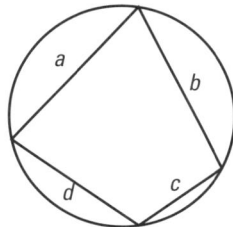

❸ Cyclic Quadrilaterals

1 In the seventh century AD an astronomer and mathematician called Brahmagupta found a formula for the area of a cyclic quadrilateral. The area of any cyclic quadrilateral with sides a, b, c and d is given by

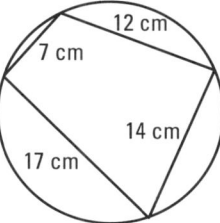

$$\sqrt{(s - a)(s - b)(s - c)(s - d)}$$

where $s = \frac{1}{2}(a + b + c + d)$.

s is half the perimeter of the quadrilateral.

Find the area of each of these cyclic shapes to one decimal place.

(a)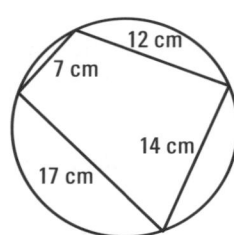

(b)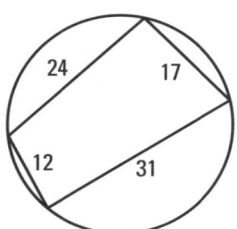

(c)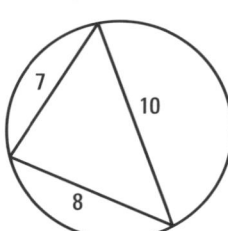

❹ Tangents

1 A tangent AB touches a circle, centre O, at B.

A$\hat{B}$C $= x$.

(a) Calculate B$\hat{D}$C in terms of x.

(b) Hence prove the alternate segment theorem.

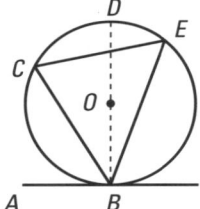

Chapter 15 *Straight-line Graphs*

---

❶ Gradient of a Straight Line

1 (a) Write down the gradient of the line, corresponding to each of the following relations:

(i) $y = 7x$ **(ii)** $y - 5x = 0$ **(iii)** $2y + x = 0$

(iv) $\dfrac{y}{x} = m$ **(v)** $y = kx$ **(vi)** $2y = mx = 0$

(b) Which of the lines **(i)**, **(ii)**, **(iii)** has the greatest gradient and which has the least?

(c) Sketch each of the lines in **(b)**.

2 (a) Draw the graph of the line $4x + 2y = 5$.

(b) Calculate the gradient by using two points on the line.

❷ Equation of a Straight Line

1 Given that $y = 2x + 3$ and $x = 3t + 5$,

(a) find the relation between y and t

(b) describe the relation.

2 If $y = m_1x + c_1$, $x = m_2t + c_2$ and $y = m_3t + c_3$, find m_3 in terms of m_1 and m_2, and c_3 in terms of c_1 and c_2.

❸ Mid-point of a Line

1 In the triangle TOF shown in the diagram,
where O is the origin and OF = X,
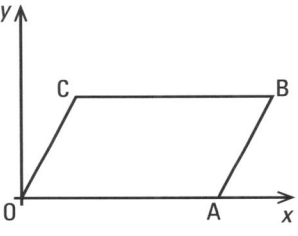
   (a) find the coordinates of the mid-point
      (i) J of TO   (ii) K of TF.
   (b) Comment on the *y*-coordinates of J and K.
   (c) Find the coordinates of the mid-points of TO and TF when the
      coordinates of T are (x_1, y_1) .
   (d) What can you deduce about the line joining J and K?

2 A parallelogram OABC is drawn as in the
diagram with coordinates O (0, 0), A (4, 0)
and B (6, 3).
   (a) Find the coordinates of C.
   (b) Work out the coordinates of the
      mid-point of (i) OB and (ii) CA.
   (c) Comment on the special property of a
      parallelogram that is illustrated.
   (d) If in another parallelogram, the coordinates of A are (5, 0) and C are
      (1, 3), find the coordinates of B.
   (e) In a third parallelogram, the coordinates of A are (6, 0) and the
      coordinates of the point of intersection of the diagonals are (2, 2).
      Find the coordinates of B and C.

❹ Length of a Line

1 (a) Prove that the distance of the point (x_1, y_1) from the origin is
      $\sqrt{(x_1^2 + y_1^2)}$
   (b)   (i) Explain why points which satisfy the equation
         $\sqrt{(x_1^2 + y_1^2)} = 10$ lie on a circle.
      (ii) State the coordinates of the centre of the circle.
      (iii) Find the radius of the circle.

2 (a) The coordinates of the vertices of the
      rectangle in the diagram are O (0, 0),
      A (*a*, 0), B (*a*, *b*) and C (0, *b*).
      (i) Find the length of OB and of CA.
      (ii) Comment on the property of
         rectangles that is illustrated.
   (b) By using a similar method, show that the
      diagonals of an isosceles trapezium are equal in length.
      (*Hint: Use the symmetry properties of the isosceles trapezium.*)

Chapter 16 *Linear Inequalities in Two Variables*

❶ Linear Inequalities in Two Variables

1 (a) On centimetre-squared paper, draw the line $y = x$.
Take 5 random points above the line and 5 random points below the line. Compare the x- and y-values for each ordered pair. Shade the region of the points that do *not* satisfy the set $\{(x, y) : x < y\}$.
Comment on the points on the line.

(b) Repeat (a), for the line $y = -x$ and the set of points $\{(x, y) : y \leqslant -x\}$.

(c) Repeat (a), for the line $y = 2x + 6$, comparing the y-values with $2x + 6$ for each point. Hence, leave unshaded the set of points where $\{(x, y) : y \geqslant 2x + 6\}$.

2 Indicate, by leaving unshaded, the region in which the solution sets lie for each of the following pairs of inequalities.

(a) $x + y > 5$
$2x - 3y < 3$

(b) $2x - y \leqslant 7$
$x + 3y > 5$

3 If $4x + 5y = K$, find the greatest value of K when (x, y) are in the set $P = \{(x, y) : 0 \leqslant x \leqslant 2\frac{1}{2}, 5y \leqslant 2x + 25\}$.

4 (a) On graph paper, draw the lines $x = 3$, $y = 1$ and $x + y = 6$.

(b) Indicate the set of points that satisfy the inequalities $x \geqslant 3$, $y > 1$ and $x + y \leqslant 6$ by shading the regions of the points that do not satisfy the inequalities.

(c) Write down all the ordered pairs of integers that satisfy these inequalities.

(d) If $u = 2x + y$, calculate the value of u at each of the above points.

(e) At which point is u greatest?

5 In the diagram on the right, the equations of the straight lines are
AB: $x + 2y = 12$
BC: $y = 2$
CA: $2x + y = 6$

(a) Write down three inequalities for the unshaded region.

(b) Find the coordinates of A, B and C.

(c) If $w = 2x + 3y$, find the value of w at A, B, and C. At which point is w greatest?

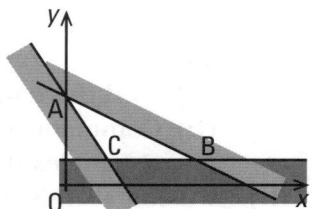

❷ Linear Programming

1 Factory A and factory B make two products, X and Y. Item X takes $\frac{1}{2}$ hour at factory A and 1 hour at factory B. Item B takes 1 hour at both Factory A and Factory B.

The profit from item X is $ 12 and from item Y is $ 16. Factory A works for 8 hours a day and factory B works for 10 hours a day.
   (a) Calculate the number of each item to be produced each day for a maximum profit.
   (b) Work out the maximum profit.

2 A cook blends two types of mixed herbs for a special dish. In mix X there are 4 units of A and 10 units of B per packet, while in mix Y there are 5 units of A and 5 units of B per packet. She needs a mixture containing at least 20 units of A and 30 units of B in $(x + y)$ packets. If mix X costs $ 5 per packet and mix Y costs $ 4 per packet, work out the cheapest way she can get the correct mix.

Chapter 17 *Quadratic Expressions*

---

❶ Expansion

1 Using squares of side x and of side y, draw a diagram to illustrate the terms in the quadratic expressions for
   (a) the perfect squares: **(i)** $(x + y)^2 = x^2 + 2xy + y^2$
   (ii) $(x - y)^2 = x^2 - 2xy + y^2$
   (b) the difference of two squares: $(x^2 - y^2) = (x + y)(x - y)$

2 Use quadratic expressions to find the value of the following without using a calculator or doing long multiplication:
   (a) 19^2 **(b)** 31^2 **(c)** $23^2 - 19^2$ **(d)** 98^2 **(e)** $75^2 - 70^2$
   (f) 1003^2 **(g)** $83^2 - 17^2$ **(h)** 85^2 **(i)** $65^2 - 35^2$ **(j)** 999^2

❷ Factorisation

1 Simplify the following expressions.
   (a) $\dfrac{x^2 - 4}{x^2 - x - 6}$ **(b)** $\dfrac{x^3 - 16x}{x^2 - 4x}$ **(c)** $\dfrac{2x^2 + 3x - 2}{x^2 - 4}$

2 Using factors, evaluate:
   (a) $0.72^2 - 0.28^2$ **(b)** $\dfrac{32}{5.4^2 - 4.6^2}$ **(c)** $\dfrac{3.6 \times 68 + 3.6 \times 32}{6.8^2 - 3.2^2}$

❸ Quadratic Functions

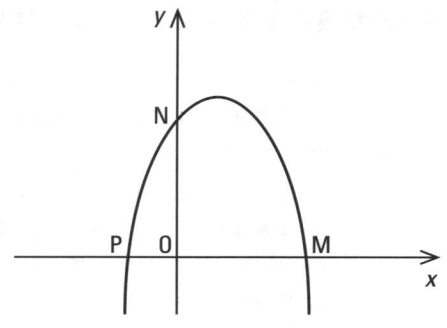

1 The diagram on the right is a sketch
graph of $y = 6 + x - x^2$. Find
   (a) the coordinates of the points N, P
   and M
   (b) the gradient of the line NM.

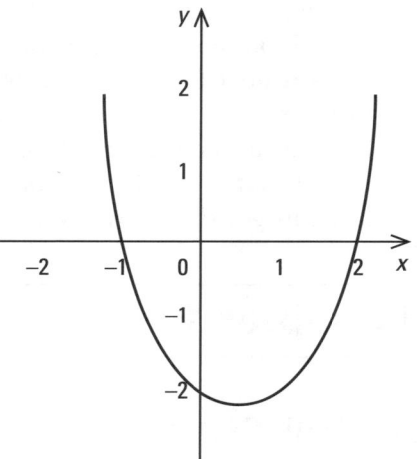

2 (a) Find the equation of the function
   represented by the graph in the
   diagram on the right.
   (b) Identify the turning point on the
   curve.
   (c) State the value of the function and
   the x-value at which it occurs.

3 Without drawing the graph of the
   relation $y = (4 - x)(2 + x)$,
   (a) write down the coordinates of the
   points where the curve cuts
      (i) the x-axis   **(ii)** the y-axis
   (b) state whether the curve has a maximum or a minimum value of y and
   write down the value of x at this point
   (c) find the corresponding value of y.

Chapter 18 *Quadratic Equations and Graphs*

---

❶ Algebraic Solution

1 (a) A boy gave the solution set of the quadratic equation
   $x^2 + 7x + 12 = 0$ to be $\{3, 4\}$. How can you tell *immediately* that
   this was not the correct set?
   (b) A girl was given the equation $x^2 + 2\frac{1}{6}x - \frac{5}{6} = 0$ to solve. She guessed
   from a sketch graph that $\frac{1}{3}$ was one of the roots. She then calculated
   that the other root must be $\frac{5}{2}$. Was her calculation correct? Show your
   working and give reasons for your answer.

2 In the general quadratic equation $ax^2 + bx + c = 0$, the roots are given by

$$x = \frac{-b \pm \sqrt{(b^2 - 4ac)}}{2a}$$

The expression $b^2 - 4ac$ is called the **discriminant** because it discriminates between three different cases.

If $b^2 > 4ac$ – there are two distinct roots.

If $b^2 < 4ac$ – there are no roots that belong to the set of *real* numbers.

If $b^2 = 4ac$ – there is one repeated root and the quadratic function is a perfect square.

(a) Use the discriminant to decide which of the following equations have two roots, one repeated root or no real roots.

  (i) $x^2 + 3x + 5 = 0$ (ii) $x^2 + 2x + 1 = 0$
  (iii) $x^2 + x - 2 = 0$ (iv) $x^2 - x - 1 = 0$
  (v) $2x^2 - x + 1 = 0$ (vi) $2x^2 - 3x - 1 = 0$

(b) If X^1 and X^2 are the roots of the equation $ax^2 + bx + c = 0$,

  show that **(i)** $X_1 + X_2 = -\dfrac{b}{a}$

  (ii) $X_1 X_2 = \dfrac{c}{a}$

(c) Given the equation $2x^2 + x - 4 = 0$,

  (i) write the sum of the roots
  (ii) write the product of the roots.

3 When the denary number 89 is represented on a three-spike abacus, there are 4 beads on the unit spike, 2 on the second spike and 3 on the third spike. Find the number base of the abacus.

4 The distance s metres travelled by a train in t seconds is given by the equation $s = ut + \frac{1}{2}at^2$, where u metres per second is its initial speed and a metres per second per second is its acceleration.

The train enters a station that is $140\,\text{m}$ long at a speed of $7\,\text{m/s}$ and travels through with an acceleration of $3.5\,\text{m/s}^2$. Find the time it will take for the train to pass through.

❷ Graphical Solution

1 The incomplete table on the right gives corresponding values for the function

x	-2	-1	0	1	2	3	4
y	-4	1	4				

$y = px^2 + 2x + 4$, for $-2 \leqslant x \leqslant 4$ where p is a constant.

(a) Use the table to find the value of the constant p.

(b) Copy and complete the table of values.

(c) Using a scale of 2 cm to 1 unit on both axes, draw the graph of the function for the given domain.

(d) Use your graph to obtain the roots of the following equations.

    (i) $px^2 + 2x + 4 = 0$

    (ii) $px^2 + 2x + 4 = 2$

(e) From your graph, write down the equation of the line of symmetry.

2 A stone is projected vertically upwards. Its position after t sec is given by the ordered pair (t, s), where s metres is the distance moved. The set of pairs representing the motion is $\{(t, s) : s = 18t - 3t^2\}$.

(a) Using a scale of 2 cm to 1 unit on the x-axis and 2 cm to 5 units on the y-axis, draw the graph of the relation for the domain $0 \leqslant t \leqslant 6$, $t \in Q$.

(b) From your graph, estimate

    (i) the time interval that the stone is in the air

    (ii) the time interval that the stone is higher than 25 m

    (iii) the time(s) at which the stone is 20 m high.

③ Simultaneous linear and quadratic equations

1 Given the equation of the quadratic curve $y = x^2 + 3x - 2$ and the equation of the straight line $y = 5x - 3$, show

(a) by using an algebraic method

(b) graphically

that the straight line is a tangent to the curve.

2 The area of an isosceles triangle is $10 \, cm^2$ while its perimeter is $20 \, cm$. Find out all you can about this triangle.

Chapter 19 *Inverse and Composite Functions*

---

① Inverse Functions

1 (a) $f : x \rightarrow 2x - 4$. Find f^{-1}.

(b) Using the same Cartesian axes, draw the graphs of

    (i) f for $2 \leqslant x \leqslant 6$ (ii) f^{-1} for $0 \leqslant x \leqslant 8$.

(c) Comment on the graphs.

2 $f(x) = \dfrac{2x + 1}{x - 4}$

    (a) Calculate x if **(i)** $f(x) = 0$ **(ii)** $f(x)$ is undefined.

    (b) Find $f^{-1}(x)$.

    (c) Hence solve the equation $\dfrac{2x + 1}{x - 4} = 5$.

3 For each of the following functions, find an expression for the inverse function, if it exists.

    (a) $f(x) = 3x$ **(b)** $f(x) = 2\dfrac{2x}{3} + 1$

    (c) $f(x) = 2x - 1$ **(d)** $f(x) = 2x^2 + 2x - 1$

    (e) $f(x) = \dfrac{x + 3}{2}$ **(f)** $f(x) = \dfrac{3x + 2}{2 - x}$

❷ Composite Functions

1 $f^2(x)$ means $ff(x)$, $f^3(x)$ means $fff(x)$, and so on.

    (a) If $f : x \rightarrow 3x - 1$, find simple expressions for $f^2(x)$, $f^3(x)$ and $f^4(x)$.

    (b) Use your expression for $f^4(x)$ to

        (i) calculate $f^4(2)$ **(ii)** find n such that $f^4(n) = 284$.

2 Find two simple functions for each of the following composite functions.

    (a) $gf : x \rightarrow 9 + 6x + x^2$

    (b) $kh : x \rightarrow \dfrac{1}{x + 2}$

    Find $kh(2)$ and $hk(2)$.

3 $f(x) = 2 + x$, $g(x) = 2x + 1$ and $k(x) = fg(x)$.

    (a) Find $k(x)$ in terms of x.

    (b) Find $f^{-1}(x)$, $g^{-1}(x)$ and $k^{-1}(x)$.

    (c) Find $f^{-1}g^{-1}(x)$ and $g^{-1}f^{-1}(x)$. Which is equal to $k^{-1}(x)$?

Chapter 20 *Non-linear Graphs*

---

❶ Gradient of a Curve

1 Two motorcyclists travel along the same highway, 240 km long, from opposite ends. The first starts at 9 am and drives south at 80 km/h, the second starts at 10 am and drives north at 96 km/h.

    (a) On the same set of axes draw a distance–time graph for each motorcyclist.

    (b) Deduce the point at which they pass one another.

2 Water is poured into a vessel at a steady rate and the height, *h* cm, after *t* sec is given in the following table.

t sec	0	0.5	1.0	1.5	2.0	2.5	3.0	3.5	4.0	4.5	5.0	5.5	6.0
h cm	0	0.1	0.3	0.6	1.0	1.7	3.0	4.3	5.0	5.4	5.7	5.9	6.0

(a) Using 2 cm to represent 1 unit on each axis, draw the graph of *h* against *t*.

(b) From your graph, write down the height after **(i)** 1.7 sec **(ii)** 4.3 sec.

(c) By drawing a suitable tangent, estimate the rate at which the height is increasing at 3.5 sec.

(d) By considering how the gradient of the curve changes, sketch the shape of the vessel.

3 Corresponding values of *x* and *y* of the function $y = \sqrt{x}$ are given for the points shown in the table below:

	A	B	C	D	E	F	G	H	J	K
x	0	1	1.1	1.2	1.3	1.4	1.5	2	2.5	3
y	0	1	1.05	1.10	1.14	1.18	1.22	1.41	1.58	1.73

(a) Using 5 cm to 1 unit on the *x*-axis and 10 cm to 1 unit on the *y*-axis, plot the points given and draw the graph for the domain $0 \leqslant x \leqslant 3$.

(b) Using the ratio

$$\frac{\textit{difference of the y-coordinates}}{\textit{difference of the x-coordinates}} = \textit{gradient of the line,}$$

complete the table below for the gradient of each chord.

line	BK	BJ	BH	BG	BF	BE	BD	BC
y-diff	0.73	0.58						
x-diff	2	1.5						
gradient	**0.37**							

(c) Draw the tangent to the curve at *x* = 1 and find the gradient of the curve at that point.

(d) Comment on the relationship between the gradient of the tangent at *x* = 1 and the gradients of the chords as the end-point of each chord moves closer to the point (1, 1). What conclusion can you draw about the relationship between the chords and tangents of a curve?

❷ Area Under a Graph

1 **(i)**

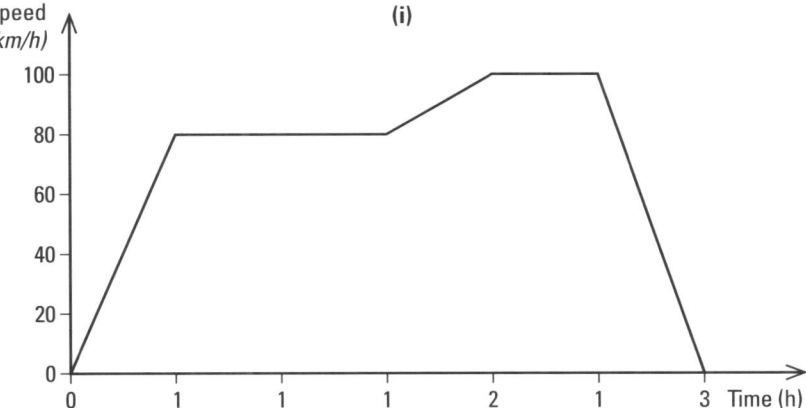

(ii)

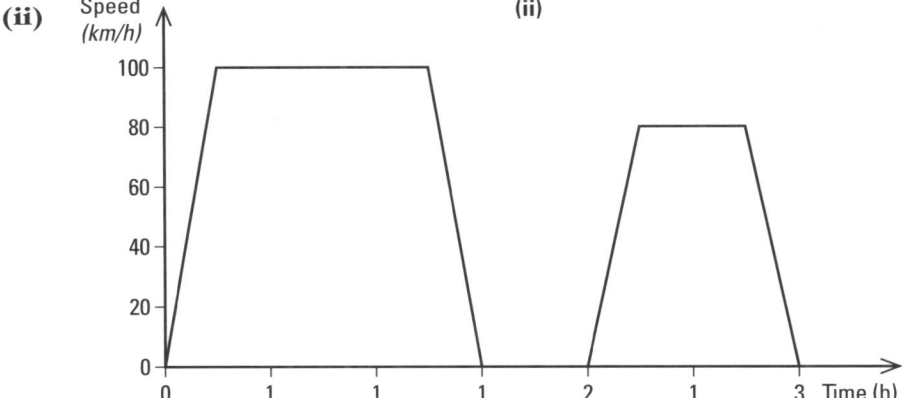

The graphs in **(i)** and **(ii)** are the speed–time graphs of two cars travelling along a highway.

(a) Describe each journey.

(b) Find the distance travelled by each car in the 3 hours.

(c) For each car calculate the average speed for the whole journey.

2 **(a)** Using 2 cm for 1 unit on each axis, draw the graph of $y = 5x - x^2$, for $0 \leqslant x \leqslant 5$.

(b) Find an approximate value for the area between the curve and the x-axis

   (i) by counting squares

   (ii) by using five trapezia.

(c) Is your answer by method **(b) (ii)** too big or too small? Explain the reason for your answer.

3 The table on the right shows the speed of a car at various times.

Time (s)	0	10	20	30	40	50	60
Speed(m/s)	0	13	20	$24\frac{1}{2}$	$27\frac{1}{2}$	$29\frac{1}{2}$	30

(a) Using 1 cm to 5 sec and 2 cm to 5 m/s, plot the points and draw the curve through the points.

(b) By drawing tangents, estimate the acceleration at
(i) 20 sec **(ii)** 40 sec

(c) Use the trapezium method to estimate the distance travelled in the 60 seconds.

❸ Cubic Graphs

1 Given the identity $x^3 - 1 \equiv (x - 1)(x^2 + x + 1)$, and by drawing the graphs of $y = x - 1$ and $y = (x^2 + x + 1)$ on the same axes, find the number of roots of the equation $x^3 - 1 = 0$. Give the reason for your answer.

2 (a) The figure on the right shows the functions $y = x^3$ and $y = 3 - 2x$. Hence, write the solution(s) of the equation $x^3 = 3 - 2x$.

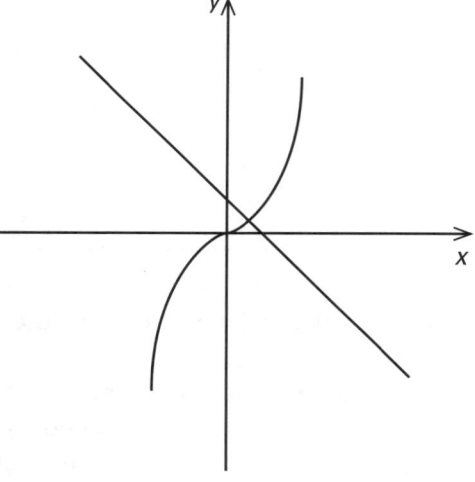

(b) Show that the equation $x^3 = 3 - 2x$ can be expressed in the form $(x - 1)(x^2 + px + q) = 0$ and find the values of p and q.

(c) Deduce from the equation $(x - 1)(x^2 + px + q) = 0$ and the values of p and q that the two graphs must intersect in a single point.
[*Hint: use the roots of a quadratic.*]

(d) Use a similar method to show that the line $y = 7x - 6$ intersects the curve $y = x^3$ in three distinct points and find the coordinates of these points.

④ Exponential Graphs

In the exponential function $y = ka^x$, k is the initial value of y when $x = 0$, and a is the factor by which the variable y changes for equal intervals in x.

a is called the *growth factor*.
In each of the following:
(a) write the initial value of the function
(b) calculate the growth factor
(c) write the formula, that is, the exponential function in the form $y = ka^x$
(d) draw a graph to illustrate the data and solve the problem.

1 Interest is compounded annually at 12% per annum on an investment of $ 10 000 over a 4-year period. Find the value of the investment at the end of **(i)** $2\frac{1}{2}$ years **(ii)** 4 years.

2 The population of a town increases at the rate of 4.5% every 5 years. In the year 2000, the population was 4000. Estimate the population at 5-year intervals for the years 2000–2020.

⑤ Inverse Variation

1 **(a)** Using a scale of 2 cm to 1 unit on each axis, draw the graph of
$$y = \frac{12}{x + 2} \text{ for } -1 \leqslant x \leqslant 6.$$

(b) Estimate the area bounded by the curve, the x-axis, and the lines
$x = -1$ and $x = 6$
  (i) by counting squares
  (ii) by using seven trapezia.

2 The equation $\qquad x^3 - 4x^2 + x + 6 = 0 \qquad$ (1)
may be written as $\qquad x^3 - 4x^2 + x = -6$

Dividing through by x $\qquad x^2 - 4x + 1 = -\dfrac{6}{x}$

Hence, the solutions of (1) are the x-coordinates of the points of intersection of the graphs $y = x^2 - 4x + 1$ and $y = -\dfrac{6}{x}$.

Draw the graphs of these two functions and state the solution set of (1).

3 Draw graphs to check your solution of the pairs of equations:
(a) $xy = 6$, $x + y = 2$
(b) $x^2 - 3 + x = y$, $2x + y = 5$
(c) $y = \dfrac{1}{x} + 1$, $x - y = 1$

Chapter 21 *Matrix Algebra*

❶ Matrices

1 Have a think about other information that can be put into a matrix.

Do you play sport? Could your league results be put into a matrix? How many rows and columns would it have?

What about your exam results for different subjects? What would be the order of the matrix?

❷ Adding and Subtracting Matrices

1 Find x, y and z if $\begin{pmatrix} x & -1 \\ 2 & 1 \end{pmatrix} + \begin{pmatrix} 1 & y \\ -4 & -3 \end{pmatrix} = \begin{pmatrix} 4 & 5 \\ -2 & z \end{pmatrix}$.

2 $P = \begin{pmatrix} -4 & 1 & -3 \\ 5 & 7 & 2 \end{pmatrix}$, $Q = \begin{pmatrix} 2 & -4 & 1 \\ 4 & -1 & -5 \end{pmatrix}$

    (a) Evaluate $P + Q$.

    (b) Evaluate $Q + P$.

    (c) Compare your results to **(a)** and **(b)**. What do you notice?
Do the same exercise for other matrices. Does the same thing always happen?

❸ Scalar Multiplication of Matrices

1 $A = \begin{pmatrix} 3 & -1 & 7 \\ -4 & 0 & 2 \end{pmatrix}$, $B = \begin{pmatrix} -2 & -5 & 3 \\ 0 & 1 & 4 \end{pmatrix}$

    (a) Show that $3A + 3B = 3(A + B)$.

    (b) Show that $k(A + B) = kA + kB$ for any value of k.

❹ Matrix Multiplication

1 $A = \begin{pmatrix} 1 & 3 \\ 2 & -1 \end{pmatrix}$, $B = \begin{pmatrix} -2 & 1 \\ 3 & 4 \end{pmatrix}$, $C = \begin{pmatrix} 3 & 2 \\ 1 & 1 \end{pmatrix}$

    (a) Find AB and BC.

    (b) Calculate $A(BC)$ and $(AB)C$.

    (c) In the calculation $A \times B \times C$, does it matter which multiplication you do first?

    (d) Try some other matrices, do you get the same result? Do you think this is true for any choice of matrices?

❺ Inverting Matrices

1 $A = \begin{pmatrix} 3 & -1 \\ 2 & 2 \end{pmatrix}$, $B = \begin{pmatrix} 1 & 0 \\ 4 & -1 \end{pmatrix}$

(a) Find A^{-1}, B^{-1}, $A^{-1}B^{-1}$ and $B^{-1}A^{-1}$.

(b) Find AB, BA and their inverses $(AB)^{-1}$ and $(BA)^{-1}$.

(c) Which of the matrix products you have found are equal?

(d) Try some otehr 2×2 matrices. Is this always true?

❻ Algebra Problems

1 (a) Write the simultaneous equations $\begin{matrix} 2x + 2y = 9 \\ x + y = 4 \end{matrix}$ in the form

$$\begin{pmatrix} p & q \\ r & s \end{pmatrix} \begin{pmatrix} x \\ y \end{pmatrix} = \begin{pmatrix} a \\ b \end{pmatrix}.$$

(b) What is the determinant of the matrix $\begin{pmatrix} p & q \\ r & s \end{pmatrix}$? What do you think this tells you about the simultaneous equations?

Chapter 22 *Vectors*

---

❶ Vectors

1 $\mathbf{a} = \begin{pmatrix} a_1 \\ a_2 \end{pmatrix}$ and $\mathbf{b} = \begin{pmatrix} b_1 \\ b_2 \end{pmatrix}$

(a) Write down $\mathbf{a} + \mathbf{b}$ as a column vector.

(b) Show that $|\mathbf{a} + \mathbf{b}|^2 = a_1^2 + a_2^2 + 2(a_1 b_1 + a_2 b_2) + b_1^2 + b_2^2$.

❷ Vector Arithmetic

1 (a) Draw any two vectors. Label them $\mathbf{a}$ and $\mathbf{b}$.

(b) Add the two vectors (using the triangle law) and put $\mathbf{a} + \mathbf{b}$ on the diagram.

(c) Compare $|\mathbf{a} + \mathbf{b}|$, the magnitude of $\mathbf{a} + \mathbf{b}$, with $|\mathbf{a}| + |\mathbf{b}|$, the sum of the magnitudes. Which is bigger?

Try a few other vectors $\mathbf{a}$ and $\mathbf{b}$. Do you think this is always true?

(d) When is $|\mathbf{a} + \mathbf{b}| = |\mathbf{a}| + |\mathbf{b}|$?

❸ Vector Geometry

1 PQRST is a regular pentagon.

$\overrightarrow{PQ} = \mathbf{p}$, $\overrightarrow{QR} = \mathbf{q}$ and $\overrightarrow{RS} = \mathbf{r}$.

Answer the following in terms of $\mathbf{p}$, $\mathbf{q}$ and $\mathbf{r}$.
  (a) Write down $\overrightarrow{SP}$.
  (b) Find $|\overrightarrow{RT}|$.
  (c) Which vector is parallel to $\overrightarrow{TS}$?

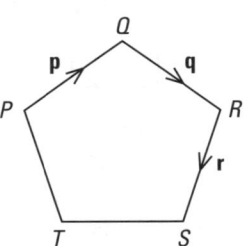

2 PQRS is a trapezium.

$\overrightarrow{RQ} = \mathbf{a}$, $\overrightarrow{RS} = \mathbf{b}$, $\overrightarrow{SP} = \mathbf{c}$ and $\overrightarrow{QP} = 3\overrightarrow{RS}$.

Show that $2\mathbf{b} = \mathbf{c} - \mathbf{a}$.

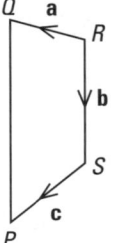

Chapter 23 *Transformations*

---

❶ Combining Transformations

1 (a) On squared paper, draw the triangle A $(4, -1)$, B $(5, -4)$ and C $(3, -3)$.
  (b) Draw the image A'B'C' of ABC after a glide reflection, with glide axis
    $x = 2$ and translation $\begin{pmatrix} 0 \\ 2 \end{pmatrix}$.
  (c) Join corresponding points in the object and image and mark their mid-points.
  (d) What do you notice about the mid-points?
  (e) Given an object and its image following a glide reflection, how can we find the glide axis? Try some other glide reflections to test your idea.

❷ Matrices and Transformations

1 Suppose a transformation maps an object A to an image A'. Then there is usually a transformation that maps A' back to A. This transformation is called the **inverse**.

Find the inverses of these transformations.

(a) Rotation through 90° clockwise about (1, 2)

(b) Translation by $\begin{pmatrix} 4 \\ -1 \end{pmatrix}$

(c) Reflection in the line $y = x$

(d) Enlargement scale factor 4, centre (–1, 4)

❸ Combining Transformations using Matrices

1 In the Finished Early exercise on Matrices and Transformations above we met inverses: a transformation that maps an image back to the object.

You might not be surprised to hear that the matrix that represents the inverse transformation is the inverse of the matrix representing the original transformation. For example, suppose a transformation is represented by a matrix T, then the inverse transformation is represented by T^{-1}.

[Remember that the inverse of a matrix $\begin{pmatrix} a & b \\ c & d \end{pmatrix}$ is $\dfrac{1}{ad - bc} \begin{pmatrix} d & -b \\ -c & a \end{pmatrix}$.]

Find the matrices that represent the inverses of these transformations.

(a) Enlargement scale factor 3, centre O.

(b) Rotation through 270° about O.

(c) Reflection in the line $y = -x$ followed by an enlargement scale factor $\frac{1}{2}$, centre O.

2 The method in question 1 doesn't work for translations. Why not?

Chapter 24 *Trigonometry 2*

---

❶ Circular Functions

1 Two trigonometric identities we haven't met yet are:
$$\sin (A + B) = \sin A \cos B + \cos A \sin B$$
$$\cos (A + B) = \cos A \cos B - \sin A \sin B$$

Use these to prove that:

(a) $\sin (\theta + 90°) = \cos \theta$

(b) $\cos (\theta + 180°) = -\cos \theta$

(c) $\sin (\theta - 180°) = -\sin \theta$

❷ The Sine and Cosine Rules

1 The line CN divides the triangle ABC into two right-angled triangles ACN and BCN.

  (a) Use trigonometry in triangle ACN to write h in terms of b and A.

  (b) Use trigonometry in triangle BCN to write h in terms of b and A.

  (c) Use parts **(a)** and **(b)** to show that $\dfrac{a}{\sin A} = \dfrac{b}{\sin B}$.

  (d) Draw another line on triangle ABC, similar to CN, that will divide it into two triangles BAN and CAN. Use these triangles to prove that

$$\frac{b}{\sin B} = \frac{c}{\sin C}.$$

  (e) Hence prove the sine rule.

2 The line CN divides the triangle ABC into two right-angled triangles ACN and BCN.

  AN $= x$ and NB $= c - x$.

  (a) Use triangle BCN to show that
  $$a^2 = (h^2 + x^2) + c^2 - 2cx$$

  (b) Use part **(a)** and triangle ACN to prove the cosine rule.

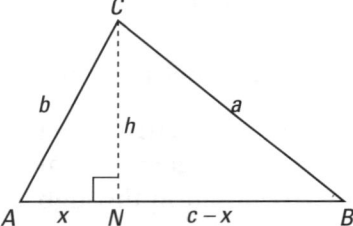

Area of a Triangle

1 (a) Find the area of the following triangles.

  (i) Triangle ABC with AB = 4 and AC = 5 and angle C = 50°.

  (ii) The same triangle but with angle C = 60°.

  (iii) The same again but with angle C = 70°.

  (b) Keep increasing angle C and finding the area of the resulting triangle. What do you notice about the areas of the triangles?

  (c) Do you think this is true for any pair of sides in a triangle? Why?

⑥ Earth Geometry

1 A and B both have a latitude of 65°. A has longitude 82°W and B has longitude 98°. Calculate the distance from A to B:
   (a) around the parallel of latitude,
   (b) around a great circle. [A diagram may help.]

You should have found that the distance around the great circle is much shorter than the distance around the parallel. In fact the shortest distance between any two points on a sphere (including the earth) is always around a great sphere.

2 Find the shortest distance between the following points.
   (a) A (72°N, 48°E), B (72°N, 132°W)
   (b) C (82°S, 0°W), D (82°S, 180°E)

3 Explain why a pilot flying from Alaska to Finland might see polar bears.

Index